Rafe Colburn

SAMS
Teach Yourself

CGI

in 24 Hours

SAMS

A Division of Macmillan USA
201 West 103rd St., Indianapolis, Indiana, 46290 USA

Sams Teach Yourself CGI in 24 Hours

Copyright © 2000 by Sams Publishing

International Standard Book Number: 0-672-31880-6

Library of Congress Catalog Card Number: 99-69271

Printed in the United States of America

First Printing: June 2000

03   02   01   00   4   3   2   1

Trademarks

Warning and Disclaimer

ACQUISITIONS EDITOR
Jeff Schultz

DEVELOPMENT EDITORS
Linda Harmony
Scott D. Meyers

MANAGING EDITOR
Charlotte Clapp

PROJECT EDITOR
Christina Smith

COPY EDITOR
Kate Givens

INDEXER
Kevin Kent

PROOFREADER
Candice Hightower

TECHNICAL EDITOR
J. Eric Slone

TEAM COORDINATOR
Amy Patton

INTERIOR DESIGNER
Gary Adair

COVER DESIGNER
Aren Howell

COPYWRITER
Eric Borgert

PRODUCTION
Darin Crone
Liz Patterson

Contents at a Glance

Contents

Hour 3 Downloading, Installing, and Debugging CGI Scripts   33

Hour 4 Writing Your First CGI Program   51

PART IV Building Basic CGI Applications 201

HOUR 13 Using Flat Files for Data Storage 203

Appendixes   425

Dedication

For Patricia

Acknowledgments

There are always too many contributors to any large effort to do an adequate job of thanking them in a space like this one. First of all, I'd like to thank the readers of my previous CGI book who took time to send comments, both positive and negative.

Secondly, I'd like to thank the editorial team that helped to produce this book. Jeff Schultz, Christina Smith, Amy Patton, Kate Givens, and J. Eric Slone are all deserving of praise, along with the other people at Sams who did a great job in facilitating the writing of this book. I'd also like to single out the book's development editor Linda Harmony for special praise. Her editorial touch improved the book in more ways than I can count.

Most of all, I'd like to thank my wife for persevering through yet another writing project.

About the Author

RAFE COLBURN is a development manager who designs and builds Web applications for Alerts.com in Raleigh, North Carolina. He's also the author of *Special Edition Using SQL* for Que, and has contributed to a number of other computer books. His personal site, rc3.org Daily, can be found at `http://rc3.org`, and he can be reached via email at `rafe@rc3.org`.

Tell Us What You Think!

As the reader of this book, *you* are our most important critic and commentator. We value your opinion and want to know what we're doing right, what we could do better, what areas you'd like to see us publish in, and any other words of wisdom you're willing to pass our way.

You can fax, email, or write me directly to let me know what you did or didn't like about this book—as well as what we can do to make our books stronger.

Please note that I cannot help you with technical problems related to the topic of this book, and that due to the high volume of mail I receive, I might not be able to reply to every message.

When you write, please be sure to include this book's title and author as well as your name and phone or fax number. I will carefully review your comments and share them with the author and editors who worked on the book.

Fax: 317-581-4770

Email: `wevdev_sams@mcp.com`

Mail: Mark Taber
        Associate Publisher
        Sams Publishing
        201 West 103rd Street
        Indianapolis, IN 46290 USA

Introduction

Now is a pretty exciting time to be writing Web applications. Just a few years ago, most people were focused on publishing static content on the Web. Web sites consisted of HTML files that people could download or read. Sometimes Web sites provided feedback forms, search functionality, or perhaps discussion boards, but for the most part, sites were built around the idea of providing static information to their users. The largest exception was online shopping sites, which generally consist of a dynamically built catalog and a shopping cart.

These days, the Web is a platform for applications just like your everyday desktop PC. People are managing their calendars, reading their email, and doing all sorts of other day-to-day tasks using Web applications. Even sites that are focused on just providing content for users to read often allow writers to submit the content using Web applications, and generate the content for users dynamically.

As standard support in browsers increases, you'll see even more dynamic applications delivered directly from the Web into users' Web browsers. More and more desktop applications will migrate to the Web. If you're a Web developer who's focused on HTML, JavaScript, and graphics design, or you're a programmer who's unfamiliar with Web programming, this book will allow you to take the first steps toward taking advantage of this trend.

The primary focus of this book is on using the Common Gateway Interface, which is built into nearly every Web server, to develop Web applications. The biggest advantage of CGI is that it supports nearly every popular programming language. So, if you already know how to program, you can probably get started writing Web applications right away. Even if you don't program, you can copy existing CGI programs and modify them to suit your own needs.

The larger focus of this book is on teaching you how Web applications are designed and built. Although you may start out writing CGI programs, there's a good chance that down the road you'll be building applications using some other platform, like Active Server Pages, Cold Fusion, or perhaps Java servlets. Even so, this book will provide you with the knowledge you need to understand how Web applications work in general, and some methods you can use to write Web applications that are easy to improve and maintain. Also, knowing CGI will enable you to quickly solve problems that you might not be able to solve using other technologies. For example, because CGI programs can be written in a wide variety of languages, often it's easiest to write Web applications that communicate with other programs using CGI.

I should also point out that most of the examples in this book are written in Perl. Perl is a scripting language that's available for most computing platforms, including UNIX, Windows, and the Mac OS. It has a number of features that make it well-suited to CGI programming, and in fact, it's the most popular language for writing CGI programs. The biggest advantage for readers of this book is that it's easy to learn Perl in bits and pieces. You don't need to understand any big concepts behind software design in order to write useful programs in Perl.

My goal in this book is to explain the Perl concepts that I use in the example programs, and not to go beyond that. I also used as few special Perl features as possible in order to apply the lessons in these examples to the programming language that you use to write CGI programs. If you don't know any programming languages, Perl is as good a starting point as any other language. I'd advise you to pick up a Perl book (like Laura Lemay's *Teach Yourself Perl in 21 Days*), or at least check out the Perl information at www.perl.com.

Hopefully this book will be the first step in sending you off on a long and successful career as a professional or amateur developer of Web applications. If you have any comments or feedback, please send them to me at rafe@rc3.org. Good luck!

PART I
An Introduction to CGI

Hour

Hour 1

Overview of CGI Programming

Do you use the World Wide Web to look up the latest stock quotes? Do you purchase items through online stores? Have you ever used a feedback form on a Web site? If the answer to any of those questions was yes, you've not only browsed a Web site, you've interacted with a *Web application*.

It didn't take long for Web developers to realize that Web sites could provide a lot of functionality above and beyond browsable content. Increasingly, you'll find that Web applications—which provide truly interactive functionality to your Web sites—are taking the place of static HTML content. If you want to accept and process user input, retrieve and present data from a database, or communicate with applications external to the Web server, you must use a Web application development platform. In this book, you will learn how to build interactive Web applications using the Common Gateway Interface (CGI)—which is the predominant platform for deploying Web applications today.

This hour will provide the introductory and background information you need before you can start writing CGI programs. The following topics will be discussed:

- Types of Web applications
- A brief history of CGI
- The definition of a CGI program
- How CGI programs work
- Pros and cons of using CGI to write Web applications
- Programming languages you can use to implement CGI programs

Types of Web Applications

A Web application is like any other application, except that the interface for it is provided through the browser. Originally, Web applications were generally used for functions that are unique to the Web — site feedback forms, online discussion boards, and shopping carts for electronic commerce sites. However, the world of Web application programming has matured, and now there are Web-based replacements for many desktop applications. People use the Web to manage their calendars and contacts, to locate places using online mapping services, and to read their email.

Although you could use JavaScript to augment a Web page with "interactivity," such as image rollovers and pull-down menus of links, you'd still be stuck with the static information the author originally placed on the page.

A History of CGI

You might be wondering where CGI was created and why it is still the most widely used platform for developing Web applications.

One of the first Web servers to be developed was NCSA HTTPD. It was developed at the National Center for Supercomputing Applications, where most of the founders of Netscape worked (and also developed the Mosaic browser). One of the most important features of NCSA HTTPD was CGI, which was added to the server with the 1.0 release.

Because NCSA HTTPD was one of the first widely used Web servers (along with the CERN server), CGI became the de facto standard for implementing Web applications. CGI support was added to the CERN server (the original Web server) in version 2.15, back in April of 1994.

At the time NCSA released HTTPD, CGI was the only way to implement Web applications. Because CGI is so simple, and the source code to NCSA HTTPD was freely available, nearly every Web server developed after NCSA HTTPD supports CGI. If you're interested, you can view the original CGI documentation at:

`http://hoohoo.ncsa.uiuc.edu/cgi/`

1

Today, all of the popular Web servers on both Windows NT and UNIX support CGI. Even Macintosh Web servers support a method of communicating with external programs that is similar to CGI.

In the years since the people at NCSA initially defined CGI and implemented it in their Web server, lots of other methods of developing Web applications have been introduced. Some Web application platforms you might be familiar with include Microsoft's Active Server Pages, Allaire's Cold Fusion, PHP, and Java servlets. These Web application development tools, among others, will be discussed in Hour 12, "Pros and Cons of Alternate Technologies."

What Is a CGI Program?

A CGI program is executed by the Web server in response to a request made by the Web browser. The Web server acts as an intermediary between the browser and the CGI program: it passes the browser's request to the CGI program, and it sends output from the program back to the Web browser for processing. For example, a program might accept a stock ticker symbol, look up the stock price associated with that symbol and return it to the user. Or, a program might accept a user's comment, and send it to the site's Webmaster in an email message. Almost any programming language can be used to write a CGI program; CGI itself is the defined interface between the Web server and the external program you want to write.

Let me discuss briefly what a CGI program doesn't do—it doesn't interact with the user in a direct way. It doesn't display or retrieve information from prompts, menus, or other interactive features. A CGI program doesn't display graphics, either. Although it may generate binary data that is, in fact, an image, it doesn't create any windows or otherwise interact with a graphical user interface.

To work properly, a CGI program must meet the following criteria:

- You must be able to execute the program from the command line by simply typing the program's name. (For example, Java programs must be executed through the Java virtual machine, by typing `java programname`. This makes them unsuitable for use as CGI programs.)
- The program must generate a valid content-type header.

Any type of content is fair game as output of a CGI program. For example, content types include HTML code, GIF images, plain text files, Microsoft Word documents, and audio files. The content-type header that's supplied by the program indicates which sort of content is being returned, so that the browser can take the appropriate action. Later in the hour, I'll discuss the details of how to create this header.

Basically, that's it. As long as the Web server can execute the program, and the program generates valid output, it's acceptable for use as a CGI program. Later in the hour, I'll discuss what qualifies as valid output, and I'll also discuss other capabilities generally associated with CGI programs.

How CGI Programs Work

Now I'm ready to get down to the nuts and bolts of how CGI programs work. The great thing about CGI is that it's an extremely simple interface. If you're familiar with UNIX-based operating systems, you will recognize the concepts that CGI is grounded in.

As I've already discussed, CGI is a set of conventions that allows Web servers and external programs to communicate. To illustrate how CGI programs work, I'm going to include a description of the entire HTTP session, so you can understand at a high level how it all fits together.

How Resources Are Requested

An HTTP session is initiated when a Web client (usually a Web browser) requests a resource from a Web server. As I'm sure you already know, these resources are identified using URLs. When you're dealing with static HTML pages, the URL simply consists of the location of a file located on a Web server. Let's say you have a URL like this:

`http://www.rc3.org/cgibook/index.html`

That URL corresponds to the file `index.html` in the `cgibook` subdirectory of the Web server's document root. If the document root is `/home/httpd/htdocs`, the path that corresponds to the URL is:

`/home/httpd/htdocs/cgibook/index.html`

If the Web server can locate and read the file, the contents of the file will be sent back to the client that requested it.

When the URL points to a CGI program, things get a bit more complicated. Let's look at a URL that points to a CGI program:

`http://www.rc3.org/cgi-bin/example.cgi`

In this case, the resource being requested is a program named `example.cgi`. What it does is unimportant. What is important is that when the Web server determines that the requested resource is a CGI program, it executes that program and returns the output of the program to the client.

This process is very different from that used for static HTML files. For one thing, a lot more can go wrong. When a CGI program is requested, the Web server must determine the following:

1. Can it locate the requested program file?
2. Does it know that the requested file is a CGI program? (I'll discuss this in Hour 2, "Setting Up Your CGI Environment.")
3. Is it allowed to execute the program?
4. Did the program execute without any errors?
5. Was the output of the program a valid response to a Web request? (I'll discuss this later in this section.)

Only if the answer to all of those questions is affirmative can the Web server successfully fulfill the request. If the answer to any of these is no, an error will be returned, or something strange will happen.

Fulfilling the Request

As stated earlier, a CGI program must supply a content-type header so the Web browser knows what type of output the program has returned. Content types for Web content are specified using MIME types. MIME is a standard that is commonly associated with email, but the naming system used for identifying the type of data stored in a MIME attachment is exactly the same as the naming system for specifying content types on the Web. Table 1.1 contains a list of common content types.

TABLE 1.1 Common Web Content Types

Identifier	Content type
text/html	HTML documents
text/plain	Plain text documents
image/gif	GIF images
image/jpeg	JPEG images
video/quicktime	A QuickTime movie
application/octet-stream	Binary files

If a CGI program generates HTML code, it produces the following content-type header:

```
Content-type: text/html
```

That information is received by the Web server, and included with the other headers that are sent back to the browser. The HTTP protocol specifies that headers are to be separated from the actual content by two linefeeds. When a browser receives two consecutive linefeeds, it knows that the headers have ended and the content to be processed has begun. So, to conclude this example, if the CGI program example.cgi produces HTML code as its output, the full output of the program might be as follows:

```
Content-type: text/html

<html>
<head><title>A simple example.</title></head>
<body>This is a simple example.</body>
</html>
```

As you can see, the required header is separated from the actual content by two line-feeds. The rest of the HTTP headers are added by the Web server, and it's all packaged up and sent to the browser for rendering. Here's the full response sent back to the browser, including the output of the script and the response line and other headers added by the Web server:

```
HTTP/1.1 200 OK
Date: Sun, 30 Jan 2000 04:21:37 GMT
Server: Apache/1.3.3
Connection: close
Content-type: text/html

<html>
<head><title>A simple example.</title></head>
<body>This is a simple example.</body>
</html>
```

HTTP Headers

Most of the information relevant to an HTTP transaction is visible to the user. The URL being requested and the information entered in a form are the visible parts of a request. Similarly, the HTML (or other) data returned by a request are displayed by the browser or saved to disk.

However, other information is exchanged that's invisible to users. This information is exchanged between the browser and server, and is used to make their jobs easier.

You're already familiar with one kind of header, the content-type header, which must be provided by every CGI program. This header tells the browser how to handle the content being returned by the CGI program. Other common headers are used to specify the types of content that browsers accept, or to indicate the name and version of the Web server or Web browser.

Passing Data to a CGI Program

In my description of how a typical HTTP session works, I left out something very important! I didn't explain how information is passed from the Web browser to the CGI program. There are several different ways that data can be passed to the Web server from a browser. For now, I'll provide an overview of how this process works, and Hour 6, "Processing Input," will discuss them in all the detail you need.

Generally speaking, the data passed to CGI programs is collected using HTML forms. (There are other ways to provide data as well.) In Hour 5, "Creating HTML Forms," I discuss how to create forms for submitting information to CGI programs, and I also discuss some alternate methods of providing data to a CGI program. The data can also be embedded in URLs used within standard hyperlinks.

Before data can be passed to a CGI program, it has to be encoded to remove any characters that might break things. Most of the time, a technique called URL encoding is used. URL encoding is a method of *escaping* certain characters that are significant to the Web server so that they're ignored and passed directly to the CGI program. For example, the ? character is used to separate the filename in the URL from the query string. If the query string itself contains a ?, passing it without escaping it could cause problems. So, the ? is translated so that it doesn't confuse the Web server.

Spaces are also confusing, they're converted into plus signs. Since plus signs are used to replace spaces, real plus signs have to be encoded as well. In Hour 6, I'm going to explain exactly how URL encoding works, and tell you about some libraries you can use to decode CGI input so that you don't have to do it manually.

Pros and Cons of CGI

There are advantages and disadvantages to writing your Web applications as CGI programs. In Hour 12, I'll discuss some of the alternatives to CGI for Web application programming and how those alternatives compare to CGI. For now I'll just talk about CGI.

I'll talk about the good stuff first—the advantages of CGI programming. The main advantage of CGI programming is that it's the ultimate cross-platform technology. It works on Web servers running both Windows NT and UNIX, and with almost every Web server. So when you write CGI programs, you can be fairly certain that they'll be portable to whatever environment you'll want to run them in. The second major advantage of CGI is that it's language independent. For the most part, you can write CGI programs in the language of your choice. There's no need to learn a new programming language just to write CGI programs. If you choose a cross-platform language, like Perl, then it's trivial to port your programs from UNIX to Windows NT, or vice versa.

Another advantage of CGI is that it's a very simple interface. It's not necessary to have any special libraries to create a CGI program, or write your programs to use a particular API. Instead, CGI programs rely on the standard UNIX concepts of standard input, standard output, and environment variables to communicate with the Web server.

Now let's take a look at the disadvantages of CGI. The single greatest disadvantage of CGI programs comes into play when you write your CGI programs in a scripting language. Every time a CGI program is requested, the interpreter for the scripting language has to be started, the script has to be evaluated, and then the script has to be executed. The fact that you have to run the Perl interpreter every time a Perl CGI script is requested is very inefficient. Whether this is a problem depends on how powerful your Web server is, how many requests there are for your CGI scripts, and how long it takes the CGI program to load.

People who write their CGI programs in a compiled language like C don't have to deal with this problem, because there's no extra overhead like that generated by an interpreter. In fact, many application servers use small, fast-executing CGI programs as a gateway between the Web server and the application server process. This allows the application server to work with Web servers that they can't communicate with through a native interface.

The other main complaint about CGI programs is that they don't make things as easy on Web programmers as some other newer Web application platforms. When you write a CGI program, in addition to all of the program logic that creates the functionality you want, you also have to write code to generate the HTML code for the page. Most of today's more popular application servers allow you to embed program logic within a standard HTML page, which can save some work when you write the programs. These application servers are also easier to learn for people who know HTML but don't know how to program. It is, however, harder to write structured, well organized programs when you use this type of technology, so the choice is really one of preference. One isn't absolutely better than the other.

CGI Programming Languages

As I've already stated, almost any programming language can be used to write CGI programs. Just because it isn't mentioned here doesn't mean that it's unsuitable for CGI programming. As long as programs written in the language can meet the criteria that I discussed earlier in this hour for CGI programs, it can be used for CGI programming. In this section of the hour, I'm going to discuss some of the more commonly used languages, but this is by no means a complete list.

Perl

Perl is the granddaddy of all of the languages used for CGI programming. Perl had the right mix of ease of use, features helpful to CGI programming, and popularity to become the dominant language for writing CGI programs when the original Web servers that support CGI were released. It's not necessarily any better suited to CGI programming than any of a number of other languages, but it's the language most CGI programmers use.

One factor that established the popularity of Perl as a CGI programming language was the availability of libraries that made it easy to write CGI programs. The CGI.pm module, which is used to make a number of CGI-related tasks easier, is now bundled with the Perl interpreter. The most important functionality provided by CGI.pm is seamless conversion of form input to a useful Perl data structure. It also provides tons of additional functionality to make it convenient to generate HTML code.

Another advantage of Perl is that there are a lot of CGI programs that have already been written in the language that have been made available for download on the Internet. In many cases, you can download an existing script and adapt it to your purposes rather than writing a new script from scratch.

In this book, nearly all of the CGI programs will be written in Perl. Perl is easy to learn, especially if you already know how to program, and is generally considered to be the de facto standard for CGI programming. However, this book is really about proper Web application design, and isn't written as a Perl tutorial. The most important thing for you to take away are the proper design techniques for creating Web applications.

UNIX Shell

When it comes to writing a simple CGI program, particularly one that is designed to interact with UNIX programs, writing it as a shell script is a common choice. Most people who write CGI programs using shell scripts do so because they're system administrators who are already familiar with shell scripting. It's easy to do a lot with a few lines of code in a shell script, particularly if it involves interfacing with other UNIX command line programs.

For example, if you wanted to write a CGI program that returns the load average for the server (using the uptime command)writing it as a shell script would make a lot of sense. The disadvantage of writing your CGI programs as shell scripts is that, in my opinion, shell scripts are best suited to quick and dirty tasks. Other languages are better suited for writing complex CGI programs.

The C Language

The C programming language is perfectly acceptable for writing CGI scripts, as are any other compiled languages that can be used to create standard command-line executable files. The main advantage of writing CGI programs in a compiled language like C is that the performance is very good. The programs execute in less time than it takes to start the Perl interpreter to run a Perl script.

Unfortunately, there are a number of disadvantages involved with writing CGI programs in C as well. These are all general software development tradeoffs, they're not specific to CGI programming. Any comparison of scripting languages to compiled languages will include the same reasons. For the benefit of people who haven't read such a discussion, I'll quickly cover the issues here.

Basically there are three areas where scripting languages have an advantage over compiled languages. The first area is speed of development. Scripting languages tend to have higher-level statements than compiled languages, which makes it easier to complete the tasks for which the scripting language was designed. For example, Perl has lots of tools that are designed to make it easy to manipulate text files. Writing a program to search through a text file for valid email addresses would require a lot fewer lines of Perl code than C code.

The second advantage is in debugging. When you work with a compiled language, you have to recompile your code every time you make a change to it. So, when you're debugging a C program, you have to compile the program, run it, and if it doesn't work, you have to change it, recompile it, and run it again. When you use a scripting language, you're saved the compilation steps. You can simply test your program, and if it doesn't work, you can make a change and test it again.

The third advantage of scripting languages is that they're easier to learn than compiled languages, generally speaking. With most scripting languages, you can learn language constructs as you need them, rather than learning an overarching language philosophy first, or learning how to structure the programs. Many languages allow you to build more structure into your programs once you learn how, but still allow you to create simple programs at first.

Now let's talk about the advantages of compiled languages over scripting languages. The primary advantage is performance. Scripting languages must be processed by an interpreter and turned into machine executable code every single time they're run. When you write scripts that you only use occasionally for various tasks, the performance issue isn't a big deal. In a high demand Web environment where a CGI program has to process hundreds of requests per hour, the overhead can make using CGI scripts prohibitive.

The other advantage of most compiled languages, and C in particular, is that they're suitable for just about any programming task. Most scripting languages are designed for a particular task, or type of task. There are many good general purpose scripting languages, but even they aren't as flexible as C. Most of the time, this flexibility doesn't come into play because scripting languages are flexible enough for the task at hand, but in some cases, C is the only language that will do.

Visual Basic

Visual Basic is an incredibly popular language for writing client/server applications. Microsoft claims that there are more Visual Basic programmers than there are for any other language. Unfortunately, for a number of reasons Visual Basic is poorly suited to the creation of CGI programs. While Visual Basic can be used with some Web servers using the wince interface, it's not really much like the standard CGI interface, and is kind of awkward for writing Web applications.

1

Fortunately, there are other options for Visual Basic programmers. Microsoft's Internet Information Server supports Active Server Pages (ASP), which allows you to embed application logic into a Web page. ASP supports a scripting language called VBScript, which is kind of a simplified version of Visual Basic. You can also write COM objects in Visual Basic than can be accessed from ASP pages. I'll discuss both of these options in Hour 12.

Python

Python is an object-oriented scripting language that's available for most popular operating systems. Like Perl, it's a general purpose language suitable for many tasks, including CGI programming. Most Python fans like it because it's easy to write readable, maintainable programs using the language. It combines many of the advantages of scripting languages, like rapid development, with some of the advantages of compiled languages, like solid program structure. One of the nicest, and most controversial, features of the language is that it uses white space to define blocks in the source code. In other words, in order to work properly, Python code has to be formatted in a sensible manner. You can learn more about Python at http://www.python.org.

Java

Java programmers are in the same boat as Visual Basic programmers when it comes to CGI programming. Earlier, I said that it's impossible to write CGI programs in Java. The reason for this is that Java programs have to be executed using a Java Virtual Machine, so there's no way to call a Java CGI program directly from the Web server. However, you can write wrapper CGI programs in another language that can be used to call the Java program using the Java Virtual Machine. If you do choose to go this route, you're then faced with the overhead of starting wrapper program, which in turn starts the Java Virtual Machine and then executes the Java program.

Again, like Visual Basic, there are other options available for Java programmers. You can use Java servlets to write Web applications. Servlets are the Java equivalent of CGI programs. A servlet engine includes a Java Virtual Machine, and runs while the Web server is up. When a request is made, the servlet engine executes the Java program that was requested, and sends the output of the servlet to the user as a response. There are also a number of application servers that use Java as their programming language. Any of these options are better for writing Web applications in Java than writing CGI programs in Java.

Summary

The purpose of this hour was to provide you with a wide ranging overview of the CGI landscape. At this point you should understand, at least at a high level, how CGI programs work, and what qualifies a program as a CGI program. You should also have a good idea which programming languages can be used to write CGI scripts, and the advantages and disadvantages of the most popular CGI programming languages. In the next hour, "Setting Up Your CGI Environment," I'm going to tell you how to set up your computer so that you can begin writing and testing CGI scripts.

Q&A

Q I've heard of Web Objects, Cold Fusion, Java Server Pages, (insert application server here)—how does it compare to CGI for writing Web applications?

A I'll discuss most of the popular Web application servers in Hour 12. Each application server has its own strengths and weaknesses and it's impossible to generalize.

Q Does the browser that my site's visitors use matter when I write CGI programs?

A For the most part, no. Because CGI is a server-side technology, as long as the browser supports the HTTP specification properly, your CGI programs should work just fine.

Q Are any security issues related to running CGI programs?

A Yes, CGI programs can make your site vulnerable to intruders in many different ways if you're not careful. Hour 22, "Securing CGI Scripts," covers the most common security issues.

Q My Internet service provider (ISP) doesn't allow me to write my own CGI programs. What can I do?

A Not a lot. Many ISPs don't allow users to supply their own CGI programs for security reasons. If this is the case, you'll have to find another ISP that does. Most Web-hosting services aimed at professional Web designers do allow their users to create their own CGI programs. You can find a list of some ISPs that support CGI at the Web site for this book at `http://rc3.org/cgibook`.

Workshop

The quiz questions are designed to strengthen the knowledge you gain each hour. For the answers to the quiz questions, refer to Appendix A, "Answers."

Quiz

1. Which was the first Web server to support CGI?
2. What is the primary advantage of compiled languages over interpreted languages?
3. What is the name of the technique used to translate special characters in query strings to characters that are acceptable to the Web server?

Hour **2**

Setting Up Your CGI Environment

In this hour, I'm going to explain what you need to do to get started in CGI programming. To write and test your CGI programs, you need to have the proper environment set up, either on your own computer or on a server that you have access to.

During this hour, I'll discuss the following topics:

- The advantages and disadvantages of running your own Web server versus using a hosting service
- Popular Web-server operating systems
- The requirements for setting up a CGI programming environment
- Step-by-step instructions for setting up a Web server under Windows for CGI development

The Web Server Itself

The first question you face as you begin to write CGI scripts is what computer to test them on. The second question is where they will reside after you've written them and you're ready to start using them. Fortunately, the answer to both of these questions does not have to be the same. Before I get started, I'd like to clear up one point of confusion. The word "server" can be used in two ways. In the first sense, a server is a computer that is used to provide various services to other computers. For example, most companies have a mail server to which all of the employees connect to retrieve their email. In this case, I'm talking about a Web server, a computer which is used to house Web content and Web applications that can be accessed using a Web browser. The other sense of the word server refers to the particular piece of software used to provide the service. Running on the computer that serves as the Web server is a program that's unfortunately also referred to as a Web server. It can also be referred to as an HTTP daemon. This program actually accepts HTTP requests and fetches the appropriate resource to respond to them.

The requirements for setting up a place where you can write CGI scripts are few. Any computer running Windows (either 95, 98, or NT) will work fine, as will any computer running a version of UNIX, including Linux or FreeBSD. As long as your computer is running one of the operating systems I just mentioned and you have the software that's necessary to run the CGI programs, you're ready to start developing software. Later this hour, I'll discuss exactly what you need to do to get your CGI programming environment up and running on a standard desktop machine running Windows.

Hosting Your CGI Scripts

After you've finished writing your CGI scripts, you have to find a place to store them so that they're accessible from the Internet, or from your intranet, depending on what you're going to use them for. If you're going to use them for an intranet application, you'll need to store them on a server that's accessible from your internal network.

If you're writing a script for use on the Internet, you have a few more options. The first option is to place the scripts on a server of your own that's connected to the Internet. The second option is to lease space on a server managed by an ISP.

Running Your Own Web Server

In some cases, you might have a server of your own on which you're going to place your CGI scripts. Perhaps your company already owns a server where all of the content is placed, or you have a server on which you're going to place the scripts. For some applications, using a server that belongs to you or your company is the only option that will work.

For example, perhaps you're writing CGI scripts for your company's intranet. If that's the case, your scripts need to be hosted somewhere on your internal network. Generally, these will be hosted on a company-wide intranet server, or perhaps a departmental server. If your application is widely used by a lot of people, or deals with particularly sensitive data, perhaps there will be a server dedicated to it.

In any case, there are advantages and disadvantages involved with using a server of your own. The single largest disadvantage of running your own Web server is the extra responsibility it entails. When you're in charge of a server, you have to make sure that everything is set up properly, that the server doesn't run out of disk space, that everything is backed up, and that the server is secure.

That's a lot of work, especially for someone who isn't trained as a system administrator. In most cases, programmers aren't in charge of all of the management tasks involved with the servers that they use. If you're writing CGI scripts for work, there are usually people in the information systems department whose job it is to take care of the servers.

Explaining in detail how to set up a computer for Web hosting is well beyond the scope of this hour. You should determine which operating system and Web server you're going to use, and then look up reference material explaining how to run them.

Web Hosting

Most Web sites on the Internet are not on servers owned or managed by the people who created the site. Rather, they're run on servers that are owned by a company that is in the business of Web hosting. These companies administer the servers themselves, and place multiple customers on each server. Although many of these companies focus on allowing users to place static HTML files on their servers, there are some who allow you to place CGI scripts on their servers as well.

High-end Web hosting companies will allow companies to place their own servers in a managed facility where they will take care of network connectivity, power, and backups, and the company that owns the server manages the content on the server and access to the server. Another option provided by some hosting companies is a dedicated server that is managed by the hosting company but is available exclusively for the use of the company that is leasing space on it.

The advantages of using a hosting company to store and serve your CGI programs (and static HTML documents) include the following:

- The hosting company takes care of all the connectivity for the server. Rather than worrying about providing enough bandwidth for all of the requests to your Web server, you can rely on the hosting company to make sure that there's plenty of bandwidth. The hosting company is able to get better rates for network connectivity than their customers could individually because they buy enough bandwidth for all their customers at once.

- The hosting company manages the Web server for you. Hosting companies are experts on keeping Web servers up and running.

- You save costs on server hardware. When you rent space on a server from a Web hosting company, the hosting company purchases the server, and you share space on it with other users.

Web-Server Operating Systems

One issue you have to deal with when you write CGI programs is which operating system you're going to use. The operating system affects which Web server software you can use, and which programming languages are available for writing CGI programs. Different Web servers are accessed and managed differently as well. I'm going to discuss three Web-server operating systems specifically in this hour. The two most popular platforms for serving Web content are Windows NT and UNIX. Less popular, but still somewhat commonly used, is the Mac OS.

UNIX

As you know from Hour 1, "Overview of CGI Programming," UNIX is the original Web server operating system. UNIX and the Internet are intimately linked. The TCP/IP protocol, upon which all Internet services run, is built into the UNIX kernel. Written for UNIX, the CERN server (one of the first Web servers) was written by Tim Berners-Lee—the inventor of the Web.

When I talk about UNIX, I'm speaking generally. There is no one operating system called UNIX. There are a number of operating systems available that are all derived from the original UNIX operating system, and that are extremely similar to one another. For the purpose of writing CGI scripts, they're almost identical. Some of the common UNIX flavors are Solaris, Linux, FreeBSD, and HP-UX.

There's little you need to do to get CGI scripts up and running under UNIX. When you install a UNIX Web server, generally it's already set up for running CGI scripts. You just need to put the scripts in the right directory and make sure that the Web server has execute permission for the scripts in order to get the scripts working. I'll discuss some of the common Web servers for UNIX a bit later in this hour.

If you're interested in experimenting with a UNIX-based operating system, there are several free options that run on standard PC hardware. Linux is the most popular free UNIX operating system, you can find out about it at http://www.linux.org. FreeBSD is also a free UNIX operating system, and is run by some of the largest sites on the Web. You can find out more about it at http://www.freebsd.org.

Windows NT

The second dominant Web server platform is Windows NT. Windows NT Server is Microsoft's server operating system. Even though Windows NT is very popular, and most Web servers for Windows NT have provided CGI support for a long time, it's not generally associated with CGI programming. At one time, it was rather difficult to write CGI programs to run under Windows NT, but this is no longer the case.

In fact, many CGI programs that are written to run on UNIX servers are very easily portable to run under Windows NT. There are versions of most of the popular UNIX scripting languages, including Perl, Python, and TCL, that run under Windows NT. Nearly all Windows NT Web servers now support CGI as it was defined for UNIX servers.

2

The CGI Environment

As you already know, CGI programs aren't like regular programs. Although they can be executed from the command line, they're really designed to be executed by a Web server in response to a request from a Web browser. There are several pieces of software that are required in order to set up a proper environment for CGI programming. A list of the software that is required, and some that is just helpful, follows:

- A Web server. In order to execute your CGI programs and send the results to a Web browser, a Web server is required. Naturally, in order to write CGI scripts, the server must support CGI.

- A language interpreter or compiler. If you write your CGI programs in a scripting language, you need the language interpreter. For example, if you write your programs in Perl, a Perl interpreter must be available. If you write them in the Bourne shell, /bin/sh must be present. Alternatively, if you write your CGI programs in a compiled language, the compiler must be available.

- Libraries or applications that automatically translate form input into a data structure native to the language that you're using. If you wish to decode the user input manually, these aren't necessary, but they can help to avoid errors and save you a lot of work.

Web Servers

The piece of software most integral to CGI programming is the Web server. The Web server handles all the requests sent by the Web browser, and retrieves the appropriate resource from disk and sends it back. It also executes CGI scripts when they're requested, and handles authentication. There are a number of Web servers available, but the two most popular are Apache for UNIX, and Microsoft Internet Information Server (IIS) for Windows. Most Web servers are extremely similar in functionality.

Web-Server Directory Structure

It's important to understand how the directories associated with a Web server are organized. Unless you understand the directory structure of the Web server, you won't know where your CGI scripts should be placed. Most Web servers share a common directory structure. They have a place to put static HTML files, and a place to put CGI scripts.

The Apache Web server, on both UNIX and Windows, uses the directory structure depicted in Figure 2.1. The htdocs directory is used to store static content, and is generally referred to as the *document root*. The cgi-bin directory is used to store CGI programs.

FIGURE 2.1

The typical directory structure for an Apache Web server.

This is simply the default configuration—if there's a directory structure you prefer more, you can easily reconfigure Apache so that you can use it. For example, if you like, you can set up Apache so that files in the htdocs directory are executed as CGI scripts if they have a certain extension. You can also create aliases so that directories elsewhere on the file system are treated by Apache as though they are below the document root.

Other Web servers use a similar directory structure by default, but nearly all Web servers allow you to configure the directories however you want. There are two important points to keep in mind when you're storing CGI scripts on a Web server. The first is that you need to make sure that your CGI scripts are in a directory where they'll be executed, and not just sent to the Web browser that requests them. If you place a script in the wrong directory, it will look something like Figure 2.2 when the browser requests it.

The second thing you should think about is how you want your Web content organized. There are sometimes good reasons for placing CGI scripts under your document root with your standard HTML files. For example, if you want the default home page for your Web site to be generated by a CGI script, you'll need to set up your server so that you can keep your CGI scripts in the home directory of the Web site.

How Scripts Are Executed

There are two separate tasks involved with processing a request for a CGI script. The first task is recognizing that the request is for a script that should be executed, and the second task is executing the script that was requested. The Web server is in charge of figuring out that the request is for a CGI script; the operating system is in charge of figuring out what needs to be done to execute the script.

FIGURE 2.2

The result of a script's source code being sent to a browser.

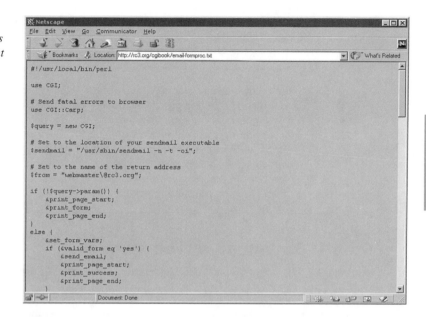

```
#!/usr/local/bin/perl

use CGI;

# Send fatal errors to browser
use CGI::Carp;

$query = new CGI;

# Set to the location of your sendmail executable
$sendmail = "/usr/sbin/sendmail -n -t -oi";

# Set to the name of the return address
$from = "webmaster\@rc3.org";

if (!$query->param()) {
    &print_page_start;
    &print_form;
    &print_page_end;
}
else {
    &set_form_vars;
    if (&valid_form eq 'yes') {
        &send_email;
        &print_page_start;
        &print_success;
        &print_page_end;
    }
```

There are a number of ways that the Web server can differentiate between requests for static files and requests for CGI programs. The most common method is specifying a directory as a `cgi-bin` directory. All the files in this directory are treated as though they are CGI programs, and the server attempts to execute them when they're requested.

Another option is to set up the Web server so that it treats files with a certain extension as CGI programs. For example, you can set it up so that any file with the extension `.cgi` is considered to be a CGI program, even if it resides in a document directory.

After the script has been requested, it's up to the operating system to figure out what to do with the request. The operating system handles the file as though its name were typed in at a command prompt. Generally, if the CGI program is running on a Windows-based server, it must have a specific extension as well. For example, when you install Perl on a computer running Windows, it associates files with the `.pl` extension with the Perl interpreter. So if you're using IIS, you should assign the `.pl` extension to Perl CGI programs.

Setting Up Your CGI Development Environment

Now that I've surveyed the landscape of Web server hardware and software, I'm going to walk you through the steps for setting up an environment where you can test your CGI scripts on a standard desktop computer running Windows. After you've followed these steps, you should be able to test almost all the scripts printed in this book on your local desktop computer.

The following steps assume that you have Windows 95, Windows 98, or Windows NT installed on your computer, and that you have TCP/IP networking installed (if you can connect to the Internet, or Web sites on your local network, you do). If you're running UNIX or the Mac OS on your local computer, the steps won't be nearly as useful to you as they are to people who are running Windows. Even though the exact technical information won't be applicable to you, the concepts involved in getting a Web server up and running are still the same.

Step 1: Download a Web Server

To test your CGI scripts, you'll need access to a Web server. Fortunately, there are many free ones available, so you won't have to spend any money.

If you don't have one installed on your system already, I recommend the Apache Web server. You could also install Microsoft's Personal Web Server, but I prefer Apache for a number of reasons. The main reason I think Apache is a good choice is that it doesn't do any permanent, irreversible damage to your system when you install it. It's a small download, and doesn't create a large footprint in your Registry or on your system. When you're done with it, it's easy to uninstall.

Another advantage of using Apache is that all the configuration directives for the Windows version of Apache are the same as those used for the UNIX version. Most computers used as Web servers run some flavor of UNIX, and UNIX is particularly popular for hosting CGI programs. If you can get your scripts working under Apache for Windows, it's not hard to migrate them to a server running Apache for UNIX. Besides, everything you learn about Apache on your local system can be transferred to a production Web server running Apache.

If your CGI script will eventually reside on a Web server running IIS, Personal Web Server is probably a better choice for you.

You can download the installer for the Apache server at the Apache Software Foundation's Web site. The URL is

```
http://www.apache.org/httpd.html
```

You should click on the download link and select the latest version of Apache for Win32 from the list. The filename will probably be something like `apache_1_3_9_win32.exe`.

Step 2: Install the Web Server

After you've downloaded the Apache installer on your local machine, the next step is to install the software. Apache uses a standard Windows software installation package, so all you have to do to install the Web server is double-click on the executable, agree to the license agreement, and choose a directory and installation type.

> The installer wants to put the server under the Program Files directory, but my recommendation is to place the Web server in a directory that doesn't include a space in the name. Although everything should work fine if you place it in the default directory as the installer suggests, I've had an easier time in the past when I installed the Web server in a directory that had no spaces in the name, like `C:\Apache`.

Step 3: Download a Perl Interpreter

This book follows the prevailing trend by focusing on Perl for CGI programming, so you'll need access to a Perl interpreter to run the programs in the book. Most UNIX systems have Perl interpreters installed already. If Perl isn't installed on your UNIX server, you should have a heart-to-heart conversation with your systems administrator, or if you're the administrator, you should download Perl at `http://www.perl.com`.

Windows users can obtain an excellent version of Perl at `http://www.activestate.com`. At one time, there were two popular versions of Perl available for Windows, the ActiveState port, and a port derived directly from the UNIX source code. Not long ago these two ports were merged to create one standard version of Perl for Windows. This had the combined advantage of putting some of the unique features from the ActiveState port into the standard distribution, and making the ActiveState version of Perl more compliant with the standard version.

One of the nicest features of the ActiveState Perl distribution is that it comes with all sorts of Perl modules that ordinarily have to be downloaded and installed individually. Because most of the installers for these programs were written with UNIX in mind, ActiveState went ahead and included the modules with their distribution of Perl so that Windows users can take advantage of them.

In any case, you should download the latest Perl build from `http://www.activestate.com`. (Insert information about navigating the Web site here.)

Step 4: Install the Perl Interpreter

After you've downloaded the latest version of Perl, you should install it on your computer. After Perl has been properly installed, you should be able to execute Perl programs by double-clicking them.

> Just as I suggested that you install Apache in a directory with no spaces in the name, I suggest the same thing for the Perl interpreter. Perl CGI programs that work with either the UNIX or Windows version of Apache are required to have the path to the executable for the Perl interpreter in the first line of the script. Spaces in the path to the interpreter break the CGI scripts, so you have to use the DOS name for any directory that has a space in the name. If you installed Perl in the directory C:\Program Files\Perl, your CGI scripts would have to begin with the following line:
>
> `#!C:\progra~1\perl\bin\perl.exe`

Step 5: Get the Web Server Up and Running

After the Web server and Perl are installed, you need to get the server up and running. With Apache, this is very easy. There are two options for running Apache; you can either install it as a service, or run it only when you need it. My recommendation is to just run the server when you need it, and only install it as a service when you want it up and running full time.

If you're only running the server for your personal testing, it makes sense to just run it when you'll be using it. If you're going to let other people view pages and test scripts on the server, it makes more sense to just keep the server up and running at all times.

Starting the server is really easy. Just double-click the apache.exe icon, and the server will start up. A DOS window will appear when the server starts. The Apache installer should also have placed an Apache Web Server folder in your Windows Start menu. That folder contains a program called Start Apache that you can select to start the server as well. To stop the server, just press Ctrl+C in the server's window, and the server will stop automatically.

To install the Apache server as a service, so that it runs all the time, you need to open a DOS window (or a command-line window under Windows NT, to use the precise terminology). Then you should change directories to the Apache directory, and type apache /s. The /s flag indicates that the server should install itself as a service. From that point onward, as long as your computer is running, Apache will run as well.

Step 6: Test the Web Server

After you have the server up and running, you can test it with a Web browser to make sure that it's working. Generally, it's easiest to test the server on your local machine rather than connecting to it from another machine. To test the server, you need to know what URL to type into the browser. If you generally connect to the Internet with a modem and an ISP, the name of your computer is probably something strange like dial813.isp.net, plus, every time you dial up again, it will change.

Fortunately, there are a couple of ways to identify the local computer without knowing the name or IP number assigned to the computer. The TCP/IP standard mandates that you be able to refer to the local computer as localhost, and that the loopback address is 127.0.0.1. So, you can use either of the two following URLs to access the Web server running on your computer:

```
http://localhost/
http://127.0.0.1/
```

When you enter one of the two URLs in your browser, you should see a page something like the one in Figure 2.3. If that page appears, Apache has been installed successfully. If not, you'll need to do some troubleshooting to determine why the installation wasn't successful.

FIGURE 2.3

The test page for the Apache server.

Step 7: Test a Perl CGI Script

After you've verified that the Apache installation was a success, you're ready to make sure that you can create and execute Perl CGI programs as well. This test involves creating a simple Perl CGI script, placing it in the appropriate directory, and verifying that it can be executed through the Web server.

The first step is to create the script. In order to create it, you'll need to know the location where you installed your Perl interpreter. Listing 2.1 contains the source code for the test script.

LISTING 2.1   A Simple Sample Program

```
#!/usr/local/bin/perl

use CGI;

$query = new CGI;

print $query->header;

print "<html><head><title>A test</title></head>\n";
print "<body>The test was successful.</body></html>";
```

You should enter the script in a text editor, save it to a file named test.pl, and place the script in the cgi-bin directory in the root directory of your Web server. The first line of the file should be changed to reflect the actual location of perl.exe on your system.

> The first line of the script is important under Unix, because it indicates which program is supposed to be used to interpret the script. Apache for Windows follows this convention and also determines how the file is supposed to be handled based on the contents of the first line of the file. Other Web servers running under Windows decide how to handle programs based on their extension, so they ignore the first line of the program.

You can then request the file with your Web browser using the following URL:

```
http://localhost/cgi-bin/test.cgi
```

If the test is successful, you'll see a page very similar to the one in Figure 2.4 in your browser window.

The test verifies that a number of components of the CGI environment are set up properly. Here's a list of the important components that the test verifies:

- The Web server is running properly and is set up to execute CGI scripts
- You've installed the CGI script in the proper directory, and the Web server is set up to treat files in that directory as CGI scripts

- Perl is properly installed on your system, and you've entered the correct path to the Perl executable in the first line of your script

- The Perl libraries that ship with Perl are correctly installed, specifically CGI.pm

FIGURE 2.4

Executing the test CGI script successfully.

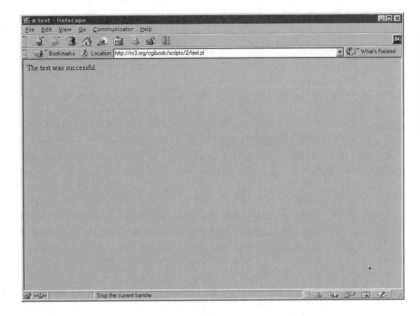

What if Something Went Wrong?

In the next hour, " Installing and Debugging CGI Scripts," I'm going to talk a lot about debugging CGI scripts, but I want to give you the information you need to debug the CGI script if it didn't work in this test.

Here are a few basic steps you can take to diagnose the problem. The first step is to make sure that you transcribed the script properly. You should execute the program from the command line to verify that it works and that the output is correct. To run the program from the command line, you need to run the Perl interpreter and pass it the name and path to your script. Let's assume that your Perl executable is in `C:\perl\bin`. To test your script, you can use the following command line:

```
C:\perl\bin\perl.exe C:\apache\cgi-bin\test.cgi
```

If the script was copied correctly, the program will generate the following output:

```
Content-Type: text/html

<html><head><title>A test</title></head>
<body>The test was successful.</body></html>
```

On executing `test.cgi` from the command line, you may first encounter the following message:

(offline mode: enter name=value pairs on standard input)

This will allow you to enter key pairs that will be passed to cgi script (something we'll be doing a lot of later in the book). For now just hit Ctrl+Z to continue.

If it wasn't copied correctly, it will probably print an error of some kind.

There's some chance that the error could be related to the presence of the CGI.pm module. If the Perl interpreter can't find CGI.pm, your program will fail to execute. You should check to make sure that Perl is installed correctly, and that CGI.pm is in the Perl library directory.

If the Perl program works correctly, in all likelihood there's a problem with the Web server. Go back again and make sure that the test in step 6 still works. If it doesn't, you've either used the wrong URL in your browser or the Web server isn't running. There's an off chance that the networking on your computer might be misconfigured. If you can view Web sites on the Internet or a local network, this isn't the case.

It's important to get this script to work before you move on to the next hour. If you can't get it working, you'll have trouble getting the rest of the scripts in the book to work too. So be sure to spend time to get this one up and running.

Summary

The purpose of this hour was to provide you with the information you need to set up an environment where you can run CGI scripts. It's pointless to write CGI scripts if you don't have anywhere to put them once they're written. This hour discussed some options for hosting CGI scripts. You also learned about the most popular operating systems for Web servers, and how Web servers work. Finally, you learned how to install the Apache Web server and ActiveState Perl on a computer running Windows, and how to test your CGI environment to make sure that it works properly.

Q&A

Q **I'm partial to O'Reilly Web site Professional(or Netscape Enterprise Server, Roxen Challenger, or thttpd). What do I need to do to get CGI scripts running?**

A Check out the documentation for your Web server. Nearly all Web servers follow the same pattern—you should be able to use CGI scripts if you put them in the cgi-bin directory for the server. Your Web server may also support other ways you can set up scripts as CGI scripts; check out the configuration instructions.

Q **I'd like to write CGI scripts for a Web server running on a Macintosh. What should I do?**

A Traditional Macintosh Web servers generally support ACGI, an alternative to CGI that works with Mac OS applications. Unfortunately, a detailed discussion of how ACGI works is beyond the scope of this book. The newest Mac OS X however, while retaining much of the feel of prior Mac OS's, is rooted in BSD Unix and even runs the Apache web server by default. For Mac OS X and above most of the information given for Unix should work with only minor modifications if any.

Q **Should I install Perl even if I plan on writing my CGI programs in another language?**

A Yes, you should. Most of the examples in this book are written in Perl. If you want to install them to see how they work, you'll need to install Perl on your Web server or your local computer.

Workshop

The quiz questions are designed to strengthen the knowledge you gain each hour. The exercises help you build on that knowledge by providing you with the opportunity to apply it to real problems. For the answers to the quiz questions, refer to Appendix A, "Answers."

Quiz

1. What are the two dominant Web server operating systems?
2. Which two URLs can be used to address the Web server on the local machine, regardless of its domain name and IP number?
3. What is the name of the directory where CGI scripts are usually installed?

Exercises

1. Get a Web server up and running on your local computer so that you can run CGI scripts.

2. Start looking into where your CGI scripts will be hosted when you finish writing them.

HOUR 3

Downloading, Installing, and Debugging CGI Scripts

Before I begin to discuss how to design and create your own CGI scripts, I thought I'd give you the opportunity to save yourself a lot of work. There are thousands of CGI scripts that have already been written and are publicly available for download over the Internet. In some cases, rather than writing a script of your own, you can download a script from the Internet and use it instead. This hour also explains some methods for debugging CGI scripts after they're installed. You can use these methods to get scripts you download to work, or to debug your own CGI scripts.

The topics covered in this hour are

- A discussion of how to download scripts from the Internet
- Information on installing and configuring scripts you download
- Information on debugging CGI scripts using a number of different techniques

Downloading Scripts From the Internet

The objective of this book is to teach you how to build your own Web applications using CGI. However, it isn't here to convince you to do unnecessary work. There are bunches of CGI scripts other people have written that you can download from the Internet and use on your own site.

These scripts are useful for two purposes. First, they can save you a lot of work. If you can find a script out there that provides the functionality you need for an application, you may want to use it instead of writing a program from scratch. Second, they can help teach you how to write better applications. You can look at existing programs to see how the author accomplished certain tasks, and decide how you might design your own programs differently, or how you might apply their solutions to problems you have to solve.

Finding the Scripts You Need

In order to find CGI programs to use on your Web sites, you need to know where to look. There are a number of popular repositories for free CGI scripts on the Internet. The best way to find the scripts you need is to search for scripts that seem to offer the functionality you require, and then download those scripts and evaluate them carefully. Some of the most popular script repositories are included in Table 3.1.

TABLE 3.1   Sites Where You Can Download Public CGI Scripts

Site	URL
http://www.cgi-resources.com	This site contains all sorts of information about CGI programming, along with a large library of publicly available scripts.
http://www.worldwidemart.com/scripts	Matt's Script Archive—one of the best known repositories of freely available scripts on the Web. The scripts in this archive are widely used and well documented.
http://www.freecode.com	A large repository of free programs, including CGI scripts.
http://www.scriptsearch.com	Billed as the world's largest library of CGI programs, this archive contains thousands of CGI scripts along with other Internet scripts.
http://www.extropia.com	These scripts originally made up Selena Sol's Public Domain Script Archive. The scripts are still all free and available to the public.

What to Look for in Publicly Available Scripts

Obviously, the first thing to look for is whether the CGI script meets the requirements for your application. Without a well-defined set of requirements, it's impossible to reasonably compare one script to another. After you're certain what the application's requirements are, you can start narrowing the field of the CGI scripts available to ones that meet those requirements.

Beyond the satisfaction of your requirements, there are some other issues that you should investigate before using a CGI script that you downloaded over the Internet. These issues surround the general reliability and maintainability of publicly distributed scripts.

Quality of the Source Code

When you download a CGI script from the Internet to use on your site, one issue you'll really want to look into is the quality of the script's source code. Before you start using the script, check out the formatting and comments in the source code. Is the program readable? Can you follow what it does? If not, it may not be worth using. If you need to fix something later, or you want to add some functionality, it's nice to be able to go right in and see where changes need to be made.

Quality source code indicates that the script's author took care when writing the script, and it is also a good sign that the code itself is of high quality. If you're reviewing a number of scripts before you look at any of them in depth, you should be able to throw away scripts that aren't written in an organized and neat manner.

Security

Any time you place a CGI script with a security hole on your server, there's a chance that some malicious person could exploit it to gain access to the server. Well-written CGI scripts don't have security holes. Unfortunately, the Web is full of CGI scripts that aren't well written, and that will introduce security holes on your site. Many of them are written by people to use on their own Web sites; some of them are distributed for use by the public.

These scripts have security holes not because the authors want to expose people who use the scripts to risks, but because writing secure software is difficult. You should be aware of the fact that any time you download someone else's program and use it on your server, there might be security problems with the program that you don't know about.

Think about it—if thousands of people are using the same insecure script, chances are somebody has figured out where the hole is. If the person who discovered the hole, or any person who's heard about the security hole, is interested in breaking into your Web server, then he can take advantage of the publicly known security flaw.

Even worse, this malicious person can use Internet search engines to find sites that use the offending CGI script, and then break into them. So it's very important to understand CGI script security when you install CGI scripts, and to review the source code for the scripts before you install them on your Web server. In Hour 22, "Securing CGI Scripts," I'll talk more about CGI security, and provide a list of sites where you can find out about security problems with scripts that you might be using.

Support

One question you'll want to get an answer to is how much support the author of the script provides. Support comes in two forms: direct support to users who are having problems, and regular improvements and updates to the program. Most people who distribute software for free don't provide much personal support, although if you treat them nicely, they'll often answer questions. On the other hand, you should look for scripts that are being actively maintained by their authors, or by someone who has taken over the maintenance of the software.

Despite the best efforts of software developers, most software has bugs, security holes, and other problems that must be fixed. If nobody is maintaining the program you use, it's up to you to maintain it yourself. For most people, it's easier to rely on the original author to maintain a script than to maintain it themselves.

Installing a Downloaded Script

After you've downloaded a script, you should install it on your local server. Usually, you'll have to make some changes to the script to get it to work in your environment. If it's written in a compiled language, like C, you'll also have to compile the script locally before you can use it. Better written scripts allow you to get them up and running simply by changing a few specific variables, and provide documentation that explains exactly what needs to be changed in order to get the scripts working.

Example: Downloading and Installing a Guestbook Script

Let's take a look at the steps required to download and install a typical CGI script on a server. For this example, I'm going to use the Guestbook script from Matt's Script Archive. The guestbook program allows users who visit your site to enter some personal information that will be published as part of your site's guestbook. Other users who visit your site can view the guestbook and add entries of their own. One nice thing about Matt Wright's scripts is that they're designed to allow users to get them up and running quickly. The documentation is clear and concise, and the scripts themselves are written so that they're easy to configure for the local computer. The guestbook script is available at:

```
http://www.worldwidemart.com/scripts/guestbook.shtml
```

The script and its attending files can be downloaded in any number of formats; you should download it in the format that's appropriate for your platform. After you've downloaded the script, you need to unpack the script in your cgi-bin directory.

> By unpack, I mean that you should use the appropriate application to extract the files from the archive. On Windows, you might use WinZip to extract the files. Under UNIX, you would most likely use gzip and tar.

Configuring the Script

After you've downloaded and unpacked the script, the next step is to get the guestbook up and running on your Web server. Because it's a Perl script, you'll have to edit it so that it works in your environment. Generally, that means editing the shebang line (the first line of the script), so that the pointer to the Perl interpreter is correct. For example, the script is set by default to look for the Perl interpreter at /usr/bin/perl. On my Web server, Perl is installed at /usr/local/bin/perl, so I changed the first line to point to the correct location. After that's done, the script should run.

> The first line of a UNIX script, the one with the pointer to the script interpreter is called the "shebang line." It's called that because the first two characters are #!. The # is sometimes called the hash character, and UNIX people call exclamation points bangs, thus shebang.

To get the script working, you have to go into the script and set some variables so they reflect your environment. These variable assignments are found in the guestbook.pl script immediately after the comments at the top. Some of the information you must enter or verify is the location of the date program on your system, the URL where the guestbook form is located, and the name of the file to be used as the guestbook log. There are also a number of options that can be set to alter the behavior of the script. These options are described in the README file.

Installing the Files and Setting Permissions

You must put all the files in the proper locations. The guestbook.pl file should reside in your cgi-bin directory, and the HTML files distributed as part of the guestbook application should reside under the document root on your Web server with the rest of your static HTML documents. Some of the variables in guestbook.pl will have to be set after you've determined the final locations for the files in the package. You also have to edit the adduser.html form and change the ACTION attribute of the FORM tag so that it points to the location where you installed guestbook.pl.

You also have to make sure that the actual guestbook file, `guestbook.html`, and the guest log, `guestlog.html`, have the proper permissions set. They must be writable by the user that the Web server runs as. You can either change the owner of the files to the Web server user (often `nobody`), or just make the files world writable. It's up to you.

These concepts are universal to all CGI scripts that write to local files, so I'll elaborate some. Under UNIX and Windows NT, all processes run as a particular user. For example, if I log into a computer running UNIX and start a Web browser, then the Web browser process will run under my user ID. When the Web server is started, the process runs under the user ID that started it, or under the user ID that's assigned to the process. For security purposes, the Web server processes are often assigned to the user ID `nobody`, which has few, if any, privileges. To change the owner of the guestbook and log file to the user ID `nobody`, the following commands are used:

```
chown nobody guestbook.html guestlog.html
```

If you opt not to deal with changing the owner of these files, you can just give all the users on the server write access to them. The big problem here is that if the computer on which the guestbook runs is used by multiple users, they'll all have the ability to modify that file. If you're worried about that, then you should change the owner to the Web server user. If that's not a concern, you can just use the `chmod` command to provide write access to the files to all users on the system. The following command is used:

```
chmod a+w guestbook.html guestlog.html
```

Testing the Script

After you're done with the installation, you should be able to run the script. If it isn't working, read over the documentation again to make sure that you've set everything up properly. Then, if it still won't work, check out the next section of the hour to find out how to debug your CGI scripts. When the script is working, the guestbook will appear in your browser as it does in Figure 3.1.

Customizing the Look and Feel

After you have the script working, you can edit all of the files associated with the guestbook to align them with the look-and-feel of your Web site. There are some instructions on customizing the files associated with the guestbook in the documentation. To view the guestbook on my Web site, use the following URL:

```
http://rc3.org/cgibook/guestbook/guestbook.html
```

In Figure 3.2, you can see the `addguest.html` script after its appearance has been changed to fit the design of my Web site.

FIGURE 3.1

The guestbook from Matt's Script Archive.

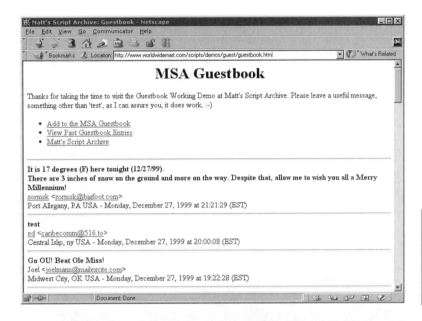

FIGURE 3.2

A customized version of the addguest.html *file.*

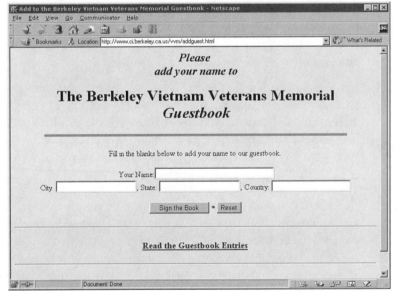

Debugging CGI Scripts

Some people would say that the toughest step in the process of creating an application is debugging it after all the functionality that you wanted is, in theory, complete. Certainly working out all of the nagging bugs in an application can take as long as getting the main functionality written.

One problem with CGI scripts is that they exist as part of a larger system. The actual CGI program is just one component of the system; there's also the operating system, the Web server, and the network connection between the Web browser and the Web server. A problem can occur with any of these components, and one of the toughest tasks facing a CGI programmer is determining where a problem occurred.

In many cases, problems crop up in the network connection between the Web server and Web browsers. In this book, I'm not going to discuss problems caused by bad Internet connections. Instead, I'm going to focus on problems that crop up on the Web server. However, you should be mindful of the fact that in some cases, the problem lies in the network connection, or even in the configuration of the browser or computer running the browser. Sometimes, when errors in your CGI scripts are reported, it turns out that the user just didn't understand how to use the script.

Finding the Source of an Error

Before you can fix an error, you have to figure out what caused it. Because this book focuses on CGI programming and not Web server administration, I'm not concerned with problems like your Web server crashing or your router preventing incoming connections. The important point to make is that if you can't connect to the Web server at all, either because the domain name in the URL you entered can't be looked up, or the server is refusing network connections, don't blame your CGI program. You've got some problem cropping up at a lower level that has to be fixed first.

Let's assume that the Web server is up and running, and there's some problem with your CGI script. Before you start digging through your program's source code, you should verify that a few common mistakes haven't been made. These mistakes plague everyone who writes CGI scripts, even people who are old hats. You can learn a lot about what went wrong by looking at the response code that's returned with the response.

Examining the HTTP Status Code

Every HTTP response is accompanied by a status code that indicates what the result of the request was. The status code is part of the response headers that are sent from the server to the browser. The most common status code by far is 200 Success. You never see or hear about this one because it means that the request was valid and returned a successful response. Whenever you request a page that is displayed properly, the response had a status code of 200.

When the status is something other than 200 Success, the Web server generally sends an error document back with the response. Often, the response code will be displayed as part of the error document. If it is not, you have to check the server's access log to find the response code for the failed request. The most common error code encountered is 404

Not Found. This code is returned when the requested resource could not be located by the Web server. Usually this error message crops up when a user clicks on a link to a file that no longer exists.

A 403 Access Denied error is returned when a user attempts to request a file that the Web server is not allowed to read. The Web server user must have read permission for a file in order to send it to a user.

When a user tries to visit a site that is password protected using basic authentication, and she enters an invalid account and password combination, she receives a 401 Unauthorized error.

None of these errors are specific to CGI programming, I'm just including them here so that you'll know what you're looking at when you see them. The most important error for CGI programmers is 500 Server Error. It indicates that something went wrong when the server tried to execute the CGI script. It doesn't necessarily mean that the program itself is broken, just that the server had trouble requesting it and getting back the proper results.

Reading the Error Log

Web servers that support CGI programs maintain an error log of some kind. Any time a request fails, the error that occurred is stored in the log so that responsible system administrators and programmers can see what went wrong when their applications failed to work properly. The error log isn't restricted to CGI-related errors. It stores any error that the Web server sends as a response to a request, so all the 404 Not Found errors and other errors associated with regular requests go there as well.

The most important feature of the error log, from a CGI programmer's standpoint, is that it goes beyond storing the error code generated by the Web server to storing the error message produced by the program itself. This works in an interesting way. When a CGI program fails, it generally displays an error message. In this case, the program doesn't generate a content-type header, which is unacceptable to the Web server. When the request for the CGI program fails, the server copies some of the output of the attempt to execute the program (in other words, the CGI program's error message) into the error log. This message is generally the most important clue for determining what went wrong with the CGI program.

The error log for the Apache Web server is generally found in the logs directory under the server root, and is usually named error_log. However, the name and location of the error log can be changed to something else, so you can't count on that being the case. You can generally get the location of this file from the server administrator, or if you're able, by checking the Web server's configuration files. Some service providers don't turn on error logging by default, and you may have to ask them to enable error logs for your site so that you can debug your programs more easily.

3

Listing 3.1 contains an excerpt from an Apache error log. I'll discuss what some of the common errors found in the error log are a bit later.

LISTING 3.1   An Excerpt from an Apache Error Log

```
[Wed Dec  1 21:33:20 1999] [error] (2)No such file or directory: exec of
➥/web/cgi-bin/bad.cgi failed
[Wed Dec  1 21:33:20 1999] [error] [client 199.72.11.45] Premature end of
➥script headers: /web/cgi-bin/bad.cgi
```

Fixing Setup Errors

Now that you've learned how to find errors, I'm going to go over some of the common errors you might encounter, and explain how to fix them. Because these common errors are generally related to features required of all CGI programs, they're easy to track down and fix. Errors in your application logic are far more insidious, and can take an awful lot longer to fix than the simpler errors listed here. I will talk about some debugging techniques later that you can use to isolate these types of bugs in your code.

Setting the Proper File Permissions

One of the most common mistakes most people make when they write CGI programs is setting the file permissions improperly. CGI scripts must be executable by the user that the Web server runs as. The easiest way around this is to make sure that all your CGI programs are executable by everyone. If the Web server isn't allowed to execute the program, the response to any request for it will be 500 Server Error.

File Permissions Under UNIX-Based Operating Systems

If your CGI programs are installed on a server running some UNIX-based operating system, you can make your program executable by everyone using the following command:

```
chmod a+x
```

You can tell if a program is executable by looking at the long version of the directory listing, which looks like this:

```
drwxr-xr-x   3 rafeco  users    512 Dec  1 00:11 ./
drwxr-xr-x  26 rafeco  users   1024 Nov 30 22:56 ../
-rwxr-xr-x   1 rafeco  users   5018 Oct 27 11:21 archive.pl*
lrwxrwxrwx   1 rafeco  users      9 Dec  1 00:11 example.sh@ ->
simple.sh
drwxr-xr-x   2 rafeco  users    512 Nov 30 22:56 guestbook/
-rwxr-xr-x   1 rafeco  users    280 Oct 24 12:44 pinggeneric.sh*
-rwxr-xr-x   1 rafeco  users    666 Aug 23 12:31 sample.cgi*
-rwxr-xr-x   1 rafeco  users   3867 Oct 27 11:07 search.pl*
-rwxr-xr-x   1 rafeco  users    156 Aug 22 23:51 simple.sh*
```

The file permissions are cryptically expressed by the string -rwxr-xr-x. Let me explain how this string is decoded. The first character, a dash in this case, indicates what type of file the current file is. The dash indicates that this is a normal file. Directories have a d in this space, and symbolic links have an l. The next nine characters are used to display the access permissions for the file.

The characters are divided into three groups of three permissions. There are three sets of people that can be granted permission for a file, and there are three types of permission for each file. From left to right, the three sets are user, group, and others.

The user permissions pertain to the owner of the file. The owner is listed in the third column of the long directory listing. The group permissions apply to the members of the group to which the file is assigned. The group associated with a file is listed in the fourth column of a long directory listing. The last group of permissions is for others. The others permissions apply to all the system's users.

When you attempt to access a file, the permissions for the most restrictive set of users of which you are a member apply to you. In other words, the others permissions are only used if you're neither the owner of the file nor a member of the group associated with it. Similarly, the group permissions do not apply to the file's owner, even if they're a member of the group associated with the file.

Now let me explain what the individual permissions mean. As I said before, there are three permissions for each set of users. The permissions are read, write, and execute. If that set of users has the permission, the appropriate letter will appear in that space. If they do not, a dash will appear there instead. For example, if the owner has the permissions rw-, he can read and write the file, but not execute it. Similarly, if others have r-x permissions, they can read and execute the file, but not modify it.

Permissions are slightly different for directories. The names of the permissions read, write, and execute are the same, but how they work differs. If you have read permission for a directory, you're allowed to list files in that directory. If you have execute permission for a directory, you can make it your current directory. If you have write access to a directory, you can create files in that directory. It's possible to access files in a directory if you have execute permission for the directory but not read permission. You just have to be allowed access to the file, and you have to know the name of it because you aren't allowed to get a listing.

So now let's go back and look at the full file permissions for a file. If a file has the permissions -rwxr-xr-x, it's a normal file, and the owner has read, write, and execute permission for the file. Both the group and others have read and execute permission, but not write permission.

3

Checking Your Headers

A common pitfall for CGI programmers is forgetting to include the code that produces the content-type header; instead the program goes straight to generating HTML or other output, causing an error.

Anytime your program won't execute because of syntax errors, or because the Web
server is unable to call it, you'll generally get an error complaining that the script didn't
print the proper header. As described earlier, the script probably sent an error message
instead, so you should look in the error log to find out what the error was.

Checking the Path to Your Script Interpreter

One very common problem you'll often find when you move scripts from one server to
another, or you install a script downloaded from the Internet, is that the path to the Perl
interpreter (or whatever script interpreter you're using) is wrong in the shebang line.

If the path to your script interpreter is incorrect, instead of seeing the output of your
script, you'll see something like the following in the error log:

```
[Wed Dec  1 21:33:20 1999] [error] (2)No such file or directory: exec of
➥/web/cgi-bin/bad.cgi failed
[Wed Dec  1 21:33:20 1999] [error] [client 199.72.11.45] Premature end of
➥script headers: /web/cgi-bin/bad.cgi
```

If you encounter one of these errors, you just need to enter the right path in the shebang
line. To do so, find the directory where your script interpreter is installed, and use that
path in your program.

If you have a UNIX shell account on the server where the CGI program
resides, you can often find the location of executable files using the which
command. The which command searches all the directories in your path for
the program you specify, and tells you where it is. For example, the following sequence illustrates how which is used to find the Perl interpreter:

```
$ which perl
/usr/local/bin/perl
```

Tools and Techniques for Debugging Your Program Code

If you've gotten past all the standard problems people run into with CGI scripts and your
script still isn't working properly, you have to start searching for bugs within your code.
This can be a much tougher job than dealing with all the common problems mentioned
previously.

Basically, errors within programs come in two flavors—syntax errors and runtime errors.
Syntax errors crop up when you use your programming language of choice improperly. If
you leave out a required semicolon or use elseif instead of elsif, your program will

not compile, or if it's an interpreted language, it won't execute all the way through. Runtime errors occur when all the syntax in your program is correct, but your program still doesn't behave as expected.

Runtime errors can cause your programs to exit with an error during execution, or they might execute but produce unexpected results. For example, if you have a mathematical construct in your program that divides a number by 0, most languages will exit and return an error during execution. On the other hand, if your program multiplies a number by 1000 when it should multiply by 100, the program will appear to work correctly but will produce invalid results.

Compiled versus Interpreted Languages

When we talk about debugging, it's important to contrast two types of languages—*compiled languages* and *interpreted languages.* The difference between the two is that there are at least two steps to get from source code to execution with compiled languages; with interpreted languages, there's only one—execution. A *scripting language,* which is a simple language designed to perform special or limited tasks, is usually interpreted.

Let me talk about an interpreted language first to give you an example. Scripts written in the Bourne shell are interpreted. When a Bourne shell script is executed, the shell reads the program command by command, and executes each command before moving on to the next one. With interpreted languages, even syntax errors are "runtime errors." In other words, if there's a syntax error on the fifth line of a shell script, the first four lines will be executed, and the program will exit with an error when it reaches the fifth line.

On the other hand, when you write a program in a compiled language, the source code must be transformed into machine readable instructions prior to execution. How this is handled differs from language to language. When you program in C, you use a compiler to transform source code into machine readable code. The code is then stored in executable format so that it can be used. When you program in Java, the source code is compiled into an intermediate format called bytecode, and is stored in that format. When you execute a Java program, the Java virtual machine translates the bytecode into machine readable code for the platform it's running on and executes the code.

The other example of a compiled language is Perl, which is a scripting language. Despite the fact that it's a scripting language, it's not an interpreted language. The difference between Perl and other compiled languages is that Perl code isn't stored in an executable format or bytecode after it's compiled. Instead, every time you run a Perl program, the source code is read by the Perl interpreter and compiled, and then executed immediately. So, it's a scripting language in the sense that to the user, compilation and execution are part of the same step, but it's a compiled language because the code is compiled before it is executed.

The difference in debugging the two types of languages is that with an interpreted language, all debugging occurs at runtime. There is no compilation step during which you can iron out all the syntax errors in your code; instead you have to run the program to find any errors in it. This really becomes a problem when your interpreted program modifies files, or makes any other changes to permanent resources. For example, let's say you've written a shell script that, among other things, submits a credit card transaction for processing. If there's a syntax error in the program after the credit card submission, you'll have to submit a credit card transaction to get to the bug, and then submit another to determine whether the bug is fixed after a change. This can make debugging interpreted programs a real hassle (fortunately, in this case, most credit card verification services provide bogus credit card numbers you can use to test your programs). Generally in these situations you comment out instructions that make permanent changes for debugging.

Running CGI Scripts from the Command Line

When you're debugging your CGI scripts, it's important to remember that they're standard command-line programs. That means that you don't have to always run them through the Web server. In many cases, it's a lot easier to run them from the command line and look at the output there to find bugs.

This is certainly true when your script is returning a `500 Server Error` result when requested. As you know, when you run into one of these errors, oftentimes you can find out what caused the error in the server's error log. You should always take a `500 Server Error` as an indication that you should test the CGI program at the command line if you can't spot the problem immediately in the error log.

Running your program at the command line will let you know immediately whether there's a syntax error in your program if it's written in a scripting language, or whether there's a runtime error in the code that prevents the program from executing if it's a compiled language. In fact, if you're writing a program in Perl, you can execute it at the command line using the `-cw` flags to compile the program without executing it, and to turn on warnings to catch coding mistakes that aren't necessarily syntax errors. For example, to compile (but not execute) the program `example.pl` with warnings, the following command line is used:

```
perl -cw example.pl
```

It's also easy to verify from the command line whether your program produces the proper HTTP header. The first two lines of the program's output should be the content type header and a blank line. This output is processed by the Web browser, so you never see it when you're testing through a server, but it's right there on the screen if you test your program at the command line.

`CGI.pm` and the Command Line

`CGI.pm`, the standard Perl tool for creating CGI scripts, is designed to make testing CGI programs from the command line very easy. When you run a program that uses `CGI.pm` from the command line, the program asks for name and value pairs that would ordinarily be sent to it using an HTML form. The interaction is shown in Listing 3.2.

LISTING 3.2 Using `CGI.pm` from the Command Line

```
$ perl archive.pl
(offline mode: enter name=value pairs on standard input)
year=1999
month=12
day=1
```

`CGI.pm` treats data received through the POST and GET methods the same, so there's no need to distinguish between them when you pass data to a script from the command line. After you're done entering the arguments, you should press Ctrl+D to indicate that you're finished, and that the program should execute.

Using Print Statements for Debugging

One of the most important and time-tested techniques for tracking down logic errors in programs is using print statements to isolate bugs and find out where incorrect values are introduced. After you have your script working well enough to produce output, you can start inserting print statements to track down logic errors.

Many programming languages include debuggers that allow you to step through the execution of your program's statement by statement. You can stop execution at any time, and examine the values of variables that have been set within the program. Unfortunately, many languages used for CGI programming don't have debuggers, and even if they do, it's sometimes easier to just use print statements for debugging.

Generally speaking, print statements are most often used to display the values of variables that are normally used internally by the program. Let me show you how print statements are used for debugging with some examples. One of the most common uses of print statements to debug is to print values as a loop executes. If you're unsure of how many times a loop iterates in a program, you can insert a print statement in the loop so that it prints either a count, or just a marker value every time through.

Another common usage for print statements is to determine where, exactly, an error is occurring. Generally, you place print statements before and after the potentially offending code, and check to see whether the text in both of the print statements gets printed out. You can place these types of "markers" throughout your code to figure out where, exactly, something is failing along the way.

Summary

In this hour, I explained how one goes about obtaining CGI scripts other people have written, and configuring so that they'll run on your Web site. Not only can these scripts save you a lot of work, but they are a good learning tool as well. Even experienced CGI programmers can use downloaded scripts to get the Web applications they need up in a quick and efficient manner.

After you've installed scripts on your server that you've written or downloaded, chances are you'll have to do some debugging before they work just right. The second half of this hour discussed methods you can use to identify and fix bugs in your CGI programs. Debugging can take up a huge amount of development time, so using proper techniques and looking for common, simple problems first can save you a lot of time in the long run.

Q&A

Q You list sites where I can find free scripts, should I look into purchasable scripts as well?

A If a purchasable script offers the functionality that you'll need, and the amount of money you spend on the script is worth the time you save by buying it, you should definitely purchase commercial software. When you're working with Web applications, you really want to pay attention to the amount of tweaking you can do to commercial software. Generally, applications have to fit within the overall design of your site, and you may want functionality that's not provided by the commercial program. It helps to be able to make changes to the software on your own.

Q Can I use a debugger to debug CGI programs?

A You can if you can run them from the command line and test them there. There's no way to run a debugger on a program being accessed over the Web, but all CGI programs should work fine at the command line as long as you pass them data in the appropriate manner. If you're accustomed to debugging software using an interactive debugger, by all means use your scripts from the command line and debug them that way.

Workshop

The quiz questions are designed to strengthen the knowledge you gain each hour. The exercises help you build on that knowledge by providing you with the opportunity to apply it to real problems. For the answers to the quiz questions, refer to Appendix A, "Answers."

Quiz

1. What does the letter d at the beginning of a UNIX file permission string indicate?

2. When you run Perl at the command line, what do the c and w flags do?

3. True or false: You can simulate both the GET and POST methods when you run CGI programs from the command line.

Exercises

1. Find out where the error log is located on your Web server. Check out the contents of the file to see what kinds of errors are being recorded there.

2. Go to one of the popular CGI program download sites, and download a few applications that look interesting. Try to get them up and running on your local server.

3

HOUR 4

Writing Your First CGI Program

In the previous hour, I explained how to make sure your CGI environment is configured and running properly, and how to adapt CGI programs downloaded from the Internet to work properly in that environment. In this hour, you'll get your first real look at developing CGI programs from scratch. I'll also provide you with a brief overview of Perl programming that will help non-Perl programmers understand how the programs in this book work. This hour covers

- The structure of a basic CGI program
- How to write a program that redirects a user to a new URL
- How redirection of input and output works
- How to deal with filehandles in Perl
- How Perl loops and conditional statements work
- How to use Perl expressions

Parts of CGI Programs

A CGI program can generally be broken down into three components. The program must process input, execute the code that gives the program its actual functionality, and generate output. The code that is sandwiched between the input and output can be thought of as the data processing functionality.

Take, for example, a program that sends form data to a particular email address. It must process the form data submitted by the browser, compose and send the email message, and then print an acknowledgement indicating that the email was sent. Or, let's say you're writing a program for your intranet that allows company employees to change their health coverage. Your program would read their form input, store their health coverage preference somewhere, and then send a confirmation indicating which health coverage they selected. The data processing functionality is the part where the user's preference is stored.

The first step in writing your CGI program is to nail down exactly what the program is supposed to do. In the example I just mentioned, the sole purpose of the program is to translate a form submission into an email message. The purpose of a checkout form on a Web site is to validate the user's payment information and insert his order into the merchant's fulfillment process. Most CGI programs have a purpose that can be stated simply like this. In other cases, you might write more complex CGI programs that can perform a number of actions based on the input that they receive.

After you've figured out what the purpose of your program is, you can figure out what input it requires and what output it should produce. Generally, the input and output requirements are easy to derive logically from the purpose of the program. If you're writing a program that displays a map of the user's neighborhood, you'll need her street address, or perhaps just her zip code, as input. You also know that regardless of what other output your program produces, you'll need to return the appropriate map to the user.

Splitting your program into sections associated with each of these three areas will make the program easier to maintain, and easier for other people to understand.

A Sample CGI Program

Let's look at an example of a CGI program that contains all three of these components. It's a simple program that accepts a user's age and tells him whether he can legally vote in the United States. The source code for the program appears in Listing 4.1.

LISTING 4.1 A Simple CGI Program

```
1: #!/usr/local/bin/perl
2:
3: # Import the CGI module and create a query object to retrieve the
4: # form input.
5: use CGI;
6: $query = new CGI;
7:
8: # Determine whether the user is of legal voting age.
9: if ($query->param('age') >= 18) {
10:     $voter = 'yes';
11: }
12: else {
13:     $voter = 'no';
14: }
15:
16: # Print out a message indicating whether the user is
17: # a registered voter or not.
18: print $query->header;
19: print "<HTML><HEAD><TITLE>Are you old enough to
    vote?</TITLE></HEAD><BODY>\n";
20: print "<H1>Are you old enough to vote?</H1>\n";
21: if ($voter eq 'yes') {
22:     print "<P>You are old enough to vote.</P>\n";
23: }
24: else {
25:     print "<P>You are not yet old enough to vote.</P>\n";
26: }
27: print "</BODY></HTML>\n";
```

Now let's look at the sections of the program, which are marked with comments to make it easier to understand. On the first line of the program, I provide the path to the Perl interpreter. When the Web server attempts to execute this program, it looks for Perl in the location specified, and if it doesn't find it there, it returns an error.

> Determining the path to the Perl interpreter based on the first line of the program is the UNIX approach. Most Windows Web servers determine which program to use to execute a CGI program based on the file's extension. The exception is the Apache Web server, which uses the UNIX approach even if you're running it under Windows.

Before we get to the program logic, the user's input has to be processed. I'm using Perl with the CGI module, so this step is very simple. First, I import the CGI module with the command use CGI. By importing the module and creating a query object (assigned to the variable $query), I automatically transfer all of the form input into a Perl data structure. That's all there is to it.

> Depending on the language that you use, this step can be more compli-
> cated. For more information on processing user input, see Hour 6,
> "Processing Input." If you're interested in how the Perl CGI module works,
> you should check out Hour 10, "Perl—The Big Kahuna of CGI." To learn how
> to process form input using languages other than Perl, see Hour 11, "Other
> Popular CGI Programming Languages."

After you've processed the user's input, the actual program logic comes into play. In this case, the logic is very straightforward. The `if` statement contains a single condition:

```
$query->param('age') >= 18
```

I check the value associated with the age parameter. If the user entered an age equal to or greater than 18, I mark him as a voter. Otherwise, I mark him as a non-voter. That's all there is to the logic. (Of course, the logic of a real-world program is often more complex.)

Finally, I print out the Web page that is sent to the user. First, I use the `header` method of the query object to print the content type for the output. Then, I print the opening tags for the page, and the page heading. To print the body of the page, I use an `if` statement to test whether the user is a voter, and print the appropriate message for each alternative.

You may wonder why I didn't just eliminate the `$voter` variable and test the user's age here. It would conserve a few lines of code, for sure. The problem is that it mingles the program's output with the program logic. In this case, the test to determine whether a user is a voter is very simple. However, there are a lot more tests I could add. Using the current design, I could have all those tests modify the value of `$voter` and leave the code that generates the program's output unchanged. If I included the test in the output section of the program, it would require more radical changes to add new tests. It makes more sense to keep all the program's functionality separate.

Let's look at a form you could use to call this script. It will work with a field that contains one field named `age`, and some means of submitting the form. The form in Listing 4.2 will work fine.

LISTING 4.2   A Form Used to Call the Voter Program

```
1: <HTML><HEAD><TITLE>Are you old enough to vote?</TITLE></HEAD>
2: <BODY>
```

```
 3: <H1>Are you old enough to vote?</H1>
 4: <P>
 5: <FORM ACTION="voter.cgi">
 6: Age: <INPUT TYPE="text" NAME="age">
 7: <INPUT TYPE="submit">
 8: </FORM>
 9: </P>
10: </BODY>
11: </HTML>
```

A URL-Redirection Program

Let's look at a simple program of a type that's used on lots of Web sites. Many sites provide pull-down menus as navigational aids. When you select an option from the menu, the browser automatically redirects you to the link that you selected. This functionality is implemented using JavaScript. In many cases, there's also a submit button associated with the field that users whose browsers support JavaScript can use to navigate using the menu. When a user clicks on the submit button, the link he chose is submitted to a CGI script, which then redirects the user to the appropriate page.

In this example, there is no intermediate processing step between processing the user input and generating the appropriate output. The program receives a URL from the form, and prints the appropriate HTTP header to redirect the user to that URL. There's no intervening logic in the middle to speak of. First, let's look at a form that works with the redirection script. It appears in Listing 4.3.

4

LISTING 4.3 A Form Used to Call a Redirection Script

```
 1: <html>
 2: <head>
 3:    <title>Redirect Form</title>
 4: </head>
 5:
 6: <body>
 7:
 8: <form action="redirect.cgi">
 9: <p>
10: Go to:
11: <select name="link">
12: <option value="http://www.genehack.org">Genehack
13: <option value="http://www.uncorked.org/medley">Medley
14: <option value="http://www.camworld.com/">CamWorld
15: <option value="http://www.stuffeddog.com">The Stuffed Dog
16: </select>
```

continues

LISTING 4.3   continued

```
17: <input type="submit" value="go">
18: </p>
19: </form>
20:
21: </body>
22: </html>
```

The page contains a form with two fields, a submit button and a pull-down list. I'll discuss how to create and use these form fields in detail in Hour 5, "Creating HTML Forms." For now, all you need to know is that you can select one option from the pull-down list and then submit the form to the CGI script using the submit button. A browser displaying the redirection form appears in Figure 4.1.

FIGURE 4.1

The site redirection form.

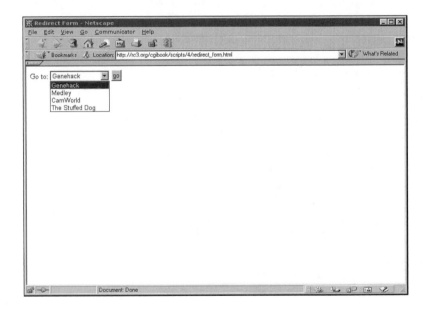

Now let's look at the CGI script that's specified in the action parameter of the form. The source code to the script appears in Listing 4.4.

LISTING 4.4   The Site Redirection Script

```
1: #!/usr/local/bin/perl
2:
3: use CGI;
4:
5: $query = new CGI;
6:
7: print $query->redirect($query->param('link'));
```

As you can see, the script is very short. The values associated with each option in the pull-down list are URLs. This script simply takes the URL submitted by the form and redirects the user to that URL. Let's look at this script line by line.

The first line of the script indicates which application is used to compile and execute the script. It points to `/usr/local/bin/perl`, the Perl interpreter. The next line imports the CGI module, which is used both to decode the form input and to redirect the user. The third line creates a new CGI object. Anytime I want to call any subroutines in the CGI module, or extract any data stored by the module, I need to reference this object.

On line 5, I call the redirect subroutine associated with the query object, and pass the value of the link parameter to that subroutine to specify which URL the user should be sent to. `$query->param('link')` is a reference to the `link` parameter from the form. It is passed as an argument to `$query->redirect`, which is a `CGI.pm` subroutine that automatically sends the user to the URL passed to it as an argument.

The functionality of this script is actually transparent to the user. When she selects a site from the list and clicks on the submit button, she is transparently redirected to the site she chose. The `CGI.pm` module makes use of the HTTP protocol to pass the user along to the new site without displaying anything in the user's browser.

How File Redirection Works

There are a few general topics that concern CGI programming that will be helpful in understanding the rest of this book, and in developing CGI programs. Most of this information isn't specific to CGI, but rather is general Perl or UNIX information that is used whenever you write CGI programs.

One of the core concepts of UNIX is file redirection. All UNIX shells support redirection, and the file redirection metaphor is utilized in most UNIX scripting languages as well (even when they're running on other platforms). Before I can explain file redirection, I have to explain standard input and standard output.

Most command-line programs running under UNIX accept their input from `standard input`, and send their output to `standard output`. By default, `standard input` and `standard output` are assigned to the console. In other words, these programs expect you to type in data using the keyboard, and send their output to the screen by default. Take the UNIX `cat` program for example. Its purpose is to read a file and print it out. Usually, you specify the name of the file to be read as a command line parameter, like this:

```
cat some_file
```

It will read `some_file` and print it out to standard output (the console in this case). Using redirection, you can print out the contents of `some_file` to another file, like this:

```
cat some_file > another_file
```

A new file named `another_file` will be created, and the contents of `some_file` will be stored in it. This is referred to as redirecting standard output. What happens if you don't supply the name of a file as a command-line parameter? The `cat` program will assume that you want to use the console as standard input. Anything you type will be echoed to standard output until you press Ctrl+D to end the file. So, if you type

`cat > yet_another_file`

everything you type (until you press Ctrl+D) will be echoed to the file `yet_another_file`. You can also use the append operator (>>) to redirect the output of a program to the end of an existing file. If the file doesn't exist, it will be created. For example,

```
cat some_file >> another_file
```

will add the contents of `some_file` to the end of `another_file`.

Now let's talk about redirecting standard input. You can redirect standard input to the `cat` program, and it will have the same effect as specifying a file on the command line. For example, you can use this command:

```
cat < some_file > another_file
```

This tells `cat` to read input from `some_file` and print it to `another_file`. Because of the way cat works, this is no different than just specifying `some_file` as a command-line parameter. However, when you're using other programs, especially programs that expect the user to type input, redirecting standard input can be very useful.

Pipes

Pipes are a slightly more complex redirection operator. Basically, a pipe redirects the standard output of one program to the standard input of another program. Here's a command line you'll see sometimes:

```
ls | more
```

The `ls` command prints a directory listing for the current directory, and the `more` command paginates whatever it receives through standard input. This command line pipes the output of `ls` to `more`. If the directory listing is more than a page long, the `more` command will automatically paginate the listing.

Working With Files in Perl

Now let's look at how files are handled from within Perl programs. Redirection operators are used when files are opened in Perl to indicate how the file will be used. Because CGI programs so often work with external files, it's important to understand how Perl handles these operations.

To access an external file from within a Perl function, the open function is used. It accepts two arguments, the filehandle that will be used to refer to the file, and the specification for the file to be opened. Here's an example:

```
open (FILE, "< some_file.html");
```

The first argument is FILE. When I want to retrieve data from the file later in the program, I'll use the filehandle FILE to do so. You don't have to make your filehandles all capital letters, but most Perl programmers do so. There's no good reason not to do it, and when you use that convention, other people who look at your program later will know that identifiers in all capital letters are filehandles. The second argument indicates that the file some_file.html should be opened for input. The < operator means that the program can read data from the filehandle only.

Usually, the open function is used with an or die clause for error handling. If the program is unable to open the file for any reason, execution of the program is terminated, and the error message specified in the or die clause is displayed. Here's an example of the or die clause:

```
open (FILE, "< some_file.html")
    or die "Can't open some_file.html";
```

When the error message associated with the or die clause doesn't end with a line feed, Perl automatically appends the name of the program and the line number on which the error was encountered to the error message you specify.

The other redirection operators can also be used when you open files. For example, to open a file for output, the > operator is used:

```
open (OUTPUT, "> log_file.txt")
    or die "Can't open log_file.txt";
```

After the OUTPUT filehandle is open, you can send output to that filehandle by specifying it in your print statements, like this:

```
print OUTPUT "This string will be printed to the file.";
```

If you plan on printing a bunch of stuff to a filehandle you opened, you can use the select statement:

```
select OUTPUT;
print "All of this";
print "will be printed";
print "to the OUTPUT";
print "filehandle.";
```

To resume sending output to the default filehandle (standard output), use the following statement:

```
select STDOUT;
```

4

You can also open files for appending so that output sent to the file will be added to the end of the file rather than overwriting the file if it exists. The >> operator is used to open a file for appending within Perl:

```
open (OUTPUT, ">> log_file.txt")
    or die "Can't open log_file.txt";
```

Let's go back to looking at files opened for input. What if you wanted to write a program that does nothing more than read a particular HTML file and send it to the browser? Listing 4.5 contains a simple program that does just that.

LISTING 4.5   A Program That Sends an HTML File to the Browser

```
1: #!/usr/local/bin/perl
2: $html_file = "example.html";
3: open (INPUT, "< $html_file")
4:     or die "Can't open $html_file";
5: print "Content-type: text/html\n\n";
6: while (<INPUT>) {P
7:     print;
8: }
9: close INPUT;
```

For convenience, I store the name of the file to be opened in a variable. For a program this simple, that's not really necessary, but in larger programs it generally makes sense to store this type of information in a variable near the top of the program, rather than referencing the filename deep within the program where it's hard to find. The program attempts to open the specified file for input.

If it fails, the program dies; otherwise, the program uses a while loop to iterate over the contents of the file one line at a time. I'll discuss how these while loops work in the next section. When you iterate over a filehandle, each line of the file is magically copied into the variable $_. Many Perl functions (including print) use $_ as their default argument. In other words, if you call the print function without telling it what to print, it assumes that you wanted to print $_. That's why this example works.

In some cases, it's easier to deal with a file in one big chunk. You can use the join function to merge all the contents in a file into a single scalar variable. This is actually a two step process that looks like this:

```
open (FILE, "< some_file.txt")
    or die;
# Read the entire contents of the file into an array
@file = <FILE>
# Convert the array into a single string
$file_contents = join ('', @file);
```

When you set a filehandle processed using the diamond (<>) operator equal to an array (in this case @file), each of the lines in the file is stored as a single element in the array. At that point, you can use the join function to copy all the elements in the array into a scalar variable. The first argument to join is the expression that should be included between each element in the array. Because each element in the array (a line from the file) ends with a line feed, I don't include anything between the array elements.

Loops in Perl

Now I'd like to briefly discuss some of the Perl language constructs that you'll see throughout this book. If you're already a Perl programmer, just skip the remaining sections of this hour. If you're not, you'll probably find these sections helpful as you read the rest of the book. Unfortunately, they won't serve as a replacement for a book dedicated to Perl or the documentation provided with Perl.

First, let's talk about the loops available in Perl. There are actually many types of loops that you can use in your Perl programs, but I'll only use a couple of them in this book. The two loops I use most often are while and foreach. Let's look at each of them in turn.

while loops are executed until a particular condition is true. Often, while loops are used with the diamond operator, which reads lines from a filehandle one at a time until it hits the end of a file marker, and returns undef (which is treated as a false result). So, if I opened a file using the filehandle FILE, I could iterate over each of the lines and print them using the command:

```
while (<FILE>) {
    print;
}
```

Any expression will work in a while loop, however. The statement:

```
while (1) {
}
```

creates an infinite loop. The expression 1 is always true. Usually, comparative expressions are used in while loops. For example, you might test a numeric value in while loop, like this:

```
$i = 0;
while ($i < 100) {
    $i++;
}
```

This loop doesn't actually do anything, it just increments $i every time the loop is executed and exits when $i gets to 99.

4

The other loop I frequently use is the foreach loop. foreach extracts each item from a list one at a time, assigns it to a variable, and then executes the body of a loop. This type of loop is generally used when you want to iterate over all the items in an array or in a hash. Let's look at a couple of examples. Here's the most basic example; it just iterates over the items in a list that I define just for the loop:

```
foreach $color ('red', 'green', 'blue') {
    print $color, "\n";
}
```

The loop is executed three times, one for each of the items in the list. The output of the program (assuming all it contains is this loop) is

```
red
green
blue
```

You can also iterate over the items stored in an array variable, as follows:

```
@colors = ('red', 'green', 'blue');
foreach $color (@colors) {
    print $color, "\n";
}
```

foreach loops are also commonly used to iterate over the contents of hashes (also referred to as associative arrays). Here's an example of such a loop:

```
%colors = (
    'red' => 'FF0000',
    'green', => '00FF00',
    'blue', => '0000FF');
foreach $color (keys %colors) {
    print $color, ":", $colors{$color}, "\n";
}
```

In this example, the keys for the associative array are extracted using the keys function, and then iterated over by the loop. The output of this program looks like:

```
red:FF0000
green:00FF00
blue:0000FF
```

The if Statement

Now let's look at one of the fundamental statements of any language, the if statement. An if statement in Perl evaluates an expression, and if that expression is true, it executes the code within the statement. Here's an example:

```
if (2 > 1) {
    print "2 is greater than 1.\n";
}
```

As you can see, the expression being evaluated is enclosed in parentheses, and the block of code to be executed appears within braces. If the block of code to be executed consists only of a single statement, you can use a shorthand version of the if statement, which looks like this:

```
print "2 is greater than 1.\n" if (2 > 1);
```

If the body of your if statement contains more than one statement, you must use the block form. You're also required to use the block form if you want to use an else block to specify code that is executed if the condition is false. Here's an example:

```
if (2 > 1) {
    print "2 is greater than 1.\n";
}
else {
    print "2 is not greater than 1.\n";
}
```

You can string together multiple if constructs using the keyword elsif, like this:

```
$color = "blue";
if ($color eq "red") {
    print "Red is for roses.\n";
}
elsif ($color eq "green") {
    print "Green is for grass.\n";
}
elsif ($color eq "blue") {
    print "Blue is for the ocean.\n";
}
else {
    print "I don't know anything about that color.\n";
}
```

If you want, you can also create statements that are executed only when the condition specified is false. These are created using the unless statement:

```
unless ($number == 7) {
    print "The number isn't 7.\n";
}
```

This is equivalent to the following statement:

```
if ($number != 7) {
    print "The number isn't 7.\n";
}
```

Because the action taken by an if or unless statement depends on a condition, these statements are also referred to as conditional statements.

4

Perl Expressions

In the expressions used by the conditional statements and `while` loops I described, various expressions were evaluated to determine how the flow of the program will work. The simplest expressions just evaluate a value and determine whether it is considered to be true or false. Any non-zero number or non-empty string is true; zero, empty strings, and the value `undef` are false. A simple `if` statement might evaluate a variable by itself, like this:

```
$var = undef;
if ($var) {
    print "The expression is true.\n";
}
```

The code inside that `if` statement would not be executed because `undef` is always considered to be false. Just as you can evaluate a variable or static value as an expression, you can also evaluate the value returned by a subroutine. Let's look at a quick example:

```
sub some_subroutine {
    return 1;
}
if (&some_subroutine) {
    print "This is true!\n";
}
```

Because the subroutine returns a nonzero number, the expression evaluates as true, and the code inside the `if` block is executed.

Now let's look at comparative expressions, which I've used throughout this hour already. Comparative expressions use an operator to compare two expressions and return true or false. The important thing here is that Perl supports separate comparison operators for numbers and strings. To test whether two numbers are equal, `==` is used. To test the equality of strings, you use `eq`. Table 4.1 contains a list of comparison operators.

TABLE 4.1   Perl Comparison Operators

Operator	Tests
==	Numeric equality
!=	Numeric inequality
>	Numeric greater than
<	Numeric less than
>=	Numeric greater than or equal to
<=	Numeric less than or equal to
eq	String equality

Operator	Tests
ne	String inequality
gt	String greater than
lt	String less than
le	String less than or equal to
ge	String greater than or equal to

You can also use Boolean operators to string together multiple expressions and create complex expressions. The Boolean operators are and, or, and not. They can also be written as &&, ||, and !, respectively.

Summary

In this hour, I explained how to write simple CGI scripts using Perl. You'll build on the concepts of simple scripts throughout the rest of this book to learn how to build powerful Web applications. I also provided a very concise introduction to Perl that will help non-Perl programmers understand some of the constructs used throughout this book. Hour 10 goes further in explaining how to use Perl in a CGI environment.

4

Q&A

Q Is it necessary to make filehandles in Perl all upper case?

A No, it's not required. However, it is a convention that's followed by nearly everyone. Making filehandles all upper case makes it easy to distinguish them from variables and function calls. You should definitely follow this convention.

Q Aren't there more types of loops supported by Perl than you list in this hour?

A Yes there are, but these are the only loops that are used in this book. There's not enough time to go into all of the loop constructs supported by Perl here.

Q I tried to use the redirection operators you discussed at the DOS prompt in Windows, but they didn't work.

A They won't work there because they're a feature specific to UNIX shells. If you like, you can download a version of the Bash shell for Windows that will provide UNIX shell functionality at http://sourceware.cygnus.com/cygwin.

Workshop

The quiz questions are designed to strengthen the knowledge you gain each hour. See Appendix A, "Answers" for the answers to the quiz questions.

Quiz

1. How do the > and >> redirection operators differ?

2. What are the two arguments passed to a `foreach` loop?

3. Under what circumstance would you use the `eq` comparison operator?

PART II

Capturing User Input

Hour

HOUR 5

Creating HTML Forms

HTML forms are used to build the interfaces for Web applications. The forms are created using tags which place various input fields on a Web page. Whether you're creating a pull-down menu of links to provide navigation options for your users, or building a multiple step checkout process for an online store, the HTML form tags provide the only interface elements you'll have access to, other than hyperlinks.

When a form is submitted, all the data entered by the user is sent to the Web server, where it is then passed along to a resource specified in the URL requested. During this hour, you'll learn how to use HTML forms to build interfaces for your CGI programs. The following topics will be discussed:

- The <FORM> tag
- Form fields based on the <INPUT> tag
- The <TEXTAREA> tag
- The <SELECT> tag
- Designing usable forms

The <FORM> Tag

The <FORM> tag is used to place a form on a Web page, and to indicate that the fields within it are all part of the same form.

Form fields can't be placed on a page at all unless they're enclosed within a <FORM> tag.

To create a form, the following syntax is used:

```
<FORM>
<!-- insert form fields here -->
</FORM>
```

There are a number of attributes associated with the <FORM> tag that control the behavior of the form. Each of the attributes has a default value, so they can all be left out, as I did in the previous example. I'll go through the attributes associated with the <FORM> tag one by one.

The ACTION Attribute

A form submission is similar to a link, in that it requests a particular URL from the server. Generally, the URL requested points to a CGI program or some other program that will process the data submitted using the form. When you create a form, the ACTION attribute is used to indicate which URL the form should be submitted to. So, the following <FORM> tag would submit the contents of the form to the program /cgi-bin/example.cgi:

```
<FORM ACTION="/cgi-bin/example.cgi">
<!-- insert form fields here -->
</FORM>
```

If you leave out the ACTION attribute, the form will be submitted to the URL of the current page. If the form appears on a static HTML page, this doesn't make much sense. However, if the form is generated by a CGI script, it's oftentimes easiest to submit the form back to the program that generated it for processing. Obviously, this is a question of application design. I'll explain why you might want to do this in Hour 6, "Processing Input."

The METHOD Attribute

The METHOD attribute is used to specify how the data in the form will be sent to the server. There are two valid methods, GET and POST. The GET method tacks all the form data onto the end of the URL being requested. The POST method submits the form data as the body of the request. Generally speaking, the two methods are interchangeable, at least when it comes to creating forms. When you write CGI scripts, there are some criteria you should think about when deciding whether to write scripts that accept data from the POST or GET methods. I'll talk about those criteria in Hour 6.

The METHOD attribute defaults to GET if it is unspecified in the <FORM> tag used to create the form.

The ENCTYPE Attribute

The ENCTYPE attribute is used to specify how form data is encoded when it is submitted to the Web server. As I discussed in Hour 1, "Overview of CGI Programming," encoding is used to sanitize data so that it can be sent to the Web server in a manner that won't break the request. Encoding types are specified as MIME types. The default encoding type is application/x-www-form-urlencoded. The other option, which is generally only used when you create a form with a file upload field, is multipart/form-data.

The TARGET Attribute

When you create a site that uses multiple frames or windows, you can use the TARGET attribute to indicate which frame (or window) the results of the form submission should be displayed in. For example, if you create a page with two frames, left_nav and main_content, you can put a search form in the left_nav frame and have the results pop in the main_content frame by including the attribute TARGET="main_content" in the <FORM> tag. By default, form submissions target the window or frame in which the form itself appears.

The <INPUT> Tag

The <INPUT> tag is used to actually create most of the HTML form fields. The TYPE attribute of this tag is used to indicate what type of field is being created, and other attributes are used to set the parameters for that field. The types of input fields available are: text fields, password fields, check boxes, radio buttons, hidden fields, and file upload fields. The <INPUT> tag is also used to create Submit and Reset buttons. I'm going to talk about each of them individually.

First, however, I want to discuss two attributes that are common to all input fields, NAME and VALUE. When the data in a form is sent to the Web server, it is organized in name/value pairs. The NAME attribute allows you to identify each field on the form. Generally speaking, form fields allow you to set the value associated with each field name. The VALUE attribute is used to predefine a value for a form field. The use of the VALUE attribute differs depending on the type of field you're creating, so I'll discuss it within the context of each field type.

In some cases, fields appear in groups, and all the fields in the group should have the same name. I'll talk about this more when I discuss the individual field types.

Text Input Fields

The default type of input field is the text input field. It allows the user to enter text in a single line. You can explicitly define an input field as a text field using the TYPE="text" attribute in the <INPUT> tag.

The VALUE attribute of a text input field is used to specify a default value for the text field. If the VALUE attribute is included in the <INPUT> tag, the value assigned to the VALUE attribute will be displayed in the text field.

The SIZE and MAXLENGTH attributes are used to set the display width of the field, and the maximum number of characters that can be typed in the field, respectively. You should place a reasonable MAXLENGTH on all your text fields, but you shouldn't count on them in your CGI programs. People can submit data to your CGI programs without using the form you provide, and you have to account for that in your programming. There are a number of ways in which this can be accomplished. For example, the user could download your form and modify it so that he can enter whatever data he wants, or he could just write a program that submits data directly to your CGI program without using the Web browser at all.

Here's an example of an <INPUT> tag for a text input field:

```
<INPUT TYPE="text" NAME="name" SIZE=30 MAXSIZE=50>
```

The field created using that tag appears in Figure 5.1.

Password Fields

Password fields are identical to text fields, except that they mask the user input so that people can't read what the person is typing in the field when they look over their shoulder. Unfortunately, the value entered in the field is not encrypted in any way when it is sent to the Web server, and if a value is assigned to the field using the VALUE attribute, it will appear in the page source as plain text.

However, this field type has two important uses. First, it prevents people watching the user type from seeing what they enter, and second, it provides a visual indication to the user that he is typing a password. The masking will make the user more comfortable with entering his password and provide the user with an interface element that he is probably accustomed to seeing. A password field that didn't hide what the user typed would, in all likelihood, be confusing to many users.

FIGURE 5.1

Text, password, radio, check box, and submit form fields.

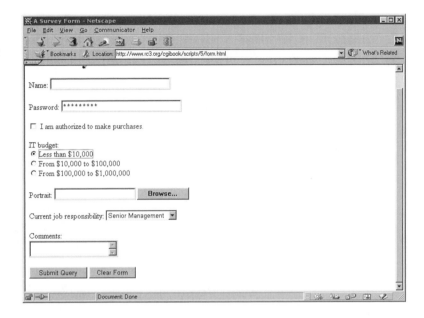

In any case, to create a password field, you must set the field type to password, using the TYPE attribute. The NAME, VALUE, LENGTH, and MAXSIZE attributes work the same for password fields as they do with text fields. The <INPUT> tag used to create the password field in Figure 5.1 looks like this:

```
<INPUT TYPE="password" NAME="password_example" VALUE="something"
SIZE=30 MAXLENGTH=30>
```

Check Boxes

A check box presents users with a binary choice, it can be either off or on. When a user clicks on a check box, the value of the field is reversed. If it's checked, it becomes unchecked, and vice versa. If a check box is checked when the form is submitted, the name/value pair associated with that field is sent to the server. If the check box is not checked, nothing is sent to the server for that field.

To create a check box field, you set the TYPE attribute to checkbox. You set the value for the field using the VALUE attribute (it's important to assign a value to the field because users can't enter one for this type). The value you enter is generally irrelevant, it's just a placeholder that you can test for in your CGI program. Usually people set the value to something like "yes" or "on".

Other than TYPE, NAME, and VALUE, the only other attribute for check boxes is CHECKED. There's no value associated with the CHECKED attribute; it's a flag. When the CHECKED

5

attribute is included in the <INPUT> tag, the check box will be checked when the form loads. Otherwise, the check box will be unchecked at load time. The check box in Figure 5.1 was created using the following <INPUT> tag:

```
<P>
<INPUT TYPE="checkbox" NAME="purchaser" VALUE="yes">
I am authorized to make purchases.
</P>
```

Radio Buttons

Radio buttons allow you to select one item from a group of possible choices. Whenever you select an item in the group, the item that was already selected becomes unselected. In this way, radio buttons are similar to a multiple choice test. They're actually named after the buttons on the old car radios. Whenever you pushed a button to select a station, the button for the station that was selected at the time was automatically unselected.

To create a radio button, you use an <INPUT> tag with the TYPE attribute set to radio. Each <INPUT> tag creates a single radio button—to create a group of buttons, you must use several <INPUT> tags, and assign the same name to them using the NAME attribute.

Like check boxes, you can make a radio button selected when the page loads by including the CHECKED flag in the <INPUT> tag for that button.

> You are permitted to use the CHECKED flag with several radio buttons in the same group, and when the form is rendered, all the buttons will be selected at once. However, because this is contrary to the design of radio buttons, it will only serve to confuse users. You should limit yourself to one CHECKED flag per radio button group.

Here's the code to create the group of radio buttons in Figure 5.1:

```
<P>
IT budget:<BR>
<INPUT TYPE="radio" NAME="budget" VALUE="10000">Less than $10,000<BR>
<INPUT TYPE="radio" NAME="budget" VALUE="100000">From $10,000 to
$100,000<BR>
<INPUT TYPE="radio" NAME="budget" VALUE="1000000">From $100,000 to
$1,000,000<BR>
</P>
```

Hidden Fields

One type of field that might not initially make much sense is the hidden form field. Hidden form fields are used to include data in a form that can't be modified by users. When you include a hidden form field on a page, nothing is actually displayed in the browser window. However, the data is stored within the source code of the page, and is submitted to the server along with the rest of the data in the form.

To create a hidden form field, you should specify the field type as hidden. The only attributes used with hidden fields are the NAME and VALUE fields. A hidden form field is created like this:

```
<INPUT TYPE="hidden" NAME="some_data" VALUE="some value">
```

Generally, hidden fields are used on dynamically generated forms to store information that the programmer wants to send to the program but doesn't want the user to see. For example, a programmer might create two forms for an online store that has a two-step checkout process. The code can place all the data from the first form into hidden form fields on the second form, and then update the order only after the second form is submitted.

In other cases, hidden form fields are used with CGI programs that are used for multiple purposes. Hidden form fields make it easier to write multiple purpose CGI scripts because they allow you to pass information to those scripts to indicate how they should be used in a given situation. For example, a search engine might have multiple collections of data available for searching. If you create a form designed for searching one of the collections, you can specify the collection to be searched in a hidden form field.

File Upload Fields

File upload fields are used to enable users to upload files through an HTML form. To create a file upload field, you should set the TYPE attribute of the <INPUT> tag to file. The user will be able to specify the location of the file on her local machine, and the contents of that file will be uploaded when she submits the form. As I stated earlier when I discussed the <FORM> tag, file upload fields must appear on forms that use the POST method, and the multipart/form-data encoding type.

There's an example of a file upload field in Figure 5.1. The appearance of these fields varies from platform to platform, but they generally consist of a text field that is used to hold the path to the file to be uploaded, and a button that opens a file selection box that can be used to locate the file to be uploaded. When a file is selected using the file selection box, its path is copied into the text field associated with the file upload field.

The <INPUT> tag used to create a file upload field is:

```
<P>
Portrait:
<INPUT TYPE="file" NAME="some_file">
</P>
```

5

Reset Buttons

A form Reset button resets all the fields on a form to their default values. No value is associated with the Reset button itself. If the VALUE attribute for a field is present, the value of that attribute will be placed in the form field. If no value is specified for a field on the form, the Reset button will empty that field. To create a Reset button, set the TYPE attribute of an <INPUT> tag to reset.

The VALUE attribute of the <INPUT> tag specifies the button label. No other attributes apply to Reset buttons. There's an example of a Reset button in Figure 5.1 that was created with this code:

```
<INPUT TYPE="reset" VALUE="Clear Form">
```

Submit Buttons

The Submit button on a form is used to send the contents of the form to the Web server to be processed. All the relevant information about how the form input should be formatted, and where the contents of the form should be submitted, is specified in the FORM tag used to create the form. To add a Submit button to a form, use the INPUT tag with the TYPE attribute set to submit. To specify a label for the Submit button, use the VALUE attribute.

You can use the NAME attribute of a Submit button to send additional information to the CGI program. If a NAME attribute is specified for a Submit button, the value specified as the VALUE attribute of that button will be sent to the server. If no name is specified for the field, the value associated with the button is not sent back to the server.

The main reason one might assign a name to a Submit button is to create a form with multiple Submit buttons, and assign different functionality to each of the buttons. For example, you could create an order management system, and for each order, place two Submit buttons in a form. You could give them both the name transaction, and assign one of them the value Refund and the other the value Credit. If the user clicks the Refund button, he will receive a refund in the mail; if he clicks Credit, the customer will receive store credit instead.

Using Images as Submit Buttons

Another option available when you design forms is to use an image as the Submit button for a form. To indicate that you want to use an image as a Submit button, use the INPUT tag with the TYPE set to image. The main advantage of using an image as the Submit button for a form is that it enables you to make your forms more aesthetically pleasing.

When you create an image-type form field, nearly all the attributes associated with the HTML IMG tag are available to you in addition to the attributes generally associated with an INPUT tag. A list of the image-related attributes that can be used with image fields appears in Table 5.1.

TABLE 5.1 Attributes Associated with the `image` Input Type

Attribute	Purpose
TYPE	If you want to create an image input field, this has to be set to `image`.
NAME	The name associated with the field when it is submitted through the form.
SRC	The location of the image that will be displayed as the form field.
HEIGHT	The vertical size of the image in pixels.
WIDTH	The horizontal size of the image in pixels.
ALT	Text to display as the image's placeholder if the browser does not support images, or has image loading turned off.
BORDER	The number of pixels in the border around the image.
HSPACE	The number of pixels to provide as a margin on the left and right of the image.
VSPACE	The number of pixels to provide as a margin on the top and bottom of the image.

There is no VALUE attribute used with an image field. If you assign a name to an image input field, the X and Y coordinates of the spot on the image where the user clicked are sent to the Web server as the value. This is only useful if you divide your image into regions that have different functionality.

Other than that, image input fields work just like Submit buttons. There's an example of an image input field in Figure 5.2.

FIGURE 5.2

A form that uses an image as a submit button.

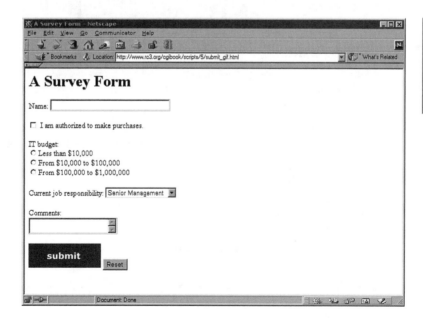

Other Form Fields

There are two other types of form fields that are not created using an <INPUT> tag. These two items are text areas and select lists. They're both a bit more complex than the fields based on the <INPUT> tag. Figure 5.3 contains examples of both types of fields.

FIGURE 5.3

A form containing a text area and two select lists.

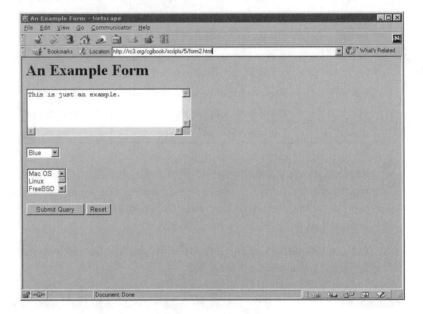

Text Areas

Standard, one-line text input fields are fine for many tasks, but for some applications, like online discussion groups and feedback forms, you need to give users more space to enter text. This is where the <TEXTAREA> tag comes into play. It enables you to create a multirow form field for text entry. Unlike the <INPUT> tag, the <TEXTAREA> tag has both an opening and closing tag. Any text that is enclosed within the <TEXTAREA> tags is displayed in the text box on the form. Take a look at this example, which is depicted in Figure 5.3:

```
<TEXTAREA NAME="example" COLS=40 ROWS=4>
This is just an example.
</TEXTAREA>
```

The COLS and ROWS attributes set the size for the text box. In the example, the box is four rows tall and 40 columns wide. As with other form input fields, the NAME attribute identifies the field when it is sent back to the server.

There's another important attribute of text boxes that is unique to them, WRAP. The WRAP attribute controls how text is displayed in the form field, and how the text is formatted when it is sent back to the server. There are three settings for the WRAP attribute, none, physical, and virtual. If WRAP is set to none, when a user enters text in the box, it is never wrapped. Each line extends to the right until the user presses Return.

The virtual setting wraps the text by inserting line feeds at the right margin of the text box. The line feeds are used for display only—to make it easier for the user to read what he typed. They are removed before the text is sent to the server. The physical setting is similar: it wraps the text at the right margin of the text box, but it includes the line feeds when the text is sent to the server. This is the only setting that actually changes what the user typed.

When you create a <TEXTAREA> tag, anything that's between the opening and closing tags is considered to be the default value for the field, including white space. So, a text box created using the following code would include a single carriage return as its default value:

```
<TEXTAREA NAME="example" WRAP="none" ROWS=3 COLS=40>
</TEXTAREA>
```

If you really want your text area to be empty (including line feeds), you have to create it as follows:

```
<TEXTAREA NAME="example" WRAP="none" ROWS=3 COLS=40></TEXTAREA>
```

Select Lists

Select lists provide the user with a menu of several choices and enable the user to select one or more of the choices before submitting the form. They are created using the <SELECT> and <OPTION> tags. The <SELECT> tag has an opening and closing tag, and is used to set up the select list. <OPTION> tags are used within the <SELECT> tag, and each <OPTION> tag adds one option to the select list.

Really, the <SELECT> tag is used to create two distinct types of form fields. The type of field that's created is based on the SIZE attribute, which specifies how many options should be displayed at once. Setting the size to 1 creates a pull-down list of options, with the selected option displayed. Setting the size to any value greater than 1 creates a list with more than one option displayed. In the latter case, a vertical scroll bar is included if the number of options exceeds the size of the display. When you create this type of select list, you can use the MULTIPLE flag to indicate that users are allowed to select more than one item at once. Both types of select lists are shown in Figure 5.3.

The NAME attribute is used to identify the select list, and the SIZE attribute indicates how many options will be displayed at once. The SIZE attribute defaults to 1. <OPTION> tags have one attribute, VALUE. The VALUE associated with an option is sent to the server when that option is selected. Here's the one line select list from Figure 5.3:

```
<SELECT NAME="color">
    <OPTION VALUE="red">Red
    <OPTION VALUE="blue" SELECTED>Blue
    <OPTION VALUE="yellow">Yellow
</SELECT>
```

The SELECTED flag is used to indicate which option in the list is selected. If it's not included, the first item in the list will be selected by default for single line select lists. If the select list displays multiple items at once, and no SELECT flags are included in the options, then nothing is selected by default when the form loads. The first items in the list are displayed.

To create a select list with multiple options, simply set the SIZE attribute to a number other than 1. If there are more options than there are lines in the multiline select list, the user will be able to scroll through them using a vertical scroll bar on the select list. The example in Figure 5.3 was created with the following code:

```
<SELECT NAME="operating_system" SIZE=3 MULTIPLE>
    <OPTION VALUE="macos">Mac OS
    <OPTION VALUE="linux">Linux
    <OPTION VALUE="freebsd">FreeBSD
    <OPTION VALUE="windows">Windows
</SELECT>
```

As you can see if you refer to Figure 5.3, the first three options are displayed by default. The last option can be accessed using the scroll bar. (If you prefer, you can use SELECTED flags to specify the options that will be pre-selected.) This select list also allows users to select multiple items at once because the <SELECT> tag includes the MULTIPLE flag. MULTIPLE select lists are very useful. In the previous case, if the user had both Linux and Windows installed on her home computer, she could select both of the options before submitting the form.

On the downside, MULTIPLE select lists can be confusing to users. Many neophyte users don't know how to properly select multiple items from one select list. In fact, the method used to select multiple items varies from platform to platform. When you're designing forms, you should take this barrier into consideration before using multiple select lists. Before using them, you should consider whether something else might work better for that application.

Workshop: Building an Entire Form

Now you've been introduced to all the fields that can be used in an HTML form. At this point, I'm going to talk about how you put these pieces together to create a usable form. Generally speaking, a form consists of more than just a group of fields—those fields need to be labeled, and often some explanation is required in order to help users understand what's going on.

In this case, I'm going to create a simple survey form, of the kind one might fill out to get a free subscription to a trade magazine. The source code for the HTML form appears in Listing 5.1.

LISTING 5.1 A Sample Survey Form

```
<HTML>
<HEAD>
<TITLE>A Survey Form</TITLE>
</HEAD>
<BODY>

<H1>A Survey Form</H1>

<FORM ACTION="/cgi-bin/survey.cgi" METHOD="post">

<P>Name:
<INPUT TYPE="text" NAME="name" SIZE=30 MAXSIZE=50>
</P>

<P>
<INPUT TYPE="checkbox" NAME="purchaser" VALUE="yes">
I am authorized to make purchases.
</P>

<P>
IT budget:<BR>
<INPUT TYPE="radio" NAME="budget" VALUE="10000">Less than $10,000<BR>
<INPUT TYPE="radio" NAME="budget" VALUE="100000">From $10,000 to
$100,000<BR>
<INPUT TYPE="radio" NAME="budget" VALUE="1000000">From $100,000 to
$1,000,000<BR>
</P>

<P>
Current job responsibility:
<SELECT NAME="job" SIZE=1>
    <OPTION VALUE="senior">Senior Management
    <OPTION VALUE="management">Management
    <OPTION VALUE="engineer">Engineer
    <OPTION VALUE="consultant">Consultant
</SELECT>
</P>

<P>
Comments:<BR>
<TEXTAREA NAME="comments" WRAP="virtual"></TEXTAREA>
</P>

<P>
<INPUT TYPE="submit">
<INPUT TYPE="reset">
</P>
```

5

continues

LISTING 5.1   continued

```
</FORM>
</BODY>
</HTML>
```

First, let's take a look at the entire form. As you can see, the form is embedded within a standard HTML page. All the form fields appear within the opening and closing <FORM> tags. You can see what the form looks like in Figure 5.4.

FIGURE 5.4

A sample form.

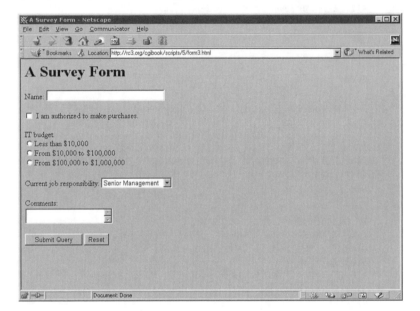

Looking at the <FORM> tag, you can see that the data entered in the form will be submitted to a program called survey.cgi in the cgi-bin directory on the server. The form uses the POST method because it contains a text box. Because users can enter lots of data in text boxes, using the POST method is more convenient because the form data is sent back to the server in the body of the request.

Elements in the Survey Form

Now I'm going to discuss the individual fields in the form. The first field in the form is a text box in which the user should enter her name. The field is 30 characters wide, and can hold a maximum of 50 characters. The name of the field is name, which is a bit confusing, but is an appropriate identifier for a field used to hold the user's name.

The second field in the form is a check box, named purchaser. The user checks this field if she is authorized to make purchases at her company. If she does check the field, the name and value are sent to the server. If not, nothing is sent to the server to represent this field.

Next is a group of radio buttons. The group is composed of several <INPUT> tags, all with the same name. They allow the user to select her company's information technology budget from a range of values. Only one value is sent to the server to represent this group of buttons.

The field that follows is a single line select list, from which the user can select the type of job that she has. The SIZE attribute was used to specify that the select list is one row high. In this case, it was optional because select lists default to a height of one row.

The final input field is a text box, named comments. The WRAP setting for the text box is virtual. Ordinarily, this setting defaults to none.

Finally, the remaining two <INPUT> tags place the Submit and Reset buttons on the form. I didn't specify values for either of them so that you could see the default labels that are placed on the buttons by the Web browser. Generally, you'll want to specify your own labels using the VALUE attribute, as the default values don't correctly describe the function of the buttons. Because no default values were specified for the fields on this form, pressing the Reset button will empty all the fields on the form.

Summary

HTML forms are the primary method by which Web programmers can create user interfaces for their CGI scripts. In this hour, I detailed all the elements that can be placed within an HTML form, and explained how they are utilized within forms. Most form elements are created using the <INPUT> tag. The exceptions are the <TEXTAREA> and <SELECT> tags.

Q&A

Q Is there a way to change the contents of a form field based on the value a user enters or selects in another form field?

A You can manipulate the contents of various form fields based on events that occur in the browser using JavaScript and VBScript. For example, if a user clicks on a check box, you can insert a value into a text field. Some browsers enable you to modify the contents of one select list based on the value selected in another. Of course, for this to work, your users' browsers must support the language you used to accomplish these tasks. JavaScript is supported by most newer Web browsers, and VBScript is supported by versions of Internet Explorer starting with 3.0.

Q Is it possible to submit a form without a Submit button?

A Yes, there are two ways to do so. If a form contains only one text field, then pressing Return while the cursor is in that field will submit the form. You can also use JavaScript to cause a form to be submitted based on an event that occurs in another form field. For example, a common navigational device involves creating a form with a single select list. The user selects a link from the list, and the form is submitted using JavaScript, directing them to that link.

5

Workshop

The quiz questions are designed to strengthen the knowledge you gain each hour. The exercises help you build on that knowledge by providing you with the opportunity to apply it to real problems. For the answers to the quiz questions, refer to Appendix A, "Answers."

Quiz

1. Why is the `password` field type insecure?
2. What is the purpose of the `MULTIPLE` attribute when used in a `SELECT` field?
3. How do you include default text in a `TEXTAREA` field?
4. True or false: a form must include a Submit button in order for the form to be submitted?

Exercises

1. Create a select list with six items that displays two of the items at any given time.
2. Create a form with a text input field, a password field, a group of radio buttons, and a Submit button.

Exercise Solutions

1. Here's an example that would work:

```
<SELECT NAME="select list" SIZE=2>
    <OPTION VALUE="red">RED
    <OPTION VALUE="green">GREEN
    <OPTION VALUE="blue">BLUE
    <OPTION VALUE="white">WHITE
    <OPTION VALUE="purple">PURPLE
    <OPTION VALUE="orange">ORANGE
```

2. Here's an example that would work:

```
<FORM>
<INPUT TYPE="text" NAME="first field">
<INPUT TYPE="password" NAME="password field">
<INPUT TYPE="radio" NAME="radios" VALUE="wfan">WFAN
<INPUT TYPE="radio" NAME=radios" VALUE="kbre">KBRE
<INPUT TYPE="radio" NAME=radios" VALUES="kilt">KILT
<INPUT TYPE="submit">
</FORM>
```

HOUR 6

Processing Input

The two things that nearly all programs have in common are input and output. This hour focuses on the input to CGI programs. First, where does the input come from? Second, how does the Web browser pass that input to the Web server? Building powerful CGI programs requires you to understand the answers to these two questions.

In this hour I'll discuss:

- How HTTP requests work
- Processing data from script arguments
- Processing data from forms
- Processing data from extra path information

A Little Bit About HTTP

Web servers accept three types of requests: GET, POST, and HEAD. A request from a program to a Web server looks like this:

```
GET /index.html HTTP/1.0
```

The first part of the request, which is GET in this case, is the method for that request. The second part, /index.html, is the URL being requested. The third part of the request, HTTP/1.0, is the protocol that the client is using.

> There are generally additional header lines that are included with the request, but the request line itself is all that is required by the Web server to service a request. The other headers contain inessential information that CGI programmers might find useful, like which browser the user is using, and what MIME types that browser accepts.

The two important request methods are GET and POST (note that they correspond to the two methods available when you create a form). The HEAD method is not normally used by Web browsers because it is a request for only the header of a response. The actual body of the response is not returned. HEAD is used by programs that need information only from a page's header. For example, programs that test links or check when pages have been updated can use the HEAD request to retrieve that information without utilizing the extra bandwidth necessary to retrieve the actual body of the request.

The GET Method

GET is the default method for Web requests. POST is only used if it is specified as the method in the form used to make the request. The important thing for CGI programmers to know about the GET method is that form data is appended to the URL when it is sent to the server. Web servers that support CGI then copy that information to an environment variable called QUERY_STRING. At that point, it's up to the CGI program to retrieve the data from the environment variable and decode it.

A URL that includes query string information looks like this:

```
http://finance.yahoo.com/q?s=aapl&d=v1
```

The ? separates the query string from the actual path to the resource being requested. The two parameters passed to the server are s and d.

The POST Method

The POST method is used when an HTML form has the METHOD attribute set to POST. Unlike the GET method, the POST method places data in the body of the request as well as in the URL. A POST request looks a lot like an HTTP response. The first line is a standard HTTP request, with the method POST specified. It includes any additional headers specified by the browser, and then the body of the request is sent, separated from the header by a blank line.

The body of a request that uses the POST method is sent to the CGI program through standard input. *Standard input* is a UNIX term that is generally associated with input read from the console. In this case, the body of the HTTP request is redirected into the program through standard input.

Information can also be sent to the server in the form of a query string following the filename in the URL. This information is still stored in the QUERY_STRING environment variable. I'll explain how standard input works, and how to handle information passed to programs from the POST method, later this hour.

Choosing Between GET and POST

Obviously, one question that CGI programmers face when designing forms is whether to use the GET or POST method. For a large percentage of tasks, they're interchangeable— either will work fine. However, in a small percentage of cases, there are advantages to using one or the other.

As you know, data submitted using GET and POST are passed to CGI programs in different ways. Fortunately, most CGI libraries convert the submitted form data into a data structure native to the programming language being used, so it's not necessary to deal with the complexity of decoding the form data. For that reason, it's not necessary to take that complexity into account when you're deciding between the two methods. More importantly, if you use a library like CGI.pm, it will parse the form data no matter how it is submitted, so your scripts can be called using the GET and POST methods interchangeably.

Here's a list of a few conditions where it makes sense to choose GET over POST, or vice versa:

- If you want your application to be capable of being called from a hyperlink, it has to support the GET method. If you use a CGI library that supports both methods interchangeably, this isn't a concern (since GET support is built in).
- If you don't want arguments passed to the script to be captured in the server's logs, you should create the form using the POST method. For example, if the form is a login form, you don't want all the usernames and passwords to be captured in the Web server's access log. You also don't want to let people see your users' passwords in plain text in a URL if they're watching over the user's shoulder.
- If the form input is very long (let's say it contains a TEXTAREA field), you'll want to use the POST method. You can use the GET method, although there are various limitations on the length of URLs imposed by browsers, servers, and operating systems (which restrict the size of environment variables). It's often easier to stick to POST.

6

- If you want users to be able to bookmark the results of a form submission, you should use the GET method. All the arguments users enter will be preserved as part of the bookmark because they're included in the URL. You can't capture form submissions that use POST in the same way. By the same token, if you don't want people to bookmark the results of a form submission, use POST. For example, you probably don't want to allow users to bookmark the results of a form that submits their credit card information and completes an order at an online store.
- If your form includes a file upload field you must use the POST method. You must also set the form's ENCTYPE to multipart/form-data.
- If you want to preserve the query string in a URL in referrer logs, you'll want to use the GET method. For example, most search applications use the GET method so that the URL to the search results page contains the search terms the user typed in the query string. That way, when a user clicks on a link on that page, the search terms will be passed to the page that the link refers to, and thus stored in the referrer log.

Handling Script Arguments

Before I get into handling data passed through the CGI interface, I'd like to talk about a simpler technique used to exchange data between Web servers and external programs. As you already know, information in a URL after the ? is not used by the Web server, but is passed on to the resource being requested. This information is generally referred to as the query string.

Most Web servers send the query string as a command line argument to the program being executed. So, you can access that data in your CGI programs using the same technique you would use to access command line arguments to a program under normal circumstances. Generally, this is only worthwhile if you're writing very simple scripts and you don't want to be bothered with decoding URL-encoded data. If the script only requires one argument, you can just append it to the URL as a query string and leave out all of that name and value business.

 Using command-line arguments with scripts this way is not part of the CGI standard; however, it is a simple technique you can use when designing Web applications. In most cases, you'll probably just want to use the query string through the CGI interface, but this method works nicely if you're writing simple shell scripts.

For example, let's say you want to write a simple script that reports whether a person is logged into the Web server (this only works on servers that run UNIX). This script is most easily written using the Bourne shell, which is used not only as the basic login shell for most users, but also provides programmers with the ability to write scripts.

> If you're not familiar with UNIX but are a Windows user, it's probably easiest to explain this by saying that the Bourne shell is equivalent to the DOS prompt, and shell scripts are like batch files. The Bourne shell is much more powerful than the DOS prompt, but they serve the same basic purpose.

The simplest method of passing data from an HTTP request to a simple shell script is to use the argument passed to the script by the Web server. In this example, the URL used to make the request is:

```
http://www.example.com/cgi-bin/finger.cgi?rafeco
```

The purpose of this script is to run the UNIX finger command to determine whether the user whose name was passed in the argument is logged in. Listing 6.1 contains the source code for the script.

LISTING 6.1   A CGI Program that Provides an Interface to the Finger Command

```
 1: #!/usr/local/bin/bash
 2:
 3: echo "Content-type: text/html"
 4: echo
 5:
 6: echo "<html><head><title>finger $1</title></head><body>"
 7:
 8: echo "<pre>"
 9: finger "$1"
10: echo "</pre>
11:
12: echo "</body></html>"
```

In shell scripts, the variable $1 returns the first command-line argument. If an argument is passed to the script, as is the case in the URL I list previously, the finger information for that account will be displayed in the browser. The command finger $1 takes care of that. The <PRE> tags ensure that the output is properly formatted. The results of the call to the finger script appear in Figure 6.1.

FIGURE **6.1**

The results of the
`finger.cgi` *script.*

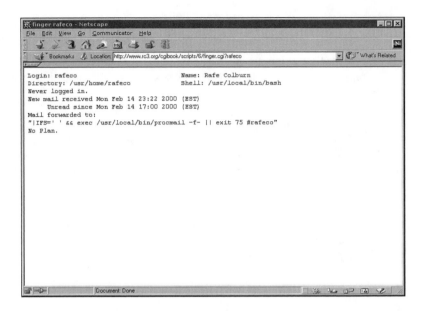

As you can see, it's possible to write scripts using arguments, but this approach is rather inflexible. The other techniques of passing data to scripts are more robust, and are better adapted to use when you write CGI scripts.

Processing Form Data

When you write a CGI program that accepts data from a form, there are several steps you must take in order to be able to use the data within your program. Regardless of what you plan on doing with the data in your CGI program, the data has to be converted to a usable format. The following general steps are used to make form data encoded with URL encoding usable within your programs:

1. Read the data passed from the form into the program.
2. Divide the form data into individual name and value pairs.
3. Split each name and value pair into a variable and a value, so that the values from the form fields can be accessed using the field name.
4. Decode the URL encoding applied to the values from the form.

Now I'm going to take a look at each of the steps in some detail.

Reading Data from the Form

Form data is passed from the Web server to the script in one of two ways, depending on the method used when the form was submitted. If the form used the GET method, the form data is passed to the Web server through the URL, and is copied to the QUERY_STRING variable by the Web server, where it can be accessed from a CGI program. To read the form data so that it can be used in your CGI program, you just need to read the contents of the environment variable, and place them in a variable that can be manipulated from within your program.

In Perl, the contents of environment variables are accessible using the hash %ENV. To copy the contents of the QUERY_STRING environment variable to a Perl variable called $query_string, the following line of code is used:

```
$form_info = $ENV{'QUERY_STRING'};
```

The read function is used to accept form data that was submitted using the POST method. First, you have to determine the size of the input stream. Then you have to read the input stream into a variable. These steps are accomplished using the following code:

```
$input_size = $ENV{'CONTENT_LENGTH'};
read (STDIN, $form_info, $input_size);
```

On the first line, the code looks at the CONTENT_LENGTH environment variable to determine the size of the body of the request. This information is read from the content-length HTTP header and placed in the CONTENT_LENGTH environment variable by the Web server when the request is processed. On the second line, the read function is used to copy the body of the request into the variable $form_info. The read function takes three arguments—the filehandle from which to read the data, the variable to place the data in, and the number of bytes of data to read. STDIN is a filehandle that's created automatically when the script is invoked, and is used to access standard input.

Dividing the Data into Name and Value Pairs

There are two characters that can be used to divide name and value pairs in a query string or the body of an HTTP request, & and ;. After you've read the form information into a variable, the next step is to create an array of name and value pairs from that information. Because a query string or HTTP request body separates the pairs by the & or ; character, splitting the information into an array is accomplished using the following code:

```
@input_pairs = split (/[&;]/, $form_info);
```

The split function has two arguments. The first argument is the expression on which to split the string in the second argument. In this case, the string is the query information stored in $form_info. Each of the pairs extracted from the form information is stored as an element in the array @input_pairs.

6

Splitting Names from Values

I'm going to use one loop to split the name and value pairs into parts, and at the same time decode the URL-encoded data. A `foreach` loop is used to iterate over all the name and value pairs, which will be stored in a hash keyed on the field names when I'm done. Inside the loop, I'll decode all of the URL encoded data as well. (See Listing 6.2.)

LISTING 6.2   Code Used to Decode URL Encoded Data

```
 1: %input = ();
 2: foreach $pair (@input_pairs) {
 3:     # Convert plusses to spaces
 4:     $pair =~ s/\+/ /g;
 5:
 6:     # Split the name and value pair
 7:     ($name, $value) = split (/=/, $pair);
 8:
 9:     # Decode the URL encoded name and value
10:     $name =~ s/%([A-Fa-f0-9]{2})/pack("c",hex($1))/ge;
11:     $value =~ s/%([A-Fa-f0-9]{2})/pack("c",hex($1))/ge;
12:
13:     # Copy the name and value into the hash
14:     $input{$name} = $value;
15: }
```

Now let's look at how the loop works. Each pair is extracted from the array and placed in the variable $pair. The first thing the script does is transform plusses into spaces using a search and replace operation. Then, the names and values are split before the data is decoded. The reason for this is that when data is URL encoded, = signs are encoded along with some other special characters. You want to split up the name and value pairs on the = signs before any other = signs that might appear in the data are decoded.

The next step is to actually decode any encoded characters. This is the most complex step in the process. A search and replace is performed on both the name and value. The script searches for a percent sign followed by two hexadecimal digits (either 0–9 or A–F). When it finds that pattern, it looks up the value of that two digit number in the ASCII table. It then replaces the entire expression (including the percent sign) with the character from the ASCII table. For example, in the ASCII table, character 20 is a space. This expression will replace every %20 with a space.

After the text has been decoded, an entry is added to the %input hash with the $name variable as the key, and the $value variable as the value assigned to that key.

A Sample Script that Manually Decodes Form Data

Now let's look at a sample script that uses the code I designed. In the end, all it does is print the name and value pairs that are submitted to the script. However, it has one important step that I didn't describe before. It determines whether to grab information from the query string or the request body depending on the value of the REQUEST_METHOD variable. If the method is GET, the script reads the QUERY_STRING environment variable. If it's POST, it reads the form information from standard input. The source code for the script appears in Listing 6.3.

LISTING 6.3 A Script that Decodes Form Input Manually

```
 1: #!/usr/local/bin/perl
 2:
 3: if ($ENV{'REQUEST_METHOD'} eq 'GET') {
 4:     $form_info = $ENV{'QUERY_STRING'};
 5: }
 6: else {
 7:     $input_size = $ENV{'CONTENT_LENGTH'};
 8:     read (STDIN, $form_info, $input_size);
 9: }
10:
11: @input_pairs = split (/[&;]/, $form_info);
12:
13: %input = ();
14: foreach $pair (@input_pairs) {
15:     # Convert plusses to spaces
16:     $pair =~ s/\+/ /g;
17:
18:     # Split the name and value pair
19:     ($name, $value) = split (/=/, $pair);
20:
21:     # Decode the URL encoded name and value
22:     $name =~ s/%([A-Fa-f0-9]{2})/pack("c",hex($1))/ge;
23:     $value =~ s/%([A-Fa-f0-9]{2})/pack("c",hex($1))/ge;
24:
25:     # Copy the name and value into the hash
26:     $input{$name} = $value;
27: }
28:
29: print "Content-type: text/html\n\n";
30:
31: print "<HTML><HEAD><TITLE>Name and Value Pairs</TITLE></HEAD><BODY>\n";
32:
33: foreach $key (keys %input) {
34:     print "<P>$key : $input{$key}</P>\n";
35: }
36:
37: print "</BODY></HTML>\n";
```

6

Using `CGI.pm` to Decode Form Data

Decoding form input manually is tedious. Every time you write a new CGI program, you have to paste the form decoding code into it, and hope that you don't create any errors. Plus, the form input decoding code described previously suffers from a number of inadequacies. It doesn't do anything at all with multiple select boxes or file upload fields. Fortunately, there is an alternative to writing and maintaining the code yourself. However, I wanted to explain it so that you can understand how the process works. Even though you probably won't need to write the code to transform a raw HTTP request into usable data, it's important to understand the steps involved in doing so.

Perl comes with a module designed to make it easier to write CGI programs. The module, written by Lincoln Stein, is called `CGI.pm`. The main purpose of `CGI.pm` is to automatically import form data, decode it, and make it available within your CGI program. It has a number of other features that will be introduced in Hour 10, "Perl—The Big Kahuna of CGI," but the most important feature for our purposes here is the decoding of form data.

To decode the data submitted to a CGI script with `CGI.pm`, all you have to do is import the `CGI.pm` module using

```
use CGI (qw: standard);
```

At that point, all the data from the CGI script is copied into a hash called `param` that is associated with the `query` object, which is referenced by the variable `$query`. So, if the user submitted a form with a field on it called `last_name`, you could access that value using the following construct:

```
$last_name = $query->param('last_name');
```

Let's look at each piece of that statement. `$last_name` is just the name of a local variable to which I want to assign the value from the form field. `$query` refers to the query object that I created for this program. The arrow operator is used to retrieve the `param` hash from the `$query` object. The value `last_name` in parentheses is used to retrieve the element from the hash `param` identified by the key `last_name`.

That's about all there is to it when it comes to decoding form input with `CGI.pm`—all the work is done for you. `CGI.pm` offers a lot of additional functionality as well, which will be described in detail in Hour 10.

A Sample Script that Uses `CGI.pm`

Now that I've explained how to access form data with `CGI.pm`, let me provide you with a simple example that shows how a full program that uses `CGI.pm` is written. This example is simple; it prints all the values submitted with a form, for any form. It does this by extracting a list of parameters passed to the script using the param() function, and then retrieving and printing all the values associated with those parameters. The source code for the script appears in Listing 6.4.

LISTING 6.4   A Script that Prints All the Form Parameters Submitted to It

```
 1: #!/usr/local/bin/perl
 2:
 3: use CGI qw(:standard);
 4:
 5: print header();
 6:
 7: print "<HTML>\n<HEAD>\n<TITLE>Form parameters</TITLE>\n</HEAD>\n";
 8: print "<BODY>\n";
 9: print "<H1>Form Parameters</H1>\n";
10:
11: if (param()) {
12:     @keys = param();
13:     foreach $key (@keys) {
14:     print $key,   ": ", param($key), "<BR>\n";
15:     }
16: }
17: else {
18:     print "<P>No form was submitted.</P>\n";
19: }
20:
21: print "</BODY></HTML>\n";
```

Let's look at how the script works. First, it imports the CGI.pm module, and uses qw(:standard) to indicate that the function-based interface should be used instead of the object-oriented interface. That means that you don't have to preface every call to a CGI.pm function with a reference to the object with which it's associated. Basically, it's a time saver you can use when you're writing simple scripts.

After the CGI module is imported, it makes all the name and value pairs submitted to the script available through the param() function. After I use the header() function to print the HTTP header and I print the HTML tags necessary to start the page, I can get down to business. I start out with an if statement that checks whether the param() function returns anything. If it doesn't, no parameters were passed to the script, and I print a message to that effect. If the param() function does return some parameter names, the next step is to print out the name and value pairs.

First, I call the param() function with no arguments, returning a list of all the parameters passed to the script. I copy that list into the array @keys. I then use a foreach loop to

6

process each of the entries in the @keys array one at a time. Each entry in the array is assigned to the variable $key, which can be accessed in the loop body. Inside the loop, I print the value of $key, and pass $key to the param() function to get the value associated with that key. I do all of this in a single print statement. After the loop has iterated over all the parameters, I just print out the ending tags for the page and I'm done.

Sending Input to CGI Programs via Extra Path Information

Extra path information provides an alternative means by which data can be passed from a Web browser to the Web server. Extra path information is separated from the rest of the URL using a /, and follows the file part of a URL. The URL looks like one long path to a file, but the filename in the URL appears somewhere in the middle of the path. For example, take a look at the following URL:

```
http://www.rc3.org/cgi-bin/epi.cgi/extra/path/info
```

The filename in the URL is epi.cgi. The extra path information is extra/path/info. The Web server is smart enough to realize that the path itself ends at epi.cgi, and that everything that follows is extra information.

The Web server copies the extra path information into the environment variable PATH_INFO. The Web server also creates a second environment variable called PATH_TRANSLATED that contains the extra path information tacked onto the path of the server's document root. So, if the document root for your Web server is /home/httpd/htdocs, the PATH_TRANSLATED for this example is:

```
/home/httpd/htdocs/extra/path/info
```

Using Extra Path Information

As you can see, there's not a lot of difference between extra path information and data passed to a script through the query string. In both cases, the data is passed from the browser to the server as part of the URL, and is eventually stored within an environment variable. One obvious difference is that extra path information has to be hard coded within a link or the TARGET attribute of a form by the programmer. Data can't be gathered from a form and passed to the script using extra path information.

The most important difference, however, is the fact that the PATH_TRANSLATED variable is created automatically whenever extra path information is passed to the script from the browser. If the extra path information contains the path to a legitimate file, the absolute location of that file (assuming it really is under the server's document root) is stored in PATH_TRANSLATED.

The usefulness of extra path information is probably best illustrated with an example. Let's say you're in charge of the Web site for a newspaper. The newspaper prints many stories every day that are formatted in a virtually identical manner. You want to keep your site as flexible as possible, so you create a very simple format to store news stories that doesn't involve any HTML. You then write a CGI program that can read one of these formatted stories, convert it to HTML in the design that your newspaper uses, and present it on the Web.

All the links on your site to stories formatted with this program would use extra path information to pass the file location of the stories to be formatted. For example, if you stored all the files in /news, and just numbered each of the stories, you could refer to them using a URL like this:

```
http://www.rc3.org/cgi-bin/story.cgi/news/0003.txt
```

The browser would request the program /cgi-bin/story.cgi, and then the CGI program would use PATH_TRANSLATED to determine which story to display. This could form the basis for a templating system, where the .txt files contain markup specific to the newspaper, and the story.cgi program converts that markup to HTML.

CGI Environment Variables

In this hour, and indeed, throughout this book, I've discussed some of the environment variables that are associated with CGI. The one I've discussed most is $QUERY_STRING, which contains the query string found in the request's URL. The Web server also copies the values from most of the HTTP headers sent by the browser into environment variables. A list of environment variables set when a CGI script is called appears in Table 6.1.

TABLE 6.1   CGI Environment Variables

Variable	Value
AUTH_TYPE	The type of authentication used to validate the remote user
CONTENT_LENGTH	The size of the body of the request in bytes
CONTENT_TYPE	The content type of the request; corresponds to the ENCTYPE set in the <FORM> tag
DOCUMENT_ROOT	The directory where Web documents are stored
GATEWAY_INTERFACE	The version of CGI that the server implements
HTTP_ACCEPT	The list of content types that the client accepts (generally the browser sends */*, indicating that it accepts all content types)

6

continues

TABLE 6.1   continued

Variable	Value
HTTP_FROM	The email address of the user who submitted the request (not set by modern browsers)
HTTP_REFERER	The URL of the document the user was viewing before he requested your program
HTTP_USER_AGENT	The browser used to make the request
PATH_INFO	The extra path information appended to the URL
PATH_TRANSLATED	The extra path information appended to the document root
QUERY_STRING	The query information passed to the script after a ? in the URL
REMOTE_ADDR	The IP address of the computer making the request (sometimes replaced with the IP address of a proxy server between the client and server)
REMOTE_HOST	The hostname of the computer making the request
REMOTE_IDENT	The username of the person making the request (not set by modern browsers)
REQUEST_METHOD	The HTTP method used to make the request: POST, GET, or HEAD
SCRIPT_NAME	The path to the script being executed
SERVER_NAME	The server's hostname or IP address
SERVER_PORT	The port on which the server is running
SERVER_PROTOCOL	The name and revision number of the protocol that the server is running
SERVER_SOFTWARE	The name and version number of the HTTP server

Summary

This hour provided an overview of the various means by which data is passed from the Web browser to the Web server, and what you can do with the data after it is received. First, I discussed the three request methods HTTP supports—GET, POST, and HEAD. I then discussed a simpler method of client-server data passing, command-line arguments. Next, I discussed some techniques you can use to decode form input. After that, I talked about extra path information, an alternative means of passing data to the server. Finally, I discussed CGI environment variables, which contain information passed to the server in HTTP headers.

Q&A

Q **This hour explained how to decode form data using Perl, but I use another language.**

A The procedure used in this hour to decode form data manually using Perl can be adapted to work in any language that supports environment variables and standard input. In Hour 11, "Other Popular CGI Programming Languages," I'll provide details on how to decode form data using the Bourne shell, C, and Python.

Q **Are there any security issues involved with accepting user input and processing it in a program?**

A Yes, quite a few actually. They're discussed in Hour 22, "Securing CGI Scripts."

Workshop

The quiz questions are designed to strengthen the knowledge you gain each hour. The exercises help you build on that knowledge by providing you with the opportunity to apply it to real problems. See Appendix A, "Answers" for the answers to the quiz questions.

Quiz

1. What is the pack function used for when manually decoding form input in Perl?
2. True or false, you can capture user input using extra path information.
3. Which character is used to separate multiple arguments when you pass information to the server using command-line arguments?

Exercises

1. Write a script that manually decodes the user's form input and redisplays the pre-filled form with the user's input.
2. Write a script that displays the contents of a file specified using extra path information.
3. Write a script that displays different content depending on which browser the user is running. (Hint: use the HTTP_USER_AGENT environment variable.)

6

HOUR 7

Validating User Input

One of the most common tasks required of CGI programs is validation of user input. Whether you're taking an order online, allowing a user to subscribe to a mailing list, or enabling the user to enter stock symbols to look up a quote, it's necessary to verify that the user entered all the required information in the form, and that the information entered is properly formatted.

There are a number of techniques that can be used for form validation, and in this hour, I'm going to cover some of the most effective ones. Over the course of this hour, you will learn:

- How to use JavaScript to validate form content
- How to design forms that require less validation
- How to design applications that efficiently incorporate form validation
- Using regular expressions to validate form content

Using JavaScript for Form Validation

Although this book is about CGI programming, I want to talk a bit about JavaScript—the first line of defense for validating user input. The most important thing to remember about using JavaScript to validate forms is that it's not completely reliable! In other words, you must validate the form content on the server side as well.

There are two advantages to using JavaScript to validate forms. One works to the benefit of the user, and the other works to the benefit of the systems administrator. Users benefit because JavaScript provides instant feedback. You can set up your form validation so that it tests the value in a form field the moment the user leaves that field, or before the form is submitted. Either way, the user doesn't have to wait until the form has been submitted and processed to figure out whether his input was valid.

Pretty much every error that is caught by JavaScript conserves one form submission. Let's say JavaScript was not used. If the user submitted a form and his name was incorrect, the CGI program would have to reject his form submission, present the form to him again, and force him to submit it a second time. If that error were caught with JavaScript, however, it could be fixed without submitting the form the first time—saving one form submission and reducing the load on the Web site.

The only real disadvantage of JavaScript is that it is somewhat unreliable. Not all Web browsers support JavaScript. Some users turn off JavaScript even if their browsers do support it. Another factor that reduces the reliability of JavaScript is that it's implemented differently from browser to browser, so it's difficult to ensure that your scripts will work in all browsers. Fortunately, the level of JavaScript support necessary to enable form validation is pretty low.

How JavaScript Works to Validate Forms

Form validation using JavaScript is *event driven*. This means the JavaScript interpreter in the browser knows when certain events occur. If there is JavaScript code associated with those events, the browser automatically executes that code. For example, form fields support the onChange event. To validate the contents of a field whenever its value changes, you just have to write an event handler to test the value. An *event handler* is nothing more than a function associated with the appropriate event.

There are lots of other events that are associated with forms as well. If you want to validate the contents of a form when the user submits the form, you can use the onSubmit event. There are also events that occur when a user enters or leaves a form field.

To react to an event, you have to add an event-handler reference to the appropriate tag. For example, if you want to trap a change in a text field, you need to refer to an onChange event handler in the <INPUT> tag for the field, like this:

```
<INPUT TYPE="text" NAME="example" onChange="check_example()">
```

Whenever the value in the field changes, the function check_example() is called. If you want to validate your form when it's submitted, you should refer to an onSubmit event handler in the <FORM> tag, like this:

```
<FORM ACTION="/cgi-bin/example.cgi" onSubmit="return verify_form()">
```

You might have noticed a difference between the references to the onChange and onSubmit event handlers. When you reference an onSumbit event handler, you have to preface the event handler name with the return keyword. The event handler itself must return a Boolean value (either true or false). If the user entered an invalid value, the event handler should return a value of false. The value returned by the function referenced in the onSubmit handler is then passed to the return command, which prevents the form from being submitted. Likewise, if the form data is valid, the event handler should return a value of true.

An Example of Form Validation

Let's take a look at a simple example in which the form is validated prior to submission. The form is very simple, it consists of a text input field and a submit button. The user is prompted to enter her zip code. If the value she enters is less than five characters long, the validation function assumes that the value entered was not valid, and instructs the user to enter a valid value before she tries to submit the form again. I'm going to examine the two main components of the script: the form and the event handler.

The Form Itself

This form includes two fields: a text field and a submit button. Here's the source code for the form, which also includes the call to the event handler that validates the form:

```
<FORM onSubmit="return check_form(this)">
    <B>Zip Code:</B>
    <INPUT TYPE="text" NAME="zip_code" SIZE=5 MAXLENGTH=5><BR>
    <INPUT TYPE="submit">
</FORM>
```

As you can see, there's not much to it. (Because this is an example, I didn't specify an action for the form.) Most importantly, the form specifies an onSubmit event handler. When the form is submitted, the check_form() function is called. If the validation code in check_form() succeeds, the function returns true and the form is submitted. If the validation fails, the function returns false and the form is not submitted.

The word this is passed to the function as an argument. In JavaScript, this is shorthand for the current object. Because the function call appears within a <FORM> tag, the this argument refers to the form. You'll see how the argument is used when I discuss the details of the event handler, in the next section.

7

The Event Handler

The JavaScript code used to validate the form in this case is very simple. It verifies that the value entered in the zip_code field is five characters long. It verifies that the user entered five characters in the field. Here's the source code:

```
function check_form(the_form) {
    if (the_form.zip_code.value.length != 5) {
        alert("The Zip Code must be 5 digits long.");
    return false;
    }
}
```

The function begins with the basic function declaration. check_form is the name of the function, and the_form indicates that the function accepts one argument, and that the value of that argument should be assigned to a variable named the_form. The function itself contains a single conditional statement that checks whether the value in the zip_code field is five characters long.

The length of the value in that field is retrieved using the identifier the_form.zip_code.value.length. The the_form variable points to the form object passed to the function from the <FORM> tag.

Designing Easily Validated Forms

You can ease the burden of form validation by writing forms that require less effort to validate. You should design your form fields so that they give the user few opportunities to make mistakes. Let me provide you with a few examples.

When you have a form that contains a field for the U.S. state, you should create a pull-down list of states that the user selects from rather than placing a text field on the page and allowing the user to enter his state abbreviation. Restricting the user to only valid options eliminates typing errors, even though it makes data entry a bit slower for experienced users. Any time you create a field that has a restricted set of options, you should use a select box or a group of radio buttons.

Any time you require a value that is of a fixed length, you should use the MAXLENGTH attribute of the text or password input field to restrict the number of characters a user can enter. For example, all United States Social Security Numbers are nine digits long. If you create a form field to allow someone to enter her Social Security Number, you should restrict the length to nine characters so that she can't inadvertently enter a value that's too large.

Another example that has less to do with data validation than with the way the data is ultimately stored is the WRAP attribute of TEXTAREA fields. Neither the none nor the virtual setting inserts line feeds into the user input. The physical setting does. When you choose a setting, you need to make sure that it corresponds to your idea of how the data should be stored. If the user's input should have a line feed at the end of each line, you might consider using the physical or none settings. The none setting will often induce users to hit return at the end of every line, and the physical setting physically inserts line feeds when each line wraps.

Incorporating Validation into the Form-Processing Code

When many people begin writing CGI programs, they wind up writing lots of extra code. For example, they create an HTML page with a form on it, and then they write a CGI script to which the form will be submitted. If that script includes code to validate the user's input, chances are they'll also write code that redisplays the form with the values the user entered and messages to indicate where the user made errors.

This is a perfectly valid method for creating Web applications, but it's probably not the most efficient method available. The main problem with this approach is that if the code to display the form already exists in the CGI script, there's no reason to reproduce it in a separate HTML file. A better strategy is to use the same CGI script to initially display the form and to process the form after it has been submitted.

That way, when you need to make a change to the fields on the form or to the form's appearance, you only have to make the change in one place. It's also easier to keep track of one file rather than two. The trick is to set up your script so that it knows whether it's being displayed for the first time.

How a Form-Processing Program Works

The first step in a form processing program is to determine whether the program should display a new form or process a form submission. To make this determination, you should test for the existence of a parameter that you know will be passed any time the form is submitted. For example, if your form contains a text field called search_term, the program can test for the existence of a query parameter named search_term to determine whether the request is a form submission. There are other methods that you can use as well, that's just the easiest.

If the request was not a form submission, the user needs to see the form for the first time. The CGI program should print out the form along with any other information associated with it. On the other hand, if the request is a form submission, the form content must be validated. If the form content is, for some reason, invalid, the form must be redisplayed

7

along with some indication of what the user did incorrectly. If the form was submitted, and the content was valid, you can move along to the main logic in the CGI program.

Take a look at the diagram in Figure 7.1. It demonstrates how an application that both generates and processes a form works.

FIGURE 7.1

The flow of logic through a form processing program.

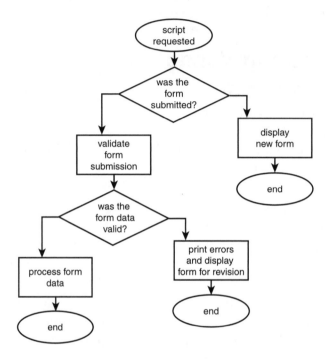

An Example of Form Processing

Now let's look at an example that demonstrates exactly how form processing works. This example consists of a simple application that displays a form, accepts the submitted form, validates the content, and displays the information (with or without an error message) back to the user.

The script itself is organized in components. The script begins with a pointer to the Perl executable. It follows by importing the CGI.pm module, and creating a new query object to import the form parameters into the Perl namespace:

```
#!C:/perl/bin/perl.exe

use CGI;
$query = new CGI;
```

The Main Script Logic

The body of the script contains the logic that determines whether to display the form for the first time, display the form with an error message, or display the results of a successful form submission. It also prints the HTML header and footer. Take a look at the code in Listing 7.1.

LISTING 7.1 The Application Logic in a Form Processing Application

```
 1: &print_page_start;
 2: if ($query->param('submitted')) {
 3:     $error_message = "";
 4:     &validate_form;
 5:     if ($error_message eq "") {
 6:     &print_form_values;
 7:     }
 8:     else {
 9:     print "<UL>\n" . $error_message . "</UL>\n";
10:     &print_form;
11:     }
12: }
13: else {
14:     &set_initial_values;
15:     &print_form;
16: }
17: &print_page_end;
```

All the constructs beginning with & are calls to user-defined subroutines. Placing the vast majority of the code in subroutines allows you to streamline the application's logic so that it's easier to read. It also enables you to reuse components of the code. I'll walk you through the application logic so that you can see how it works.

First, there's a call to the subroutine print_page_start. This code prints the HTTP content type header, the HTML heading, and the headline for the page. The next step is a conditional statement that tests for the presence of the submitted parameter, which is a hidden field that appears in the form. The only purpose of the hidden field is to indicate that the form has been submitted. It can be tested regardless of the values entered in the other fields.

If the query has been submitted, the next step is to test the values entered to make sure that they're valid. The first thing I do is define a variable called $error_message. If any of the values entered in the form are invalid, error messages will be placed in this variable. To check the values, I call the validate_form subroutine.

7

If the $error_message variable is still empty after validate_form has executed, the values the user entered were okay. The print_form_values subroutine is called, and the values that the user entered are displayed. If this CGI script had a real purpose, then at this point, the real functionality would be implemented.

If the $error_message variable is not empty, there was some problem with the user's input. The script prints the error message stored in the $error_message variable, and redisplays the form with the values that the user entered, using the &print_form subroutine.

Let's skip back to the beginning. If a user arrived at the page without submitting the form, the form is displayed for the first time. This is accomplished using two subroutines. The first subroutine, set_initial_values, sets the default values for the form. In this case, all the variables are set to blank values. Then, the form is printed using the subroutine print_form. At that point, the print_page_end subroutine is called, and execution of the script concludes.

The Input Validation Subroutine

Now let's look at the important subroutines from the script. The first interesting subroutine is validate_form. Listing 7.2 shows the source code.

LISTING 7.2   The validate_form Subroutine

```
 1: sub validate_form {
 2:     $name = $query->param('name');
 3:     $quest = $query->param('quest');
 4:     $fav_color = $query->param('fav_color');
 5:     if ($name eq "") {
 6:     $error_message .= "<LI>You must enter a name.\n";
 7:     }
 8:     if ($quest eq "") {
 9:     $error_message .= "<LI>You must enter your quest.\n";
10:     }
11:     if ($fav_color eq "") {
12:     $error_message .= "<LI>You must select your favorite color.\n";
13:     }
14: }
```

The first part of the subroutine just copies the form parameters into variables that are more convenient to access from within the script. This makes the code a bit more readable. Then, each field is tested to verify that the user entered or selected a value. The code could be as complex as you want at this point. We could test to make sure there are two words in the name field, or that the quest field contains only letters and numbers with no punctuation.

> The complexity of the form validation code is entirely up to the application developer. Because the point of this script is to demonstrate how form validation fits into the overall plan for the application, the validation code itself is very simple.

The Output Subroutine

The output subroutine for this script just prints out the values that the user entered or selected for all the form fields. This is the slot where the real application logic would appear in an application that had a legitimate purpose. For example, if this were an order entry system, at this point the script would actually store the user's order in the database. The code in this program is very simple:

```
sub print_form_values {
    print "<b>Name:</b> " . $name . "<br>\n";
    print "<b>Quest:</b> " . $quest . "<br>\n";
    print "<b>Favorite Color:</b> " . $fav_color;
    print "<br>\n";
}
```

The script just prints the name of each form field on a line, and the value assigned to that field afterward. Because the form validation subroutine is always called before the print_form_values subroutine, you can use the shorter variable names from that subroutine here.

The Form Creation Subroutine

The key subroutine in this script is &print_form. Not only is it by far the most complex subroutine in this script, but it's the whole reason for this exercise. It demonstrates how the same code can be used to generate both the initial form for an application, and follow-up forms that allow users to correct their errors.

> In most applications, the code used to display the form will not be the most complex code in the application. Instead, the actual application logic will comprise the bulk of the complexity.

Listing 7.3 shows the source code for the subroutine print_form.

7

LISTING 7.3   The print_form Subroutine

```
 1: sub print_form {
 2:     @colors = ('red', 'green', 'blue');
 3:     print "<FORM>\n";
 4:     print "<INPUT TYPE=\"hidden\" NAME=\"submitted\" VALUE=\
➥"yes\">\n";
 5:     print "<b>Name:</b>";
 6:     print "<INPUT TYPE=\"text\" NAME=\"name\" VALUE=\"$name\
➥"><BR>\n";
 7:     print "<b>Quest:</b>";
 8:     print "<INPUT TYPE=\"text\" NAME=\"quest\" VALUE=\"$quest\
➥"><BR><BR>\n";
 9:     print "<b>Favorite Color:</b><br>\n";
10:     foreach $color (@colors) {
11:     print "<INPUT TYPE=\"radio\" NAME=\"fav_color\" ";
12:     print "VALUE=\"$color\"";
13:     if ($fav_color eq $color) {
14:         print " CHECKED";
15:     }
16:     print ">$color<BR>\n";
17:     }
18:     print "<BR>\n";
19:     print "<INPUT TYPE=\"submit\">\n";
20:     print "</FORM>\n";
21: }
```

The subroutine begins with a statement that creates an array containing all the colors that will be provided as options for the user's favorite color. The advantage of setting the script up this way is that it's very easy to add or remove colors from the form. You just modify the list to reflect the change you want to make.

> If this script were longer and more complex, it would have been a good idea to create the @colors array at the very beginning of the program, shown in Listing 7.4. That way programmers don't have to dig through the source code to change the list of colors.

Then, the opening <FORM> tag is presented. The tag has no attributes because this form will use the GET method, and will be submitted to itself. The next statement prints the hidden field submitted. This field is just a marker with a known value that enables you to determine whether a request for the script is a form submission, or just a standard request.

The next four lines create the name and quest fields. Creating both of the fields is identical conceptually. Just print out the label for the field, and then the <INPUT> tag itself. If the field has a value (because the form was submitted), that value is included in the VALUE attribute. If the form was displayed for the first time, the VALUE attribute will be empty (but will still be included).

The third field, fav_color, is a bit more interesting. This field is created with a group of radio buttons. As you no doubt remember, the list of colors that are options for the fav_color field was created earlier in the subroutine. I use a foreach loop to create the radio buttons. The foreach loop pulls out all the elements of an array one at a time, and assigns them to a variable, in this case, $color. I use the $color variable within the loop body for both the label on the form, and for the VALUE attribute in the <INPUT> tag I create. Because this is a radio button group, all the tags have the same NAME attribute.

In the body of the loop, there's a test that compares the current value of $color to the value of $fav_color. If the script is processing a form submission, the $fav_color variable is set to the color that the user selected on the form. If $color and $fav_color are the same, the CHECKED attribute is included in the <INPUT> tag to indicate that the button will be selected by default when the form is displayed.

After the radio button group has been displayed, all that's left is to print the submit button for the form, and end with the closing form tag.

The Full Source Code

The remaining subroutines in the script aren't particularly complex; they consist of simple print statements or variable assignments. The full source code for the script appears in Listing 7.4.

LISTING 7.4 The Full Source Code for the Form-Processing Example

```
 1: #!C:/perl/bin/perl.exe
 2:
 3: use CGI;
 4: $query = new CGI;
 5:
 6: &print_page_start;
 7: if ($query->param('submitted')) {
 8:     $error_message = "";
 9:     &validate_form;
10:     if ($error_message eq "") {
11:     &print_form_values;
12:     }
13:     else {
```

continues

7

LISTING 7.4 continued

```
14:     print "<UL>\n" . $error_message . "</UL>\n";
15:     &print_form;
16:     }
17: }
18: else {
19:     &set_initial_values;
20:     &print_form;
21: }
22: &print_page_end;
23:
24: sub set_initial_values {
25:     $name = "";
26:     $quest = "";
27:     $fav_color = "";
28: }
29:
30: sub validate_form {
31:     $name = $query->param('name');
32:     $quest = $query->param('quest');
33:     $fav_color = $query->param('fav_color');
34:     if ($name eq "") {
35:     $error_message .= "<LI>You must enter a name.\n";
36:     }
37:     if ($quest eq "") {
38:     $error_message .= "<LI>You must enter your quest.\n";
39:     }
40:     if ($fav_color eq "") {
41:     $error_message .= "<LI>You must select your favorite color.\n";
42:     }
43: }
44:
45: sub set_form_values {
46:     $name = $query->param('name');
47:     $quest = $query->param('quest');
48:     $quest = $query->param('fav_color');
49: }
50:
51: sub print_form {
52:     @colors = ('red', 'green', 'blue');
53:     print "<FORM>\n";
54:     print "<INPUT TYPE=\"hidden\" NAME=\"submitted\" VALUE=\"yes\">\n";
55:     print "<b>Name:</b>";
56:     print "<INPUT TYPE=\"text\" NAME=\"name\" VALUE=\"$name\"><BR>\n";
57:     print "<b>Quest:</b>";
58:     print "<INPUT TYPE=\"text\" NAME=\"quest\" VALUE=\"$quest\
        ➥"><BR><BR>\n";
59:     print "<b>Favorite Color:</b><br>\n";
60:     foreach $color (@colors) {
```

```
61:        print "<INPUT TYPE=\"radio\" NAME=\"fav_color\" ";
62:        print "VALUE=\"$color\"";
63:        if ($fav_color eq $color) {
64:            print " CHECKED";
65:        }
66:        print ">$color<BR>\n";
67:        }
68:        print "<BR>\n";
69:        print "<INPUT TYPE=\"submit\">\n";
70:        print "</FORM>\n";
71: }
72:
73: sub print_form_values {
74:        print "<b>Name:</b> " . $query->param('name') . "<br>\n";
75:        print "<b>Quest:</b> " . $query->param('quest') . "<br>\n";
76:        print "<b>Favorite Color:</b> " . $query->param('fav_color');
77:        print "<br>\n";
78: }
79:
80: sub print_page_start {
81:        print "Content-type: text/html\n\n";
82:        print "<html>\n<head>\n";
83:        print "<title>A Form Example</title\n";
84:        print "</head>\n<body>\n";
85:        print "<h1>A Form Example</h1>\n";
86: }
87:
88: sub print_page_end {
89:        print "</body>\n</html>\n";
90: }
```

Validating Values

It's not enough to know which technique should be used to process form input; you also need to know what sorts of things you can validate in form fields. In the sample script, I checked to make sure that the user entered something in each of the fields. That sort of check is better than nothing, but it doesn't really do much to ensure that the user entered the type of data that you expected in the field.

In some cases, validation beyond making sure that the field is populated is unnecessary. For example, if you're just letting the user enter feedback about the Web site, it's not so important what they enter in the form field for comments. Or, such a wide variety of values is allowed that there's no reliable way to make sure that they entered the right thing in the form field. On the other hand, there are many fields that require specific types of data that can be easily validated.

7

I'll give you a few examples. All Social Security Numbers must contain nine digits, so you can write code to make sure that the user submitted a string nine characters long, and that all nine of those characters are numbers. Another good example of data that's easily validated is credit card numbers. Not only do credit card numbers have a fixed number of digits, but most of them have numbers that can be verified using a checksum. A *checksum* is a number derived by performing a calculation on the digits in a number. Credit card numbers follow a pattern that enable them to be verified using the checksum, which can be used to discriminate between valid credit card numbers and random.

Regular Expressions

Regular expressions are a special language used for pattern matching against strings. They were originally created as part of the UNIX utility grep, which is used to extract all the lines containing a particular pattern from a text file. Since then, implementations of regular expressions have appeared in many scripting languages, utilities, and applications for most computing platforms. For example, many text editors allow you to search the contents of files using regular expressions.

There are two problems with regular expressions: they're rather cryptic and hard to understand, and they're implemented differently from language to language. The upside is that they're the most powerful pattern matching language available.

I'm going to discuss how to use regular expressions to validate form content in Perl. Chances are, the language you use to write Web applications will support regular expressions, but you'll have to use different syntax to use them within the program.

Regular expressions are collections of meta-characters. The meta-characters are used as wildcards of various kinds, or to match specific parts of a string that aren't visible. For example, the ^ meta-character matches the beginning of a string, and $ matches the end of a string. More important, though, are the various wildcards.

There are two types of wildcard characters or groups of characters. The first type defines what to match; the second type defines how many characters should be matched. The period is a wildcard that matches any character. The * meta-character indicates that the wildcard that appears before it should match 0 or more characters (or groups of characters) that match the wildcard. That may sound somewhat confusing, but I think I can clear things up a bit with an example. Take a look at this regular expression:

```
/p.*q/
```

The slashes on both sides are just delimiters. They're generally used to indicate that the text inside is a regular expression. Anyway, that expression will match pshoesq, pq, or p'"?>,q. It won't match pb, pabst, or portal. Let's say it's passed a string like:

```
The horse prances quickly.
```

The expression will match "prances q" inside the longer string. If the expression were changed to /^p.*q$/, it wouldn't match the sentence above at all. That's because the ^ character matches the beginning of the string, and $ matches the end of the string, meaning that the first character of the string must be p, and the last must be q. The p and q occur in the middle of the sentence, so ^p and q$ aren't matched.

Let's look at another meta-character, +. The + meta-character is like *, except that it matches one or more characters, instead of zero or more. The only difference between the expression /p.+q/ and /^p.*q$/ is that it won't match the string pq. The + dictates that one character must appear between the two characters listed.

Another important wildcard is ?, which matches any single character. It doesn't require a character afterward to list how many characters to match. The expression b?t will match bit, or bat, but not boot. Because the ? will match any character, it will also match something like b&t.

At this point, I should tell you how to escape characters. As you can see, the list of meta-characters piles up quickly. So what happens when you want to match one of the meta-characters when it appears in a string? For example, how do you write an expression that matches the string "Mr. Colburn"? The answer is that you escape the period to indicate that it won't be treated as a meta-character. The appropriate expression to match that string is /Mr\. Colburn/. The backslash is used to escape meta-characters in regular expressions.

There are also a number of grouping operators that can be used with regular expressions to create more advanced expressions. For example, one problem with the . operator is that it will match literally any character. It doesn't care if the character is a letter, number, symbol, tab, or line feed. In some cases, you need to constrain the list of characters to be matched. Brackets are used to create groups of characters to be matched. For example, [aeiou] will match any lowercase vowel. [aeiou]* will match 0 or more lowercase vowels, and [aeiou]+ will match one or more lowercase vowels. Some regular expression engines, including the one in Perl, will also allow you to define a series of characters, using a hyphen. For example, [a-zA-Z] will match any upper- or lowercase letter. [0-9] will match any digit.

Another grouping operator supported by most regular expression engines allows you to create an expression that will match any one of several substrings using parentheses. For example, let's say you wanted to match one of several email addresses using a regular expression. The following expression matches several addresses at my Internet domain:

```
/(rcolburn|rafe|webmaster)@rc3.org/
```

7

That expression matches rcolburn@rc3.org, rafe@rc3.org, and webmaster@rc3.org. Needless to say, such an expression can save a lot of typing, and make your expressions more readable.

These are just some of the basic functions that most regular expression engines support. Most support lots more advanced functionality as well. Appendix E, "Summary of Regular Expressions" contains a detailed reference for the regular expression engine that's built into Perl.

An Example that Uses Regular Expressions

Let's look at a very simple example that uses a regular expression for form validation. In this example, a regular expression will be used to validate a Social Security Number. The source code for the program appears in Listing 7.5.

LISTING 7.5 A Program that Validates a Social Security Number

```
 1: #!c:/perl/bin/perl.exe
 2:
 3: use CGI qw ( :standard );
 4:
 5: print header;
 6: print "<HTML><HEAD><TITLE>SSN Validator</TITLE></HEAD>\n";
 7: print "<BODY>\n";
 8:
 9: if (param) {
10:     $ssn = param('ssn');
11:     if ((length($ssn) == 9) && ($ssn =~ /^[0-9]+$/)) {
12:     print "Valid Social Security Number.\n";
13:     }
14:     else {
15:     print "Invalid Social Security Number.\n";
16:     }
17: }
18: else {
19:     print "<FORM>\n";
20:     print "Social Security Number: \n";
21:     print "<INPUT TYPE=\"text\" NAME=\"ssn\">\n";
22:     print "<INPUT TYPE=\"submit\">\n";
23:     print "</FORM>\n";
24: }
25:
26: print "</BODY></HTML>\n";
```

This program follows the format that I introduced earlier in the chapter; it both displays the form and processes it. It's a lot simpler, though, because it doesn't redisplay the form if the user didn't enter a valid Social Security Number. The purpose of this example is to show you how to validate a value using regular expressions. Here's the validation code:

```
if ((length($ssn) == 9) && ($ssn =~ /^[0-9]+$/)) {
    print "Valid Social Security Number.\n";
    }
    else {
    print "Invalid Social Security Number.\n";
    }
```

The part that actually validates the user input is in the `if` statement. It performs two tests on the value. First, it checks whether the input is exactly nine characters long, using the `length()` function. Then, it uses a regular expression to determine whether the user entered anything other than numbers in the field. Here's the relevant code:

```
$ssn =~ /^[0-9]+$/
```

The binding operator, `=~`, compares the value in the variable to the left of the operator to the pattern match on the right. The purpose of the operator is to determine whether the string contains the pattern. If it does, the entire expression returns a true value; otherwise it returns false. The operator is designed for cases just like this one where you need to determine whether one string is part of another.

In this case, the regular expression begins with `^` and ends with `$`, which means that the expression must match the entire value in `$ssn`. The expression searches for a group of one or more characters ranging between 0 and 9. This is just a check to make sure that the user entered only numbers. The number of characters the user entered is checked in the first expression of the `if` statement.

If the value entered is both the right length and matches the expression, the Social Security Number is considered valid. If either of the expressions is false, it's considered invalid and an error message is displayed.

Summary

A large chunk of the CGI programs on the Web are used for one thing—processing form input. The objective of this hour was to provide you with a basic architecture that will work for the vast majority of forms processing scripts, and to explain how you can build data validation code into those scripts. When you write CGI programs, especially ones that will be gathering data that will be stored permanently, it's important to make sure that the data that's entered is valid. One tool that you can use to create expressions that will validate a wide variety of data is regular expressions. This hour contained a brief explanation of some regular expression functionality, to give you an idea of how it can be used.

7

Q&A

Q **You mentioned validating credit card numbers with checksums earlier; where can I find out more?**

A There is a formula, called the Luhn check, that you can apply to credit card numbers to check for mistyped numbers. Information on using the Luhn check can be found at:

`http://www.beachnet.com/~hstiles/cardtype.html`

You can also use the `Business::CreditCard` Perl module to verify credit card numbers using the checksum formula for each credit card type rather than writing the code to do it yourself.

Workshop

The quiz questions are designed to strengthen the knowledge you gain each hour. The exercises help you build on that knowledge by providing you with the opportunity to apply it to real problems. See Appendix A, "Answers" for the answers to the quiz questions.

Quiz

1. What are the two primary advantages of using JavaScript for form validation?

2. Why is it important to validate user-submitted data in your CGI programs even if your forms are validated with JavaScript?

3. What is the difference between the + character and the * character in regular expressions?

Exercises

1. Write a JavaScript function that verifies that a user checked a checkbox.

2. Write a Perl subroutine that verifies that the user entered a nine digit Social Security Number, and that all of the characters the user entered are digits.

Hour **8**

Creating an Email Feedback Form

Web browsing isn't the most popular Internet application—email is. There are many circumstances under which you might want to send email from a CGI script. You might want to send the data submitted by a user to the person who has to process it, or you might want to acknowledge a user's form submission by sending them an email message. In this hour, I'll explain how you can send Internet email from a CGI program. The following topics will be discussed:

- Real-world examples that illustrate why you'd want to send email from CGI scripts

- A brief overview of how Internet email works

- How to use sendmail to send email messages from the command line of a UNIX-based system

- How to use sendmail within a CGI program running on a UNIX-based server

- How to use Blat to send Internet email from a Web server running Windows

What Kinds of Applications Entail Sending Email?

Several types of applications benefit from sending email programmatically. Consider a feedback form on a Web site that is used to solicit comments from users. The easiest way to pass the feedback to the designers is to send it to them via email each time the form is submitted. Email sent to users is often utilized by online stores. When a user places an order, usually a receipt is sent to them via email so that they can keep it for their records.

Another real-world example involves a bank that allows customers to apply for various bank products online. The application process is handled through HTML forms, but ultimately the applications must be processed by a human being. The CGI script that processes the user submissions formats all the data, encrypts it using PGP (Pretty Good Privacy, an encryption program for email), and sends it to the customer service department at the bank via email. At that point, the human being processes the application and sends the appropriate information back to the user via the postal service.

Even if your CGI script stores user-submitted data in a database rather than emailing the data directly to the appropriate person, you might want to send an email to someone notifying them that the data was submitted. For example, if you run an electronic commerce site, you probably store all the orders in a database. You might also want to send email to the person in charge of fulfilling orders to let him know that an order has been placed.

How Email Works

Before I explain how to send email from within a CGI script, let me first explain how Internet email works at a very high level. First, email messages are usually generated using a *mail client*. Popular mail clients include Outlook Express, Eudora, and Pine. However, a mail client is really any program from which an email message originates. In this hour, the email client is the CGI program that sends the email message.

Internet email delivery is facilitated by software called a *mail transfer agent*. A mail transfer agent, or MTA, is different than mail clients, like Eudora or Microsoft Outlook. A mail transfer agent's job is to examine email messages, determine what the next step toward delivering them is, and then performing that step. When you send mail using a mail client, it just passes the email off to a mail transfer agent, which then moves the message along in the delivery process. When I discuss *mail servers* in this context, I'm talking about computers on which MTAs reside.

8

There are two ways that email messages can be passed to MTAs for delivery. The first method, the one we'll use in this hour for the most part, is to execute the MTA and pass the new email message to it for delivery. The most commonly used MTA is sendmail, which is an executable on UNIX systems. To send a message, you just pass it to sendmail, which in turn evaluates the mail headers and sends the message on its way. The second method used to send email is to use the SMTP protocol. sendmail is also available for Windows, but does not provide the same command line interface that it does on UNIX systems.

SMTP, the Simple Mail Transfer Protocol, is the protocol that MTAs use to talk to each other. It can also be used by mail clients, or any other program, to initiate the process of sending an email message. Your program just has to connect to port 25 of an SMTP server, send the necessary commands to indicate that a message is being sent, and then send over the body of the message.

Irrespective of which method you use to initiate the email sending process, after the MTA has the message, it starts doing all the work. Much like HTTP requests and responses, email messages have headers that should have all the information necessary to indicate where the message should be delivered. Just like physical mail handled by the postal service, all messages should have a destination address and a return address. The destination addresses are specified in the To: header, and the return address is specified in the From: header. There are headers that can be used to specify other recipients as well, like CC: and BCC:.

When the MTA receives the email, it examines the recipients' addresses and uses DNS (Domain Name Service, which is usually used to translate domain names to IP numbers) to determine which mail server is associated with the domain names in the addresses. The DNS database should include a record, called an MX record, that specifies the mail server for every domain. For example, if the email is addressed to rafe@rc3.org, it looks up the MX (mail exchange) record for rc3.org, and discovers that the mail server associated with that domain is umbar.pair.com. At that point, it opens a connection to umbar.pair.com, and transfers the message. Then the MTA at umbar.pair.com invokes a program that places the message in the inbox for rafe, or, if rafe isn't a valid user for that mail server, returns the message to the sender with an error.

What CGI programmers need to know is that to get an email message delivered, they need to address the message properly, and then place it into the mail delivery stream by passing it off to an MTA on the local computer, or by connecting to an SMTP server and sending it from there. If you're using a UNIX server, it's usually easier to pass the message off to the local MTA. If you're running a Web server on another computer, it's sometimes easier to send the message via SMTP rather than invoking the local MTA, which may not exist. Both options will be discussed later in this hour.

Mail Message Composition

An email message consists of two parts—a set of headers and the message body. This is analogous to the structure of HTTP requests and responses. Just as the response from a Web server consists of headers that describe the response, and then the body of the response, an email message consists of headers that describe the message and the body of the message.

The most important headers in the email message are those that relate to addressing. Another header is used to indicate what the subject of the mail is. As the email message is passed from host to host on its way to the final recipient, headers are added to specify how the email message was routed. Also, mail clients can add any headers they want, by prepending them with X-. Listing 8.1 contains all the headers and the body for a typical Internet email message.

LISTING 8.1   A Typical Internet Email Message

```
From rafeco@rc3.org  Sat Dec  4 18:44:06 1999
Received: from issmtp01.interpath.net (issmtp01.interpath.net
[216.48.1.21]) by umbar.pair.com (8.9.1/8.6.12) with ESMTP id
SAA06974 for <rafeco@rc3.org>;
Sat, 4 Dec 1999 18:44:05 -0500 (EST)
X-Envelope-To: <rafeco@rc3.org>
Received: from rc3.org ([199.72.11.37]) by issmtp01.interpath.net
          (Netscape Messaging Server 3.61)  with ESMTP id AAA6977
          for <rafeco@rc3.org>; Sat, 4 Dec 1999 18:44:04 -0500
Message-ID: <3849A79D.234C712A@rc3.org>
Date: Sat, 04 Dec 1999 18:45:33 -0500
From: Rafe Colburn <rafeco@rc3.org>
X-Mailer: Mozilla 4.61    (Win98; I)
X-Accept-Language: en
MIME-Version: 1.0
To: rafeco@rc3.org
Subject: Test message
Content-Type: text/plain; charset=us-ascii
Content-Transfer-Encoding: 7bit

This is the body of a test message.
```

As you can see from the listing, there are all sorts of headers in the message that don't have anything at all to do with identifying who the message is to or from. When you're constructing email messages to be sent, you only need to worry about the To: and From: headers. Generally, you'll want to include the Subject: header as well.

Using sendmail

sendmail is the most popular UNIX MTA. Most computers that run a UNIX-based operating system use sendmail for two reasons. It can run as a daemon, listening on port 25 for SMTP connections. It can also be run as an executable, to send email messages over the Internet. Configuring the behavior of sendmail when it's set up to run as a daemon is a monumental task, and is well beyond the scope and subject matter of this book. In this hour, you will learn how to execute sendmail at the command line to send email messages from within your CGI programs.

Let's take a look at how sendmail is executed from the command line. I'm going to use the same command line options that you would use if you were calling sendmail from within a script. The sendmail session is captured in Listing 8.2.

LISTING 8.2   Running sendmail from the Command Line

```
$ sendmail -n -t -oi
From: rafe@rc3.org
To: rafe@rc3.org
Subject: A subject

This is the message body.
```

I use three command line arguments when I invoke the sendmail program to enhance the security of the script. The -n flag indicates that sendmail shouldn't try to interpret aliases from the addresses. This requires a bit of explanation. On most UNIX systems, there's a file called etc/aliases that is used to map various account names to other addresses. For example, /etc/aliases usually includes a pointer from the account name postmaster to the email account of the email administrator. The -n flag just indicates to sendmail that it shouldn't compare the recipients of the email to the contents of the aliases file before sending.

> For most Web applications, this flag isn't important because the aliases file is only applied to email addresses on the local mail server. Users shouldn't be entering email addresses associated with the local server, so /etc/aliases shouldn't be consulted anyway. Even so, it's better to leave this in place for insurance.

The -t flag indicates that the addressing information should be taken from the actual message content, rather than from the command line, which prevents the user from embedding escapes to shell commands and committing other malicious trickery from the command line. Ordinarily, users can enter the address of the recipient (or a group of recipients) on the command line when they invoke sendmail.

The -oi flag tells sendmail not to take a line with a single dot on it as a message terminator. Ordinarily, email messages can be terminated using a line that contains only a dot in the first column. Because I know I'm not going to use that notation to indicate that I'm terminating the message, I use the -oi flag. This prevents users from terminating the email message inadvertently. Instead, the email message is terminated when an end of file marker is passed to it. This is the easiest way to end an email message from within a program. When you enter an email message on the command line, the Control-D character is used as the end of file marker. Once you're done entering the message, you just hit Control-D to send it. Within programs, the file is ended automatically when you close the filehandle, or when execution of the program ceases. I always close filehandles manually, as you'll see in the examples that follow.

After the sendmail program has been invoked, the next step is to pass the actual email message to the program. Email messages are just like HTTP requests and responses in that the headers are separated from the message body by a blank line. In this case, I typed only three headers: the sender, recipient, and subject. There are many other headers that could be included, but these are the only three that are really necessary.

Using sendmail with Perl

Now that you've seen how sendmail is called from the command line, you will learn how to call sendmail from within a Perl program. To call sendmail from within a Perl program, you have to create a filehandle that opens a pipe to the sendmail executable. After the filehandle is created, any print statements sent to that filehandle are passed on to sendmail.

Briefly, this is how everything works. Any time you want to send the output of a Perl program somewhere other than to the console, you have to open a filehandle. A filehandle is just a pointer to a file, or a program where the output will be sent. When you open the filehandle, you specify where output sent to that filehandle will go. In this case, the filehandle is opened using a pipe. A *pipe* is a UNIX construct that uses the output of one program as the input for another. In this case, we're using the output of the CGI program that's sent to the filehandle as the input for the sendmail program.

After the filehandle is open, you can use print statements to generate the headers and body of the email message. Closing the filehandle will close the pipe, and cause sendmail to process the message. The code that communicates with sendmail appears in Listing 8.3.

8

LISTING 8.3   Sending Email from a Perl Program

```
open (MAIL, "| /usr/lib/sendmail -n -t -oi");
print MAIL "From: rafe@rc3.org\n";
print MAIL "To: rafe@rc3.org\n";
print MAIL "Subject: A subject\n\n";
print MAIL "This is the message body.\n";
close MAIL;
```

That's all there is to it. The call to the open function creates a filehandle called MAIL. The second argument to the function is this:

```
"| /usr/lib/sendmail -n -t -oi"
```

This argument uses the pipe character, |, to indicate that the filehandle type is a pipe. The full path to sendmail is included, as are the command arguments that I discussed earlier. After the filehandle is open, the output of print statements is directed to it by specifying the filehandle before the actual text to be printed. After the full email message has been printed, the close function is used to close the filehandle and send the message.

Example: Sending Email from a CGI Script

Let's look at a simple example that illustrates how email is sent using a CGI script. I've written a CGI script (email-form.pl) that presents users with a form that requests their email address, a subject, and a message body. When the user fills out the form fields and submits the form, an email message with the subject and body that they entered is sent to the email address they specified. Theoretically, the email address is their own, but that's not necessary. What this means is that you shouldn't put this script on your Web site unmodified. For one thing, it's not really very useful. For another, it will allow people to send email messages to whomever they like, and they will appear to be from the return address specified in the script. The full source code for the script appears in Listing 8.4.

LISTING 8.4   The source code for email-form.pl

```
 1:#!/usr/local/bin/perl
 2:
 3:use CGI;
 4:
 5:# Send fatal errors to browser
 6:use CGI::Carp;
 7:
 8:$query = new CGI;
 9:
10:# Set to the location of your sendmail executable
```

continues

LISTING 8.4 continued

```
11:$sendmail = "/usr/sbin/sendmail -n -t -oi";
12:
13:# Set to the name of the return address
14:$from = "webmaster\@rc3.org";
15:
16:if (!$query->param()) {
17:    &print_page_start;
18:    &print_form;
19:    &print_page_end;
20:}
21:else {
22:    &set_form_vars;
23:    if (&valid_form eq 'yes') {
24:    &send_email;
25:    &print_page_start;
26:    &print_success;
27:    &print_page_end;
28:    }
29:    else {
30:    &print_page_start;
31:    &print_error_message;
32:    &print_form;
33:    &print_page_end;
34:    }
35:}
36:
37:sub print_page_start {
38:    print $query->header;
39:    print "<HTML>\n";
40:    print "<HEAD>\n";
41:    print "<TITLE>Email Form</TITLE>\n";
42:    print "</HEAD>\n";
43:    print "<BODY>\n";
44:    print "<H1>Email Form</H1>\n";
45:}
46:
47:sub print_page_end {
48:    print "</BODY>\n";
49:    print "</HTML>\n";
50:}
51:
52:sub set_form_vars {
53:    $address = $query->param('address');
54:    $subject = $query->param('subject');
55:    $body = $query->param('body');
56:}
57:
58:sub print_form {
59:    print "<FORM METHOD=\"post\">\n";
60:    print "<P>\nYour email address:\n";
```

8

```
61:    print "<INPUT TYPE=\"text\" NAME=\"address\" VALUE=\"$address\">\n";
62:    print "</P>\n";
63:    print "<P>\nEmail subject:\n";
64:    print "<INPUT TYPE=\"text\" NAME=\"subject\" VALUE=\"$subject\">\n";
65:    print "</P>\n";
66:    print "<P>\nEmail body:<BR>\n";
67:    print "<TEXTAREA NAME=\"body\" WRAP=\"physical\" ROWS=5 COLS=70>";
68:    print $body;
69:    print "</TEXTAREA>\n</P>\n";
70:    print "<P>\n<INPUT TYPE=\"submit\" VALUE=\"Send Email\">\n</P>\n";
71:    print "</FORM>\n";
72:}
73:
74:sub valid_form {
75:    $success = "yes";
76:    if (!$subject) {
77:    $subject_error = "<P>You need to enter a subject ";
78:    $subject_error .= "for your message.</P>\n";
79:    $success = "no";
80:    }
81:    if (!$address) {
82:    $address_error = "<P>You need to specify a recipient for ";
83:    $address_error .= "the message.</P>\n";
84:    $success = "no";
85:    }
86:    if ($address !~ /^[\w-.]+\@[\w-.]+$/) {
87:    $address_error = "<P>The email address you entered is invalid, ";
88:    $address_error .= "please enter a valid address. </P>\n";
89:    $success = "no";
90:    }
91:    if (!$body) {
92:    $body_error = "<P>You need to enter some text in the ";
93:    $body_error .= "body of your message.</P>\n";
94:    $success = "no";
95:    }
96:    return $success;
97:}
98:
99:sub print_error_message {
100:    if ($address_error) {
101:    print $address_error, "\n";
102:    }
103:    if ($subject_error) {
104:    print $subject_error, "\n";
105:    }
106:    if ($body_error) {
107:    print $body_error, "\n";
108:    }
109:}
110:
111:sub print_success {
```

continues

LISTING 8.4   continued

```
112:    print "<P>An email with the subject \"$subject\" was sent to ";
113:    print "$address.</P>\n";
114:}
115:
116:sub send_email {
117:    open(MAIL, "| $sendmail") or
118:    die "Couldn't open sendmail: ";
119:    print MAIL <<EOF;
120:From: $from
121:To: $address
122:Subject: $subject
123:
124:$body
125:
126:EOF
127:    close MAIL;
128://}
```

Setting Things Up

The first few lines of the script are used to import some libraries that you'll need, and set a few variables that are used later in the program (see Listing 8.4).

A *library* is just a body of code that someone else has written that you can import into your own program and use. Perl and most other programming languages come bundled with libraries that provide lots of functionality needed by many programmers.

As is the case with all Perl CGI scripts, the first line is a pointer to the Perl interpreter. On line 3, the CGI module is imported to read the form data into the CGI program. The next command imports the CGI::Carp module. This module is used to send errors to the browser instead of printing them on the console of the Web server. This module is discussed further in Hour 10, "Perl—The Big Kahuna of CGI." Next, set two variables. The first, $sendmail, is set on line 11 and contains a pointer to the sendmail executable on the Web server. The second, set on line 14, is used to specify the address that will appear in the From: field of the outgoing email.

When most people need to run an executable file under UNIX, they rely on the directory in which it resides being included in their $PATH variable. Whenever a filename is typed at a command prompt, the shell searches all the directories in $PATH for that file, and then executes it if it can be found. Unfortunately, sendmail is usually stored in a directory outside those included in most people's $PATH variable. That's why it's best to specify the exact location of sendmail in your scripts. If you're having trouble finding it, you might try looking in the /usr/lib, /lib, /usr/sbin, and /sbin directories.

The Application Logic

After the script has been set up, there's some overarching application logic used to determine what the script should do at any given point in time. The main application logic starts on line 16 and ends on line 35. If no form submission has been made, the script prints an empty form. If the form was submitted, the script validates the input. If it's valid, the script sends the email message and the user receives confirmation that the script was successful. If the input was invalid, the script indicates the errors and redisplays the form for revision.

Let's take a closer look at how all of this works. The application logic is created using one conditional statement nested inside another. The if statement on line 16 tests for the existence of $query->param(), which contains all of the form fields passed to the script. If it exists, that indicates that the form has been submitted.

If the form was not submitted, the script prints the form for the first time. Three subroutines are called on lines 16-18 to print the page, &print_page_start, &print_form, and &print_page_end. The &print_page_start and &print_page_end subroutines are called no matter what the outcome of the script was. They're just used to begin and end the HTML document. The &print_form subroutine is used to print the form, and is used to print a new form and to redisplay the form in case of erroneous input.

If the form has been submitted, the code on lines 22-34 is executed. The values are moved from $query->param() to normal variables using the &set_form_vars subroutine. Then, the values the user entered are validated using the &valid_form subroutine. The if statement on line 23 checks whether the form input is valid. If the form input is valid, the email is sent, and a success message is displayed. The &send_email subroutine calls sendmail and creates the outgoing mail message. The two subroutines &print_page_start and &print_page_end are used to set up the page, and &print_success lets the user know that the form submission was successful.

Validating the Form

Form validation is particularly important when you're dealing with email. The subroutine `valid_form`, which begins on line 74 and ends on line 97, is used to validate the user's input. The most important thing is to make sure that the user enters a valid email address. Many Web applications don't do any more than cursory testing on email addresses to make sure that they're valid—perhaps they just check to make sure that the address contains an @ sign. Unfortunately, doing so just leads to more problems later. These problems take the form of bounced email messages, or, if the user is malicious, they can lead to the user gaining access to the Web server.

The validation for the `body` and `subject` fields is simple. As long as something's there, the values are considered to be valid. The validation for the email address is a bit more complex. It uses a regular expression to make sure that the email address matches a specific pattern. To match the pattern, the email address must consist of one of a specific set of characters, followed by an at sign (@), followed by one or more of a specific set of characters. Included in the set of characters are letters, numbers, dashes, periods, and underscores. This will throw out all obviously invalid email addresses, and will throw out any email address that contains characters that aren't allowed to appear in an email address. Let's look at the pattern:

```
/^[\w-.]+\@[\w-.]+$/
```

I'll go ahead and break down the pattern so that you can understand how it works. The / characters at the beginning and end are just delimiters; the actual regular expression is everything in between. The expression begins with the ^ character, which matches the beginning of the string. The $ at the end matches the end of the string. Using these two characters indicates that the expression must match the entire string, not just a part of it. The expression `[\w-.]` appears twice in the pattern. The brackets group all the characters within into one expression. Any character that matches any of the characters inside the brackets is considered to be a match. The characters inside the brackets are `\w`, `-`, and a period. The `\w` matches any "word character." Word characters include letters, numbers, and underscores. Because the pattern then includes a hyphen and a dot, these characters are also matches. The + signs following the expressions in brackets indicate that only a group of one or more characters that match the smaller expression should be considered a match.

However, it doesn't check for full compliance with RFC 822, the standard for Internet email messages. (RFC stands for Request for Comments. These documents are used to specify standards for various Internet applications.) The code necessary to verify that an email address is compliant with RFC 822 is long and involved. Any time an invalid value is encountered, the value of the variable `$success` is set to "no".

8

Sending the Email Message

The most important subroutine for our purposes is the one that actually sends the email message. The mail is sent by the `send_email` subroutine, which begins on line 116 and ends on line 128. This subroutine opens the pipe to the `sendmail` program, and then prints out the email message and closes the filehandle.

The subroutine begins by opening a pipe to the `sendmail` executable. The variable `$sendmail`, which was initialized at the beginning of the program, is used to provide the full path to `sendmail`, and all the required command-line flags. If, for some reason, the program can't open the `sendmail` executable, execution ceases and an error is printed. Because I imported the `CGI::Carp` module at the beginning of the program, the error is sent to the browser. After the filehandle is open, all I have to do is print the text of the email to the filehandle, `MAIL`. Closing the filehandle sends the email message.

Using Blat

When it comes to sending Internet email, programmers with Web servers that run a UNIX-based operating system have it easy. Except under special circumstances, all these operating systems have MTAs installed by default. Generally, the mail transfer agent is `sendmail`.

Unfortunately, people who use Windows NT don't have it so easy. They have to rely on products that aren't installed by default to send Internet email. Many of the MTAs for Windows NT are commercial products that you have to pay for to use. One free MTA for Windows is a program called Blat. Blat is a simple command-line program that acts as an SMTP client. You can download Blat at the following URL:

```
http://gepasi.dbs.aber.ac.uk/softw/Blat.html
```

Blat works a bit differently than `sendmail`. Unlike `sendmail`, which can read messages passed to it through standard input, Blat reads the email message to be sent from a text file, and accepts the name of the SMTP server to use, mail recipient, and mail sender as command-line arguments. The command-line arguments Blat accepts are listed in Table 8.1.

Command-line arguments are parameters that are passed to a program when it is invoked at a prompt (either a UNIX shell prompt or a DOS prompt). For example, if you want a wide directory listing under DOS, you type:

```
dir /w
```

The /w is a command-line argument that indicates that a wide directory listing should be displayed.

TABLE 8.1   Command-Line Arguments Accepted by Blat

Argument	Purpose
<filename> (or -)	The filename of the file to be sent as the body of the email message. A - indicates that the message should be read from the console. (required)
-t *<recipient list>*	A comma separated list of email addresses to which the message should be sent. (required)
-s *"subject"*	The subject of the email message.
-f *<sender address>*	Used to specify a sender address other than the default (the SMTP server must recognize this address).
-i *<address>*	The email address that will appear in the From: header.
-c *<recipient list>*	List of carbon copy recipients, comma separated.
-b *<recipient list>*	List of blind carbon copy recipients, comma separated.
-o *<organization>*	The organization to be placed in the Organization: header.
-q	Suppress all output.
-noh	Omit the URL for the Blat home page from the X-Mailer header.
-noh2	Omit the X-Mailer header completely.
-server *<hostname>*	Use the specified SMTP server instead of the default.
-port *<port>*	Connect to the specified port on the SMTP server instead of the default port.
-mime	MIME encode the message for transfer.
-uuencode	Send binary file UUEncoded.
-base64	Send binary file Base64 encoded.
-try *<number>*	The number of times Blat should try to send the message.
-attach *<file>*	Attach the specified binary file to the message.
-attacht *<file>*	Attach the specified text file to the message.

Using Blat from Perl

To send mail using Blat from a Perl program, you have to use a couple of extra steps that aren't necessary when you use sendmail. The first is that you have to save a copy of the message to a text file, and then pass the location of that text file to Blat in order to send that content in an email message. The second is that rather than opening a filehandle that points to Blat, you have to actually make a system call to Blat using backtics or the system() function.

> A system call is a command that launches a program from within another program. If I wanted to get a directory listing using dir from within a Perl program, I would make a system call to dir. Two common methods of making system calls are the system function, which executes the command line passed to it as an argument, and backtics. Backtics just execute whatever appears between them. So, `dir` would execute the directory command.

8

Listing 8.5 contains a simple program that will send an email using Blat. To use it within a CGI program, you should adapt the code to replace the sendmail-based code in the sample program in this hour.

LISTING 8.5   Using Blat in a Perl Program

```perl
#!c:/perl/bin/perl.exe

$blat = 'blat.exe';
$server = 'smtp.interpath.net';
$to = 'rafe@rc3.org';
$from = 'rafe@rc3.org';
$temp_file = 'tempmsg.txt';
$subject = 'A test message';

open (MESSAGE, "> $temp_file")
    or die "Can't open temp file: ";

print MESSAGE "This is just a test message.\n\n";

close MESSAGE;

$command = "$blat $temp_file ";
$command .= "-s \"$subject\" ";
$command .= "-t $to -i $from ";
$command .= "-server $server";

system($command);

unlink $temp_file;
```

That's really all there is to it. Rather than just setting the subject and body of the message statically within your CGI programs, you'll probably want to read them from some form input, but other than that, using Blat to send email messages is just that easy.

Summary

Email and Web browsing are the two most popular Internet applications, so it isn't very surprising that there are all sorts of situations where you'll want to use them together. Mail is generally sent using a program called a mail transfer agent (MTA). On servers running UNIX, the most popular MTA is sendmail. Using pipes, you can call sendmail from within your scripts, and use it to send email messages. Windows users have it a bit tougher because Internet email is not as well-integrated into the operating system as it is on UNIX. You need to use a third-party program as an MTA. One such program is Blat, a free product that enables you to send email from a command prompt under Windows.

Q&A

Q Are there MTAs available for UNIX other than sendmail?

A Yes, there are quite a few. Two popular alternatives to sendmail are qmail and postfix. sendmail has a reputation not entirely unjustified for being insecure and is also notoriously difficult to configure. Other MTAs that have appeared address both of those problems. Because sendmail has been around so long and is so well-known, it's still the most popular MTA by far. It is also very well maintained, and security holes are closed as fast as they are found. Even so, some sites have chosen to go with these other MTAs. You can find out more information about qmail at http://www.qmail.org. You can also find out more information about postfix at http://www.postfix.org.

Q What other tools for sending Internet mail from Windows are available?

A Because Windows does not share the common history with the Internet that UNIX does, no support for Internet email is integrated with Windows. For that reason, many third parties have created SMTP servers and MTAs for Windows. Currently, Microsoft ships an SMTP service with Internet Information Server 4.0 that can be addressed using COM. There's also a version of sendmail available for Windows these days. For information on more Windows-based Internet mail tools, you should search the Internet.

Q Is it ethical to send email to everyone who visits my Web site, or all of my customers?

A Funny you should ask…seriously, though, it is often tempting for people to send "bulk email" to large groups of people in order to pique their interest in a new feature on their site, or let them know about a great deal they're offering. You should resist this temptation. You should never send bulk email to people who haven't given you permission to include them on your mailing list. Regardless of whether such a practice is ethical, doing so will make you extremely unpopular with a significant number of people. It can also cause you to find yourself on a list like the Realtime Blackhole List (`http://maps.vix.com/rbl`), a list of mail servers from which all messages are automatically discarded because "spam" has originated from them.

Workshop

The quiz questions are designed to strengthen the knowledge you gain each hour. The exercises help you build on that knowledge by providing you with the opportunity to apply it to real problems. For the answers to the quiz questions, refer to Appendix A, "Answers."

Quiz

1. Which RFC document defines the standard for Internet email messages?

2. What does the `-t` flag for `sendmail` indicate?

3. Which two roles does `sendmail` play on a typical server?

4. Why must temporary files be used with Blat?

Exercises

1. Find out where `sendmail` is located on your Web server (if it's a UNIX server).

2. Find out which SMTP server is used by computers in your Web server's domain (if it's a Windows NT Web server).

3. Adapt the sample program from this hour so that the user can choose an address from a select box, and have the email sent to that address.

PART III

CGI Programming Languages and Tools

Hour

HOUR 9

CGI and Simple Shell Scripting

Many UNIX users write shell scripts to accomplish simple tasks they want to repeat. Using shell scripts, you can also write full-fledged programs, including CGI programs. This hour is targeted at people who are already familiar with shell scripting, and would like to create CGI programs using a UNIX shell. Even if you don't know how to write shell scripts, you'll learn how to write simple shell CGI programs that interface with UNIX utilities. In this hour, I'm going to cover:

- How shell scripts work in a CGI environment
- Passing the output of shell commands to the Web browser
- Dealing with the query string and handling form input
- Using the Un-CGI tool to process form input

Writing Shell Scripts

When you think about UNIX shells, you usually think about the interactive command-line environment available to UNIX users. When you use Telnet to connect to a computer running UNIX, or you're sitting at a computer running UNIX, you enter all your commands into a shell. The closest equivalent to a UNIX shell on a computer running Windows is the MS-DOS prompt.

One of the ingenious things about the UNIX shells is that they provide a full-featured programming environment. All the UNIX shells provide the programming constructs that you'd expect from any scripting environment, and can be used for application development. This hour is concerned with writing CGI programs using a UNIX shell.

All the programs in this hour will be written in the Bourne shell (generally found at /bin/sh on UNIX systems). There are two reasons for this. The first is that the Bourne shell is available on every system running UNIX. The programs in this hour should run on every computer running UNIX with no alterations. The second is that the Bourne shell is generally considered to be the best shell for programming. Lots of people also write programs in the C Shell (/bin/csh), but there are some good reasons not to do that. Those reasons are outlined in the seminal article "Csh Programming Considered Harmful," which can be found at:

```
http://www.faqs.org/faqs/unix-faq/shell/csh-whynot/
```

How Shell Scripts Work

Shell scripts are truly interpreted, unlike scripts written in Perl. The scripts are processed and executed one line at a time; they aren't compiled before they are executed. In that sense, they differ from Perl in an important way. The script has no prior knowledge of what lies ahead in the script at runtime. You can't place function definitions later than calls to those functions in the script.

Shell scripts begin just like all UNIX scripts. The first line is the shebang line, which points to the application used to execute the script. (The line is called the shebang line because the first character is sometimes referred to as the "hash" character, and exclamation points are often referred to as "bangs." So, shebang is a useful mnemonic reminder of how the line is constructed.)

If you're writing a Bourne shell script, the first line should be:

```
#!/bin/sh
```

The next step, of course, is to print the content type header, which is required of all CGI scripts, regardless of the language they're written in. The echo command is used for printing in shell scripts, and automatically appends a line feed to its output, unless it's executed with the -n flag. To generate the content type header, the following lines of code are used:

```
echo 'Content-type: text/html'
echo
```

After you've printed the header, you can print out the actual HTML document. You can use any shell command you like within a shell script, so if the HTML is stored in another file, you can just print it using the cat command, like this:

```
cat whatever.html
```

The contents of the file would be read from the disk and printed. If you prefer, you can just use echo to generate the HTML for your document. Here are some echo statements that print HTML:

```
echo "<html><head><title>Example</title></head><body>"
echo "Just an example.</body></html>"
```

A full script looks like this:

```
#!/bin/sh
echo 'Content-type: text/html'
echo
echo "<html><head><title>Example</title></head><body>"
echo "Just an example.</body></html>"
```

Creating Gateways to UNIX Commands

One of the most common uses of shell scripts in CGI programming is to create Web gateways to UNIX commands. Rather than logging into a server using Telnet or SSH every time you want to find out some of the vital statistics for the machine, it might be easier just to write a CGI script that executes the commands you're interested in and prints the results to an HTML document. Shell scripts consist mostly of UNIX commands, so using shell scripts to create these kinds of CGI programs is an obvious choice.

Let's look at a script that executes several commands that are of use to system administrators and that provide a general picture of how the computer is doing. You'll execute the uptime command to see how busy the server's processor is. You'll use df to see whether any of the file systems are running out of space. Then you use uname -a to check out the system type for the server. The script itself is very simple. It doesn't accept any arguments and just prints out the output of those commands inside <pre> tags so t hat the layout of the output is preserved. The source code for the script appears in Listing 9.1.

LISTING 9.1 A Shell Script That Executes UNIX Commands

```
1: #!/bin/sh
2:
3: echo "Content-type: text/html"
4: echo
5:
```

continues

LISTING 9.1 continued

```
 6: echo "<html><head><title>System Status</title></head><body>"
 7: echo "<h1>System Status</h1>"
 8: echo "<h3>uptime</h3>"
 9: echo "<pre>"
10: uptime
11: echo "</pre>"
12: echo "<h3>drive space</h3>"
13: echo "<pre>"
14: df -k
15: echo "</pre>"
16: echo "<h3>system type</h3>"
17: echo "<pre>"
18: uname -a
19: echo "</pre>"
20: echo "</body></html>"
```

As you can see, the three shell commands appear as bare words in the script. They're executed as they're encountered. echo is also a shell command, and is in this case used to print out the HTML tags and HTTP header information. The df -k command prints out a list of the drives connected to the system, and how much capacity they have remaining. The -k flag indicates that the values in the output should appear in kilobytes. The uname -a command prints out all the values associated with uname. The output of the script appears in Figure 9.1.

FIGURE 9.1

The output of a shell script that executes UNIX commands.

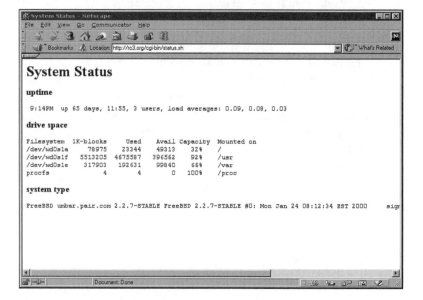

Decoding Form Data

It is possible to decode form data using a shell script. Unfortunately, doing so is not trivial. There are no easy-to-use libraries available for decoding form data in a shell script, and the shell code that I've seen that decodes form data generally doesn't handle all the special cases you can run into, like multiple select boxes and file uploads. If you're going to be doing any complex form handling, my recommendation is to write your program in another language, like Perl, Python, or C.

Frank Pilhofer wrote a shell script that processes form data, and you might want to look at it just to see how it works. In the documentation for the script, he explains why the script doesn't work very well, and some alternatives to it that are available. You can find his script at:

`http://www.informatik.uni-frankfurt.de/~fp/Tools/ProcCGIInput.html`

Working with Query Strings

As an alternative to processing form data, you can work with raw query strings in your shell CGI programs. When you execute a script from the shell prompt, the arguments passed to the script are made available in numbered environment variables. The first argument to the script is stored in $1, the second in $2, and so on. The query string in a request for a CGI program is passed to that program as a command-line parameter. So, if you request the URL `http://localhost/cgi-bin/test.sh?foo`, the $1 variable will be set to foo.

Sending multiple arguments is easy, too. All you have to do is separate each argument with a space. You can URL-encode the spaces in one of two ways. Web servers will convert plusses into spaces. So to send the arguments foo, bar, and baz to a script, you would use the URL:

`http://localhost/cgi-bin/test.sh?foo+bar+baz`

To URL-encode a space, you can also use the code %20, the ASCII code for a space. However, using %20 isn't as reliable. Some Web servers will not split the arguments on %20. So, if you use the following URL, all the arguments will be stored in $1:

`http://localhost/cgi-bin/test.sh?foo%20bar%20baz`

Writing a Program That Uses the Query String

Now that you know how to pass data to a shell script through the query string, let's look at some programs that might use that data. Often, shell programs are used to provide a Web interface to UNIX programs. For example, you could write a program that accepts the path to a file and then deletes that file. That probably wouldn't be such a good idea, though, because it would allow any user to delete files on your server. Another example might be a program that lists the users currently logged into a server.

When you write programs that allow you to run shell commands over the Web, you have to be extremely mindful of the security concerns involved. These issues are discussed in detail in Hour 22, "Securing CGI Scripts." The main thing you have to prevent is the use of shell meta-characters in the arguments passed to the script. For example, let's say you've written a script that uses the finger command to get information about one of the system's users. The name of the user to finger is passed to the script as its argument. What happens if the URL looks like this:

```
http://localhost/cgi-bin/finger.sh?user;rm%20-rf%20/
```

If the script were set up to paste the argument into a shell command, the finger command would work as expected, the semicolon would be interpreted as the break between two commands, and the CGI script would also attempt to execute the command rm -rf /. UNIX users know that this command attempts to delete every file on the root file system with prejudice. (Of course, even if you wrote your script badly and allowed this command to be executed, you wouldn't be running your Web server as the root user, so this command wouldn't work anyway, right?)

The easiest way to prevent malicious people from executing dangerous commands through your shell CGI scripts is to perform all your environment variable expansions inside double quotation marks. In other words, finger "$QUERY_STRING" is not dangerous, but finger $QUERY_STRING is. Needless to say, in the sample program, I'll stick to the former usage.

So let's look at using the query string to pass arguments to the script. The purpose of this script is to use the finger command to retrieve information about one of the system's users. The source code for the script is shown in Listing 9.2.

LISTING 9.2   A Shell Script That Receives Its Arguments in the Query String

```
 1: #!/bin/sh
 2:
 3: echo "Content-type: text/html"
 4: echo
 5: echo "<html><head><title>finger $1</title></head><body>"
 6: if [ -n "$1" ]; then
 7:     echo "<h1>finger $1</h1>"
 8:     echo "<pre>"
 9:     finger "$1"
10:     echo "</pre>"
```

```
11: else
12:     echo "You must specify the name of the user you want to finger."
13: fi
14: echo "</body></html>"
```

Let's look at the script. First, on line 3, the script prints out the HTTP header. The echo statement on line 4 prints a blank line to separate the header from the body of the response. Line 5 prints the beginning HTML for the page and the page title.

You only want to attempt to finger a user if he supplied an account name in the query string. On line 6, I test the contents of $1 (the first argument to the script) to determine whether an account name was supplied. The -n test is true if the string provided as an argument is not null. If the string is empty, the condition evaluates as false. Note that $1 is enclosed in double quotation marks in order to avoid security problems.

If an argument was specified, the script passes the specified username to the finger command. The output of the finger command is sent to the browser. The $1 variable is placed within double quotation marks for security reasons. It doesn't affect how the finger command works.

Un-CGI

Un-CGI is a tool that processes form data by copying the data into environment variables. The tool itself, which is written in C, can be used with any UNIX programming language. As long as your CGI scripting language can access environment variables and print output to the console, your CGI scripts can use Un-CGI.

Here's how Un-CGI works. When you call a script that will use Un-CGI to process incoming form data, the URL actually points to Un-CGI but includes the name of the script as extra path information. So, if you wanted to call a script named email.sh, using Un-CGI to first process the form data and copy it into environment variables, the URL would look like:

```
http://rc3.org/cgi-bin/uncgi/email.sh
```

The first part of the path, /cgi-bin/uncgi calls the Un-CGI program. Un-CGI then processes the form data and calls the program provided in the extra path information—in this case, email.sh. The nice thing about this is that the script that's targeted doesn't have to be a shell script; it can be written in C, Perl, or almost anything else. Most languages have nice libraries or modules that you can use to handle form data from within your programs, but if your language of choice doesn't, Un-CGI provides an easy alternative to writing code to handle form data yourself.

Installing Un-CGI

Un-CGI is distributed in source code form. To install it, you must download it and then compile it on your local system. Fortunately, this is a pretty simple process if you've compiled UNIX software before. The program is distributed with a source code file, a Makefile, and a README file. To install it, you should read the README file to determine which changes you need to make to the Makefile. After you've edited the Makefile to correspond to your local configuration, just type `make install` in the Un-CGI directory (assuming the `make` program is in your path), and Un-CGI will be compiled and installed in the location you specify in the Makefile. You can download the Un-CGI source code at:

`http://www.midwinter.com/~koreth/uncgi.html`

There's a lot of information on the Un-CGI home page that you'll find helpful if you run into any problems with the installation. I'd like to address one of the specific changes you have to make to the Makefile. In the Makefile, you must specify where Un-CGI will look for the CGI scripts it uses. This is the directory name that the extra path information will be appended to when Un-CGI tries to execute scripts after it's called. Let's say that you specify the directory `/usr/www/cgi-bin/uncgi-bin` in the Makefile. If the URL I used as an example earlier were requested, Un-CGI would try to execute this program:

`/usr/www/cgi-bin/uncgi-bin/email.sh`

The point here is that you must install all the CGI programs that will work with Un-CGI in the directory that you specify.

How the Form Data Is Handled

Now let's look at what happens to form data that's submitted to Un-CGI. Un-CGI makes the value from each form field into its own environment variable. Listing 9.3 contains a simple form that's submitted to Un-CGI.

LISTING 9.3 A Sample Form

```
 1: <html>
 2: <head>
 3: <title>A Sample Form</title>
 4: </head>
 5: <body>
 6: <form action="/cgi-bin/uncgi/sample.sh">
 7: Latitude: <input name="latitude"><br>
 8: Longitude: <input name="longitude"><br>
 9: Altitude: <input name="altitude"><br>
10: <input type="submit">
11: </form>
12: </body>
13: </html>
```

When the form in Listing 9.3 is submitted to the server, Un-CGI will create three environment variables that correspond to each of the fields in the form. The environment variables will be named WWW_latitude, WWW_longitude, and WWW_altitude. As you can see, the pattern that Un-CGI follows is to translate the form fields into environment variables with the same name as the field, prepended with WWW_ to avoid conflicts with other variables in the CGI program's environment. A sample program that reads these environment variables appears in Listing 9.4.

LISTING 9.4 A Shell Script That Reads the Environment Variables Set by Un-CGI

```
1: #!/bin/sh
2: echo 'Content-type: text/html'
3: echo
4: echo '<html><head><title>Results</title></head><body>'
5: echo "The latitude is $WWW_latitude<br>"
6: echo "The longitude is $WWW_longitude<br>"
7: echo "The altitude is $WWW_altitude<br>"
8: echo "</body></html>"
```

I can use Un-CGI with Perl programs as well. The Perl program in Listing 9.5 contains the same functionality as the shell script in Listing 9.4.

LISTING 9.5 A Perl Program That Reads the Environment Variables Set by Un-CGI

```
1: #!/usr/local/bin/perl
2: print "Content-type: text/html\n\n";
3: print "<html><head><title>Results</title></head><body>";
4: print "The latitude is ", $ENV{'WWW_latitude'}, "<br>\n";
5: print "The longitude is ", $ENV{'WWW_longitude'}, "<br>\n";
6: print "The altitude is ", $ENV{'WWW_altitude'}, "<br>\n";
7: print "</body></html>\n";
```

Un-CGI also provides some special features to make it easier to handle form data. When Un-CGI encounters a form field that begins with an underscore, it reformats the data in the field to make it easier to use. It strips all whitespace from the beginning and end of the value, and converts all the line endings in the data to UNIX line feeds. The leading underscore is removed when the environment variable is created, so a field named _name will still be converted to an environment variable named WWW_name.

Handling Multivalue Fields

Un-CGI handles multiple select boxes and check boxes with the same name by including all the values the user selected in the environment variable, separated with hashes (#). So, if the user selects the values red, green, and blue in a multiple select list named color, the WWW_color environment variable will contain red#green#blue.

That leaves it to the programmer to split the values into their individual components. There are a number of ways to accomplish this, and the methods vary depending on whether you know how many selections the user will make. I'll provide source code that enables you to handle cases where you know how many choices can be made and also handle cases where the user can make any number of selections.

Let's first look at the case where the user can make as many selections as he wants. In this case, the sample script will just print out the list of options that the user selected. I included the following fields in the sample form to create a situation where the user could submit multiple values with the same name:

```
<b>Weather:</b><br>
<input type="checkbox" name="weather" value="sunny">sunny<br>
<input type="checkbox" name="weather" value="cloudy">cloudy<br>
<input type="checkbox" name="weather" value="rain">rain<br>
<input type="checkbox" name="weather" value="hot">hot<br>
<input type="checkbox" name="weather" value="snowing">snowing<br>
```

As you know, if the user selects more than one of these check boxes, multiple name and value pairs with the name weather will be included in the form submission. The same condition occurs when the form includes a select list that allows multiple selections. The code used to process the form submission appears in Listing 9.6.

LISTING 9.6   A Shell Script That Supports Multivalue Fields

```
 1: #!/bin/sh
 2: echo 'Content-type: text/html'
 3: echo
 4: echo '<html><head><title>Results</title></head><body>'
 5: echo "The latitude is $WWW_latitude<br>"
 6: echo "The longitude is $WWW_longitude<br>"
 7: echo "The altitude is $WWW_altitude<br>"
 8: echo "<br><br>"
 9: echo "Current weather:<br>"
10: IFS=#
11: for s in $WWW_weather ; do
12:         echo "$s<br>"
13: done
14: echo "</body></html>"
```

The code on lines 10–13 handles the multivalue field. On line 10, I set the IFS variable to #. The IFS variable is the internal field separator. On line 11, I start a for loop that processes the fields in the variable $WWW_weather. It splits the value in the variable on the field separator, and processes those values one at a time. In this case, the variables are simply printed using an `echo` statement.

Summary

The purpose of this hour was to provide an explanation of how UNIX shell scripts can be used in a CGI environment. In it I discussed how to process command line arguments using a shell program, and why processing form data with a shell script generally doesn't work very well. You also learned how to use Un-CGI to process form data and make it available to your shell scripts.

9

Q&A

Q Can I write CGI shell scripts that run under Windows NT?

A Not easily. More importantly, one wonders why you would want to do such a thing. Most of the advantages of writing your CGI programs in a UNIX shell are tied to the command-line oriented paradigm of UNIX. Windows NT does not provide the advanced command-line functionality that UNIX does, so it really doesn't make sense to write shell scripts in that environment.

Q What about batch files? Can I write CGI programs as batch files?

A Yes, you can. The only problem is that there are some known, unavoidable problems associated with using batch files in a CGI environment. For that reason, I recommend that you not use batch files as CGI programs.

Q Are there any advantages to writing CGI programs as shell scripts instead of in Perl?

A If you aren't an expert shell scripter, and you already know Perl, I don't really think there are any advantages to writing CGI programs using shell scripts. There are some things that are easier to do in a shell program than they are to do in Perl, but there are lots more tasks associated with CGI programming that Perl makes easier than shell scripting. You can call any shell command within Perl that you can call from a shell script, so there's no advantage there. If you want to write a very simple program that just sends the output of a UNIX command to the browser, using a shell script instead of a Perl program probably makes sense.

Workshop

The quiz questions are designed to strengthen the knowledge you gain each hour. The exercises help you build on that knowledge by providing you with the opportunity to apply it to real problems. See Appendix A, "Answers" for the answers to the quiz questions.

Quiz

1. Why must you not pass unprotected user input to a shell command?

2. How does Un-CGI know which script to execute when it is called from a Web browser?

3. What special handling does Un-CGI perform on form fields with names that begin with an underscore?

Exercises

1. Create a script that uses the `traceroute` command to print the traceroute to a remote system on the network through a CGI script.

2. Get Un-CGI up and running on your Web server.

HOUR **10**

Perl—The Big Kahuna of CGI

Because Perl is the most commonly used language for writing CGI scripts, developers have created many tools to simplify Perl programming. Although teaching you the Perl language itself is beyond the scope of this book, I will discuss some tools and recommend some resources that can help out. In this hour, I'll cover the following topics:

- Taking care of common programming tasks with `CGI.pm`
- Using `cgi-lib.pl`—the precursor to `CGI.pm`
- Handling errors with `CGI::Carp`
- Finding out more about Perl programming

`CGI.pm`

As you already know, `CGI.pm` is a Perl module specifically designed to take care of common CGI programming tasks, saving you work in writing CGI programs. All recent versions of Perl come with `CGI.pm` as part of the standard distribution. This has cemented the position of CGI.pm as the de facto standard for creating CGI scripts in Perl. (Earlier versions of Perl required you to download and install the CGI.pm module.)

CGI.pm is most often used to decode data submitted through HTML forms. However, it provides extensive additional functionality to make it easy for programmers to generate HTML using Perl. How much of this functionality is used generally depends on whether the programmer is more familiar with Perl or HTML. People more familiar with HTML tend to just create HTML tags with print statements.

I'll briefly cover the most important features of CGI.pm in this hour. For the full documentation of the module, you can read the Perl documentation using the command:

```
perldoc CGI
```

Extensive documentation is also provided online at the URL:

```
http://stein.cshl.org/WWW/software/CGI
```

Accessing CGI.pm from Your Program

The first step in using CGI.pm from within the program is importing the module. As long as the CGI.pm file is in one of the standard library directories with your installation, you can import it using the command

```
use CGI;
```

CGI.pm has an object-oriented interface, which requires you to create a new CGI object, and then reference all the data structures and functions associated with CGI.pm using that object.

A discussion of the nature of object-oriented programming is beyond the scope of this book. Suffice it to say that when you use the object-oriented interface to CGI.pm, you keep the subroutine names and variable names associated with CGI.pm completely separate from the rest of your program. It also lets you easily identify calls to CGI.pm subroutines within your program.

The object is created by initializing a variable and assigning it to a reference to a new CGI object. If you want to create a CGI object called $query, the following statement is used:

```
$query = new CGI;
```

If you use the object-oriented interface, any time you want to use any of the methods (methods are just what you call subroutines associated with a particular object) supported by CGI.pm, like the param method, which returns parameters passed to the program, you have to reference them using the query object. For example, to retrieve the value of a parameter called name, you have to use the following syntax:

```
$name = $query->param('name');
```

There's also a standard interface to CGI.pm that you can use if you don't want to deal with creating the query object and referencing it whenever you call any of the methods in CGI.pm. To import the CGI module in standard mode rather than object-oriented mode, use the following line:

```
use CGI qw(:standard);
```

10

When you use CGI.pm in standard mode, you can leave the references to the CGI object out. So, to retrieve the value of a parameter called name in standard mode, you can call the param subroutine directly, like this:

```
$name = param('name');
```

The standard interface is fine in almost all cases. On larger projects, I prefer to use CGI.pm in object-oriented mode because it allows me to differentiate between calls to subroutines contained in CGI.pm and subroutines of the same name in other modules or those that I've written myself.

Decoding Form Data via CGI.pm

The most common usage of CGI.pm is to decode form data. In fact, in many CGI programs, that's all it's used for. As soon as you import the CGI.pm module, all the input from the form is automatically translated and made accessible through the param subroutine.

In most cases, the translation from form field to Perl variable is obvious. A group of radio buttons called favorite_color is accessible through param('favorite_color'). A text input field called name is accessible through param('name'). There are three special cases that merit individual discussion when it comes to translating form input into a Perl data structure. These three cases are image input fields for which names are specified, select lists that allow you to select multiple options, and file upload fields. Let's take a look at how each of these are handled.

Named Image-Input Fields

As you learned in Hour 5, "Creating HTML Forms," when you use an image as a submit button on a form, and you specify a name for that field, the X and Y coordinates where the user clicked on the image are sent back to the server. Rather than sending one parameter back to the server, the input from the field is split into two separate parameters, representing the X and Y values. If the field is named button, the two parameters sent back are button.x and button.y. The two values are accessed using the param function using these parameter names. To retrieve the X and Y values, the following code is used:

```
$x = $query->param('button.x');
$y = $query->param('button.y');
```

Multiple Select Lists

When you create a multiple select list on a form and the user selects more than one option, multiple name and value pairs with the same name are sent to represent that field. For example, here's a URL request from a form that includes a multiple select list with two items selected:

```
http://rc3.org/cgibook/scripts/10/mult_select.html?color=green&color=blue
```

As you can see, the color parameter is passed twice, with two different values. CGI.pm handles this by placing the contents of that field in an array instead of a scalar variable. If you call the param subroutine to retrieve the values in the color field, the proper way to call it is like this:

```
@colors = $query->param('color');
```

Called in this manner, the two values from the field color will be placed in the array @colors. Let's look at what happens if you call it like this:

```
$color = $query->param('color');
```

The value of $color will be the first of the parameters, and the remaining selections that the user made will go unaccessed.

File Upload Fields

As you might imagine, handling file uploads from HTML forms is a bit more complex than handling values in other form fields. First, as I mentioned back in Hour 5, if you want to use file upload fields, your form must be created with the ENCTYPE attribute set to multipart/form-data. If you use the default ENCTYPE, only the file's name will be accessible within your CGI program.

The param subroutine can be used to obtain the name of the uploaded file. If the file upload field on a form is named portrait, you can grab the filename of the uploaded file using the following code:

```
$portrait = $query->param('portrait');
```

The contents of the file itself are accessible through a filehandle that is automatically created with the name of the uploaded file. To print out the contents of the uploaded file, you can use the following code:

```
while (<$portrait>) {
    print;
}
```

The while loop prints each line of the uploaded file in turn because print, like many other functions, accepts the implied $ argument that contains the current line of the filehandle being processed. What about binary files that the user uploaded and you want to save to disk? You can use the same filehandle to access the contents of the file, but you have to use the binary read function to extract data from the filehandle.

Let's assume that the portrait the user uploads is expected to be a binary file. You want to write the file to disk using the name of the file that the user uploaded, assuming that there's not already a file stored under that name. The source code for the program appears in Listing 10.1.

10

LISTING 10.1   A Program That Processes File Uploads

```
 1: #!/usr/local/bin/perl
 2:
 3: use CGI;
 4: $query = new CGI;
 5:
 6: $upload_directory = "portraits";
 7:
 8: if ($query->param('portrait')) {
 9:     &print_page_start;
10:     &write_file;
11:     &print_page_end;
12: }
13: else {
14:     &print_page_start;
15:     &print_form;
16:     &print_page_end;
17: }
18:
19: sub print_page_start {
20:     print $query->header;
21:     print "<HTML><HEAD><TITLE>Portrait Upload</TITLE>\n</HEAD>\n<BODY>\n";
22:     print "<H1>Portrait Upload</H1>\n";
23: }
24:
25: sub print_page_end {
26:     print "</BODY></HTML>\n";
27: }
```

continues

LISTING 10.1   continued

```
28:
29: sub print_form {
30:     print "<FORM ACTION=\"upload.pl\" METHOD=\"post\" ";
31:     print "ENCTYPE=\"multipart/form-data\">\n";
32:     print "<INPUT TYPE=\"file\" NAME=\"portrait\"><BR>\n";
33:     print "<INPUT TYPE=\"submit\" VALUE=\"upload file\"><BR>\n";
34:     print "</FORM>\n";
35: }
36:
37: sub write_file {
38:     $filename = $query->param('portrait');
39:     if ($filename =~ /.*[\/\\](.*)/) {
40:         $out_filename = $1;
41:     }
42:     else {
43:         $out_filename = $filename;
44:     }
45:     print "$filename<BR>\n";
46:     $counter = 0;
47:
48:     while (-e "$upload_directory/$out_filename") {
49:         $counter++;
50:         $out_filename =~ s/^(.+)\.(.+)$/$1$counter\.$2/;
51:     }
52:     print "$filename<BR>\n";
53:
54:     open (OUTFILE, "> $upload_directory/$out_filename");
55:     while ($bytesread = read ($filename, $buffer, 1024)) {
56:         print OUTFILE $buffer;
57:     }
58:     close $filename;
59:     close OUTFILE;
60: }
61:
62: sub print_success {
63:     print "<P>The file was saved successfully.</P>\n";
64: }
```

This program is actually somewhat complex. Not only does it process a file that has been uploaded using a form, but it also makes sure that it has a unique name and then saves it to disk. Let's look at how all that works.

Most of the script is straightforward. First, the program determines whether the request includes the portrait parameter. If it does, it assumes that a file has been uploaded; otherwise, it prints the form. In the print_form subroutine, which begins on line 30, note that the form uses the post method and multipart/form-data encoding. Both of these are necessary for files to upload properly.

The most interesting part of the script is the `write_file` subroutine, which actually saves the uploaded file to disk. There's a lot going on in this subroutine, so let's look at it closely. First, the filename of the upload file sent by the browser is extracted using `param` on line 39. Then, the actual filename is extracted from the full path of the file and stored in the variable `$out_filename`. That's the name that will be used for the file when it's stored on disk.

After the base name of the output file has been derived, the program checks to make sure that the file doesn't already exist. If it does exist, the number in a counter is appended to the filename and that number is checked, until an unclaimed filename is found. This is accomplished using the `while` loop that begins on line 48.

When the final name of the output file has been generated, the filehandle `OUTFILE` is opened, pointing to the location of the new file. On line 55, another `while` loop is used with the `read` function to read data from the filehandle pointing to the uploaded file. That data is then printed to the `OUTFILE` filehandle. After the entire file has been printed, both filehandles are closed.

After the file has been written to disk, the program prints a message indicating that the file has been saved successfully, prints the ending HTML tags, and exits.

Generating HTTP Headers and HTML Tags via `CGI.pm`

One use of `CGI.pm` is to generate HTTP headers and HTML tags so that you don't have to write them out in print statements yourself. The ability to generate HTML using `CGI.pm` is particularly useful for people who are Perl programmers and aren't proficient with HTML. I would recommend learning HTML to anyone who's serious about CGI programming, but if you're a Perl programmer, you can use `CGI.pm` to generate lots of HTML for you. One serious flaw with this approach is that anyone wanting to change the layout of pages you generate using `CGI.pm` in this way will have to know Perl, which can be a problem if you are working on a team that includes designers who are familiar with HTML and not Perl.

Throughout this book, I use `CGI.pm` to generate HTTP headers so that I don't have to print them myself. On the other hand, I don't use `CGI.pm` to generate HTML that appears in my Web documents because I don't want this book to focus too closely on `CGI.pm`.

10

How to Generate HTTP Headers

As you know from Hour 3, "Downloading, Installing, and Debugging CGI Scripts," a CGI script is required to provide a content-type header before it produces any actual content. The `header` subroutine provided by `CGI.pm` takes care of this for you. In most of the CGI programs written in Perl in this book, I include the following line:

```
print $query->header;
```

This line uses the `header` method to generate a content type header with a default MIME type of `text/html`. If the output of your script is not HTML, you can change the content type in the header by passing an argument to the `header` method. To indicate that the script's output is a GIF image, for example, the following line would be used:

```
print $query->header('image/gif');
```

There are other properties to the `header` method as well; if you want to use them, you should include the property names along with the values.

> A property is an attribute of an object. The CGI header object, for example, has a number of properties that can be altered before the header is produced. For example, hanging the -type property allows you to change the content-type in the header.

For example, if you want to send a cookie stored in the variable `$cookie` to the user and set the content type to `text/plain`, the following code is used:

```
print $query->header(-type=>'text/plain',
                     -cookie=>$cookie);
```

> Cookies are discussed in full detail in Hour 15, "Session (State) Management."

The `expires` property is used to indicate to browsers and proxy servers how long the document generated by the CGI script should be cached before a new copy is requested. To tell the proxy servers to store the page for three days, use the following call to the `header` method:

```
print $query->header(-expires=>'+3d');
```

Oftentimes, Web developers use a `<META>` tag to indicate when documents should expire. On pages that should not be cached, you will often find the following `<META>` tag:

```
<META HTTP-EQUIV="expires" CONTENT="now">
```

You can achieve the same effect using the `header` method:

```
print $query->header(-expires=>'now');
```

Another property of the `header` method is status. The HTTP status code `200 Success` is normally sent to the browser with successful requests. You can override this status with any status code you choose by setting the `status` property, as follows:

```
print $query->header(-status=>'204 No Response');
```

The `204 No Response` code indicates that the request was successful but that no document is being sent as a response. The browser should remain at the current URL.

How to Generate HTML Tags

`CGI.pm` provides methods that can be used to generate almost any tag in the HTML lexicon. For example, to generate a top-level heading, you can use the following code:

```
print $query->h1('This is a top level heading');
```

There are similar methods used to produce most other HTML tags. If you're interested in them, I'll let you look them up in the `CGI.pm` documentation yourself. However, I would like to talk about how you can use `CGI.pm` to generate HTML forms. I'm not going to use this technique elsewhere in the book, but I do use it when I'm writing CGI scripts for my own use.

The nicest thing about the form generation methods in `CGI.pm` is that they make it very easy to redisplay a form with values that were submitted through a script. For example, you can set a default value for a form field when you call the method to create that field. If there is a parameter that is already in existence with the same name, the value of that parameter will be used instead of the default value you specify.

Let's look at a quick example. Listing 10.2 contains a simple CGI program that creates a form with one field and a submit button. All the HTML in the file is generated using the methods in `CGI.pm`.

LISTING 10.2 A Program That Uses `CGI.pm` to Generate a Form

```
1: #!/usr/local/bin/perl
2:
3: use CGI;
4: $query = new CGI;
5:
6: print $query->header;
7:
```

continues

LISTING 10.2   continued

```
 8: print $query->start_html('A form generated by CGI.pm'), "\n",
 9:     $query->h1('A form generated by CGI.pm'), "\n";
10:
11: print $query->start_form, "\n";
12:
13: print $query->p, "Favorite color: ";
14: print $query->textfield(-name=>'color',
15:                         -default=>'red');
16: print $query->p, "\n";
17:
18: print $query->submit, "\n";
19: print $query->end_form, "\n";
20:
21: print $query->end_html, "\n";
```

When you view the page, the source code in Listing 10.3 is generated.

LISTING 10.3   The HTML Generated by the `form.pl` Script

```
 1: <!DOCTYPE HTML PUBLIC "-//IETF//DTD HTML//EN">
 2: <HTML><HEAD><TITLE>A form generated by CGI.pm</TITLE>
 3: </HEAD><BODY>
 4: <H1>A form generated by CGI.pm</H1>
 5: <FORM METHOD="POST"  ENCTYPE="application/x-www-form-urlencoded">
 6:
 7: <P>Favorite color: <INPUT TYPE="text" NAME="color" VALUE="red"><P>
 8: <INPUT TYPE="submit" NAME=".submit">
 9: </FORM>
10: </BODY></HTML>
```

As you can see, all the calls to methods in CGI.pm are translated into HTML tags when the program is executed. The default value specified for the color field is inserted into the form field, as you'd expect. What happens if the user enters a value in the field and submits the form? The value entered overrides the default value that's set and appears instead. A post-submission screen shot appears in Figure 10.1.

As you can see, the new value that was entered replaces the default value. If you want the default value to override user entered values when the form field is displayed, you must set the override property for that field to 1. When you add the override property to the color field, the code used to create it looks like this:

```
print $query->textfield(-name=>'color',
                        -default=>'red',
                        -override=>1);
```

FIGURE **10.1**

A CGI.pm-*generated form after submission.*

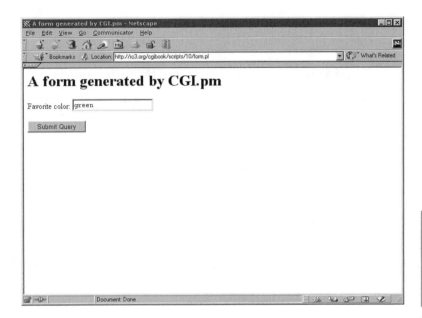

cgi-lib.pl

At one time, the most popular Perl library used by authors of CGI scripts was cgi-lib.pl. cgi-lib.pl has been around a lot longer than CGI.pm, and was the dominant CGI library for Perl 4. After Perl 5 was released, CGI.pm became the most popular Perl library and, even though it's bundled with the standard Perl distribution, lots of people still write CGI programs using cgi-lib.pl. The official home page for cgi-lib.pl is:

http://cgi-lib.berkeley.edu/

The number one advantage of cgi-lib.pl is that it's relatively simple, especially compared to CGI.pm. By way of comparison, CGI.pm is about 180k. cgi-lib.pl is about 15k. Of course, it offers an awful lot less functionality than CGI.pm does. To use cgi-lib.pl in your program, you have to process it using the require subroutine, like this:

```
require "cgi-lib.pl";
```

The most important subroutine in cgi-lib.pl is ReadParse. It's the subroutine used to copy all the form data into a data structure. To copy all the form data into a hash called input, the following code is used:

```
&ReadParse(*input);
```

You can then access any form field by name. For example, if the submitted form contained a field called address, you could access it as follows:

```
print $input{'address'};
```

Calling ReadParse with no argument will place all of your form data in the hash called
%in.

Replacing `cgi-lib.pl` with `CGI.pm`

When CGI.pm was released, nearly all CGI scripts used cgi-lib.pl to decode form input.
In order to get people to convert their scripts to use CGI.pm, Lincoln Stein added functionality to CGI.pm so that it would function as a drop-in replacement for cgi-lib.pl. I'm not
recommending that you replace cgi-lib.pl with CGI.pm if cgi-lib.pl is working for
you, but there are a lot of reasons why one might want to move to CGI.pm. For example,
CGI.pm handles cookies in a very robust manner, whereas cgi-lib.pl has no support for
cookies. Also, there are a few methods in cgi-lib.pl that don't have drop-in replacements in CGI.pm and will actually require you to change your code so that it uses the
CGI.pm methods for accomplishing those tasks, but they're few and far between.

In any case, if you want to replace cgi-lib.pl with CGI.pm, you don't have to change
much in your programs. Just replace the line:

```
require "cgi-lib.pl";
```

with:

```
use CGI qw(:cgi-lib);
```

That's all there is to it. Everything else can remain the same in your programs. For more
information on porting CGI programs from cgi-lib.pl to CGI.pm, check out the following URL:

```
http://stein.cshl.org/WWW/software/CGI/cgi-lib_porting.html
```

Handling Errors with `CGI::Carp`

One of the most useful tools for Web developers who are trying to figure out how to fix
broken CGI scripts is the server's error log. If a CGI program dies due to a runtime error,
the error message that the program generated when it died is stored in the error log.
Unfortunately, these error messages generally aren't time stamped or marked with the
name of the program that generated them. The CGI::Carp module solves that problem.

When you add the line:

```
use CGI::Carp;
```

at the beginning of a CGI program, the module traps the die and warn functions, adds a time stamp and program identification information to the error message, and saves the message in the error log. Here's an error log entry for a program that does not use CGI::Carp:

```
Can't open test.file:  at /home/httpd/cgi-bin/test.pl line 5.
[Wed Feb  9 15:14:01 2000] [error] [client 10.0.0.105] Premature end of
    script headers: /home/httpd/cgi-bin/test.pl
```

When you add the CGI::Carp module to the program, the error message looks like this:

```
[Wed Feb  9 15:14:18 2000] test.pl: Can't open test.file:
    at /home/httpd/cgi-bin/test.pl line 6.
[Wed Feb  9 15:14:18 2000] [error] [client 10.0.0.105]
    Premature end of script headers: /home/httpd/cgi-bin/test.pl
```

As you can see, in the second case the error report contains more detail than the first. In these two isolated cases, the difference doesn't seem to matter much, but when your error log is 1500 lines long, the extra identifying information is a big help.

Sending Fatal Errors to the Browser

When you're developing CGI scripts, sometimes it's better to just avoid the error log entirely. Using CGI::Carp, you can instead redirect fatal errors to the browser directly. To use CGI::Carp in this mode, you should import it in fatalsToBrowser mode, like this:

```
use CGI::Carp qw(fatalsToBrowser);
```

Then, when you try to access a script that contains a fatal error, instead of getting a standard 500 Server Error, you'll actually get the message that's normally printed to the server's error log. Figure 10.2 shows what an error message redirected to the browser in this way looks like. When you use fatalsToBrowser, the failed request is transformed into a successful request by CGI::Carp, so the actual server error will no longer be logged to the server's error log. However, the error message generated by the script itself (along with the identifying information added by CGI::Carp) will still be appended to the error log.

Sending errors to the browser is fine when your script is still in development mode, but you should turn that feature off when you make the script available over the Web. Error messages can provide information to users that you probably don't want to make public.

FIGURE 10.2
*Sending error mes-
sages to the browser
with* CGI::Carp.

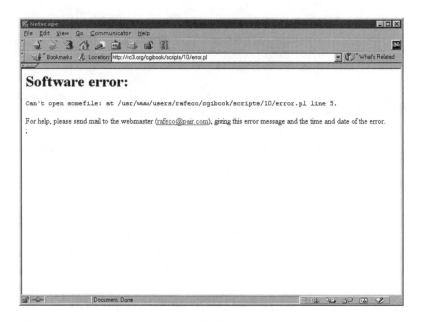

Resources for Perl Programmers

So far, I've described three tools that can make your life easier as a Perl programmer. You
might be wondering where you can find information about other tools or about the Perl
language itself. In this section, I'll discuss the built-in Perl documentation, various Web
sites, and two book resources. I'll also take a look at CPAN—the Comprehensive Perl
Archive Network, a huge archive of Perl modules that you can use to save yourself work.

Perl Documentation

First of all, when Perl is installed on a system, lots of documentation is installed with it.
This documentation takes three forms: man pages, POD files, and HTML documentation.

Man pages are the standard online documentation on computers running UNIX. If you
want to find out how to use the ls command, just type **man ls**. If you want to find out
about perl, type **man perl**. Most Perl modules, including CGI.pm and CGI::Carp, install
man pages when they are installed. When you look up documentation on a Perl module,
you leave off the .pm extension. For example, to find information about CGI.pm, you just
type **man CGI**.

POD files are the native format for Perl documentation (POD stands for Plain Old
Documentation). One nice thing about POD files is that the POD information can actually
be stored inside a Perl program using a specialized markup language. You can use a POD

reader to extract that information from a program that has the POD information built in. Even if a module doesn't install a man page when it's installed, it might still have POD information. Under UNIX and Windows, the POD reader is the `perldoc` program.

There are a lot of POD files that come with the Perl distribution. For a list of them, just type **perldoc perl**. One POD file you might find particularly useful is the `perlfunc` POD file, which contains documentation for all the functions built into Perl. To read Perl documentation for a module, use `perldoc` and the name of the module in the same way you'd use the `man` command. `perldoc CGI` will get the documentation for `CGI.pm`, and `perldoc CGI::Carp` will display the documentation for `CGI::Carp`.

Finally, there's also HTML documentation that's installed when you install Perl under Windows. This documentation is actually generated by a program that comes with Perl called pod2html. Under UNIX, you can create HTML documentation from your POD files yourself using pod2html. The ActiveState distribution of Perl for Windows does this for you. The HTML documentation is stored under the `html` subdirectory of the directory where Perl is installed. So, if you install Perl on a Windows machine in the directory `C:\perl` you can find the HTML documentation in `C:\perl\html`.

Perl Information On the Web

The best spot for finding out more about Perl in general is `http://www.perl.com`, the official Perl home page. Not only can you access all sorts of Perl documentation and information, but you can also read the latest Perl news and find out about the latest releases.

There's also a magazine devoted to Perl—The Perl Journal. You can read articles from the magazine and subscribe at `http://www.itknowledge.com/tpj`. Web Techniques is a magazine concerned with Web development in general that covers Perl and CGI programming very well. You can read articles from the magazine at `http://www.webtechniques.com`.

Perl Books

There are an awful lot of Perl books on the shelves, and I'd like to recommend a couple with which I am familiar. The book you should buy depends greatly on what you're looking for. If you don't know Perl and want to learn it, I recommend *Teach Yourself Perl in 21 Days* by Laura Lemay. It's very well written and provides a gentle introduction for novices. At the same time, it delves into deeper issues than most introductory books.

For reference purposes, the number one title by far is *Programming Perl* (commonly referred to by Perl programmers as the "Camel Book"), written by the author of Perl itself, Larry Wall, along with Tom Christiansen and Randal L. Schwartz. The book is a bit esoteric for the true novice, but if you have a decent handle on Perl you'll find the book indispensable. It's the book I keep next to my desk when I'm doing all of my Perl programming.

The Comprehensive Perl Archive Network

If you're writing programs in Perl and you've never heard of CPAN, you're missing out. CPAN is an online archive of hundreds of Perl modules designed for all sorts of tasks. Long before `CGI.pm` was part of the standard Perl distribution, it was available through CPAN. There are CPAN modules for date arithmetic, sending email, generating random numbers, and everything else in between.

The modules in CPAN are written by individuals who want to contribute their source code to the Perl community, and thus the quality of the modules varies widely. That said, I've never downloaded anything from CPAN that didn't work. There are a number of ways to access CPAN. The two most common are via the Web and using the CPAN shell.

To access CPAN over the Web, go to the following URL:

```
http://www.perl.com/CPAN-local/README.html
```

When you're there, there are a number of ways to navigate the hierarchy of modules. You can search the archive, review a list of all the modules on a single page, or traverse the tree of modules by author, category, name, or date of submission. After you've found the module you want, it's up to you to download it and install it. There are some instructions on how to install modules at:

```
http://18.85.40.23/INSTALL.html
```

The other option for installing modules is to use the CPAN shell. The CPAN shell is part of the module `CPAN.pm`, which was written by Andreas Konig. The nicest feature of the CPAN shell is that when you select a module, it will automatically take the steps necessary to download, build, and install the module. If there are prerequisites for the module, it will download, build, and install them as well. To start the shell, just type the following at a command prompt:

```
perl -MCPAN -e shell;
```

The first time you launch the CPAN shell, you have to answer a few questions. The vast majority of users can accept the default answers to the questions, at least until they get to the point where they have to enter the URL for their favorite CPAN site. At that point, you should pick one from the list at:

```
http://www.perl.com/CPAN-local/SITES.html
```

After you're in the shell, you can start working with CPAN. You can get help on how to use CPAN from within the shell by typing **h** at the cpan> prompt. You can also find out more about how to use CPAN by typing **man CPAN** or **perldoc CPAN** at a prompt.

> The CPAN shell only works reliably on systems running UNIX.

Summary

In this hour, you took a closer look at the tools and resources you can use to assist you in writing CGI programs in Perl. First, I discussed some of the capabilities of `CGI.pm`. I then contrasted it with `cgi-lib.pl`, a simpler library for decoding form data. Next, I looked at `CGI::Carp`, a tool to assist programmers in debugging CGI programs. Finally, I talked about some places where you can look for more information on Perl.

Q&A

Q What is the performance difference between `CGI.pm` and `cgi-lib.pl`?

A Under some situations, using `cgi-lib.pl` instead of `CGI.pm` can reduce compilation time for CGI programs by half. If performance is a big issue, you might consider using `cgi-lib.pl`. Most Perl programmers who are confronted with performance constraints tend to lean toward using `mod_perl` to execute their programs. This alternative is discussed in Hour 12, "Pros and Cons of Alternate Technologies."

Q Is it okay to use code downloaded from CPAN on commercial sites?

A This varies depending on the license for the individual module you're downloading. However, as a general rule, if it's okay to use Perl for a task, it's okay to use modules downloaded from CPAN for that task.

Workshop

The quiz questions are designed to strengthen the knowledge you gain each hour. The exercises help you build on that knowledge by providing you with the opportunity to apply it to real problems. See Appendix A, "Answers" for the answers to the quiz questions.

Quiz

1. Which method in `CGI.pm` is used to generate the `<FORM>` tag that begins forms?
2. Which subroutine in `cgi-lib.pl` is used to import form variables into a CGI program?
3. True or false: `cgi-lib.pl` supports cookies.

Exercises

1. Check out the documentation for CGI.pm, and create a document that produces all the HTML tags using methods from CGI.pm.

2. Search CPAN for a module that will perform a task that you would ordinarily write code to perform yourself. Download and install that module.

Hour **11**

Other Popular CGI Programming Languages

One of the most powerful features of CGI is its language independence. Any programming language that meets a few simple criteria can be used to develop CGI programs. In this hour, I'm going to explain how to write CGI programs in two languages other than Perl and the Bourne shell.

In this hour, you'll learn

- What criteria permit a language to be used for CGI programs
- How to write CGI programs in C
- How to use the `cgic` library with your C programs
- How to write CGI programs in Python

Will My Favorite Language Work for CGI?

One big question most programmers face when they start to learn about CGI is whether their favorite programming language will work for writing CGI scripts. If that language is Perl or the Bourne shell, the answer is a resounding yes. However, the truth is that many languages are suitable for use in writing CGI programs; they just have to meet a few simple criteria.

These criteria are easy to deduce when you think about how CGI programs work. First, let's look at how CGI programs are called. CGI programs are invoked by the Web server. The key here is that the server must be able to call the program by name alone. In other words, if your program must be called by passing the program name as an argument to the program interpreter, or with particular arguments, it isn't going to work in the CGI environment. That's a big reason why Java won't work for writing CGI scripts. (You have to call Java programs using the Java virtual machine.)

Next, let's look at how CGI programs accept input. Data can be passed to a CGI script in one of two ways. Either the data can be stored in an environment variable, or it can be passed to the program via standard input. To use a programming language to write CGI programs, it must be able to access and process data passed to it using either of these methods.

Finally, let's look at the output of CGI programs. When any computer program is executed as a CGI program, all the data printed to standard output is returned to the browser. As long as your program is capable of printing text data and sending it to standard output, you're fine here.

As you can see, CGI is associated with command-line programs. Programming environments like PowerBuilder and Visual Basic are unsuitable for CGI programming because they are geared toward creating programs that allow the user to interact with them via a graphical interface. Simpler scripting languages that work from the command line tend to work best.

Writing CGI Programs in C

C is one of the most popular programming languages in the world. It's the language in which operating systems, applications, and even other programming languages are written. It's a compiled language and a very low level language. For these reasons, C programs offer great performance. Because C is generally associated with system programming and has been around for a very long time, C compilers are also tuned to compile applications that offer the best performance possible.

The main problems with C from the CGI programmer's perspective are the things that make it great for system programming. Most CGI programmers prefer higher level languages that provide lots of built-in functions that make writing CGI programs easy. C, on the other hand, is a low level language suited to any task. Unfortunately, that means that you have to write code to perform tasks that are greatly simplified in many popular scripting languages. The other problem with C for CGI programmers is that it's a compiled language. Compilation adds another step to the development cycle that can slow development significantly.

For many applications, the performance gains obtained by using programs written in compiled languages rather than scripting languages are crucial. Generally speaking, in the CGI environment this just isn't so. If CGI does become a bottleneck, generally it's easier to port your programs to a development platform that does not use the CGI interface than it is to rewrite all your programs in C. Besides, CGI has other disadvantages aside from raw performance that can be avoided by moving to another interface.

The `cgic` Library

`cgic` is a CGI library for C written by Thomas Boutell (`http://www.boutell.com/cgic`). Like `CGI.pm` and `cgi-lib.pl`, it is used to decode data submitted by the user and make it available within your CGI program. The only difference is that this library is written to work with C programs instead of programs written in Perl or any other language.

Before you can use `cgic`, you have to import it into your C program. Generally, it is loaded into your CGI program using a line like:

```
#include "cgic.h"
```

Programs written to work with `cgic` differ from standard C programs in some ways. All C programs must contain a function named `main()` in order to compile and execute properly. When you write programs that use `cgic`, you eliminate the `main()` function and instead start with a function called `cgiMain()`.

`cgic` provides the `main()` function so that it can perform all of the setup necessary to get the environment ready for your code. The `main()` function takes care of parsing all the form data and reading in data from environment variables; it then calls the `cgiMain()` function, which you provide.

Printing Headers

`cgic` provides three functions for generating HTTP headers from your script. Usually, you'll use the `cgiHeaderContentType()` function, which accepts the content type of the data your script generates as an argument. If your script generates HTML, you'd call it as follows:

```
cgiHeaderContentType("text/html");
```

If you want to redirect the user to a different location, the `cgiHeaderLocation()` function is used. It accepts the URL to which the user should be redirected as an argument.

11

To send a status code other than 200 (the default), you can use `cgiHeaderStatus()`, which accepts a status code as an argument. You can only use one of the header functions in your program.

Printing Output

Rather than just using standard `printf` statements, it is recommended that you use `fprintf` statements to write output to `cgiOut` in programs that use `cgic`. `cgiOut` is basically a wrapper for standard output; the advantage of using it is that it makes your programs more portable. If at some point it's advantageous for CGI programs to print to somewhere other than standard output, `cgic` will be updated so that `cgiOut` sends its output there instead, and you won't need to make updates to your programs.

Let's look at a typical `fprintf` statement used with `cgic`:

```
fprintf(cgiOut, "<HTML><HEAD>\n");
```

Right now, this is equivalent to

```
printf("<HTML><HEAD>\n";
```

As I said, using the `fprintf` method puts you in better shape for the future.

Handling Form Input

One of the big differences between C and a scripting language like Perl is that C is more rigorous about how its variables are defined. When you're dealing with a string in Perl, you can just stuff it into a scalar variable. You don't have to predefine the variable, specify how big it is, or indicate what type of data is stored in it. String handling in C is significantly more complex. I won't discuss it here because it's assumed that if you're interested in writing CGI programs in C, you're already a C programmer. However, I will explain how form input, which generally consists of strings, is handled with `cgic`.

Handling String Data

When you want to handle string data from a form, the first thing you need to do is declare a variable in which to store the data. C strings are arrays of characters, and it's extremely important to make sure that your arrays are large enough to hold all of the data submitted by the user. If more data is submitted than can be stored in the memory that you allocate, a buffer overflow occurs. Buffer overflows are a huge security problem, so you should take every measure you can to avoid them.

Let's say your form contained a field called `name` that you specified with a `MAXLENGTH` of 80 characters. The following code is used to copy it into a variable in your program called `name`:

```
char name[81];
cgiFormStringNoNewlines("name", name, 81);
```

First, I declare an array of characters called name that can store up to 81 bytes of information. The first 80 characters are allocated for storage of the user's input, and the last character is used to store the null character that marks the end of the string. On the next line, I use cgiFormStringNoNewlines to retrieve the data that the user submitted. The function accepts three arguments: the name of the form field, the name of the buffer in which the form data should be stored, and the maximum size of the string to be retrieved. If the value submitted is larger than the number of bytes you specify, the value will be truncated and cgiFormStringNoNewlines() will return a different value.

By allowing me to specify the amount of information to retrieve, cgic allows me to avoid buffer overflows. As you already know, a malicious user is not constrained by MAXLENGTH attributes in forms. They can easily submit more data than you request in a number of ways. The functions that retrieve form values in cgic protect you from this sort of activity by constraining the amount of data they return. An additional feature of cgiFormStringNoNewlines() is that it strips any line feeds from the data it returns. If you're retrieving data from a <TEXTAREA> field, you might want to use cgiFormString(), which preserves line feeds in the user submitted data.

Handling Numeric Data

As you know, C discriminates between numeric data and character data. If you want to treat data submitted by a user as a number, you have to retrieve it using numeric functions. There are four numeric functions associated with cgic. cgiFormInteger() and cgiFormDouble() are used to retrieve integer and floating point data respectively. cgiFormIntegerBounded() and cgiFormDoubleBounded() retrieve integer and floating point data with bounds checking. Let's look at the cgiFormDoubleBounded() function; you can find out more about the rest of the numeric functions in the cgic documentation.

The cgiFormDoubleBounded() function accepts five arguments. They are the name of the form field, the address of the variable to store the value in, the data's lower bound, the data's upper bound, and the default value to return. A call to cgiFormDoubleBounded() looks like this:

```
double state_tax_rate;
cgiFormDoubleBounded("tax_rate", &state_tax_rate, .05, .65, .25);
```

The value is retrieved from the tax_rate field and stored in the variable state_tax_rate. The value cannot be less than .05 or more than .65. If the value is outside the specified bounds, it is automatically changed to the bound that it violates. If the user entered the number 1000 in the field, it would be changed to .65. If the parameter is missing or no value was entered, the default value is returned, in this case .25.

11

Handling Single Check Boxes

The methods of accessing form data I just described work perfectly for text, password, hidden, submit, and textarea fields. Let's look at how checkbox fields are handled. As you know, when a checkbox field is included on a form, if it is checked, the name and value pair associated with the field are sent to the server. If it's not checked, that name and value pair are just left out. cgic provides a function that makes it easy to handle single check boxes. The cgiFormCheckboxSingle function tests for the existence of a particular parameter, and if it exists, returns cgiFormSuccess. If it doesn't exist, it returns cgiFormNotFound. Code to test whether a checkbox field named citizen was checked looks like this:

```
if (cgiFormCheckboxSingle("citizen") == cgiFormSuccess) {
    fprintf(cgiOut, "Glad you're a citizen!\n";
}
else {
    fprintf(cgiOut, "Wish you were a citizen.\n";
}
```

Handling Single Select Fields

Select lists without the MULTIPLE flag and radio button groups allow users to select one of a group of options. The simplest method of handling these fields is to use the cgiFormStringNoNewlines() function to copy the value that the user selected into a string variable and use it from there, just as you would with a text-based input field. However, cgic also lets you define a list of options for a particular field in your program and then correlate the user's input with that list of values.

Let's look at how this code works. First, I have to create an array that contains a list of options that were presented to the user:

```
char *counties[] = {
    "Wake",
    "Orange",
    "Chatham",
    "Johnston"
};
```

To determine which option the user chose, I use the cgiFormSelectSingle() function as follows:

```
int user_county;
cgiFormSelectSingle("county", counties, 4, &user_county, 0);
```

The arguments to cgiFormSelectSingle() are the query parameter from which to retrieve the value, the name of the array containing the list of options, the number of options in the array, the variable in which to store the retrieved value, and the array index of the default option. The index of the option that the user chose is stored in the specified variable. If the user's choice is not in the list, the default value specified is stored in the variable.

There's also a function meant for handling radio button groups called `cgiFormRadio()`. Although it might seem counterintuitive, the only difference between `cgiFormRadio()` and `cgiFormSelectSingle()` is the name. In other words, you can use either function for a single select list or for a radio button group.

> Even though `cgiFormSelectSingle()` and `cgiFormRadio()` are identical today, you should use the appropriate function for the field in your form in case changes are made later to differentiate the two functions.

Handling Multiple Select Fields

The `cgiFormSelectMultiple()` and `cgiFormCheckboxMultiple()` functions are used to handle form fields from which the user can select multiple values. They each work with two types of fields[md]select lists that allow you to select multiple items, and multiple check boxes with the same name. Both of these send back multiple parameters with the same name to the CGI script. Handling this type of field is moderately complex, at least compared to how the other data handling functionality works.

`cgiFormSelectMultiple()` and `cgiFormCheckboxMultiple()` work exactly the same way. Each function accepts five arguments. The first argument is the name of the parameter that was submitted to the script. The second argument is a pointer to an array of possible values associated with the parameter. The third argument is the number of elements in the array of possible values. The fourth argument is the name of an array of integers with the same number of elements as the array of possible values. Each element in this array will be set to true or false depending on whether the user submitted the corresponding value in the array of possible values. The final argument is an integer variable that will be set to the number of values submitted that aren't in the list of possible values.

Let's take a look at how to handle the counties field if multiple selections were allowed:

```
char *counties[] = {
    "Wake",
    "Orange",
    "Chatham",
    "Johnston"
};
int selected_counties[4];
int invalid;
cgiFormSelectMultiple("county", counties, 4, selected_counties, &invalid);
```

As you can see, three variables have to be defined in order to use `cgiFormSelect Multiple()` or `cgiFormCheckboxMultiple()`. The counties array contains a list of possible values that can be submitted. The selected_counties array is an array of integers that the `cgiFormSelectMultiple()` function stores its results in, and invalid is an integer variable used to store the number of submitted values that aren't in the list supplied to the function.

Let's say that the user submitted the form with the options Wake and Chatham selected. When the `cgiFormSelectMultiple()` function is executed, the selected_counties array is updated so that the first and third elements are set to true. These elements actually have 0 and 2 as indexes because array elements in C are numbered beginning with 0.

There's also a simpler, less reliable method for extracting data in cases where multiple parameters with the same name are submitted. The `cgiFormStringMultiple()` function accepts two arguments, the name of the field to retrieve data from, and an array to stuff the data into. Each of the values is stored in a separate element of the array. This method isn't as failsafe as the more complex method described previously because it operates under the assumption that the user isn't malicious and won't send data that isn't in the form. This function is used in the example below.

A C Example

This is a simple example of a form handling program written in C. It accepts user input submitted through a form, and prints the values that the user entered. The source code for the program appears in Listing 11.1.

LISTING **11.1**   A Sample CGI Program Written in C

```
 1: #include <stdio.h>
 2: #include "cgic.h"
 3:
 4: int cgiMain() {
 5:    cgiHeaderContentType("text/html");
 6:    fprintf(cgiOut, "<HTML><HEAD>\n");
 7:    fprintf(cgiOut, "<TITLE>C Example</TITLE></HEAD>\n");
 8:    fprintf(cgiOut, "<BODY><H1>C Example</H1>\n");
 9:    Name();
10:    Secure();
11:    Operating_System();
12:    Browser();
13:    fprintf(cgiOut, "</BODY></HTML>\n");
14:    return 0;
15: }
16:
17: void Name() {
18:    char name[81];
19:    cgiFromStringNoNewLines("name", name, 81);
20:    fprintf(cgiOut, "Name: %s<br>\n", name);
```

```
21: }
22:
23: void Secure() {
24:   if (cgiFormCheckboxSingle("secure") == CgiFormSuccess) {
25:     fprintf("<p>Your browser supports secure connections.</p>\n");
26:   }
27:   else {
28:     fprintf("<p>Your browser does not support secure connections.</p>\n");
29:   }
30: }
31:
32: char *operating_systems[] = {
33:   "Mac OS",
34:   "Windows",
35:   "Linux"
36: };
37:
38: void Operating_System() {
39:   int os_choice;
40:   cgiFormSelectSingle("operating_system", operating_systems, 3,
41:              &os_choice, 0);
42:   fprintf(cgiOut, "<p>The operating system you use is %s.</p>\n",
43:       operating_systems[os_choice]);
44: }
45:
46: char *browsers[] = {
47:   "Netscape Navigator",
48:   "Mozilla",
49:   "Opera",
50:   "Internet Explorer"
51: };
52:
53: void Browser() {
54:   int i;
55:   int result;
56:   int valid;
57:   char **browsers;
58:
59:   fprintf(cgiOut, "<p>Browsers chosen:<br>\n");
60:   result = cgiFormStringMultiple("browser", &browsers);
61:   if (result == cgiFormNotFound) {
62:     fprintf(cgiOut, "No browsers selected!<br>\n");
63:   }
64:   else {
65:     int i = 0;
66:     while (browsers[i]) {
67:       fprintf(cgiOut, "%s\n<br>", browsers[i]);
68:       i++;
69:     }
70:   }
71:   print "</p>\n";
72: }
```

11

This script uses several of the functions provided by `cgic` to process the form data that is submitted. As required by `cgic`, the program is built around the `cgiMain()` function, with separate functions to handle each field on the form. In the `cgiMain()` function (which begins on line 4), I call the `cgiHeaderContentType()` function to print out the header. (I could just as easily print the header myself, but it's better programming to let the library take care of it.)

After the header is printed, I use the `fprintf` statements on lines 6-8 to start the HTML on the page. When I get to the page body, I start calling the form processing functions. The first function I call is the `Name()` function, which begins on line 17. It uses the `cgiFromStringNoNewLines()` function to extract a value of up to 80 characters from the form data, and prints it out.

The second function called is the `Secure()` function, which processes a check box and begins on line 23. It uses the `cgiFormCheckboxSingle()` function, which returns either `cgiFormSuccess` or `cgiFormNotFound`, depending on whether the check box was checked on the form. I test the value returned by the function, and print the appropriate message.

The next field to be processed is handled by the `Operating_System` function on line 38, which deals with a single item select list. It uses `cgiFormSelectSingle()` to extract the value the user entered, and then displays it.

The final function is the `Browser()` function, which handles a group of check boxes submitted from the form. It uses the simpler `cgiFormStringMultiple()` to retrieve the user input, and places it in the `browsers` array. I store the value returned by the `cgiFormStringMultiple()` function so that I can determine whether the user checked any of the check boxes. If they didn't, I print out a message indicating so. If they did, I use a `while` loop to iterate over the `browsers` array and print out each of the elements. After the `Browsers()` function has been executed, I print out the closing HTML tags for the page, and the program exits. The form used to submit data to this script appears in Listing 11.2.

LISTING 11.2   The Form Used to Submit Data to the Sample Program

```
1: <html>
2: <head>
3:     <title>C CGI Script Test</title>
4: </head>
5: <body>
6:
7: <h1>CGI Example</h1>
8:
9: <form action="/cgi-bin/cprogram">
```

```
10: <p>
11: Name: <input type="text" name="name">
12: </p>
13:
14: <p>
15: <input type="checkbox" name="secure" value="yes">
16: My browser supports secure connections.
17: </p>
18:
19: <p>
20: <select name="operating_system">
21:     <option value="Mac OS">Mac OS
22:     <option value="Windows">Windows
23:     <option value="Linux">Linux
24: </select>
25: </p>
26:
27: <p>
28: I use these browsers:<br>
29: <input type="checkbox" name="browser" value="Netscape Navigator">
30: Netscape Navigator<br>
31: <input type="checkbox" name="browser" value="Mozilla">
32: Mozilla<br>
33: <input type="checkbox" name="browser" value="Opera">
34: Opera<br>
35: <input type="checkbox" name="browser" value="Internet Explorer">
36: Internet Explorer
37: </p>
38:
39: <p>
40: <input type="submit">
41: </p>
42:
43: </form>
44:
45: </body>
46: </html>
```

11

Writing CGI Programs in Python

Python is a scripting language that is in some ways similar to Perl. Many people prefer Python because it's highly object oriented, which makes it easy to write highly structured, maintainable programs. This section of the chapter is written for people who already know how to program in Python, but have never used Python for CGI programming.

Writing a CGI program in Python is as simple as writing one in any other language. As long as your program prints a valid content type header and generates content that conforms to that content type, you're out of the woods. The most difficult part of writing a CGI program in any language is processing form input. Unsurprisingly, there's a module for translating form data using Python. It's called cgi.py.

Let's look at how form parameters are decoded and accessed using cgi.py. Dot notation is used to access methods and properties of objects in Python. The first step is to import the cgi.py module using the import statement:

```
import cgi
```

As you might imagine, this imports the CGI module into your program. At that point, you can create an object that contains all the form data by calling the FieldStorage() method of the CGI object. Here's how that code looks:

```
form = cgi.FieldStorage()
```

At this point, all the form data is stored in the object form. form is what's known as a dictionary object[md]it's like a hash in Perl. To access an item in a Python dictionary, you just pass the name of the object to retrieve the value. For example, to retrieve the county field you'd use the following code:

```
county = form["county"]
```

To print the value in that field, you could use the following print statement:

```
print county.value
```

If your form contains multiple check boxes with the same name, or a select list that allows multiple selections, the FieldStorage() function will return a list of values for that field rather than a single value. You can then access the list of values using a for loop, like this:

```
counties = form["counties"]
county_list = ""
    # Iterate over all of the counties that the user selected
    # for county in counties:
    # If the county_list already contains an item, insert a
    # comma before adding the next one
    if county_list:
        county_list = county_list + "," + county.value
    # In this case, no counties have been added to the list
    else:
        county_list = county.value
```

If the form the user submitted contains a file field, you can access the file in the same way you access any other data. First, you can retrieve the field from the form object:

```
uploaded_file = form["file_field"]
```

Then, you can access the file using the property of the field object, like this:

```
uploaded_file.file.readline()
```

A Python Example

Now let's look at an example written in Python. If the user's form input contains the hidden field action, the script processes that information. Otherwise, it prints a new form to be filled out. The source code for the script is in Listing 11.3.

LISTING 11.3   A CGI Script Written in Python

```
 1: #!/usr/local/bin/python
 2:
 3: import cgi
 4: form = cgi.FieldStorage()
 5:
 6: def print_page_start():
 7:     print "Content-type: text/html\n\n"
 8:     print "<html><head><title>Example Form</title></head><body>\n"
 9:     print "<h1>Example Form</h1>"
10:
11: def print_page_end():
12:     print "</body></html>\n"
13:
14: def print_form():
15:     print "<form>\n"
16:     print "<input type=\"hidden\" name=\"action\" value=\"process\">\n"
17:     print "Name: <input name=\"name\"><br>\n"
18:     print "Age: <input name=\"age\"><br>\n"
19:     print "<input type=\"submit\">\n</form>\n"
20:
21: def process_form(form):
22:     try:
23:         name = form["name"].value
24:     except:
25:         print "You must enter your name.\n"
26:         print_page_end()
27:         raise SystemExit
28:
29:     try:
30:         age = form["age"].value
31:     except:
32:         print "You must enter your age.\n"
33:         print_page_end()
34:         raise SystemExit
35:
36:     print "<p>Your name is " + name + ".</p>\n"
37:     print "<p>Your age is " + age + ".</p>\n"
38:
39: # Check for the existence of the action parameter
40: try:
```

11

continues

LISTING 11.3   continued

```
41:     action = form["action"].value
42: except:
43:     action = None
44:
45: print_page_start()
46:
47: # If the form was submitted, process it.  Otherwise, print the form
48: if action == "process":
49:     process_form(form)
50: else:
51:     print_form()
52:
53: print_page_end()
```

The script starts the same way CGI scripts written in Perl do—with a pointer to the interpreter used to execute the script. In this case, there's a pointer to the Python interpreter. Next, I import the Python CGI module, and copy the form parameters into the form object using the FieldStorage() method of the CGI module.

At that point, I define a few subroutines. The print_page_start and print_page_end subroutines are very similar to the subroutines I include in my Perl programs. The print_form subroutine is used to generate the form if the user requested the script without submitting the form. The process_form subroutine is where the action takes place. I'll go back to it in a bit.

After I define all the subroutines I'm going to use, I get to the main body of the script. First, I use an if statement to check whether the action parameter exists. If it does, I set the action variable equal to the action parameter's value. If it doesn't, I set the variable to None.

I then use print_page_start to print the first chunk of HTML in the program. After that, I check whether action is equal to process. If it is, I call the process_form subroutine, and if it isn't, I print the form.

The process_form subroutine is where most of the action takes place. The user is required to enter both their name and age. The program attempts to read the values into variables, and if there are no values, an error occurs when the code in the except blocks is executed. These blocks print an error message, called the print_page_end subroutine, and then raise SystemExit to stop the execution of the program.

Summary

This hour was directed at people who are familiar with C or Python programming, and would like to use one of those languages to write CGI scripts. It introduced libraries you can use with those languages to make it simpler to write CGI programs.

Q&A

Q My favorite programming language still hasn't been covered!

A It's possible to write CGI programs in almost any programming language. You should research your favorite programming language on the Web to find out how to use it to write CGI programs.

Workshop

The quiz questions are designed to strengthen the knowledge you gain each hour. See Appendix A, "Answers" for the answers to the quiz questions.

Quiz

1. What is the difference between the `cgiFormSelectSingle()` and `cgiFormRadio()` functions in `cgic`?

2. Why is it important to make sure that you allocate enough space for strings in CGI programs written in C?

11

Hour 12

Pros and Cons of Alternate Technologies

The real goal of this book is not to just teach you how to write CGI programs, but how to build Web applications. CGI programming is just one means to that end. However, there are plenty of other platforms available upon which you can build Web applications. Most of them offer some distinct advantages over CGI programming, and also generally have some weaknesses when compared with CGI. In this hour, I'm going to provide a broad survey of some of the more popular Web application platforms that you can use.

In this hour you will learn:

- Why CGI alternatives developed
- Types of CGI alternatives
- Active Server Pages
- Allaire ColdFusion
- Apache mod_perl and FastCGI
- PHP

- Server Side Java
- NSAPI and ISAPI

Looking Back

CGI was quite a breakthrough in the early days of the World Wide Web. It was the first enabling technology that let people create truly dynamic Web pages. Before CGI was implemented in NCSA HTTPD, Web sites were simply collections of static files. The Web was a valuable resource, but without CGI there were no search engines, connections to existing databases, or Web-based gateways to other Internet services.

CGI provided a simple way to build these new features into the Web interface and made the Web a much better place to do research, conduct electronic commerce, or even just look for interesting reading. In fact, thanks to CGI and its descendants, the Web now provides a common interface to what once were custom applications, like client/server database applications. By building applications using Web servers and Web browsers, businesses can lower development and maintenance costs and provide their users with an interface to their data with which they are already familiar.

Why CGI Alternatives Appeared

Although CGI was truly a breakthrough, like any new technology it has some inherent limitations. The number one problem is performance. Every time a user requests a CGI script, the server must launch the CGI program, which takes processor time. When the CGI program is written in Perl, the server must run the entire Perl interpreter and compile the program before it can be run, which takes even more processor time. This isn't an issue for many Web sites because they don't serve enough users to be affected by these performance problems, but for busy sites running complex applications, the limitations of CGI were once difficult to outmaneuver.

The other problem with CGI is the complexity of writing CGI programs. Although CGI itself isn't particularly complex, CGI programs are somewhat complex in that you have to write a program that not only contains all of your application logic but also generates all the HTML for a page in order for it to work properly. This means that Web-page designers who don't know how to program have to learn how to edit HTML contained within print statements in your script, or your programmers have to include the HTML from the designers in their programs. Neither solution is optimal. Many application platforms have been created to specifically address this problem. For example, both Active Server Pages and ColdFusion allow you to create applications by embedding code within standard HTML pages. The goal is to simplify Web application development.

Getting Past CGI's Limitations

Most of the newer solutions also tackle some of the problems with CGI. They take care of some of the performance problems by hooking your application directly into the Web server so that the server doesn't have to request an external application every time a user requests a dynamic page. They also simplify or automate many of the tasks that must be written manually if you're using CGI.

One of the main advantages of these newer technologies is that they are designed from the ground up to provide seamless connectivity to relational databases. One of the most significant weaknesses of CGI is that writing programs to connect to databases is fairly complex. Using software specifically designed for that purpose makes things a lot easier.

As you know, every time a user requests a CGI script the server runs the script and captures its output. If the CGI script is designed to gather data from a database, every time the CGI script runs it must also connect to the database and log in. This can really slow down the performance of your Web site and slow down your database with the overhead of opening and closing connections repeatedly, as well. Most of the more modern tools simply open a database connection, or pool of connections, when they're initially started and reuse those connections to service the requests that they receive.

Another limitation of CGI is that there was no happy medium between writing static HTML pages and building pages dynamically using CGI scripts. Many CGI replacements enable you to embed code into your HTML Web pages that can do the same types of things for which CGI scripts are commonly used.

Server Side Includes can be used to place commands within your HTML pages, but they are not particularly flexible or powerful.

12

Types of CGI Alternatives

I would place CGI alternatives into three categories: those that allow you to embed actual code within your HTML documents, those that allow you to place tokens in your documents that call external code, and application programming interfaces for Web servers. For example, Microsoft's Active Server Pages, Allaire's ColdFusion, and PHP work by enabling you to embed special tags in your HTML that provide CGI-like functionality. Application servers like WebObjects fit the second type. You write programs that contain the code for your Web site, and when the pages are served, they are scanned for tokens that refer to functions in those programs. By token, I mean any string of text that is understood by the application server. For example, an application server might understand that the token [get_user_name] should be read as a call to the function that returns the user's real name. Technologies such as mod_perl, NSAPI, and ISAPI enable you to write applications that interface directly with your server software, instead of forcing you to go through the CGI interface.

As you might imagine, the type of Web application framework you use depends on what you want to accomplish and what type of interface you're more comfortable using. The application frameworks that are basically HTML extensions make it really easy to add commands to your Web pages to make them more dynamic and to retrieve external data and embed it in the page. They also provide few entry barriers to people who already know HTML and are interested in spicing up their pages.

The token parsing application servers are popular with people who want to separate the code for their site from the page templates. Generally, these types of systems are associated with object oriented programming languages. For example, you can write a number of components in Java, and then place tokens that call those components in your Web pages.

The application programming interfaces that are built into Web servers, such as NSAPI and ISAPI, are perfect for programmers who are comfortable developing software and are undertaking large, complex projects. For seasoned programmers, writing one large application can sometimes be less daunting than adding code to most of the pages on a Web site.

Active Server Pages

Active Server Pages, or ASP, provides a framework for building Web applications using HTML, scripts, and ActiveX components. You create an ASP page by embedding scripts in your HTML page. When a user requests an ASP page, the server executes the scripts embedded within the page, and the output of the scripts is included as part of the HTML so that any browser can view the page.

ASP supports VBScript and JavaScript by default, and support is available for other languages, including Perl. The first time a user downloads an ASP page, the scripts in the page are compiled. The server stores the compiled source until the code changes, at which time the code is recompiled and stored again. By using this caching method, ASP avoids many of the performance issues that plague CGI programming because the scripts don't need to be recompiled to respond to every request.

Look at the three separate parts of ASP: ActiveX components, scripts, and HTML pages. One of the difficulties in describing ASP is the sheer volume of acronyms that Microsoft uses to describe their technologies, as you'll soon find out.

ActiveX Components

The underlying piece of the ASP puzzle is the ActiveX component. An ActiveX component is a piece of software that runs within the context of a runtime environment, in this case IIS. Most people are familiar with ActiveX components that can be downloaded and executed in Microsoft's Internet Explorer Web browser, but there are also ActiveX components that provide functionality to the Web server. ASP pages work by interfacing with these components.

 ActiveX components are also referred to as *ActiveX controls.*

For example, one of the most commonly used ActiveX components conforms to the Microsoft technology known as Active Data Objects (ADO). An ADO component acts as the middle man between an ASP page and a relational database. For example, if you want to retrieve records from a Microsoft Access database, your scripts call the ADO component, which in turn requests the data from the Access database.

ASP components support Microsoft's Component Object Model (COM), and they can be written in most programming languages, including C++, Java, Visual Basic, and Cobol.

To extend the functionality of ASP, all you must do is write new components. Even better, many third-party components are available, and more are being written every day. A list of third-party components is available at the ASP developers' site (http://www.genusa.com/asp/).

A tactic that has become quite popular with ASP programmers is to create components in Visual Basic or C++ to encapsulate all of the functionality required for the Web application. Rather than writing code in ASP and placing it within your pages, you can create COM components and reference them from within your ASP pages. This allows you to write most of your logic in a compiled language that's easier to test and maintain. You can catch a lot of the errors in your code when it's compiled, rather than letting them slip through until runtime. Also, most application programming environments have an advantage over technologies like ASP: they make it easier to write structured, sensible code.

Scripts

ASP scripts are embedded in HTML documents and are used to interface with ASP components. The scripts are compiled by the Web server and are executed by the server when the page is requested. The output from the script is inserted into the Web page in place of the script code, so users downloading the page see what appears to be a normal HTML page.

12

The scripts can be written in any of several languages, including VBScript and JScript (Microsoft's version of JavaScript). Microsoft has also added support for third-party scripting languages, like ActiveWare's PerlScript, which can be used to embed Perl scripts into your Web pages.

Look at the sample code in Listing 12.1. In this example, I've embedded some ASP script statements in a document. The if statements print an error message if an error was produced by a script statement from a previous part of the document. The first if statement checks to see whether there was an error, and if there was it prints an error message based on the value of the last_error variable.

LISTING 12.1   An ASP Code Sample

```
[ve]
last_error = 1
[ve]
<% if (last_error <> "") then  %>
<TABLE>
    <TR>
        <TH><FONT COLOR=#FFFFFF>ERROR:</FONT>
            <% if (last_error = 1) then %>
                <FONT COLOR=#FFFFFF>Invalid Login</FONT>
            <% End If %>
            <% if (last_error = 2) then %>
                <FONT COLOR=#FFFFFF>Invalid Social Security Number</FONT>
            <% End If %>
        </TH>
    </TR>
</TABLE>
<% End If %>
```

As you already know, HTML tags are enclosed in greater-than and less-than signs, like this: <TAG>. To set ASP script statements apart from standard HTML tags, percent signs are used within the greater-than and less-than signs, like this: <% script code %>.

An HTML document containing ASP scripts can also include client-side scripts, which are designed to be executed in the browser. The separate coding method that ASP scripts use (with the percentage signs) make it easy to differentiate server-side from client-side scripts.

HTML Pages

No matter how you create your ASP components and scripts, by the time they get to the browser they look like normal HTML pages. All the code you insert into your pages is compiled and executed by the server, and the output is included in the page as normal HTML code.

One of the main advantages of ASP is that you can do most of your coding in HTML and add functionality by adding a small amount of ASP code to the pages. Instead of writing programs to build your pages, you can build your pages and augment them through small programs.

Other ASP Platforms

Since its release, ASP has gained popularity as a tool for creating Web applications. To take advantage of this popularity, Chili!Soft has created Chili!ASP, which adds ASP functionality to Netscape's FastTrack and Enterprise servers for Windows NT. O'Reilly has also added ASP support to its WebSite Professional Web server for Windows NT. You can learn more information on Chili!ASP at `http://www.chilisoft.net`.

Allaire ColdFusion

ColdFusion is an application server that was originally available for Windows NT Web servers. Since its release, it has been ported to Solaris and HP-UX, and a Linux version is forthcoming. It supports a number of Web server programming interfaces, including Netscape's NSAPI, Microsoft's ISAPI, and CGI. There's also a Cold Fusion Apache module for both Windows NT and UNIX. Cold Fusion is similar to ASP in the way that it operates. To create dynamic pages, you simply embed the special Cold Fusion tags into your Web pages, and the Cold Fusion application interprets those tags and inserts standard HTML in their place before the document is sent to the user.

The main difference between Cold Fusion and ASP is that each "program statement" in Cold Fusion is contained in a single tag, whereas in ASP, the programmer can create blocks of code that look more like traditional statements. This makes it easier to write more structured programs in ASP; on the other hand, people who know HTML but not a programming language will have an easier time adapting to ColdFusion.

ColdFusion Sample Code

Let's look at some sample code to explain how ColdFusion works. I know that I haven't explained how to use CGI with relational databases yet, so bear with this example. An overview of SQL is provided in Hour 15, "Session (State) Management. The strength of ColdFusion is its ability to easily interface with relational databases, and process the

12

results of a query. ColdFusion uses a custom set of tags to embed application logic in a Web page. This set of tags is referred to as CFML—the Cold Fusion Markup Language.

For example, let's look at a query that retrieves a list of addresses from a database, and then prints them out. The first part of the example connects to the database and executes a SQL query which returns a list of addresses. The second part of the example loops over the results of the query and displays them on a page. The sample code appears in Listing 12.2.

LISTING 12.2 CFML that Queries a Database and Displays the Results of the Query

```
<CFQUERY NAME="get_addresses" DATASOURCE="address_book">
    SELECT name, address, city, state, zip
    FROM Addresses
</CFQUERY>

<CFOUTPUT QUERY="get_addresses">
    <P>
    #name#<BR>
    #address#<BR>
    #city#, #state#  #zip#
    </P>
</CFOUTPUT>
```

Now let me explain how the code works. The `<CFQUERY>` tag is used to execute a query against a particular data source, in this case, `address_book`. Data sources are set up in the ColdFusion Administrator, so the server already knows which database, username, and password are associated with the `address_book` data source. The query is also assigned a name so that the results can be accessed later.

Inside the `<CFQUERY>` tag is a SQL `SELECT` statement that retrieves all the addresses from the table `Addresses`. After the query has been executed, the `<CFOUTPUT>` tag is used to display the results of the query. The existence of the `QUERY` attribute in the `<CFOUTPUT>` tag indicates that the tag should loop over the results of the query, one row at a time (the query returns the results as one address per row). The actual text and HTML to be displayed is placed within the `<CFOUTPUT>` tags. The expressions surrounded by hash symbols (#) are evaluated and replaced with the values assigned to them. So `#name#` is replaced with the value in the name column from the current row, and so on.

The Apache `mod_perl` Module

The Apache Web server is built using a group of programs referred to as modules. When the Apache Web server receives a request for a particular document, it is sent to several modules, which check to see whether they are supposed to handle the request. To extend the Apache Web server, a user can write new modules in C. Of course, writing new modules in C to extend the functionality of your Web server is not an easy task. Chances are, if you're doing this type of thing you probably aren't interested in *Teach Yourself CGI Programming 24 Hours*.

On the other hand, a particular module called mod_perl combines the Perl interpreter with the Apache server. Among other things, this enables you to run your Perl CGI scripts using the mod_perl module, which eliminates the overhead of starting Perl and compiling your scripts every time they're requested. Running your scripts through the embedded Perl interpreter instead of the regular Perl interpreter can improve the performance of your scripts drastically, and many Perl CGI scripts will run under mod_perl without any changes.

mod_perl also provides Perl programs with access to Apache's API (Application Programming Interface), so even if you don't know how to program in C, you can use Perl to write extensions to your Web server. The API provides hooks that you can use to extend or modify any of the functionality built into the Web server.

Apache is the most popular Web server on the Internet. In a recent survey, Apache had more than 50 percent of the Web server market. Apache is written and maintained entirely by a group of volunteers and is always on the leading edge of Web technology. Despite the fact that it is available for free, it offers some of the most advanced features of any Web server and offers performance comparable with any commercial Web server. For more information on the Apache project, check out its home page at http://www.apache.org.

To learn more about Perl/Apache integration and mod_perl, you should visit the Perl/Apache Integration Project at http://perl.apache.org.

Porting Your Scripts from CGI to mod_perl

Thanks to the Apache::Registry module, you don't have to do much work to move your Perl scripts from CGI to the mod_perl interface. You can set up the Apache Web server to execute files with certain extensions using the mod_perl interface, or you can register certain directories as containing files that should be executed through mod_perl.

You can run into a few snags when you run existing Perl scripts using mod_perl; be on the lookout for them. All of these snags arise from the very capability that provides the biggest advantage: the Perl interpreter used by mod_perl doesn't exit after your script is finished running.

Because the interpreter stays active all the time, things don't necessarily get cleaned up properly after it executes a script. The global variables retain their values, and unclosed files stay open. Because of this, flaky behavior can sometimes occur when a program

12

expects a variable to be empty but it contains the value that was placed there the last time the script ran. To avoid these types of problems, remember to be tidy with your code. The easiest way to enforce tidiness on yourself is to run all your scripts by launching the Perl interpreter with the -w flag, which provides warnings for all types of problems that might not seem obvious. You should also include the line use strict; at the beginning of your programs, which makes sure that you don't create errant global variables.

Another programming practice that you should avoid is using the exit() function in your mod_perl scripts. The exit() function closes the Perl interpreter, so the next time a mod_perl script is called, the Perl interpreter must be restarted. This can rapidly eliminate any performance gains from using mod_perl. You should write your scripts so that they exit naturally (by running out of statements to execute) instead of ending them in the middle. If you want to cheat, you can set a label at the very end of the program, and replace the calls you would have made to exit() with goto statements that point to the label.

PHP

PHP is one of the oldest embedded scripting languages for Web pages. It includes a fairly extensive set of commands that enable you to process forms, gather information from databases, and include conditional statements (like if...else) in your Web pages. For PHP documentation and examples, as well as the actual software distribution, you should see the PHP home page at http://www.php.net.

PHP can run on any UNIX Web server that supports CGI, like the CERN server or NCSA HTTPD. It also ships as an Apache module, so if you use the Apache server, you can compile the PHP engine into your Web server for better performance. On other servers, the PHP CGI script works by appending extra path information on the end of the path to the php.cgi program. Best of all, PHP is completely free and is distributed as open source software.

Although PHP works fine as a CGI program, it doesn't really shine unless it's run as an Apache module. Naturally, there can be performance issues when you run the CGI version of PHP because the Web server must launch the php.cgi program, which in turn must load the page and parse all the PHP commands. In addition to improved performance, the Apache module provides a lot of features that the CGI version doesn't, like enhanced security and advanced configuration options. Finally, you can write extensions to PHP to add functionality to the Apache server without writing new modules.

Another powerful feature of PHP is its capability to provide native connectivity to many relational databases, including Oracle, Sybase, Postgres, MySQL, and Adabas. It also supports ODBC, which is a standard database interface supported by many databases.

Examples Using PHP

The PHP scripting language is actually quite robust. It provides all the functions and commands that one would expect in a regular language, and the syntax is somewhat similar to C or Perl. Here's a basic example from the documentation.

First, suppose you created a simple form like this:

```
<FORM ACTION="display.php3" METHOD=post>
<INPUT TYPE="text" NAME="name">
<INPUT TYPE="text" NAME="age">
<INPUT TYPE="submit">
</FORM>
```

The `action` attribute sends the output from the form to the `display.php3` file, which is an HTML file with embedded PHP script commands. The PHP interpreter automatically translates the output from the form into variables that can be accessed from within the `display.php3` page. For example, the command to print the value that the user entered in the name and age fields of the form is

```
<?echo "<P>Hi $name, you are $age years old!</P>" ?>
```

Now, look at a slightly more advanced script. Using `if...else` statements, you can print specific messages depending on the value the user entered in the age field of the form:

```
<?
    if ($age > 50);
        echo "<P>Hi $name, you are ancient!</P>";
    elseif ($age > 30);
        echo "<P>Hi $name, you are very old!</P>";
    else;
        echo "Hi $name.";
    endif;
?>
```

Finally, examine PHP's database support. Listing 12.3 demonstrates how to connect to a MySQL database.

LISTING 12.3 An Example of a PHP Script that Includes a Database Connection

```
<?     $hostname = "dbhost.example.com";
       $username = "dbuser";
       $password = "dbpassword";

       mysql_connect($hostname, $username, $password);
       mysql_select_db("some_database");

       $query = "select name, address, city, state, zip ";
       $query = $query . "from addresses ";
```

continues

12

LISTING 12.3   continued

```
$result = mysql_query($query);
$rows = mysql_numrows($result);

$i = 0;

while ($i < $rows) {
        $name = mysql_result($result, $i, "name");
        $address = mysql_result($result, $i, "address");
        $city = mysql_result($result, $i, "city");
        $state = mysql_result($result, $i, "state");
        $zip = mysql_result($result, $i, "zip");

        print "<p>\n";
        print "$name<br>\n";
        print "$address<br>\n";
        print "$city, $state  $zip\n";
        print "</p>\n\n";
        $i++;
}
?>
```

First, the program assigns some variables that are passed to the `mysql_connect` function as arguments. Then, the `mysql_select_db` function is used to indicate which database is to be used on the server it just connected to. The `$query` variable is initiated, and the SQL query to be executed is assigned to it. The value of `$query` is then passed to the `mysql_query` function to execute the query against the database. The number of rows retrieved is fetched using the `mysql_numrows` function.

At that point, you're ready to display the results of the query. A `while` loop is used to iterate over all the rows in the results, and display the address from each row. `$i` is a counter that is incremented every time through the loop, which stops executing when `$i` is equal to `$rows`, the number of rows retrieved using the query.

Of course, many more functions and capabilities are built into the PHP package. To learn more about them, you should visit the PHP home page.

Server-Side Java

Java has attained popularity as a language useful for building applets, which are small applications that run in Web browsers. As Java's popularity has increased, however, it has become more popular for writing all kinds of applications. One example of the widening reach of the Java platform is servlet technology. *Servlets* are Java applications that are executed by Web servers to provide additional functionality.

As I've stated elsewhere, one of the problems with many CGI replacements is that they lock you in to a particular Web server. If you write your programs for the Netscape Server API, you must port all your code to another language or API if you want to change to another Web server. The same can be said for Apache modules, ASP pages, or many of the other technologies discussed in this hour.

Sun has created the Java Servlet Development Kit to try to get around this problem. The number one benefit of the Java environment is portability. Sun has made the Java Virtual Machine, which is used to execute Java applications, available on a wide number of platforms. If a computer has the Java Virtual Machine installed, it should be capable of running any Java application, regardless of where the application was compiled. Sun refers to this in its marketing literature as "Write Once, Run Anywhere." The JSDK provides the API necessary to write Java classes that function as Web applications.

The JSDK includes the reference implementation of the servlet engine. The reference implementation is not designed for production Web servers, rather it implements the entire Java servlet standard. It is useful for testing servlets, and is the model upon which other servlet engines are based. There are a number of commercial products that can be used with Web servers to add servlet support. One of the most popular is New Atlanta's ServletExec product (`http://www.newatlanta.com`), which provides support for servlets for a number of popular Web servers, including Apache, IIS, and Netscape Web servers. The Apache Software Group is also building an Apache module, `mod_jserv`, to add Java support to the Apache Web server. The advantage of `mod_jserv` is that it's free, open source software. You can find out more at `http://java.apache.org`.

There are also a number of other application servers that support servlets. For more information on servlets, you might want to check out `http://www.servlets.com`. To download the official JSDK and get the official word on servlets from Sun, go to `http://java.sun.com/products/servlet`.

12

Summary

As you can see from this hour, there are plenty of ways not to use CGI and still build powerful Web-based applications. Much like CGI, there are tradeoffs that come with all these technologies. One thing that you give up as you move away from CGI is portability. CGI is available for nearly every Web server, and the languages used to write CGI programs (such as C, Perl, and UNIX shell scripting) are very portable as well. As you move to proprietary application platforms, you might find yourself locked into a solution that's not the best choice for the long run.

Q&A

Q Are any of the packages described in this hour preconfigured for particular applications, like electronic commerce?

A No. This hour discussed open platforms usable for creating pretty much any type of Web application. There's another, even longer list of products that are designed for specific applications like publishing Web content or developing electronic commerce sites. Some of those products are built on top of the products mentioned here.

Q Does my ISP support (insert CGI alternative here)?

A I don't know. Many CGI alternatives are complicated and expensive. Others pretty much require that you have a server dedicated to your application. That means that you won't be able to host your application in a shared hosting environment the way you can with static HTML files or basic CGI scripts. On the other hand, there are many ISPs that do support some of the popular application servers, including PHP, Cold Fusion, and ASP. You just need to do some research to find out if your ISP is one of them.

Q Are more CGI alternatives available?

A Of course. This hour is really only the tip of the iceberg when it comes to CGI alternatives. Application back-ends for Web sites are one of the hottest areas of growth in the software industry right now. Although the technologies described in this hour can give you a good starting point, you should always be on the lookout for technologies that can make the job of building Web applications easier and better.

Workshop

The quiz questions are designed to strengthen the knowledge you gain each hour. The exercises help you build on that knowledge by providing you with the opportunity to apply it to real problems. For answers to the quiz questions, refer to Appendix A, "Answers."

Quiz

1. What is the difference between technologies like ISAPI and CGI?
2. What are the three parts of ASP pages?
3. True or false: PHP is only available as an Apache module.
4. True or false: Java servlets are a closed standard supported only by a Sun product.

Exercises

1. Before you choose a particular product to use, you should first define the problem you're trying to solve. When you have in mind what exactly you're trying to do, you can select the product that makes the most sense in solving the problem. Therefore, before running out and trying all these technologies, determine what the Web application you're going to create will do.

2. The great thing about most of these application servers is that there are free versions available to download for evaluation. (Some of them, like PHP and ASP, are just free, period!) You should try downloading one for your Web server platform and seeing how you like it.

12

PART IV

Building Basic CGI Applications

Hour

HOUR 13

Using Flat Files for Data Storage

One thing most applications of any complexity require is persistent data storage. Whether you're creating an online message board, a catalog, or just allowing users to register, your programs need to be able to retrieve existing data and store new data entered by users. There are a number of ways to add data storage capabilities to your programs. One of the simplest is to store the data in a flat-file database—which is nothing more than a plain text file.

In this hour you will learn:

- What, exactly, a database is
- What defines a flat-file database
- How to build an application that retrieves data from a flat-file database and displays it using HTML
- How to build applications that add, delete, and modify data in a flat-file database

What Is a Database?

In the simplest terms, a database is simply a place to store multiple chunks of similar data. Each chunk of data is known as a *record,* and each piece of information in a record is known as a *field.* Every record in a database contains the same number and type of fields. If you use an address book with your email client, for example, the file that stores all the addresses is a database. In this case, the database contains a record for every user, and the fields might be the user's real name and email address. If your database were a Rolodex, each card in the Rolodex would be a record, and each separate piece of information on the card would be a field.

Of course, there are also enormous databases that store millions of records, like the ones that banks use to keep track of all their accounts. Although your email address book and the bank's account database might not have much in common, they do share the fact that they're repositories for multiple incidences of the same type of record.

There are different types of databases, but the two most common are flat-file databases and relational databases. I am going to discuss flat-file databases in this hour, and then relational databases in Hour 19, "Working with Relational Databases."

Flat-File Databases

A *flat-file database* is simply a plain text file that stores multiple records separated by delimiters. A *delimiter* is a character, or group of characters, that indicates where one record (or field) ends and another begins. Flat-file databases ordinarily use one delimiter to indicate the breaks between records, and a different delimiter to indicate the breaks between the fields that make up a record. Alternatively, if you know what size each field is going to be, you can split the data up by assigning a width to each field.

If you know, for example, that the colon (:) character isn't going to appear within the data in your file, you could use the colon to separate the fields in each record. Another popular method of delimiting fields is to separate each field with a tab. In most character sets, a tab is an individual character, not just a set number of spaces.

> More often than not, in a flat-file database, the end of line character is used as a delimiter between records.

Delimiting Data Using Characters

Let's look at a common database that uses characters to delimit data fields, the UNIX password file. On almost every computer running the UNIX operating system, there is a file that contains a list of the users who can log in to the system. It contains their usernames, an encrypted version of their passwords, their real names, their home directories, and some other information. All this information is stored in a flat-file database (usually located at /etc/passwd). Each line of the file is a separate record, because the linefeed character is the delimiter between records. The fields are separated using colons. Let's take a look at a snippet from a typical password file:

```
jsmith:VFSRFd2adlS8g:998:100:Joe Smith:/usr3/home/jsmith:/bin/tcsh
rjones:BglAiMro/BHJQ:999:100:Robert Jones:/usr3/home/rjones:/bin/tcsh
bwhite:tQ6pGzsWB6.FQ:587:100:Beth White:/usr3/home/bwhite:/bin/tcsh
```

The fields are as follows: username, encrypted password, user ID number, group ID, real name, home directory, and shell. Although the UNIX password file is a good example of a flat-file database, it's not something you want to provide access to over the Web!

Delimiting Data Using Field Widths

Now let's take a look at a file that is broken up based on the widths of the data fields. In this case, let's say that the file is a check register. Each line in the database represents a separate check. A line contains the account number (10 digits), the check number (four digits), the date the check was cashed (six digits), and the amount of the check (eight digits). Here's some sample data:

```
01234567890001120497003505O
11223344550005110497002551l
```

Let's take a look at the first line. The account number is 0123456789, the check number is 0001, the date is April 12, 1997, and the check was written for $350.50 (we assume that the last two digits of the amount are supposed to be after the decimal point).

You might notice from this data that the database is somewhat "brittle." What I mean by this is that the field layout governs what types of values can be placed in each field. For example, what happens if the check number is above 9999? It will be too large for the field in the record that is meant to hold it. If you try to make that field larger, you have to change all the programs that know how to read data stored in this format.

The main advantage of using data that is delimited according to field width in is conservation of space. Because you know how much data each record can hold, you know exactly how much space your database takes up, no matter what appears in the records. However, it's not often that I have such an apt and obvious example of why writing applications in a particular way can be really bad. The only reason I mention this method is that many existing systems do provide data formatted this way, so you should understand how it works in case you have to use these types of files with your CGI programs. I wouldn't advocate storing your own data in this manner.

13

File Operations

Before I go into a specific example of an application, let me explain how accessing a flat-file database works in general. There are four operations that you might want to perform—reading a record, adding a record, deleting a record, and modifying a record. Let's look at the steps required to perform each of these operations.

Retrieving Records from a Database

1. Find some information that will allow you to identify the record or records you need to retrieve.
2. Open the file in which the data is stored.
3. Search through all the records in the file until you find the ones that match the information you're looking for.
4. Copy the data from the file into a data structure that can be accessed from within your program.
5. Close the file.

Inserting a Record into a Database

1. Adapt the data that will be stored in the record to the format used by records in the database.
2. Lock the file so that no other processes can write to the file while it's open. (I'll discuss file locking later in the hour.)
3. Open the database file for writing.
4. Write the record to the end of the file (also known as *appending* the record).
5. Close the file.
6. Unlock the file.

Deleting Records from a Database

1. Find some information that you can use to identify the record or records that you want to delete.
2. Lock the file so that no other process can write to the file while it's open.
3. Open the file for reading and writing.
4. Read all the records into memory.
5. Remove all the records from the file.
6. Write all the records that are stored in memory, except those to be deleted, to the file.
7. Close the file.
8. Unlock the file.

Modifying a Record in a Database

1. Find some information that you can use to identify the record you want to modify.

2. Lock the database file.

3. Open the file for reading and writing.

4. Read all the records into memory.

5. In memory, replace the information in the record that you want to modify with the updated information.

6. Remove all the records from the file.

7. Write all the records that are stored in memory to the file.

8. Close the file.

9. Unlock the file.

> Note that when you modify a record in a flat file, the easiest method is to read all of the records into memory and then write them all back to the file after modifying the appropriate record. If your database is very large, this can cause your program to run very slowly. If you begin running into performance problems when you modify records, you should consider moving to a more robust type of database, like a relational database.

File Locking

I mentioned file locking in the descriptions of some of the flat-file database transactions. Locking a file grants the locking process exclusive access to the file until the lock is released. This prevents various problems involved with two processes trying to write information to the same file at the same time.

Locking is important when you use flat-file databases in a CGI environment because the probability of receiving concurrent requests that modify the same file is high. If you don't use file locking to keep multiple instances of the same program from stomping on each other, you can wind up losing data, or worse, with a corrupt database file. File locking ensures that updates are never lost, and that concurrent writes are avoided.

The problem generally associated with the need for file locking is referred to as the *lost update problem*. This problem arises when two transactions try to modify the same record concurrently. Let's say that two travel agents are both trying to reserve the last seat on a flight at the same time. Both check the availability and see that one seat is available. The first agent checks the availability and finds that there is an opening, then the second agent

13

checks the availability and also sees that there's an opening. The first agent then reserves the seat. Since the second agent checked the availability between the first agent's checking the seat and posting the reservation, they also reserve the seat, overwriting the first agent's registration. The first agent's update is lost.

If some locking scheme were implemented, then the interaction would go quite differently. The first agent would obtain a lock on the file (or table, if this were a relational database application), check the availability, and then post the reservation. In the meantime, the second agent would attempt to obtain a lock on the resource but would have to wait until the first agent's transaction is complete. At that point, the reservation would already be posted and the second agent would not be able to book the seat.

After you've opened the file and have obtained an exclusive lock on it, you should perform all the operations on the file as quickly as possible. When a file is locked, all the other processes that want to write to the file have to wait. If there are bunches of Web requests coming in at the same time, you can really slow down access to your CGI program with file locking because it's a bottleneck. Any way you can minimize the amount of time that the file is locked will help.

Building a Database Application

Now that you know which steps you need to take to perform various operations on flat-file databases, and you know how to use file locking to give your programs exclusive access to files when you modify them, I'm going to explain how to perform each of those operations using Perl programs. When appropriate, the examples use file locking to gain exclusive access to the files, and wrap the file modification code in an `eval` construct so that any errors can be trapped and reported to users in a friendly manner.

The Sample Database

Before I can demonstrate any scripts that make use of a database, I need to explain the structure of the sample database itself. This database is very simple. It contains one record per line, and each record contains three fields: name, email address, and browser preference. The fields are delimited by single tab characters. The sample database, which contains three records, is included in Listing 13.1.

LISTING **13.1**   The Sample Flat-File Database

```
Rafe Colburn     rafe@rc3.org     Netscape
John Doe     nobody@rc3.org     Internet Explore
Tom Sawyer     tom@rc3.org     Opera
```

Retrieving Records from the Database

The first example demonstrates how to retrieve records from a flat-file database. This program allows the user to enter a name to search for, and then returns all the records from the file with names that contain the string the user entered. So, if they enter the string "john" in the form, any users whose names contain "john" will be returned. The search is not case-sensitive. Names like "John Smith" and "Samuel Johnson" will be matched by that search.

This script follows a structure that should be familiar to you. If a request for the program is received without a query, the form is displayed. If the query has been submitted, the database is loaded and the names in the file are compared to the value submitted by the user. Any records from the database with names that match the value submitted will be displayed.

The source code to the script appears in Listing 13.2. I'll walk you through the code to explain exactly how it works, but I'm going to skip the parts that you should already know about from previous hours. On line 6, I set the variable $guest_file to the name of the file that serves as the guest database. If the file was stored in a directory other than the directory in which the script resides, this variable would also contain the path to that file.

LISTING 13.2   The Source Code to the `retrieve.pl` Script

```
 1: #!c:/perl/bin/perl
 2:
 3: use CGI;
 4: $query = new CGI;
 5:
 6: $guest_file = "guests.txt";
 7:
 8: &print_page_start;
 9:
10: if ($query->param()) {
11:     $search_name = $query->param('search_name');
12:
13:     # Wrap this code in an eval block in order to trap
14:     # errors.
15:     eval {
16:     open (GUESTS, "< $guest_file") or
17:         die "Can't open $guest_file: $!";
18:     while (<GUESTS>) {
19:             chomp;
20:         ($name, $email, $browser) = split /\t/;
21:         if ($name =~ /$search_name/i) {
22:         print "$name<BR>\n$email<BR>\n$browser<BR>\n<HR>\n";
23:             }
```

13

continues

LISTING 13.2   continued

```
24:        }
25:        }
26: }
27: else {
28:        print "<FORM>\n";
29:        print "<INPUT TYPE=\"text\" NAME=\"search_name\"><BR>\n";
30:        print "<INPUT TYPE=\"submit\">\n";
31:        print "</FORM>\n";
32: }
33:
34: chomp $@;
35: if ($@) {
36:        print "ERROR: $@<BR>\n";
37: }
38:
39: &print_page_end;
40:
41: sub print_page_start {
42:        print $query->header;
43:        print "<HTML>\n<HEAD>\n<TITLE>Search for Records</TITLE>\n";
44:        print "</HEAD>\n<BODY>\n";
45:        print "<H1>Search for Records</H1>\n";
46: }
47:
48: sub print_page_end {
49:        print "</BODY>\n</HTML>\n";
50: }
```

Lines 10–32 contain the main logic for the application. The if statement in line 10 tests for the existence of query parameters, and if none exist, the query form is displayed. If query parameters do exist, the script proceeds to search the database and display matching records.

Line 15 opens an eval block. These blocks are used to encapsulate the code within them so that if a problem occurs during the execution of the code within the block, the program won't exit. Instead, the exception will be trapped, and execution of the program continues after the eval block is closed (in this case, on line 24). The eval block ensures that execution of the program can continue even if the program is unable to access the database file.

Lines 16 and 17 open the database file for input. The < operator indicates that the file should be used as input for the program. I assign the filehandle GUESTS to the open file. The or die construct throws an error if the database can't be opened. The program might not be able to open the file because the Web server process doesn't have read access to it, or because it doesn't exist. Under normal circumstances, the program would exit if the die function was called, printing the message in quotation marks. (The variable $! is a special variable containing the operating system's error message.) Because the code appears inside an eval block, the die command is trapped and the error message is stored for later.

After the filehandle is open, you have to parse through the records in the file one by one and compare them to the search term entered by the user. The while loop that begins on line 18 does just that. while (<GUESTS>) is a Perl expression that pulls lines out of the GUESTS filehandle one at a time, and makes them available within the loop using the special variable $_.

One interesting thing about the variable $_ is that many Perl functions know they should use it as an argument if no other argument is specified. When you're iterating over the lines in a text file, the current line being processed is automatically stored in $_. For example, line 19 contains only a call to the chomp function. An argument of $_ is implied. The chomp function removes the line feed at the end of the current record.

Line 20 splits the record into individual fields using the split function. Ordinarily, the split function accepts two arguments, the field delimiter and the expression to be split. However, like the chomp function, it will automatically split the value in $_ if no expression to be split is passed to it. The first argument is the delimiter; in this case, the delimiter is /\t/. The \t meta-character indicates that the record should be split on tabs.

After the record has been split into fields, the if statement on line 21 uses the binding operator to figure out whether the search term is part of the name field, which is stored in the variable $name. If it is, the record is printed using the print statement on line 22.

After the main program dling code, which spans lines 34–37, is executed. $@ is a special variable used to store any error message returned by the eval block. If that variable was set (due to an error being trapped by eval), the error message is displayed. After errors are handled, the end of the HTML is printed. The results of a database search with the name field left empty are displayed in Figure 13.1.

Inserting a Record into the Database

The next task is to insert a record into the database. This script is a bit more complex than the retrieval script because it has to lock the file before the new record can be inserted. It also includes some validation code to make sure that the user enters something in every field. The other significant difference is that the form contains three fields instead of one. The full source code for the script appears in Listing 13.3.

13

FIGURE **13.1**

*The results of a suc-
cessful search with*
retrieve.pl.

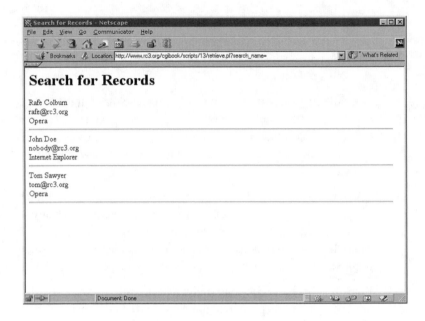

LISTING 13.3   The Source Code for insert.pl

```
 1: #!c:/perl/bin/perl
 2:
 3: use CGI;
 4: $query = new CGI;
 5:
 6: $guest_file = "guests.txt";
 7: @browsers = ("Netscape", "Internet Explorer", "Opera");
 8:
 9: &print_page_start;
10:
11: if ($query->param()) {
12:     if (&valid_form) {
13:     # Create the record to be inserted
14:     $record = $query->param('name') . "\t";
15:     $record .= $query->param('email') . "\t";
16:     $record .= $query->param('browser') . "\n";
17:
18:     # Wrap this code in an eval block in order to trap
19:     # errors.
20:     eval {
21:         open (GUESTS, ">> $guest_file") or
22:         die "Can't open $guest_file: $!";
23:         flock GUESTS, 2;
24:         print GUESTS $record;
25:         close GUESTS;
26:         print "<P>New record inserted.</P>\n";
```

```
27:      }
28:      }
29:      else {
30:      &print_form;
31:      }
32: }
33: else {
34:      &print_form;
35: }
36:
37: # If an error occurred, let the user know.
38: chomp $@;
39: if ($@) {
40:      print "ERROR: $@<BR>\n";
41: }
42:
43: &print_page_end;
44:
45: sub print_page_start {
46:      print $query->header;
47:      print "<HTML>\n<HEAD>\n<TITLE>Search for Records</TITLE>\n";
48:      print "</HEAD>\n<BODY>\n";
49:      print "<H1>Search for Records</H1>\n";
50: }
51:
52: sub print_form {
53:      print "<P>\n<FORM>\n";
54:      if (!$query->param()) {
55:      print "Name: <INPUT TYPE=\"text\" NAME=\"name\"><BR>\n";
56:      print "Email: <INPUT TYPE=\"text\" NAME=\"email\"><BR>\n";
57:      print "Browser:<BR>";
58:      foreach $browser (@browsers) {
59:          print "<INPUT TYPE=\"radio\" NAME=\"browser\" ";
60:          print "VALUE=\"$browser\">$browser<BR>\n";
61:      }
62:      }
63:      else {
64:      print "Name: <INPUT TYPE=\"text\" NAME=\"name\" ";
65:      print "VALUE=\"", $query->param('name'), "\"><BR>\n";
66:      print "Email: <INPUT TYPE=\"text\" NAME=\"email\" ";
67:      print "VALUE=\"", $query->param('email'), "\"><BR>\n";
68:      print "Browser:<BR>";
69:      foreach $browser (@browsers) {
70:          print "<INPUT TYPE=\"radio\" NAME=\"browser\" ";
71:          print "VALUE=\"$browser\"";
72:          if ($browser eq $query->param('browser')) {
73:          print " CHECKED";
74:          }
75:          print ">$browser<BR>\n";
76:      }
77:      }
```

13

continues

LISTING 13.3   continued

```
 78:        print "<INPUT TYPE=\"submit\">\n";
 79:        print "</FORM>\n</P>\n";
 80: }
 81:
 82: sub valid_form {
 83:        $return_code = 1;
 84:        if (!$query->param('name')) {
 85:        print "You must enter a name.<BR>\n";
 86:        $return_code = 0;
 87:        }
 88:        if (!$query->param('email')) {
 89:        print "You must enter an email address.<BR>\n";
 90:        $return_code = 0;
 91:        }
 92:        if (!$query->param('browser')) {
 93:        print "You must select a browser.<BR>\n";
 94:        $return_code = 0;
 95:        }
 96:        return $return_code;
 97: }
 98:
 99:
100: sub print_page_end {
101:        print "</BODY>\n</HTML>\n";
102: }
```

There's a bit less to explain with this script than the last one because some parts are very similar. For example, in this script, on line 6, the $guest_file variable is set, just like in the last script. On the next line, an array called @browsers is created. On the form, there's a list of browsers from which the user can choose their favorite. The options for that list are set using this array. Adding or removing browsers is as simple as editing the list.

The main script logic runs from lines 11–35. First, there's a condition to check whether parameters have been passed to the script. If not, the subroutine print_form is used to print out the form for the first time. If parameters were received, the valid_form subroutine is called in line 12. If the form is valid, the record is appended to the file. If the form is not valid, the form is printed again so that the user can make the necessary corrections.

The valid_form subroutine itself (lines 82–97) just checks to make sure that the user entered a value in all three form fields. If this script was more than just an example in a book, you might want to perform more extensive validation on the form fields to make sure that the user entered something that actually looks like a name and an email address, but to save space, I just checked to make sure they entered something.

The code used to print the form the first time, and print an error and reprint the form in the case of bad input, isn't anything exciting. The code is in the print_form subroutine, which runs from lines 52–80.

The important part of the script is the code that appends a new record to the database file. This code is in an eval block that begins at line 20 and ends at line 27. Before the record is inserted, it has to be created. The variable assignment statements on lines 14, 15, and 16 copy the values from the parameters to the variable $record, which is used to store the new record for the database.

Now let's look at the inside of the eval block. Like the previous script, this one uses the open function to open a filehandle called GUESTS that accesses the file named in the $guest_file variable. In this case, the filehandle is opened for appending, not for input. The >> operator indicates that anything printed to the GUESTS filehandle should be appended to the end of the file. As in the previous example, the or die construct is included to handle errors.

In line 23, the flock function is used to get a lock on the GUESTS filehandle. (If necessary, flock waits for any other process that has already locked the file.) The flock function itself accepts two arguments, the filehandle that points to the file to be locked, and the type of lock to obtain. In CGI scripts, you want an exclusive lock, so the second argument is 2.

On line 24, the $record variable is printed to the GUESTS filehandle, appending the record to the end of the file. On line 25, the filehandle is closed. When the filehandle is closed, Perl automatically releases the lock on the file, allowing other processes to obtain a lock on the file and modify it.

Figure 13.2 shows the form used to enter a new record, and Listing 13.4 is a listing of the database with a new record for Bill Clinton appended to it.

LISTING 13.4 The Updated Guest Database

```
Rafe Colburn     rafe@rc3.org      Opera
John Doe         nobody@rc3.org    Internet Explorer
Tom Sawyer       tom@rc3.org       Opera
Bill Clinton     president@whitehouse.gov      Netscape
```

13

Deleting Records from the Database

Now let's look at a script that's used to delete records from the database. It's again a bit more complicated than the previous script. Because it has to modify the existing contents of the file, and not just add a record onto the end, it has to open the file in read/write mode. It's similar to `retrieve.pl` in that the form accepts all or part of a name as input, and performs an operation (in this case, deletion) on all the records that match that name.

FIGURE 13.2

The new record form in the insert.pl *script.*

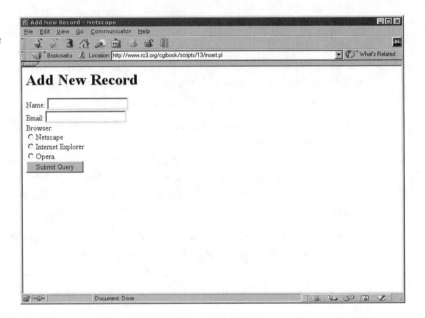

Let's take a look at the source code to the script. The full source code appears in Listing 13.5.

LISTING 13.5   The Source Code for the `delete.pl` Script

```perl
 1: #!c:/perl/bin/perl
 2:
 3: use CGI;
 4: $query = new CGI;
 5:
 6: $guest_file = "guests.txt";
 7:
 8: &print_page_start;
 9:
10: if ($query->param()) {
11:     $search_name = $query->param('search_name');
12:
13:     # Wrap this code in an eval block in order to trap
14:     # errors.
15:     eval {
16:     open (GUESTS, "+>> $guest_file") or
17:         die "Can't open $guest_file: $!";
18:     flock GUESTS, 2;
19:
```

```
20:     seek GUESTS, 0, 0;
21:     my @guests = <GUESTS>;
22:     my @new_guests = ();
23:
24:     foreach $guest (@guests) {
25:         ($name, $email, $browser) = split /\t/, $guest;
26:         if ($name !~ /$search_name/i) {
27:             push @new_guests, $guest;
28:         }
29:     }
30:     seek GUESTS, 0, 0;
31:     truncate GUESTS, 0;
32:     print GUESTS @new_guests;
33:     close GUESTS;
34:
35:     print "Record(s) deleted.\n";
36:     }
37: }
38: else {
39:     print "<FORM>\n";
40:     print "<INPUT TYPE=\"text\" NAME=\"search_name\"><BR>\n";
41:     print "<INPUT TYPE=\"submit\">\n";
42:     print "</FORM>\n";
43: }
44:
45: chomp $@;
46: if ($@) {
47:     print "ERROR: $@<BR>\n";
48: }
49:
50: &print_page_end;
51:
52: sub print_page_start {
53:     print $query->header;
54:     print "<HTML>\n<HEAD>\n<TITLE>Search for Records</TITLE>\n";
55:     print "</HEAD>\n<BODY>\n";
56:     print "<H1>Search for Records</H1>\n";
57: }
58:
59: sub print_page_end {
60:     print "</BODY>\n</HTML>\n";
61: }
```

13

Most of this script should be familiar to you, as it's not much different than the previous two scripts. The most important part of the script occurs within the eval block (lines 15–36) where the file is opened, locked, and modified.

The filehandle is opened on line 16. The operator +>> is used to open the file in this case. The + before the append operator indicates that the file should be opened in read/write mode. Because the file is opened in read/write mode, it is handled differently.

First, the process obtains an exclusive lock on the file using the `flock` function in line 18. In line 20, the program moves the pointer to the beginning of the file using the `seek` function. On line 21, the program copies the entire contents of the file into the array `@guests`. On the next line, I create a new array called `@new_guests`.

On line 24, a `foreach` loop begins that is used to process all the records retrieved from the file. It moves each record into a variable named `$guest`, which is then evaluated in the body of the loop. On line 25, the record is split into fields, and then on line 26, the name field is compared to the value the user entered, and if they don't match, the record is inserted into the `@new_guests` array. If the records do match, the record is left out of the array, and is thus deleted.

After all the records have been evaluated and the ones to be deleted have been discarded, the cursor is returned to the beginning of the file in line 30. In line 31, all the contents of the file are deleted using the `truncate` function. Then, in line 32, the contents of the array `@new_guests` are printed to the file. This prints all the records except those that were supposed to be deleted. After the records have been printed back into the file, it's closed on line 33.

Modifying a Record in the Database

Modifying a record in a flat file is a three step process. First, you have to select a record to modify. Second, you have to enter the new data for that record, and third, you have to store that data in the database. I'm going to use one script to implement all three steps. First, take a look at the source code for the script in Listing 13.6.

LISTING **13.6**   The `modify.pl` Script

```
 1: #!c:/perl/bin/perl
 2:
 3: use CGI;
 4: $query = new CGI;
 5:
 6: $guest_file = "guests.txt";
 7: @browsers = ('Netscape', 'Internet Explorer', 'Opera');
 8:
 9: &print_page_start;
10:
11: if ($query->param()) {
12:     if ($query->param('new_name')) {
13:     if (&valid_form) {
14:         # Wrap this code in an eval block in order to trap
15:         # errors.
16:         eval {
17:         open (GUESTS, "+>> $guest_file") or
18:             die "Can't open $guest_file: $!";
19:         flock GUESTS, 2;
```

```
20:
21:          seek GUESTS, 0, 0;
22:          my @guests = <GUESTS>;
23:          my @new_guests = ();
24:
25:          foreach $guest (@guests) {
26:              chomp $guest;
27:              ($name, $email, $browser) = split /\t/, $guest;
28:              if ($name eq $query->param('name') &&
29:              $email eq $query->param('email') &&
30:              $browser eq $query->param('browser')) {
31:                  $name = $query->param('new_name');
32:                  $email = $query->param('new_email');
33:                  $browser = $query->param('new_browser');
34:                  $guest = "$name\t$email\t$browser";
35:                  }
36:              $guest .= "\n";
37:              push @new_guests, $guest;
38:          }
39:          seek GUESTS, 0, 0;
40:          truncate GUESTS, 0;
41:          print GUESTS @new_guests;
42:          close GUESTS;
43:
44:          print "<P>Record(s) modified.</P>\n";
45:          print "<A HREF=\"retrieve.pl\">Retrieve records.</A>\n";
46:          }
47:      }
48:      else {
49:          &print_form;
50:      }
51:      }
52:      else {
53:      &print_form;
54:      }
55: }
56: else {
57:      &print_record_list;
58: }
59:
60: chomp $@;
61: if ($@) {
62:      print "ERROR: $@<BR>\n";
63: }
64:
65: &print_page_end;
66:
67: sub print_page_start {
68:      print $query->header;
69:      print "<HTML>\n<HEAD>\n<TITLE>Modify Records</TITLE>\n";
70:      print "</HEAD>\n<BODY>\n";
```

13

continues

LISTING 13.6   continued

```
71:      print "<H1>Modify Records</H1>\n";
72: }
73:
74: sub print_form {
75:      print "<P>\n<FORM>\n";
76:      if (!$query->param()) {
77:      print "Name: <INPUT TYPE=\"text\" NAME=\"new_name\"><BR>\n";
78:      print "Email: <INPUT TYPE=\"text\" NAME=\"new_email\"><BR>\n";
79:      print "Browser:<BR>";
80:      foreach $browser (@browsers) {
81:          print "<INPUT TYPE=\"radio\" NAME=\"new_browser\" ";
82:          print "VALUE=\"$browser\">$browser<BR>\n";
83:      }
84:      }
85:      else {
86:          if ($query->param('new_name')) {
87:          print "Name: <INPUT TYPE=\"text\" NAME=\"new_name\" ";
88:          print "VALUE=\"", $query->param('new_name'), "\"><BR>\n";
89:          print "Email: <INPUT TYPE=\"text\" NAME=\"new_email\" ";
90:          print "VALUE=\"", $query->param('new_email'), "\"><BR>\n";
91:          print "Browser:<BR>";
92:          foreach $browser (@browsers) {
93:          print "<INPUT TYPE=\"radio\" NAME=\"new_browser\" ";
94:          print "VALUE=\"$browser\"";
95:          if ($browser eq $query->param('new_browser')) {
96:              print " CHECKED";
97:          }
98:          print ">$browser<BR>\n";
99:          }
100:     }
101:     else {
102:         print "Name: <INPUT TYPE=\"text\" NAME=\"new_name\" ";
103:         print "VALUE=\"", $query->param('name'), "\"><BR>\n";
104:         print "Email: <INPUT TYPE=\"text\" NAME=\"new_email\" ";
105:         print "VALUE=\"", $query->param('email'), "\"><BR>\n";
106:         print "Browser:<BR>";
107:         foreach $browser (@browsers) {
108:         print "<INPUT TYPE=\"radio\" NAME=\"new_browser\" ";
109:         print "VALUE=\"$browser\"";
110:         if ($browser eq $query->param('browser')) {
111:             print " CHECKED";
112:         }
113:         print ">$browser<BR>\n";
114:         }
115:     }
116:     }
117:     print "<INPUT TYPE=\"hidden\" NAME=\"name\" ";
118:     print "VALUE=\"" . $query->param('name') . "\">\n";
119:     print "<INPUT TYPE=\"hidden\" NAME=\"email\" ";
120:     print "VALUE=\"" . $query->param('email') . "\">\n";
```

```
121:        print "<INPUT TYPE=\"hidden\" NAME=\"browser\" ";
122:        print "VALUE=\"" . $query->param('browser') . "\">\n";
123:        print "<INPUT TYPE=\"submit\" VALUE=\"Update record\">\n";
124:        print "</FORM>\n</P>\n";
125: }
126:
127: sub valid_form {
128:        $return_code = 1;
129:        if (!$query->param('new_name')) {
130:        print "You must enter a name.<BR>\n";
131:        $return_code = 0;
132:        }
133:        if (!$query->param('new_email')) {
134:        print "You must enter an email address.<BR>\n";
135:        $return_code = 0;
136:        }
137:        if (!$query->param('new_browser')) {
138:        print "You must select a browser.<BR>\n";
139:        $return_code = 0;
140:        }
141:        return $return_code;
142: }
143:
144: sub print_record_list {
145:        open (GUESTS, "< $guest_file") or
146:        die "Can't open guest file: $!";
147:        while (<GUESTS>) {
148:        chomp;
149:        ($name, $email, $browser) = split /\t/;
150:        print "<P>\n";
151:        print "<FORM>\n";
152:        print "Name: $name<BR>\n";
153:        print "Email: $email<BR>\n";
154:        print "Browser: $browser<BR>\n";
155:        print "<INPUT TYPE=\"hidden\" NAME=\"name\" VALUE=\"$name\">\n";
156:        print "<INPUT TYPE=\"hidden\" NAME=\"email\" VALUE=\"$email\">\n";
157:        print "<INPUT TYPE=\"hidden\" NAME=\"browser\" VALUE=\"$browser\">\n";
158:        print "<INPUT TYPE=\"submit\" VALUE=\"Edit this entry\">\n";
159:        print "</FORM>\n";
160:        print "</P>\n";
161:        }
162: }
163:
164: sub print_page_end {
165:        print "</BODY>\n</HTML>\n";
166: }
```

Let's take a look at how the script works. First, if no parameters are passed to the script, it fetches all the records from the file, and prints a page with a form for each record in the file. To edit a particular record, the user just has to choose one from the list and click on Edit This Entry. The &print_record_list subroutine is called on line 57. The subroutine (lines 144–162) opens the file listed in $guest_file, and prints the contents of each record. It also prints a form for each record, storing the values in the fields in hidden form fields.

When a user clicks one of the form buttons to edit a record, a form is printed with all the current values of each of the fields so that the user can edit them. The values are also stored again in hidden fields, so that the program can determine which record should be updated. When the form is submitted, both the old and new values will be submitted to the program.

After the form used to edit the record is submitted, the values in the form are validated. The form validation code is identical to the code used to validate the form in the insert.pl script. If the user failed to enter something in any of the fields, the form is sent back to the user with an error message. If all the form fields contain values, the program attempts to update the record in the database.

A lot of this code will look familiar to you as well. The code that deals with the guests.txt file is wrapped in an eval block so that errors can be trapped. On line 17, I open a read/write filehandle for the guests database. I lock the file on line 18, and on line 20 move the pointer to the beginning of the file. All the records in the file are read into the array @guests on line 21. On line 22, I create a new array, @new_guests to store the future contents of the file.

The foreach loop that begins on line 25 and ends on line 38 is where things get really different. Like the delete.pl script, it evaluates the records one at a time. On line 26, the line feed at the end of each record is removed. On line 27, the fields are broken out into individual variables. The if statement on line 28 is the crux of the entire script. It checks to see whether the old values for each field submitted from the form are equal to the fields in the current record. If they are, that's the record to be modified.

When all the fields are equal, the current values in the record are replaced by the new values submitted with the form. Whether the record was the one to be modified or not, after the if statement executes, the line feed is added back onto the end of the record, and record is placed in the @new_guests array on line 37. After the foreach loop is complete, all the records in the file are stored in the @new_guests array.

On lines 39–42, the file is emptied and the new set of records is printed to the file. The filehandle is closed to release the lock, and the program finishes up by printing out a success message and the closing HTML tags.

Summary

Flat-file databases are a useful way to store rudimentary data structures between executions of a program. In this hour, I explained how flat-file databases are designed, and how to access them using Perl programs. I also explained, step by step, the four most common operations performed on data stored within a flat file. I also explained how to use file locking to protect your databases from being damaged by simultaneous access from multiple processes.

Q&A

Q Flat-file databases seem pretty easy to use; why shouldn't I use them instead of more powerful database applications?

A One of the main reasons is performance. In order to retrieve a specific piece of information from a flat-file database, you have to search every record in order to find it. Relational databases are designed explicitly with fast retrieval of data in mind, so they provide better performance. Flat-file databases are also very crude if the record contains lots of fields, or contains fields that hold a lot of data. On the other hand, flat-file databases are almost infinitely easier to set up and administer than relational databases. If you need only one table, a flat-file database is probably the right choice.

Q I already have information stored in a database; how can I connect it to the Web?

A Because databases are such powerful and important applications, many different commercial database packages are available for every platform. Unfortunately, this means that I probably can't explain how to use your particular database on the Web in the space that I have. A couple of common standards, however, make it easier for programs to get data from databases: ODBC (Open Database Connectivity), and SQL (Structured Query Language). I'm going to discuss both in the next hour.

Workshop

The quiz questions are designed to strengthen the knowledge you gain each hour. The exercises help you build on that knowledge by providing you with the opportunity to apply it to real problems. For the answers to the quiz questions, refer to Appendix A, "Answers."

13

Quiz

1. How do you open a file for output in Perl?
2. What is a delimiter?

Exercises

1. Write a program that searches the guests database and prints the results of the search. You should use the same `while` loop that was used in the last sample program in this hour, and use the bind operator to search the lines and then print the ones that match.

2. Write a CGI application that creates a flat-file database of your own. Flat-file databases are simple, but they are powerful enough for many data storage tasks.

HOUR 14

Creating a CGI-Based Message Board

One feature found on many Web sites is a discussion group where the site's users can discuss topics of common interest and share information. This hour's lesson consists of a walkthrough of a Web discussion group application that you can adapt for use on your own site. Not only is the application useful on its own, but it also demonstrates how flat files are used for data storage in a real application, and illustrates the following topics:

- Creating flat files from a Web application
- Creating a file format for data storage
- Parsing through a text file to extract information
- Modifying a structured text file
- Generating unique filenames dynamically

The Structure of the Application

The message board is implemented using two Perl programs. One is used to display a list of topics; the other is used to post new topics and responses to existing topics. Each topic with its responses is stored in a text file. All the topic files are stored in a common directory.

All the topics could have been placed in a single file, but that would have made it a bit more confusing.

The topic files themselves are plain text files, which are formatted in a very simple markup language that I designed specifically for this application. The program used to create and modify topics generates files in this format, and the Web discussion group application understands how to parse files created using that format. The data format is much like HTML, in that it delimits each field using specific tags, rather than white space.

The File Format

First, let's look at the file format that I designed. A topic file with one response appears in Listing 14.1. You'll see the custom tags I created for this file format.

LISTING 14.1   The Topic File Format for the Web Discussion Application

```
 1: <title>This is a sample topic.</title>
 2: <author>Rafe Colburn</author>
 3: <last_modified>946324591</last_modified>
 4: <post>
 5: Just some information you might find interesting.</post>
 6: <response>
 7: <response_author>John Doe</response_author>
 8: <response_body>This is a response to the sample topic.^M<BR>
 9: </response_body>
10: </response>
```

Let's look at the tags that appear in the file. The `<title>` tag surrounds the topic title. The `<author>` tag surrounds the name of the topic's author. The date and time of the last modification of the topic appears in the `<last_modified>` tag. The date is presented as the number of seconds since the UNIX epoch, the value returned by the Perl `time` function.

The `time` function in Perl returns the number of seconds since the UNIX epoch regardless of which platform the program is running on. It's consistent across platforms.

You can convert that number to a properly formatted time using the Perl `localtime` function:

```
perl -e "print scalar localtime(946324591);"

Mon Dec 27 14:56:31 1999
```

The `<post>` tag encapsulates the actual text of the topic itself. Each response resides within an individual `<response>` tag. Inside the response tag are the two other tags, `<response_author>` and `<response_body>`.

The Display Script

The script used to display the topics has two modes. If it's passed a topic ID through the `topic` parameter, it attempts to display that specific topic. If no parameters are passed to it, it displays a list of the topics available to read. The topic list is generated by listing all the files in the topic directory and extracting the title and author from those files. The topic IDs correspond to the names of the files in the topic directory.

If the `topic` parameter is supplied, the full text of the topic is displayed. Each of the responses is displayed on the same page as the original topic, and a form used to respond to the topic is also displayed. The full source code for the `display.pl` script appears in Listing 14.2.

LISTING 14.2   The `display.pl` Program

```
 1: #!c:/perl/bin/perl
 2:
 3: use CGI;
 4: $query = new CGI;
 5:
 6: $topic_directory = "topics";
 7:
 8: if ($query->param('topic')) {
 9:     $topic = $query->param('topic');
10:     &file_error unless (&open_topic);
11:     &format_error unless (&parse_topic);
12:     &print_page_start;
13:     &print_topic;
14:     &print_response_form;
15:     print "<P>Return to the <A HREF=\"display.pl\">topic list</A>.</P>\n";
16:     &print_page_end;
17: }
18: else {
19:     $page_title = "Topic Index";
20:     &print_page_start;
```

14

continues

LISTING 14.2   continued

```
21:        &print_topic_index;
22:        &print_page_end;
23: }
24:
25: sub print_page_start {
26:        print $query->header;
27:        print "<HTML>\n<HEAD>\n<TITLE>$page_title</TITLE>\n</HEAD>\n";
28:        print "<BODY>\n<H1>$page_title</H1>\n";
29: }
30:
31: sub print_page_end {
32:        print "</BODY>\n</HTML>\n";
33: }
34:
35: sub print_topic_index {
36:        eval {
37:        opendir (TOPICS, "$topic_directory")
38:            or die "Can't open $topic_directory";
39:        @topics = grep (/^.+\.txt$/, readdir (TOPICS));
40:        foreach $topic (@topics) {
41:            $topic =~ s/(.+)\.txt/$1/;
42:            &open_topic;
43:            &parse_topic;
44:            print "<A HREF=\"display.pl?topic=$topic\">";
45:            print "$page_title</A>, $topic_author<BR>\n";
46:        }
47:        };
48: }
49:
50: sub open_topic {
51:        $topic_file = "$topic_directory/" . $topic . ".txt";
52:        eval {
53:        open (TOPIC, "< $topic_file")
54:            or die "Can't open $topic_file";
55:        @topic_text = <TOPIC>;
56:        };
57:        if ($@) {
58:        $error = $@;
59:        return undef;
60:        }
61:        else {
62:        return 1;
63:        }
64: }
65:
66: sub parse_topic {
67:        $topic_text = join '', @topic_text;
68:        # Extract the topic title from the topic
69:        if ($topic_text =~ /<title>(.*)<\/title>/s) {
70:        $page_title = $1;
```

```
 71:      }
 72:      else {
 73:      $err = "title";
 74:      return undef;
 75:      }
 76:
 77:      # Extract the author from the topic
 78:      if ($topic_text =~ /<author>(.*)<\/author>/s) {
 79:      $topic_author = $1;
 80:      }
 81:      else {
 82:      $err = "author";
 83:      return undef;
 84:      }
 85:
 86:      # Extract the date when the file was last modified
 87:      if ($topic_text =~ /<last_modified>(.*)<\/last_modified>/s) {
 88:      $last_modified = $1;
 89:      }
 90:      else {
 91:      $err = "lastmod";
 92:      return undef;
 93:      }
 94:
 95:      # Extract the first post from the topic
 96:      if ($topic_text =~ /<post>(.*)<\/post>/s) {
 97:      $post = $1;
 98:      }
 99:      else {
100:      $err = "post";
101:      return undef;
102:      }
103:
104:      @response_list = ();
105:      while ($topic_text =~ /<response>(.*?)<\/response>/sg) {
106:      $response = $1;
107:      if ($response =~ /<response_author>(.*)<\/response_author>/s) {
108:          push @response_list, $1;
109:      }
110:      else {
111:          $err = "response author";
112:          return undef;
113:      }
114:      if ($response =~ /<response_body>(.*)<\/response_body>/s) {
115:          push @response_list, $1;
116:      }
117:      else {
118:          $err = "response body";
119:          return undef;
120:      }
121:      }
```

14

continues

LISTING 14.2 continued

```perl
122:
123:        # Return a value so that the parse was considered successful.
124:        1;
125: }
126:
127: sub print_topic {
128:        print "<P>Author: $topic_author</P>\n";
129:        print "<P>Most recent response: ";
130:        print scalar localtime($last_modified), "</P>\n";
131:        print "<P>$post</P>\n";
132:        print "<HR>\n";
133:        $part_type = "author";
134:        foreach $response_part (@response_list) {
135:        if ($part_type eq "author") {
136:            print "<P>Author: $response_part</P>\n";
137:            $part_type = "body";
138:        }
139:        else {
140:            print "<P>$response_part</P>\n";
141:            print "<HR>\n";
142:            $part_type = "author";
143:        }
144:        }
145: }
146:
147: sub print_response_form {
148:        print "<FORM METHOD=\"post\" ACTION=\"post.pl\">\n";
149:        print "<INPUT TYPE=\"hidden\" NAME=\"action\" VALUE=\"response\">\n";
150:        print "<INPUT TYPE=\"hidden\" NAME=\"response_to\" ";
151:        print "VALUE=\"$topic\">\n";
152:        print "Author: ";
153:        print "<INPUT TYPE=\"text\" NAME=\"author\" ";
154:        print "SIZE=40 MAXLENGHT=72 VALUE=\"$author\"><BR>\n";
155:        print "Message body: <BR>\n";
156:        print "<TEXTAREA ROWS=10 COLS=60 NAME=\"post\" WRAP=\"virtual\">";
157:        print "</TEXTAREA><BR>\n";
158:        print "<INPUT TYPE=\"submit\" VALUE=\"post topic\"><BR>\n";
159:        print "</FORM>\n";
160: }
161:
162: sub format_error {
163:        print $query->header;
164:        print "<HTML>\n<HEAD>\n<TITLE>Format Error</TITLE>\n</HEAD>\n";
165:        print "<BODY><H3>Format Error</H3>\n<P>$err</P>\n</BODY>\n</HTML>\n";
166:        exit;
167: }
168:
169: sub file_error {
170:        print $query->header;
171:        print "<HTML>\n<HEAD>\n<TITLE>File Error</TITLE>\n</HEAD>\n";
```

```
172:      print "<BODY><H3>File Error</H3>\n<P>$error</P>\n</BODY>\n</HTML>\n";
173:      exit;
174: }
```

Utility Subroutines

There are a few utility subroutines in the script that you can look at before you dig into the meat of the script. You should already be familiar with print_page_start and print_page_end. They just print out the HTML tags needed to start and end an HTML page. The print_page_start subroutine uses the page title specified in the $page_title variable.

There are also a couple of subroutines written for error handling. If an error occurs when the program attempts to open a topic file, the program uses the file_error subroutine to print an error message for the user. If the topic file is improperly formatted, the format_error subroutine is used to send an error message to the browser. How these errors are trapped will be discussed later.

Parsing a Topic File

The most important functionality found in this program is the code used to parse topic files. After a topic file is open, the parse_topic subroutine is used to extract all the information from that file and store it in regular variables so that it can be printed. When topic files are opened, all the lines in the file are copied into an array, @topic_text. The first thing that the program does is copy all those lines into a single scalar variable called $topic_text, on line 67. The join function is used to concatenate all the text in an array into a single string. The empty string passed to the join function is the delimiter to place between array elements. In this case, no delimiter is inserted.

After all the text in the file is copied into a variable, the script searches for the predefined tokens and extracts the needed data. The first piece of data the script tries to extract is the topic title. On line 69, the regular expression /<title>(.*)<\/title>/s is used to extract the title from the file. If the title tag is not present, the parse function returns undef, the undefined value. That indicates that the parsing of the topic failed, and the program calls the format_error function and exits.

Let's look at a couple of features of the regular expression. After the regular expression, the s flag is supplied. This indicates that matches should span line feeds. The wildcard in the regular expression, which matches everything between the opening and closing title tags, is surrounded by parentheses. In a regular expression, when an expression is surrounded by parentheses, it indicates that the value the expression matches should be preserved. The values are preserved by being copied into variables. The first expression so preserved is copied into the variable $1, the value of which I assign to the variable $page_title on line 70.

14

The same technique is used to extract the author, date last modified, and body text from the topic. In any of these cases, if the proper opening and closing tags can't be found, the script exits with an error.

The code for extracting responses is a bit more complex. The first four elements found in a topic can only appear one time. There's only one date last modified, only one author, and only one title. On the other hand, there can be any number of responses to a particular topic. That makes extracting responses a two step process. The first step is to extract all the responses one at a time, the second step is to extract the information from each response and store it in an array so that it can be displayed later.

A special type of loop is used to extract all the responses from the topic. The loop begins on line 105. Let's take that line of code apart piece by piece. The loop is a `while` loop, so it is executed until the loop condition is false. In this case, the loop condition uses the binding operator. Under normal circumstances, the expression will evaluate as true as long as the expression to the right of the operator can be found in the variable to the left of the operator. That means that an infinite loop would be created if the response tag were present, or that the loop would not execute at all if the topic has no responses.

However, I use the g flag at the end of the expression. The g flag causes a regular expression to iterate over the instances of that expression in a string, rather than matching the first instance in the string every time. When all the instances of the matching string are exhausted, the binding operator returns false, and execution of the `while` loop ceases.

Let's look at one other feature of this regular expression. The actual wildcard in the expression is (.*?). The question mark tells the wildcard to be "non-greedy." By default, Perl regular expressions match the largest possible number of characters. So, if a topic had multiple responses and you didn't include the question mark, the expression would match the opening tag of the first response and the closing tag of the last response, and treat them like one big response. The question mark indicates that the first </response> encountered should be treated as the end of the match, not the last </response> encountered.

After a response has been matched, it is copied into the variable $response (on line 106). At that point, the author and body of the response are extracted and appended to the array @response_list. There's no differentiation between authors and actual response text in the @response_list array; I just know that I alternated the two types of data when I printed out the responses.

The parsing routine leaves me with several scalar variables that contain data associated with the topic, and one array that contains all the responses. At that point, I'm ready to present the data in the format that I choose.

Printing the Topic List

Now that you understand how the topic files are parsed, I can take you through the various execution paths through the script. First, let's look at what happens when no topic is specified and a list of topics is presented. The code from lines 19–22 is executed if no topic ID is supplied. On line 21, the print_topic_index subroutine is called. That subroutine, which begins on line 35, parses all the files in the topic directory and extracts the titles and authors of those topics.

The entire contents of the subroutine are wrapped in an eval statement so that any errors that occur can be trapped and handled gracefully within the program. In this case, I haven't built an error handler for errors that occur when accessing the directory.

Let's look at the code that reads the files from the directory. First, I use opendir to open a directory handle for the topic directory. Conceptually directory handles are very similar to filehandles. The thing to remember is that completely separate functions are used to deal with the contents of a directory after it's open. In this case, I read a list of all the files in the directory at once on line 48.

Line 48 reads the list of files in the directory, and filters out all the files that don't have an extension of .txt. The command used to do this is somewhat complex, so let me explain it in detail. First of all, the list of files is stored in the array @topics. This is important because the entire expression is accessed in the list context. Later, when I use readdir, it will read all the files at once (instead of just reading the next file in the directory) because the function is called in the list context.

> In Perl, there are two contexts in which a function can be called, the list context and the scalar context. Some functions behave differently depending on the context. For example, if you call the localtime function in the scalar context, it returns a nicely formatted string. If you call it in the list context, it returns a list of all the components of a date and time.

The @topics array isn't just assigned the contents of the full list of files returned by readdir. Instead, the list of files is filtered using the grep function and a regular expression. The grep function takes the list of files returned by readdir and discards all the filenames that don't match the regular expression. In the end, the @topics array is filled with a list of names of files that are assumed to be topics for the discussion group. (Any file that lives in the topics directory and has an extension of .txt is assumed to be a discussion group topic.)

14

After all the topic filenames are placed in @topics, a foreach loop is used to iterate over those files. The open_topic subroutine is used to open each file, and the parse_topic file is used to extract all the topic information from the file. At that point, all that's left is to print a link for the topic. The query string with the proper topic ID for each topic is embedded into the links. The topic list appears in Figure 14.1.

FIGURE 14.1

The topic list for the discussion group.

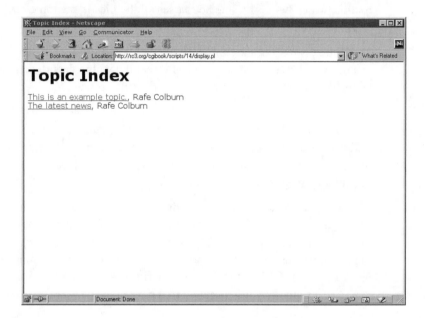

Printing a Topic

When a user clicks a link to a particular topic, that topic file is opened and parsed, and then the program prints out the topic. The print_topic subroutine, which runs from line 127–145, formats all the data from the parsed topic using HTML and sends it to the browser. The only interesting part of this subroutine is the code that prints responses. As you know, both the authors and response text were placed in the same array. This subroutine uses a foreach loop to extract each element from the array and print it. The program knows that the first element is an author, the second is a response body, the third is an author, and so on. It uses a test in the foreach loop to determine which type of data it's printing and format it appropriately. Figure 14.2 contains an example of a topic.

After the topic is printed, the print_response_form subroutine is called to print out the form the user can use to enter a response for the topic. The form is submitted to the post.pl program, which I'll discuss in a bit. The complete response form appears in Figure 14.3.

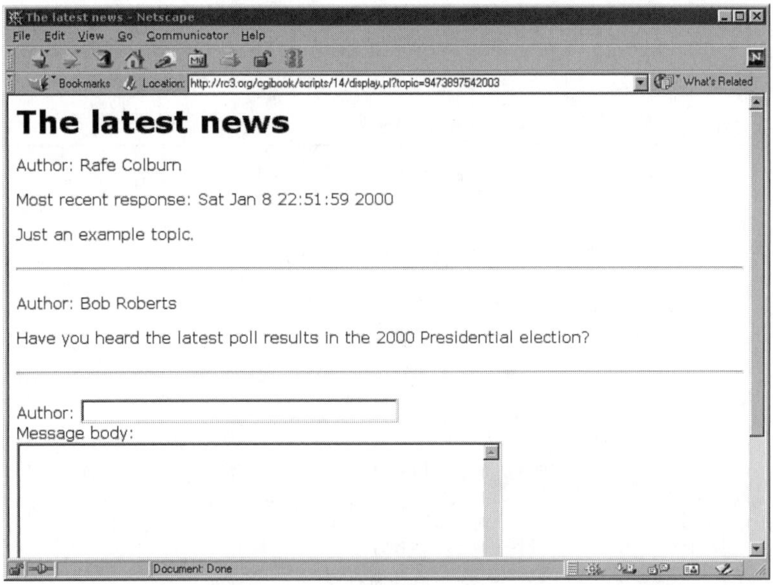

FIGURE **14.2**

A topic rendered by the display script.

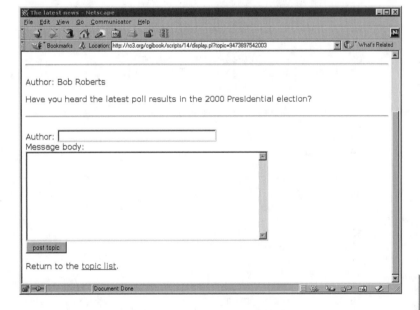

FIGURE **14.3**

The response form.

The Posting Script

Now that you've seen how topics are displayed, let's take a look at how new topics are created and how responses are added to existing topics. The post.pl script serves two

14

purposes. First, it is used to create new topics, and second, it's used to append responses to existing topics. The source code for the script appears in Listing 14.3.

LISTING 14.3   The Source Code for `post.pl`

```perl
1: #!c:/perl/bin/perl
2:
3: use CGI;
4: use CGI::Carp qw(fatalsToBrowser);
5: $query = new CGI;
6:
7: $topic_directory = "topics";
8:
9: if ($query->param('action')) {
10:     &set_variables;
11:
12:     # The form to create a new topic has been submitted
13:     if ($action eq "new") {
14:     if (&valid_form) {
15:         &write_new_topic;
16:         $page_title = $title;
17:         &print_page_start;
18:         &print_success;
19:         &print_page_end;
20:     }
21:     else {
22:         $page_title = "New Topic";
23:         &print_page_start;
24:         &print_error;
25:         &print_form;
26:             &print_page_end;
27:     }
28:     }
29:     elsif ($action = "response") {
30:     &set_variables;
31:     if (&valid_form) {
32:         &write_response;
33:         $page_title = "New response entered";
34:         &print_page_start;
35:         &print_response_success;
36:         &print_page_end;
37:     }
38:     else {
39:         $page_title = "New response";
40:         &print_page_start;
41:         &print_error;
42:         &print_form;
43:         &print_page_end;
44:     }
45:     }
46: }
```

```
47: else {
48:     $action = "new";
49:     $page_title = "Enter new topic";
50:     &print_page_start;
51:     $topic_type = "new";
52:     &print_form;
53:     &print_page_end;
54: }
55:
56: sub set_variables {
57:     $action = $query->param('action');
58:     $title = $query->param('title');
59:     $author = $query->param('author');
60:     $post = $query->param('post');
61:     $response_to = $query->param('response_to');
62: }
63:
64: sub print_page_start {
65:     print $query->header;
66:     print "<HTML>\n<HEAD>\n<TITLE>$page_title</TITLE>\n</HEAD>\n";
67:     print "<BODY>\n<H1>$page_title</H1>\n";
68: }
69:
70: sub print_page_end {
71:     print "</BODY>\n</HTML>\n";
72: }
73:
74: sub print_form {
75:     print "<FORM METHOD=\"post\">\n";
76:     print "<INPUT TYPE=\"hidden\" NAME=\"action\" VALUE=\"$action\">\n";
77:     if ($action eq "response") {
78:     print "<INPUT TYPE=\"hidden\" NAME=\"response_to\" ";
79:     print "VALUE=\"$response_to\">\n";
80:     }
81:     if ($action eq "new") {
82:     print "Topic: ";
83:     print "<INPUT TYPE=\"text\" NAME=\"title\" ";
84:     print "SIZE=40 MAXLENGTH=72 VALUE=\"$title\"><BR>\n";
85:     }
86:     print "Author: ";
87:     print "<INPUT TYPE=\"text\" NAME=\"author\" ";
88:     print "SIZE=40 MAXLENGHT=72 VALUE=\"$author\"><BR>\n";
89:     print "Message body: <BR>\n";
90:     print "<TEXTAREA ROWS=10 COLS=60 NAME=\"post\" WRAP=\"virtual\">";
91:     print "$post</TEXTAREA><BR>\n";
92:     print "<INPUT TYPE=\"submit\" VALUE=\"post topic\"><BR>\n";
93:     print "</FORM>\n";
94: }
95:
96: sub valid_form {
97:     $error_message = '';
```

14

continues

LISTING 14.3   continued

```perl
 98:      if ($title eq '' && $action eq 'new') {
 99:      $error_message .= "You must enter a title.<BR>\n";
100:      }
101:      if ($author eq '') {
102:      $error_message .= "You must enter an author.<BR>\n";
103:      }
104:      if ($post eq '') {
105:      $error_message .= "You must enter a message.<BR>\n";
106:      }
107:      if ($error_message eq '') {
108:      return 1;
109:      }
110:      else {
111:      return undef;
112:      }
113: }
114:
115: sub write_new_topic {
116:      $topic_file = time . $$ . '.txt';
117:      open (TOPIC, "> $topic_directory/$topic_file")
118:      or die "Can't open $topic_directory/$topic_file";
119:      print TOPIC "<title>$title</title>\n";
120:      print TOPIC "<author>$author</author>\n";
121:      print TOPIC "<last_modified>" . time . "</last_modified>\n";
122:      print TOPIC "<post>\n";
123:      $post =~ s/\n/<BR>\n/g;
124:      print TOPIC $post;
125:      print TOPIC "</post>\n";
126:      close TOPIC;
127: }
128:
129: sub write_response {
130:      $topic_file = $response_to . '.txt';
131:      open (TOPIC, "+>> $topic_directory/$topic_file")
132:      or die "Can't open $topic_directory/$topic_file";
133:      flock TOPIC, 2;
134:      seek TOPIC, 0, 0;
135:      my @topic_text = <TOPIC>;
136:      my $topic_text = join '', @topic_text;
137:      my $current_time = time;
138:      $topic_text =~ s/<last_modified>(\d+)<\/last_modified>/<last_modified>
139:      ➥$current_time<\/last_modified>/;
140:      seek TOPIC, 0, 0;
141:      truncate TOPIC, 0;
142:      print TOPIC $topic_text;
143:      print TOPIC "<response>\n";
144:      print TOPIC "<response_author>$author</response_author>\n";
145:      $post =~ s/\n/<BR>\n/g;
146:      print TOPIC "<response_body>$post</response_body>\n";
```

```
147:       print TOPIC "</response>\n";
148:       close TOPIC;
149: }
150:
151: sub print_success {
152:       "<P>New topic created.</P>\n";
153: }
154:
155: sub print_response_success {
156:       print "<P>New response entered.</P>\n";
157: }
158:
159: sub print_error {
160:       print "<FONT COLOR=#CC0000>\n";
161:       print "<P>Please correct the following errors:<BR>\n";
162:       print "$error_message\n</FONT></P>\n";
163: }
```

The action parameter, which is included in the response form and new topic form, is tested to determine whether the user is creating a new topic, has submitted a new topic, or has submitted a response. If the action parameter is missing, the program displays the form used to create a new topic. If the action parameter is set to new, the program assumes that the form for creating a topic was filled out and that it has been submitted. If the action is response, the program assumes that a response to an existing topic has been submitted. Now let's take a look at each of the options in detail.

Presenting the New Topic Form

If the action parameter is omitted, or it's not set to new or response, the new topic form is displayed. The print_form subroutine is used by all the actions—if no action is specified, it just prints all the fields with no values prefilled. The new topic form appears in Figure 14.4.

Processing a New Topic Submission

Let's look at what happens when a user submits a new topic. Like most form processing scripts, post.pl validates the user's input to make sure that the new topic is acceptable. It uses the valid_form subroutine, which just checks to make sure that the user entered an author, title, and body text. Of course, you could add any additional validation to this subroutine that you wanted. If the form submission is not valid, the print_error subroutine lets the user know what the problems were with his form input, and the form is redisplayed with the values the user entered inserted into the fields. The results of an invalid form submission appear in Figure 14.5.

14

FIGURE **14.4**

The new topic form.

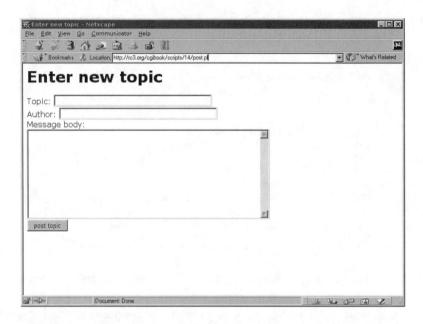

FIGURE **14.5**

An invalid form submission.

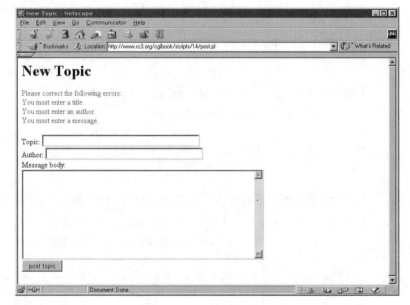

If the form submission is valid, the program goes on to create the new topic file. The topic file is created by the `write_topic_file` routine, which begins on line 115.

The first step in the process is to create a name for the topic file. The only important thing about the name of the topic file is that it must be unique. The easiest way to create a unique filename in a Perl CGI program is to append the output of the time function (which returns the number of seconds since the UNIX epoch to the process ID of the current instance CGI script). In most cases, just the time would be enough, but there's an off chance that two processes will try to create a file at the same time, and then you'd have a conflict. It's safer to include the process ID in the filename to avoid this problem.

> If you use a utility like FastCGI or mod_perl to create persistent Web applications, you'll have to use another method of generating unique filenames; the same process services all the requests for the application.

After the filename has been created, a filehandle is opened to write to the file with the new name. All the information associated with the topic is printed to the new file, and the file is then closed. Of course, the predefined topic file format that I created is used so that the display.pl script can successfully parse it later.

Adding a Response

The code used to add a response is a bit more complex than the new topic creation code. When a response is submitted, the values in the response are validated, just as they are when a new topic is submitted. The valid_form subroutine does not require responses to have a title because the response form contains no title field. If the user's input from the response form was valid, the write_response subroutine is called.

If the write_response subroutine just appended the response to the topic file without altering any of the other content, there wouldn't be anything to it. I would just open an appended filehandle for the topic file, and print the new response at the end of the file. In this case, the response has to be added, and the date the response was last modified must also be updated.

On line 131, the file is opened in read/write mode. Line 133 locks the response file so that it doesn't get damaged if multiple users try to respond to the same topic at the same time. Lines 135 and 136 copy the entire contents of the file into a single scalar variable. And line 138 replaces the last modified date in the file with the current time. Line 139 moves back to the beginning of the file. On the next line I truncate the contents of the file, and on line 141, I copy the new, modified information with the new last modified date into the file. Then I tack on the response, and close the file, saving it and releasing the lock.

14

Summary

This hour contains the first in-depth example in the book. It demonstrated how to use several programs in concert to create a fairly robust online message board that you can use on your Web site. It also demonstrated how to apply a number of important concepts in real-world applications, including how to create unique filenames and how to create and modify files from within a CGI script. It also contained an example of a simple parser that was used to translate topics from an established format to a data structure accessible from a Perl program. Even if the discussion board isn't useful to you directly, you can mine useful information out of this hour that applies to the scripts that you are writing.

Q&A

Q Isn't it easier to just download a prebuilt discussion group package from the Web and use that?

A Probably, but then you wouldn't have the benefit of learning how the discussion group works. If you add some navigation to the discussion group application in this hour, it will work fine for most tasks. If you're looking for something more robust, you may want to check out Ultimate Bulletin Board (`http://www.ultimatebb.com`), a very nice discussion group package that will run on UNIX or Windows NT.

Workshop

The quiz questions are designed to strengthen the knowledge you gain each hour. The exercises help you build on that knowledge by providing you with the opportunity to apply it to real problems. For the answers to the quiz questions, refer to Appendix A "Answers."

Quiz

1. Why are both the time and process ID included in filenames generated by `post.pl`?

Exercises

1. Create an application that will allow you to delete topics from the message group.

2. Insert code in the message group application that will store the date/time for each response in a topic, and that will display those response times when topics are printed.

HOUR **15**

Session (State) Management

Online shopping malls, sites that want to remember users between visits, and sites with customizable interfaces can only work if you have a way to uniquely identify users and keep track of their activities. In other words, to build complex Web-based applications, you need to store data that *persists* between requests. This hour therefore discusses different methods for creating *sessions,* which enable you to store transaction data from one request to the next. This hour also discusses *cookies,* which store small amounts of data on the user's computer for later use by the Web site.

This hour will:

- Define session management
- Discuss the rationale behind using session management
- Explain basic authentication
- Cover the usage of hidden form fields
- Explain how cookies work
- Demonstrate how to use cookies in your Web site

Why Use Session Management?

Session management is a means by which a user's identity can be preserved between requests. Session management in a Web environment works by passing an identifier to the user with a response, and then having the user pass back that identifier with subsequent requests to keep track of their session. This identifier can then be used to correlate the user with information relating to their activity. For example, if the user is shopping on your site, you can keep track of all of the items they've placed in their shopping basket using session management.

As you've already learned, HTTP is a connectionless protocol. When a user requests a Web page, the server sends the page and forgets that the browser ever asked. If a Web site could only serve one user at a time, there wouldn't be any problems with session management. The individual user would begin using the site, the server could keep track of where the user was and what she was doing, and the user could work through her transaction until it was complete.

Alternatively, a Telnet server or FTP server *can* service multiple users and keep track of all of them by allowing each user to open a persistent connection to the server. Every user has his own socket connection, so the server differentiates the users by the ports from which they connected.

Unlike Telnet and FTP, the connection to a Web server is only open long enough to accept the request from the browser and send the response. Therefore, there are no session management mechanisms built into the HTTP standard. Ordinarily, this isn't a problem. When a user is visiting a static Web site, all the server needs to know is which document the user is requesting. However, there are some situations where session management can make life much easier for users and for site administrators.

Let's say you run a Web-based conferencing system that requires the user to log in before browsing the site or posting any messages. HTTP is connectionless, so if the server doesn't store any information about the user, it will "forget" that the user already logged in and require her to enter her user ID and password every time he wants to access a page on the site.

By using a session management mechanism, however, the server can keep track of where the user has been and who he is—without forcing him to identify himself every time he visits a page.

Actually, most session management mechanisms do require user identification for every page visit to a page, but the identification occurs in the background without any explicit action from the user.

Perhaps the classic session management usage is in the creation of a "shopping cart." Without session management, a user would have to remember all the items he wanted to order and enter them in the order form when he was done shopping. By using session management, you can allow a user to add items as he browses the catalog. When he checks out, all the items that he selected along the way will appear on the final ordering screen. All he has to do is enter his name, address, and credit card number to order the items.

Basic Authentication

One of the earliest mechanisms for preserving client *state* is basic authentication. By state, I mean the current status of the user's activity or transaction. Basic authentication is used to protect subdirectories of a Web server by user ID and password, and was implemented on some of the earliest Web servers. The only element of the session's state that basic authentication maintains is the username and password they used to log in.

The way basic authentication works is that the server expects to receive an Authorization: header with requests. If the Authorization: header is not present or the user ID and password sent in the header are not valid, the request is rejected. The user sees a 401 Unauthorized response code, along with the WWW-Authenticate: header that indicates the realm for which the user should provide authorization. When most browsers receive this code, they display a dialog box where the user can enter a user ID and password that will be sent with a new request for the page. If the user ID and password are valid, they are sent with every subsequent request within that realm.

Realms are documents on a Web server that are grouped together under the same authentication system. In other words, the same user IDs and passwords can be used to access any document within a realm.

Most Web servers include support for basic authentication, although they vary widely in how it is configured. For information on setting up realms and configuring authentication, you should refer to the documentation provided with your Web server.

Let's take a look at the actual header lines that are exchanged in the course of an authenticated Web session (these examples are taken from RFC 1945, the HTTP 1.0 specification). First the server sends the WWW-authorize: line:

```
WWW-Authenticate: Basic realm="WallyWorld"
```

This line indicates that Basic is the type of authentication required, and the document is in the WallyWorld realm. If the user enters the user ID Aladdin and the password open sesame, the following authorization header is returned:

```
Authorization: Basic QWxhZGRpbjpvcGVuIHNlc2FtZQ==
```

The Authorization: line indicates that it is using Basic authentication and sends the user ID and password, encoded using Base64 encoding.

In one sense, Basic Authentication is a very simple session management system. It keeps track of the user's identity between requests. Once a user enters the username and password for an authentication realm in their browser, that username and password are sent with every request for a URL in that authentication realm until they close their browser. Although basic authentication is pretty useful for managing access to resources on a server, it's not very useful for keeping track of who a user is and what he is doing. To do that, you have to write your own session tracking mechanism (or use one provided by whatever application server you're using).

Hidden Fields in Forms

As you learned back in Hour 5, "Creating HTML Forms," you can use hidden form fields in your forms. Each of these fields contains a name and value that is passed to the CGI script along with the other visible form fields. You can use these hidden form fields to save the state of a transaction from one form to the next.

Let's say you're building a Web page that allows a user to register, and you want to ask the user additional questions based on the information he provides in the registration form. If the user responds that he has a TV in his home, you may want to ask how much TV he watches in a week. If he has a dog, you could ask what his favorite brand of dog food is.

In order to store all the information that the user enters in the registration form until you actually save it to a database when he submits the second form, you can transfer it from the first form to the second using hidden fields in the form. Figure 15.1 illustrates how to preserve information between forms using hidden form fields.

FIGURE 15.1

Processing an order using two forms and hidden form fields.

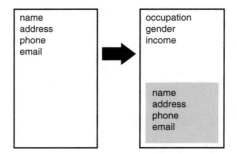

As you can see in Figure 15.1, using multiple forms can break up the data a user must enter into logical "chunks" so that the user isn't confronted with a large, confusing form. By passing the data the user has already entered from one form to the next using hidden fields, you save yourself the trouble of storing the information temporarily on the server. It also saves you from writing to your transaction database twice.

Hidden Form Fields Example

I'm going to use a very simple example to illustrate how hidden form fields can be used to preserve client state from one form to the next in a multiple form application. This example is simplified by leaving out all form validation code, and by using very few form fields.

If form validation was included, the application would have to verify that the user input in each stage of the application was valid before moving on to the next form. Adding more form fields is easy—you just have to determine which form to place them in, and be sure that you replicate them in each following form using hidden form fields.

In this case, the example is ostensibly a registration script for the Web site. The application is designed to capture three pieces of information—the user's name, the user's email address, and the name of the company that the user works for. The first form is used to capture the user's name and email address, and the second form is used to capture his company name.

In this example, I'm going to use the same basic logic that I introduced back in Hour 6, "Processing Input." The only difference is that I'm building on that logic by including multiple forms. The full source code listing for the program appears in Listing 15.1.

LISTING 15.1   A Script that Maintains Sessions with Hidden Form Fields

```
 1: #!c:/perl/bin/perl
 2:
 3: use CGI;
 4: $query = new CGI;
 5:
 6: if ($query->param()) {
 7:     if ($query->param('company')) {
 8:     &set_variables;
 9:     $title = "Registration Results";
10:     &print_page_start;
11:     &print_results;
12:     }
13:     else {
14:     &set_variables;
15:     $title = "Registration Form, Part 2";
16:     &print_page_start;
17:     &print_second_form;
18:     }
19: }
20: else {
21:     $title = "Registration Form, Part 1";
22:     &print_page_start;
23:     &print_first_form;
24: }
25:
26: &print_page_end;
27:
28: sub set_variables {
29:     $name = $query->param('name');
30:     $email = $query->param('email');
31:     $company = $query->param('company');
32: }
33:
34: sub print_page_start {
35:     print $query->header;
36:     print "<HTML>\n<HEAD>\n<TITLE>$title</TITLE>\n</HEAD>\n<BODY>\n";
37:     print "<H1>$title</H1>\n";
38: }
39:
40: sub print_first_form {
41:     print "<FORM>\n";
42:     print "Name: <INPUT TYPE=\"text\" NAME=\"name\"><BR>\n";
43:     print "Email: <INPUT TYPE=\"text\" NAME=\"email\"><BR>\n";
44:     print "<INPUT TYPE=\"submit\" VALUE=\"Continue\"><BR>\n";
45:     print "</FORM>\n";
46: }
47:
48: sub print_second_form {
49:     print "<FORM>\n";
50:     print "<INPUT TYPE=\"hidden\" NAME=\"name\" VALUE=\"$name\">\n";
51:     print "<INPUT TYPE=\"hidden\" NAME=\"email\" VALUE=\"$email\">\n";
```

```
52:     print "<INPUT TYPE=\"text\" NAME=\"company\">\n";
53:     print "<INPUT TYPE=\"submit\" VALUE=\"Register\">\n";
54:     print "</FORM>\n";
55: }
56:
57: sub print_results {
58:     print "Name: $name<BR>\n";
59:     print "Email: $email<BR>\n";
60:     print "Company: $company<BR>\n";
61: }
62:
63: sub print_page_end {
64:     print "</BODY>\n";
65:     print "</HTML>\n";
66: }
```

Application Logic

This CGI program begins the way all the other CGI programs written in Perl do—with a pointer to the Perl interpreter. In this program, I'm using the object-oriented interface to CGI.pm, so I import the module and create a new query object. After that is complete, the script determines whether to show the first form, show the second form, or process the user input. Listing 15.1 shows the code that implements that logic.

On line 6, the script checks to see whether the form was submitted at all. If the script was called without a form submission, the initial form is displayed. Otherwise, on line 7 the script checks to see whether the form submission was from the first or second form by checking for the presence of the company parameter. If that parameter is present, all the user input is processed. In this case, the &print_results function is used to process the full user input. If the parameter company is not present, the second form is displayed by the function &print_second_form.

The $title variable is used to store the title of the page. The &print_page_start subroutine includes the value in $title in both the page title and in the page heading.

Printing the Hidden Fields

The most important part of this script is the subroutine &print_second_form, which begins on line 48. It transfers the values entered in the first form into hidden fields in the second form.

The subroutine &set_variables is called before this one to move the values from the param() data structure to normal variables. Then, the second form is printed with the values from the first stored in hidden fields. The HTML source generated when the second form is displayed appears in Listing 15.2.

LISTINGS 15.2   HTML Generated by `register.pl`

```
 1: <HTML>
 2: <HEAD>
 3: <TITLE>Registration Form, Part 2</TITLE>
 4: </HEAD>
 5: <BODY>
 6: <H1>Registration Form, Part 2</H1>
 7: <FORM>
 8: <INPUT TYPE="hidden" NAME="name" VALUE="Rafe Colburn">
 9: <INPUT TYPE="hidden" NAME="email" VALUE="rafe@rc3.org">
10: <INPUT TYPE="text" NAME="company">
11: <INPUT TYPE="submit" VALUE="Register">
12: </FORM>
13: </BODY>
14: </HTML>
```

Using Cookies

The release of Netscape Navigator 2.0 was a watershed event for the Web. It contained a plethora of new features, including support for frames, JavaScript, and cookies. As stated earlier, cookies are used by servers to store information with the client that they can retrieve later.

Cookies didn't get a whole lot of press at first, but these days they're used behind the scenes at most of the popular Web sites. To get a sense of how many Web sites use cookies to store information about their users, set the preferences on your browser to notify you anytime a site sends you a cookie. You'll wear out your mouse-clicking finger responding to all the "cookie alert" dialog boxes (see Figure 15.2).

FIGURE 15.2

If you have your browser set to warn you before accepting cookies, this is the kind of dialog box displayed every time you receive one.

Before you learn the technical details of using cookies to build better Web sites, you need to understand the political issues surrounding them. You probably know that a lot of savvy Web surfers distrust cookies. There are also plenty of users who don't know that they even exist, or who know what they are but don't care whether sites use them or not. Cookies are like any other technology, in that the problems don't stem from the technology itself but the way it's used.

For example, one common use of cookies is to store passwords for accessing Web sites. For low-security sites, like those that require free registration, cookies can save users from being forced to enter their usernames and passwords every time they visit. This is a fairly innocuous use of cookies, making things more convenient for users. On the other hand, some Web advertising companies use cookies to track which sites users visit and build profiles of their surfing habits. Although this certainly isn't illegal, many users consider it to be unethical to gather information about them without their knowledge or consent.

Before you use cookies on your site, you should ask yourself what you're trying to accomplish. If you're using cookies to make the lives of your users easier or to provide enhanced features through your Web site, most users won't mind. On the other hand, if you use cookies to monitor user activity or otherwise spy on your users, chances are that there will be a backlash.

The most important thing to remember is that because some users are concerned about protecting their privacy, they surf with cookies turned off. You should always make sure that your site will still work for users that don't accept cookies, for whatever reason.

How Cookies Work

Now that we've gotten the politics of cookies out of the way, we can get down to the nuts and bolts of how they work. Cookies are just another header sent with a request or response. Here's how they work.

When a browser sends a request to a site that uses cookies, the server sends a cookie to the user in the response header. The cookie is stored by the client. Anytime the user visits a page in the domain specified with the cookie, it sends the information in the cookie back to the server. The server can send up to four kilobytes of information in a cookie, and browsers will not store more than 20 cookies per domain.

To use cookies for session management, Web sites usually send a unique ID number to a user, which is returned every time the user requests a page stored in the domain specified in the cookie. The Web server can save information like the user's name and password, his interface preferences, or the contents of his shopping cart under that unique ID. Generally speaking, these IDs should be truly unique—meaning that once one is assigned, it should never be assigned to anyone else. This can be accomplished by letting users pick their own account name (notifying them of conflicts with existing account names, of course) or by using an algorithm that generates unique identifiers. If your sessions expire after a specific time period, then you can recycle session identifiers if you wish, but using unique session IDs can save you trouble down the line if you change your site so that session IDs persist over longer periods of time. Let's take a look at a sample cookie:

```
Set-cookie: Session_ID=00001; path=/; domain=.mcp.com; expires=Saturday,
➡01-Aug-98 10:00:00 GMT
```

The parts of the cookie are as follows:

`name=value`

Both the name and value of a cookie are set by the server. In the previous example, I named the cookie `Session_ID` and set `00001` as the value of the cookie. The maximum size of the cookie cannot exceed four kilobytes. Neither the name nor value can contain a space, tab, or semicolon. If you're going to include lots of information in a cookie, you can use URL encoding to store the information. It's a format that doesn't use any of the characters that are prohibited in cookie values, and it automatically converts whitespace to its hexadecimal equivalents.

`domain=.mcp.com`

The domain is specified to indicate the servers to which the cookie should be sent. For example, if the browser has received the cookie in the previous example, anytime it connects to a server in the `mcp.com` domain, like `www.mcp.com`, `sams.mcp.com`, or even `www.sams.mcp.com`, it sends the cookie. On the other hand, you can specify a specific server in the cookie and the cookie will only be returned to that server. For example, if the cookie used `domain=home.netscape.com`, the cookie would only be returned to that particular server.

> By default, cookies are sent back only to the server that set them. To get a server to send the cookie to every computer in that domain, you have to specify the domain parameter with the cookie. Some browsers allow users to only send cookies back to the originating server. In those cases, even if you specify that your cookie should be sent back to the entire domain, it will only be sent back to the server that set it.

The server that is sending the cookie must be part of the domain specified in the cookie in order for it to be accepted by the browser. For example, if you wrote a CGI script and stored it on the server `www.mcp.com`, but you tried to set a cookie with the domain `.netscape.com`, the cookie would not be set. Some old browsers will accept cookies that are set for different domains than the one that is sending the cookie, but this has been phased out.

`path=/`

Just as the domain specifies which servers a cookie should be sent to, the path specifies which entities on the server should receive the cookie. For example, if you want a cookie you've set to be returned to your CGI programs only, you could use `path=/cgi-bin/` in

15

the cookie. Most of the time, however, you will probably just want to use path=/, which indicates that the cookie should be sent regardless of the location of the requested file on the server.

```
expires= Saturday, 01-Aug-98 10:00:00 GMT
```

The expires field indicates when the cookie should be deleted automatically by the Web browser. If you don't provide an expiration date with the cookie, it will be deleted when the user closes her Web browser. Cookies with no expiration date are useful for tracking a single Web session. On the other hand, if you want to save information with the client for an extended period of time, you should include an expiration date for the cookie. The amount of time the cookie should persist is up to you. Many sites set the cookies to expire several years in the future.

Using Cookies to Save User Information

One common use of cookies is to save user information so that the user doesn't have to enter it every time she visits the site. For example, popular sites like *The New York Times* and My Yahoo! use cookies to store users' login IDs and passwords.

Let's take a look at the headers you receive when you connect to www.hotwired.com:

```
HTTP/1.1 200 OK
Date: Wed, 15 Oct 1997 17:07:22 GMT
Server: Apache/1.2.0 HotWired/1.2
Vary: accept
Set-Cookie: p_uniqid=0QE++M4NFJ7Cpb1v+A; path=/; domain=.hotwired.com;
➥expires=Fri, 31-Dec-99 23:59:59 GMT
Set-Cookie: s_uniqid=0QE++M4NFJ7Cpb1v+A; path=/; domain=.hotwired.com
Cache-Control: no-cache="Set-Cookie"
Connection: close
Content-Type: text/html
```

The site sets two cookies: one that doesn't expire until December 31, 1999, and another that expires as soon as you leave the browser. The cookies contain unique IDs that can be keyed to database entries or site logs. They could have stored all the information in the cookie instead, but it makes more sense to store the information locally and just use the cookie to connect the user with the information. Listing 15.3 contains a script that sets a cookie.

LISTING 15.3   A Script That Sets a Cookie

```
1: #!c:/perl/bin/perl
2:
3: $cookie = "menus=on; expires=Wed, Feb-09-2000 00:00:00 GMT; path=/; ";
4: # $cookie .= "domain=.rc3.org";
```

continues

LISTING 15.3   continued

```
 5:
 6: print "Set-cookie: $cookie", "\n";
 7: print "Content-type: text/html", "\n\n";
 8:
 9: print "<HTML><HEAD><TITLE>Example</TITLE></HEAD>\n";
10: print "<BODY>";
11: print "This is an example page that sets a cookie.\n";
12: print "</BODY></HTML>";
```

The cookie, which expires on Wednesday, February 9, 2000, will be saved by the client. It contains the name and value pair menus=on. The site could use this cookie to determine whether to display full or condensed menus to the user when she visits the site.

There's really no more to setting cookies than that. If you want to include more information in the cookie, all you have to do is add it to the name=value pair.

Creating cookies with CGI.pm is even easier. All you have to do is use the cookie method of the query object and set the appropriate parameters for the cookie you're creating. Listing 15.4 contains the source code for the previous program, written using CGI.pm instead.

LISTING 15.4   A Script That Sets a Cookie Using CGI.pm

```
 1: #!c:/perl/bin/perl
 2:
 3: use CGI;
 4: $query = new CGI;
 5:
 6: $cookie = $query->cookie(-name=>'menus',
 7:                   -value=>'on',
 8:                   -expires=>'+30d',
 9:                   -path=>'/');
10: print $query->header(-cookie=>$cookie);
11: print $query->start_html(-title=>'Example');
12: print "This is an example page that sets a cookie. \n";
13: print $query->end_html;
```

One big advantage of using CGI.pm to set cookies is that you don't have to calculate the date when you want the cookie to expire. Instead, you can use constructs like +30d to set an expiration date 30 days in the future, or +8h to expire in eight hours.

Using Cookies to Retrieve User Information

Setting cookies is only half the job. After you've stored the data on the user's computer, you need to retrieve it and do something with it. Listing 15.5 contains a program that extracts all the cookies sent with a request and prints them onscreen.

LISTING 15.5   A Program That Prints All the Cookies Associated with a Request

```
 1: #!/usr/bin/perl
 2:
 3: print "Content-type: text/html", "\n\n";
 4: print "<HTML>\n";
 5: print "<HEAD><TITLE>Cookies</TITLE></HEAD>\n";
 6: print "<BODY>\n<H3>Here are all the cookies that were sent \n";
 7: print "by the browser. </H3>\n";
 8: print "<HR><PRE>";
 9: $raw_cookie = $ENV{'HTTP_COOKIE'};
10: @cookies = split /;/, $raw_cookie;
11: foreach $cookie (@cookies) {
12:     print $cookie, "\n";
13: }
14: print "</PRE>\n";
15: print "</BODY></HTML>\n
```

Naturally, after you've extracted the cookies from the environment variable, you can do anything you like with them. In this case, they're just displayed in the browser. The output of the script appears in Figure 15.3.

FIGURE 15.3

The output of the cookie display script.

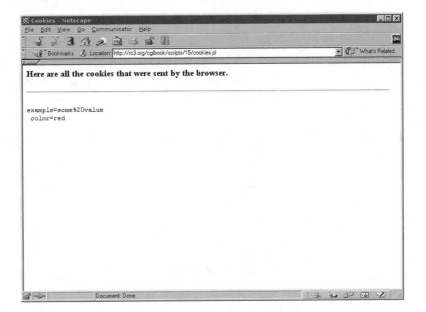

You can also use cookies to set up a Web Caller ID system of sorts. Looking back at the headers from the Hotwired Web site, you can see that the site sets a permanent cookie, named p_uniqid, that stores a unique ID for the user. Whenever that user returns to the

site, the Web site will receive the cookie. It can then look up the user's unique ID in a database, see which pages he's viewed in the past, and log which pages he visits this time. This paves the way for sites that can automatically select news stories that will be of the most interest to the user, or provide other customized content based on the user's actions in the past. Right now, many advertisers who advertise on multiple sites use cookies to track users and make sure that the same user doesn't see the same ad all the time.

Setting and Retrieving Cookies with JavaScript

If you know that your site's visitors all use browsers that support JavaScript, or your site will still work properly without cookies, you can bypass CGI and use JavaScript to handle your cookies. There are some disadvantages to this, the largest of which is that the users can view all your source code if they want to. Another disadvantage is that because the JavaScript code is executed within the client, your program only has access to the resources that are available from within the client's environment. It can't read input from files on the server or connect to databases. Setting and retrieving cookies with a JavaScript program is simple. The `document.cookie` method is used to create cookies and to retrieve the values of existing cookies. For example, to set the cookie used in the previous example with JavaScript, all you have to do is include the following line within the `<SCRIPT>` tags in the header of your document:

```
document.cookie="menus=on; expires=Fri, Nov-14-97 00:00:00 GMT; path=/"
```

Assuming the person visiting the site has already been here before, you can read the cookie using the `document.cookie` method as well. Listing 15.6 contains an example of how to grab a cookie that you've already set.

LISTING 15.6   Some JavaScript Code That Sets and Reads Cookies

```
 1: // First make sure that there are cookies being sent back
 2: // to the server.
 3: if(document.cookie) {
 4:     // Now check to see whether the menus cookie exists
 5:     index = document.cookie.indexOf("menus");
 6:     // If the cookie doesn't exist, set it to on.
 7:     if (index == -1) {
 8:         // I'm only setting the name, value, and expiration;
 9:         // all the other properties will be set to the
10:         // default values.
11:         document.cookie = "menus=on"
12:         cookie_val = "on";
13:     }
14:     // If the cookie exists, set up the variables to extract
15:     // the cookie's value.
16:     else {
17:         str_begin = (document.cookie.indexOf("=", index) + 1);
18:         str_end = (document.cookie.indexOf(";", index));
```

```
19:         if (str_end == -1) {
20:             str_end = document.cookie.length;
21:         }
22:         cookie_val = document.cookie.substring(str_begin, str_end);
23:     }
24:     // If the menus are on, print the first message.  If they
25:     // are not, print the second.
26:     if (cookie_val == "on") {
27:         document.write("This would be a menu.");
28:     }
29:     else {
30:         document.write("Menus are off.");
31:     }
32: }
```

You don't need to include all the attributes with a cookie. All that's required is the name attribute; the others all have default values and can be left out, as demonstrated in Listing 15.6.

Cookies that are set and read using JavaScript are no different than cookies created with CGI programs. You can use JavaScript to read cookies that were set by CGI, and vice versa.

Session Management with Cookies

Now that you've seen how to create cookies and how to retrieve them after they've been stored, I can show you how to create and maintain sessions using cookies. You're going to create what in all likelihood is the world's smallest shopping site, because the catalog only contains two items. The way the site works is that there is a separate cookie for each unique item in the catalog. The cookie stores the quantity of the item that the user is going to order. When the user checks out of the store, the check-out program looks at the cookies that are sent back by the browser and builds a list of items that the user has ordered.

This isn't how a real shopping site would work; if there were thousands of items in the catalog there would be thousands of different cookies to set. Real sites store a unique identifier in a cookie, and then store all the information associated with the user's session in a database or some other persistent data structure. Every time the user requests a page, their identifier is sent back to the server and the information about their session is looked up.

The Catalog Page

The first program serves as the catalog for the site. Because all the shopping cart information is stored in cookies, you could have any number of pages that work just like this one does. This CGI program displays a page with two forms on the screen (shown in Figure 15.4), one for each item in the catalog. When the user clicks on the Add Item to Cart button, he receives a cookie that specifies how many of the items he wants to add to the cart, and the page is reloaded so he can order other items. When he is done ordering, he can click on Check Out to complete the transaction. The source code to the script appears in Listing 15.7.

LISTING 15.7 The Product Selection Page in the Online Store

```
 1: #!c:/perl/bin/perl
 2:
 3: use CGI;
 4: $query = new CGI;
 5:
 6: if ($query->param(item) eq "deluxe") {
 7:     $cookie = $query->cookie(-name=>'deluxe',
 8:                   -value=>$query->param('quantity'));
 9: }
10: elsif ($query->param(item) eq "standard") {
11:     $cookie = $query->cookie(-name=>'standard',
12:                   -value=>$query->param('quantity'));
13: }
14:
15: if ($cookie) {
16:     print $query->header(-cookie=>$cookie);
17: }
18: else {
19:     print $query->header;
20: }
21:
22: print <<EOF;
23: <HTML>
24: <HEAD>
25: <TITLE>Mall Example</TITLE>
26: </HEAD>
27: <BODY>
28: <H1>Mall Example</H1>
29:
30: <TABLE BORDER=0 CELLPADDING=10 WIDTH=400>
31: <TR VALIGN=top ALIGN=left>
32: <FORM METHOD="post">
33: <TD>
34: <B>Deluxe Widget</B><BR>
35: The deluxe widget is the finest of its kind. Purchase yours today
```

15

```
36: for the low price of \$1,995.
37: </TD>
38: <TD>
39:     <SELECT NAME="quantity">
40:         <OPTION VALUE=1>1
41:         <OPTION VALUE=2>2
42:         <OPTION VALUE=3>3
43:     </SELECT>
44: </TD>
45: <TD>
46:     <INPUT TYPE=hidden NAME="item" VALUE="deluxe">
47:     <INPUT TYPE=submit VALUE="Add to Cart">
48: </TD>
49: </FORM>
50: </TR>
51:
52: <TR VALIGN=top ALIGN=left>
53: <FORM METHOD="post">
54: <TD>
55: <B>Standard Widget</B><BR>
56: The standard widget is really pretty boring. Purchase yours today
57: for the low price of \$995.
58: </TD>
59: <TD>
60:     <SELECT NAME="quantity">
61:         <OPTION VALUE=1>1
62:         <OPTION VALUE=2>2
63:         <OPTION VALUE=3>3
64:     </SELECT>
65: </TD>
66: <TD>
67:     <INPUT TYPE=hidden NAME="item" VALUE="standard">
68:     <INPUT TYPE=submit VALUE="Add to Cart">
69: </TD>
70: </FORM>
71: </TR>
72: <TR>
73: <TD COLSPAN=3 ALIGN=center>
74:     <FONT SIZE=+1><A HREF="checkout.pl">Check Out</A></FONT>
75: </TD>
76: </TR>
77: </TABLE>
78:
79:
80: </BODY>
81: </HTML>
82: EOF
```

FIGURE 15.4

*A page that contains
a very small online
catalog.*

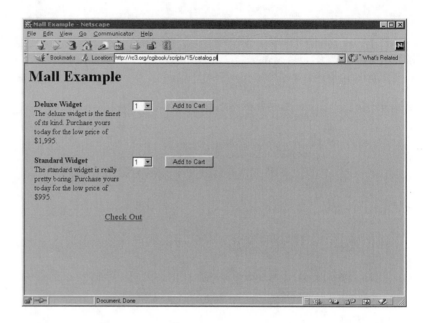

The first thing the program does is check to see whether it has received any input from
the forms contained in the page. If it has, it sets a cookie that specifies how many of an
item the user wants to buy, and then redisplays the page so that the user can select other
items. If it does not receive input from a form, it just displays the page.

The Checkout Form

After the user is done with the page, he can click on the Check Out link to complete the
order. The checkout.pl program simply checks to see whether there is a cookie set for
each item in the catalog. If there is, it adds a line to the invoice for that item, containing
the name of the item, the quantity ordered, the price, and the total cost. The source code
to the checkout.pl script appears in Listing 15.8.

LISTING 15.8   The Checkout Script

```
 1: #!c:/perl/bin/perl
 2:
 3: use CGI;
 4: $query = new CGI;
 5:
 6: print $query->header;
 7: print $query->start_html(-title=>'Check Out');
 8: print "<H1 ALIGN=center>Checking Out</H1>\n";
 9: print "<DIV ALIGN=center>\n";
10: print "<TABLE CELLPADDING=4 BORDER=1>\n<TR>\n";
```

15

```
11: print "<TH>Item</TH><TH>Quantity</TH><TH>Price</TH><TH>Amount</TH></TR>\n";
12: if ($query->cookie('standard')) {
13:     $quantity = $query->cookie('standard');
14:     print "<TR><TD>Standard Widget</TD><TD ALIGN=right>$quantity</TD>\n";
15:     print "<TD ALIGN=right>\$995</TD><TD ALIGN=right>";
16:     print "\$", 995 * $quantity;
17:     print "</TD></TR>\n";
18: }
19: if ($query->cookie('deluxe')) {
20:     $quantity = $query->cookie('deluxe');
21:     print "<TR><TD>Deluxe Widget</TD><TD ALIGN=right>$quantity</TD>\n";
22:     print "<TD ALIGN=right>\$1995</TD><TD ALIGN=right>";
23:     print "\$", 1995 * $quantity;
24:     print "</TD></TR>\n";
25: }
26: print "</TABLE>\n</DIV>\n";
27: print $query->end_html, "\n";
```

The checkout page (shown in Figure 15.5) is very simple in this example. If this was a real commerce site, you would probably require the user to enter his name, address, telephone number, credit card number, and a bunch of other stuff at this point. If you were really on the ball, you would have a database of users based on cookies, and you'd automatically print out all the information for each user every time she visits the site. Then he would only have to enter the information the first time he visits the site, and update his record with any changes made after that.

FIGURE 15.5

The checkout page from an online shopping site.

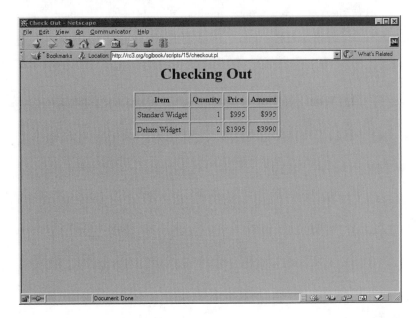

Why CGI and Cookies Don't Mix

Now that I've shown you all sorts of cool things you can do with cookies, I'm going to explain why cookies and CGI really don't mix. The problem with combining cookies and CGI is that much of the time, cookies are used by every page on your site. For example, if you want to log a user's session ID every time he visits a page on your Web site, you have to run all those pages using CGI, which is extremely slow.

If you want to use session management across your entire site, you may benefit by using an application development platform like ASP, ColdFusion, or PHP that lets you embed code snippets into standard HTML pages. These platforms provide fast application servers that integrate directly with the Web server, and also enable you to spend most of your time designing your pages and then go in and add the session management code once you're done. These platforms are discussed in Hour 12, "Pros and Cons of Alternate Technologies."

Summary

Session management is one of the key building blocks of interactive, large-scale Web applications. The capability to conduct transactions that span more than one page, and to create individual sessions for each user who visits your Web site, make applications like Amazon.com's online bookstore possible. This hour discussed two ways to add session management to your applications—using hidden form fields, and using cookies. Using cookies is the more robust method; it enables you to manage sessions that comprise all the pages on your site.

Q&A

Q What can I do to manage user sessions if they have cookies turned off?

A Unfortunately, if your site's visitors are using a browser that doesn't support cookies, or they have cookies turned off, there isn't an easy alternate method for session management. One option is to include session identifiers as part of the URL on your site. To use this strategy, every link on your site has to be generated dynamically with the user's session ID included as part of the URL. This is a lot of work, but if you want to support all users, it's necessary. One site that uses such a scheme is Amazon.com. Session IDs are stored in a cookie, but they are also included in all of the links on the site.

Q Can cookies be used to steal my email address, find out my real name, or list the files on my hard drive?

A There are a lot of rumors surrounding cookies, but the bottom line is that they can only be used to store information that the user has provided to the Web site. Cookies can only store information, not gather it. The main privacy issue with cookies is that they can be used to store a history of Web pages you've visited, but remember that cookies are only sent back to the domain from which they originated. A cookie can't be used to gather information from sites other than the one that sent it. Unfortunately, cookies can be included with images and other files as well as with HTML documents. So, if an image on a page is served from a domain other than that which is serving the actual Web document, it can send you a cookie as well. Some ad banner networks are using this to track user activity across all of the sites that participate in their network.

Workshop

The quiz questions are designed to strengthen the knowledge you gain each hour. The exercises help you build on that knowledge by providing you with the opportunity to apply it to real problems. For the answers to the quiz questions, refer to Appendix A, "Answers."

Quiz

1. What is the purpose of the domain attribute of a cookie?
2. How are the names and passwords for basic authentication encoded?
3. How can users spoof hidden form fields and send values other than those that you've specified?
4. How do you remove an existing cookie?

Exercises

1. Create a CGI program that asks a user for his name the first time he visits the page, and then sets a cookie and welcomes him by name every time he comes back.

HOUR 16

Building a Simple Shopping Cart

Nearly all Web sites that sell merchandise over the Internet include that ubiquitous element—the shopping cart. Most shopping cart applications work by assigning the user a session identifier, and associating the user's purchase choices with that identifier. The application keeps track of the user's activities by carrying the identifier from page to page within the site. When the user is ready to "check out," the application retrieves all the items to be purchased.

This hour demonstrates how to build a simple shopping cart by discussing the following topics:

- How shopping cart applications work
- How to build a catalog
- How to build a shopping cart
- How the checkout procedure for an online store works

How the Sample Shopping Cart Works

The sample shopping cart application has three components. In this case, they're rather simplified, but the concepts are the same whether you're selling five items or you're Amazon.com. The first component is the catalog. The catalog contains the ID, name, and price for all the items that are sold by the online store. Generally, the catalog is the most sophisticated component of the site. At Amazon.com, not only is the basic name and pricing information included in the catalogs, but so is lots of other information, including reader reviews, editorial reviews, and images of the book covers.

In this case, the catalog is stored in a single flat text file. In Hour 20, "Creating an Online Store," I'll explain how to create an online catalog using a relational database. Relational databases are really ideal for the storage of information associated with online stores, but many smaller sites use flat files for data storage. In any case, in this sample application, flat files will be used. The main reason is that this application is designed to illustrate how session management is used to create a shopping cart, not how to use relational databases.

The structure of the `products.txt` file, which contains a list of products sold on the site, appears in Listing 16.1.

LISTING 16.1   The `products.txt` File

```
1:      64 megabyte SIMM        99.00
2:      3D Video Card    199.00
3:      DVD-ROM Drive    79.00
4:      500mhz Athlon processor 249.00
5:      Ethernet adapter        19.00
6:      19 inch monitor 319.00
```

As you can see, the product catalog for this application is very simple. For every product, there's only a product ID, product description, and product price.

The rest of the data associated with the application is stored in a file called `cart.txt`. This file contains the shopping cart information for all the users using the site at any given time. The following code is a snippet of the `cart.txt` file:

```
946771592332    1       2
946771592332    4       1
946771592332    3       1
```

The cart file contains three fields per record—a session ID, a product ID, and a quantity. Whenever a user adds a new item to his cart, a new record is added to the file. If a user adds an item that's already in his cart, or alters the quantity of an item in the cart, the appropriate record is modified. If the user removes an item, the corresponding record is removed from the file. When a user checks out and places his order, the order is stored elsewhere and all the cart information is expunged from the file.

There's one significant problem that isn't covered by this application, and that is the expiration of unpurchased content from the file. Consider the following scenario: a user arrives at the site and adds a bunch of stuff to his shopping cart. Instead of checking out or removing all the stuff in the cart, he just leaves and never comes back. The items he placed in his shopping cart remain there forever. The best solution for this problem is to log the date and time that items were placed in the cart, and automatically remove them after a certain amount of time passes.

The Catalog

First let's take a look at the catalog script. It serves two purposes—it lists the products on the screen, and it adds selected products to the shopping cart. Each item in the cart has its own form, which the user can submit to add an item to the cart. The form fields are passed back to the catalog.pl script through the query string.

Like many of the scripts presented in this book, it decides what to do based on the parameters it receives in the query string. If a product ID is passed to the script, it retrieves the user's session ID or assigns a new one, and attempts to add that product to her cart. If no product ID is passed to the script, it just displays the product listing without altering the contents of the user's cart. The source code for the catalog.pl script appears in Listing 16.2.

LISTING 16.2 The catalog.pl Script

```
 1: #!/usr/local/bin/perl
 2:
 3: use CGI;
 4: use CGI::Carp qw( fatalsToBrowser );
 5:
 6: $query = new CGI;
 7:
 8: $catalog_file = "products.txt";
 9: $cart_file = "cart.txt";
10:
11: if ($query->param('product_id')) {
12:     if ($query->cookie('session_id')) {
13:         $session_id = ($query->cookie('session_id'));
14:     }
15:     else {
```

continues

LISTING 16.2   continued

```
16:          $session_id = time . $$;
17:      }
18:      &set_variables;
19:      &add_to_cart;
20:      &print_page_start;
21:      &open_catalog;
22:      &display_catalog;
23:      &print_page_end;
24: }
25: else {
26:      &print_page_start;
27:      &open_catalog;
28:      &display_catalog;
29:      &print_page_end;
30: }
31:
32: sub add_to_cart {
33:      open (CART, "+>> $cart_file")
34:          or die "Can't open shopping cart file";
35:      flock CART, 2;
36:      seek CART, 0, 0;
37:      @records = <CART>;
38:      @new_records = ();
39:      $found = 'no';
40:      foreach $record (@records) {
41:          chomp $record;
42:          ($rec_session_id, $rec_product_id, $rec_quantity) =
43:              split /\t/, $record;
44:          if (($session_id eq $rec_session_id) and
45:              ($product_id eq $rec_product_id)) {
46:              $new_quantity = $quantity + $rec_quantity;
47:              $new_record = "$session_id\t$product_id\t$new_quantity";
48:              $record = $new_record;
49:              $found = 'yes';
50:          }
51:          $record .= "\n";
52:          push @new_records, $record;
53:      }
54:      seek CART, 0, 0;
55:      truncate CART, 0;
56:      print CART @new_records;
57:      if ($found eq 'no') {
58:          print CART "$session_id\t$product_id\t$quantity\n";
59:      }
60:      close CART;
61: }
62:
63: sub set_variables {
64:      $product_id = $query->param('product_id');
```

16

```perl
65:        $quantity = $query->param('quantity');
66: }
67:
68: sub open_catalog {
69:     eval {
70:         open (CATALOG, "< $catalog_file")
71:             or die "Can't open $catalog_file";
72:     };
73: }
74:
75: sub display_catalog {
76:     print "<CENTER>\n<TABLE BORDER=1 CELLPADDING=4>\n";
77:     print "<TR>\n<TH>Description</TH>\n<TH>Price</TH>\n</TR>\n";
78:
79:     while (<CATALOG>) {
80:         ($product_id, $product_desc, $product_price) = split /\t/;
81:         print "<TR>\n";
82:         print "<FORM>\n";
83:         print "<INPUT TYPE=\"hidden\" NAME=\"product_id\" ";
84:         print "VALUE=\"$product_id\">\n";
85:         print "<TD>$product_desc</TD>\n<TD>$product_price</TD>\n";
86:         print "<TD><INPUT TYPE=\"text\" NAME=\"quantity\" ";
87:         print "VALUE=\"1\" SIZE=2></TD>\n";
88:         print "<TD><INPUT TYPE=\"submit\" VALUE=\"add\"></TD>\n";
89:         print "</FORM>\n";
90:         print "</TR>\n";
91:     }
92:     print "</TABLE>\n</CENTER>\n";
93: }
94:
95: sub print_page_start {
96:     if ($session_id) {
97:         $cookie = $query->cookie(-name=>'session_id',
98:                                 -value=>$session_id);
99:         print $query->header(-cookie=>$cookie);
100:     }
101:     else {
102:         print $query->header;
103:     }
104:     print "<HTML>\n<HEAD>\n<TITLE>PC Product Catalog</TITLE>\n";
105:     print "</HEAD>\n<BODY>\n";
106:     print "<H1 ALIGN=\"center\">PC Product Catalog</H1>\n";
107: }
108:
109: sub print_page_end {
110:     print "<P><CENTER><B>";
111:     print"<A HREF=\"cart.pl\">view cart</A></B></CENTER></P>\n";
112:     print "</BODY>\n</HTML>\n";
113: }
```

In this script, as in most, there's some setup that takes place before the actual processing of user data gets under way. As is the case in all the scripts I write, first I import the CGI module, and create a query object. Then, I create variables that contain the locations of the shopping cart and catalog files. The Web server must have read access for the catalog file (it doesn't write to the file), and must have read and write access to the shopping cart file.

Printing the Catalog

Before we look at manipulating the shopping cart, let's take a look at how the catalog is presented to users. The presentation of the catalog is a two-step process. First, I use the open_catalog subroutine to create a file handle named CATALOG in order to read the list of items from the file. The open statement is wrapped in an eval block, but in this sample program, there's no error-handling code to specifically handle any errors trapped by the eval block. The open_catalog subroutine runs from line 68 to line 73.

After the catalog file is open, the next step is to print all the records in the file. The display_catalog subroutine, which begins on line 75, does this job. The catalog itself is formatted using an HTML table, so on lines 76 and 77, I begin the table and print the table headings.

The actual contents of the catalog file are processed and printed using the while loop that begins on line 79. Each line is pulled from the file and processed by the loop. When you process a form using a loop and file handle in this way, each line of the file is automatically copied into the special variable $_ as it is processed by the loop. Many Perl functions process $_ if no argument to replace it is specified. For example, on line 80, the chomp function, which removes the line feed from the end of a string, has no arguments specified. Because no string to chomp is passed to it, it assumes that it's supposed to chomp $_.

The next line works exactly the same way. It splits the current value of $_ into several variables by assuming that tabs are field delimiters. When you're working with $_, it's not necessary to pass the string to split to the split function. After the individual fields have been extracted from the record, the catalog item can be printed.

Each row of the table is actually an individual form. Each form contains three fields—a hidden field with the product ID, a text field where the user can enter a quantity for the product, and a submit button. To add products to her cart, the user just has to enter a quantity in the text box (the default is 1) and click on the submit button. Next, I'll explain what happens if a user does add an item to the shopping cart.

Adding Items to the Shopping Cart

Now let's look at what happens when a user submits a form in the catalog to add an item to the cart. It's important to point out that users can't add more than one type of item to his cart at a time. Each item in the catalog has a form unto itself, and while the user can add any quantity of that item to his cart at any given time, he can't add several different items at the same time.

When a user submits a form to add an item to the cart, two parameters are passed to the script—the product ID of the item being added, and the quantity of that item that should be added. When a user adds an item to the cart, the script first searches the cart file to see if the user already has that item in his cart. If he does, the new quantity is added to the existing quantity of that item, and that record in the cart file is updated. If the item being added isn't already in the cart, a new record is added to the file with the session ID, product ID, and quantity.

The addition of items to the shopping cart is handled by the add_to_cart subroutine. This subroutine opens the cart file, determines whether an existing record needs to be updated or a new record needs to be created, and updates the cart file. First, the subroutine opens the file in read/write mode, and locks the file. The file is actually opened using the append (>>) operator, but that only affects where the file pointer is located when the file is opened. After the file is opened, the file pointer is moved to the beginning of the file, and all the records are read into the array @records. A new variable, $found, is defined so that you can keep track of whether you've located a record that matches the product being added to the cart. If the session ID of the user adding the item, and the product ID of the item being added, match a record that's already in the cart file, the $found variable is set to 'yes', so you know not to create a new record later.

After all the variables are set up, I iterate over all the records in the cart file to find one that matches. As each record is evaluated, it's placed in the @new_records array, which will eventually be written back to the file. If a record is a match, the quantity being added is added to the current quantity in the record, and it is pushed into the @new_records array. The $found variable is also set to indicate that the record was found.

One bit of code that's not built into this application is a check that determines whether the user entered a valid quantity in the form. If the user entered non-digits, that value can't be added to the current quantity. If the user entered a negative number, that item could actually wind up with a negative quantity in the cart file, and could actually receive a credit when they check out. If this were a real application, you'd have to check for those types of conditions.

16

After all the records in the file have been processed, the existing file is truncated and the records are then printed to the now empty file. At that point, if a matching record wasn't found, a new record is appended to the file containing the session ID and product that was to be added. After all the records have been printed to the file, it is closed.

The Contents of the Shopping Cart

The cart.pl file is used to view the contents of shopping carts, and to allow users to remove items from the cart if they no longer intend to purchase them. If the script receives no parameters, it just retrieves the list of items in the user's shopping cart and displays them. Each item in the cart is accompanied by a form that can be used to remove that item from the shopping cart. If the action parameter is set to remove, it attempts to remove the specified item from the cart. The full source code for the script appears in Listing 16.3.

LISTING 16.3   The Source Code for cart.pl

```
 1: #!/usr/local/bin/perl
 2:
 3: use CGI;
 4: use CGI::Carp qw( fatalsToBrowser );
 5:
 6: $cart_file = "cart.txt";
 7: $catalog_file = "products.txt";
 8: $query = new CGI;
 9:
10:
11: if ($query->cookie('session_id')) {
12:     $session_id = ($query->cookie('session_id'));
13: }
14:
15: if ($query->param('action')) {
16:     if ($query->param('action') eq 'remove') {
17:         $page_title = "Shopping Cart";
18:         &remove_item;
19:         &print_page_start;
20:         &get_cart_contents;
21:         if (@user_cart) {
22:             &get_product_list;
23:             &print_cart;
24:         }
25:         else {
26:             &print_no_cart;
27:         }
28:         &print_page_end;
29:     }
30: }
31: else {
32:     $page_title = "Shopping Cart";
```

```perl
33:     &print_page_start;
34:     &get_cart_contents;
35:     if (@user_cart) {
36:         &get_product_list;
37:         &print_cart;
38:     }
39:     else {
40:         &print_no_cart;
41:     }
42:     &print_page_end;
43: }
44:
45: sub remove_item {
46:     open (CART, "+>> $cart_file")
47:         or die "Can't open cart file";
48:     flock CART, 2;
49:     seek CART, 0, 0;
50:     @records = <CART>;
51:     @new_records = ();
52:     foreach $record (@records) {
53:         chomp $record;
54:         ($rec_session_id, $rec_product_id, $rec_quantity) =
55:             split /\t/, $record;
56:         unless (($rec_session_id eq $session_id) and
57:                 ($rec_product_id eq $query->param('product_id'))) {
58:             push @new_records, $record . "\n";
59:         }
60:     }
61:     seek CART, 0, 0;
62:     truncate CART, 0;
63:     print CART @new_records;
64:     close CART;
65: }
66:
67: sub get_cart_contents {
68:     open (CART, "< $cart_file")
69:         or die "Can't open shopping cart file";
70:     @records = <CART>;
71:     @user_cart = ();
72:     foreach $record (@records) {
73:         chomp $record;
74:         ($rec_session_id, $rec_product_id, $rec_quantity) =
75:             split /\t/, $record;
76:         if ($rec_session_id eq $session_id) {
77:             push @user_cart, $record;
78:         }
79:     }
80: }
81:
82: sub get_product_list {
```

continues

16

LISTING **16.3**   continued

```
83:        open (CATALOG, "< $catalog_file")
84:            or die "Can't open catalog file";
85:        %product_names = ();
86:        %product_prices = ();
87:        while (<CATALOG>) {
88:            ($cat_product_id, $product_name, $product_price) =
89:                split /\t/;
90:            $product_names{$cat_product_id} = $product_name;
91:            $product_prices{$cat_product_id} = $product_price;
92:        }
93:        close CATALOG;
94: }
95:
96: sub print_cart {
97:        print "<CENTER>\n<TABLE>\n<TR>\n";
98:        print "<TH>Product ID</TH>\n<TH>Product Name</TH>\n";
99:        print "<TH>Price</TH>\n<TH>Quantity</TH>\n</TR>\n";
100:        foreach $cart_item (@user_cart) {
101:            ($rec_session_id, $rec_product_id, $rec_quantity) =
102:                split /\t/, $cart_item;
103:            print "<TD>$rec_product_id</TD>\n";
104:            print "<TD>", $product_names{$rec_product_id}, "</TD>\n";
105:            print "<TD>", $product_prices{$rec_product_id}, "</TD>\n";
106:            print "<TD>$rec_quantity</TD>\n";
107:            print "<TD>\n<FORM>\n";
108:            print "<INPUT TYPE=\"hidden\" NAME=\"action\" VALUE=\"remove\">\n";
109:            print "<INPUT TYPE=\"hidden\" NAME=\"product_id\" ";
110:            print "VALUE=\"$rec_product_id\">\n";
111:            print "<INPUT TYPE=\"submit\" VALUE=\"remove\">\n";
112:            print "</TD>\n";
113:            print "</TR>\n";
114:        }
115:        print "</TABLE>\n";
116: }
117:
118: sub print_page_start {
119:        print $query->header;
120:        print "<HTML>\n<HEAD>\n<TITLE>$page_title</TITLE>\n";
121:        print "</HEAD>\n<BODY>\n";
122:        print "<H1 ALIGN=\"center\">$page_title</H1>\n";
123: }
124:
125: sub print_no_cart {
126:        print "<P>There are no items in your shopping cart.</P>\n";
127: }
128:
129: sub print_page_end {
130:        print "<P><CENTER><B>";
131:        print"<A HREF=\"catalog.pl\">return to catalog</A></B></CENTER></P>\n";
132:        print "</BODY>\n</HTML>\n";
133: }
```

Printing the User's Cart

You'd think that printing the contents of the user's cart would be pretty simple, but in fact it's a relatively complex process. In order to properly display the contents of a cart, data must be retrieved from multiple files and correlated so that records are displayed correctly. Take a look at the shopping cart in Figure 16.1. Each line of the shopping cart contains the product ID, quantity, description, and price for the product on that line.

16

FIGURE 16.1

A user's shopping cart.

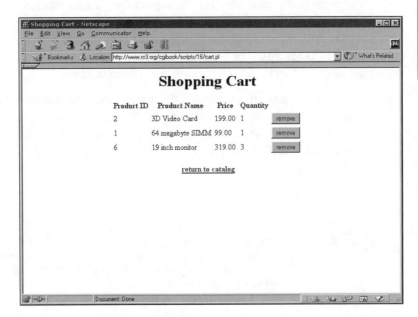

Now let's take a look at the steps required to display a user's shopping cart. The first step in displaying the user's shopping cart is retrieving a list of all the items in her cart from the cart file. This is accomplished in the get_cart_contents subroutine. In that subroutine, all the records in the cart file are read into the @records array, and the matching records are stored in the @user_cart array. To determine which records match, each record is broken out into its individual fields, and the session ID in each record is compared to the user's session ID.

After all the matching records have been extracted, the program determines whether there are, in fact, any items in the user's cart. If there aren't, a message is printed indicating that the cart is empty and the user is directed back to the catalog. If the cart is not empty, the get_product_list subroutine is called to fetch the prices and descriptions for the items in the catalog so that they can be printed in the cart listing.

Because this book is about CGI programming and not data structures, I use a relatively simple data structure to store all the product information when I retrieve it from the catalog. I create two hashes (also known as associative arrays). In this case, there are two hashes. The first keeps track of the descriptions of each product; the second keeps track of prices. The product ID is used as the key for both hashes. After all the product information has been retrieved, the contents of the cart can be displayed.

The `print_cart` subroutine is used to print the contents of the shopping cart. First, it prints the beginning tags for the table and column headings, and then a `foreach` loop is used to print the actual contents of the cart. The columns in the table are, from left to right, the product ID, the product description, price, and quantity. The far right column contains a button used to remove that item from the cart.

When the columns are printed, the description and price are retrieved from the hashes created in the `get_product_list` subroutine. Information is retrieved from a hash by referencing the hash using the appropriate key. For example, to retrieve the description of a product with the ID 1, the following code is used:

```
$product_names{'1'}
```

> When you want to reference a single element in a hash, you prefix the name of the hash with $. To reference a hash as a whole, you prefix the hash name with a %. To extract an item from the hash product_names, the usage is: $product_names{KEY}. To create it initially, the notation is: %product_names.

There's also a form embedded in every row of the table. It contains hidden fields that specify the product ID and action. In this case, the action is always `remove`. After the `foreach` loop has processed all the contents of the user's cart, the table is closed, and the `print_page_end` subroutine is used to display the closing HTML tags for the page.

Removing an Item from the Cart

Removing an item from the shopping cart is just another example of code that removes records from a flat file database. The `remove_item` subroutine is used to remove the record associated with a particular item in the cart. The `remove_item` subroutine uses the pattern seen in all the code used to modify records in a flat file database.

It opens the file, locks it, and retrieves all the records. Then it deletes the entire contents of the file, and prints all the records except for the one that is supposed to be removed. This record is identified using the product ID found in the form in the shopping cart, and the user's session ID, which is retrieved from the session_id cookie. After all the records have been printed back into the file, the cart file is closed, and the new contents of the shopping cart are printed.

There is no form validation for this function because all the values in the form are hard coded in the shopping cart page. Of course, this form could be spoofed by altering the URL used to call the page, but the damage the user could potentially do is very low. Even so, in a production application, you would want to include some error-checking code to make sure that the user isn't abusing the application.

16

Checkout

From the shopping cart, the user is allowed to check out. In this case, the user is simply asked for his address and payment information, which is then stored so that the order can be fulfilled. Let's look at the general case for online stores first. After a user has selected some items from an online catalog, and is ready to purchase them, certain information must be collected. After the information has been gathered, there are several steps that generally also occur. Not all sites use all these steps, but I'll list them anyway. First, let's look at the information gathered:

- The user's name and billing address
- The address to which the items being purchased should be shipped
- The method of payment for the shipment
- If the method of payment is a credit card, you must get the user's credit card number, expiration date, and the name on the credit card
- You might also want to ask whether the purchase is a gift
- If it is a gift, you might want to ask for a message to place on the invoice, and whether the gift should be wrapped

There's a lot more information that could also be gathered, if you choose. For example, you might allow the user to enter discount codes or coupon IDs if your site offers such promotions. In addition to gathering all the information associated with the order, you must also perform the steps necessary to verify that the order is valid and that it should be fulfilled. You must also calculate the final cost of the order based on the information that the user enters. These steps might include:

- Verifying that the user filled out all the required fields on the form and that the data the user entered seems to be appropriate for those fields
- Verifying that the user entered a valid credit card number
- Taking into account any discounts or credits the user is entitled to

- Contacting a payment processing service to verify that the credit card is valid and that the user has enough credit available to accept the charge for the order

- Determining shipping costs based on the user's preference and their geographical location

- Determining whether sales tax should be charged for the order, and if so, what percentage should be added

After you've calculated the final total for the order and have confirmed that you do in fact want to accept it, the next step is to move the order into the queue for fulfillment. How this is accomplished varies widely depending on how your site is built, and more importantly, on how your order fulfillment process works. For simpler sites, the most common process is to bundle all the order information up and email it to the person who is responsible for making sure the order is fulfilled. Sites with more complicated back-end systems might use some remote procedure calling scheme to insert the order into an automated order fulfillment system.

The Checkout Script for this Example

Let's look at the simple checkout script for this example. In this case, I just ask the user to fill out a few forms, verify that they entered the information that was requested, and then just append their order information to a file. In theory, if this were a real site, some person or program would periodically read that file and move the orders along in the fulfillment process. Because this is just an example, we don't really care what happens to that information down the road. The source code for the checkout script is in Listing 16.4.

LISTING 16.4 The source code for checkout.pl

```perl
#!/usr/local/bin/perl

use CGI;
use CGI::Carp qw(fatalsToBrowser);
use DBI;

$cart_file = "cart.txt";
$catalog_file = "products.txt";
$query = new CGI;

%cc_types = ('AMEX' => 'American Express',
             'VISA' => 'Visa',
             'MC' => 'Mastercard',
             'DISC' => 'Discover');

if ($query->cookie('session_id')) {
    $session_id = $query->cookie('session_id');
}
```

```
else {
    $page_title = "Checkout: Error";
    &print_page_start;
    &print_no_cart;
    &print_page_end;
    exit;
}

&get_cart_contents;

if (@user_cart) {
    if ($query->param('cc_type')) {
        &set_variables;
        if (! &valid_form) {
            $page_title = "Checkout Complete";
            &print_page_start;
            &insert_order;
            &empty_cart;
            &print_success;
            &print_page_end;
        }
        else {
            $page_title = "Checkout: Please correct errors";
            &print_page_start;
            &print_error;
            &print_form;
            &print_page_end;
        }
    }
    else {
        $page_title = "Checkout";
        &print_page_start;
        &print_form;
        &print_page_end;
    }
}
else {
    $page_title = "Error: Your cart is empty";
    &print_page_start;
    &print_no_cart;
    &print_page_end;
}

sub get_cart_contents {
    open (CART, "< $cart_file")
        or die "Can't open shopping cart file";
    @records = <CART>;
    @user_cart = ();
    foreach $record (@records) {
        chomp $record;
```

continues

LISTING 16.4   continued

```perl
            ($rec_session_id, $rec_product_id, $rec_quantity) =
                split /\t/, $record;
            if ($rec_session_id eq $session_id) {
                push @user_cart, $record;
            }
        }
    }
}

sub insert_order {
    1;
}

sub empty_cart {
    open (CART, "+>> $cart_file")
        or die "Can't open cart file";
    flock CART, 2;
    seek CART, 0, 0;
    @records = <CART>;
    @new_records = ();
    foreach $record (@records) {
        chomp $record;
        ($rec_session_id, $rec_product_id, $rec_quantity) =
            split /\t/, $record;
        unless ($rec_session_id eq $session_id) {
            push @new_records, $record . "\n";
        }
    }
    seek CART, 0, 0;
    truncate CART, 0;
    print CART @new_records;
    close CART;
}

sub print_empty_cart {
    print "<P>You cannot check out until you have placed items ";
    print "in your shopping cart.</P>\n";
    print "<P>Return to the <A HREF=\"catalog.pl\">catalog</A>.</P>\n";
}

sub set_variables {
    $name = $query->param('name');
    $address = $query->param('address');
    $city = $query->param('city');
    $state = $query->param('state');
    $zip = $query->param('zip');
    $cc_type = $query->param('cc_type');
    $cc_number = $query->param('cc_number');
    $exp_month = $query->param('exp_month');
    $exp_year = $query->param('exp_year');
}
```

```perl
sub valid_form {
    $error_message = '';
    $error_message .= "<LI>You must enter your name\n"
        if ($name =~ /^\s*$/);
    $error_message .= "<LI>You must enter your address\n"
        if ($address =~ /^\s*$/);
    $error_message .= "<LI>You must enter your city\n"
        if ($city =~ /^\s*$/);
    $error_message .= "<LI>You must enter a valid zip code\n"
        if ($zip !~ /^\d+$/);
    $error_message .= "<LI>You must enter a valid month of expiration\n"
        if ($exp_month > 12 || $exp_month < 1);
    $error_message .= "<LI>You must enter a valid year of expiration\n"
        if ($exp_year < 2000 || $exp_year > 2010);
    $error_message .= "<LI>You must enter a valid credit card number\n"
        if ($cc_number !~ /^\d+$/);
    return $error_message;
}

sub print_error {
    print "<P>Please correct the following errors:</P>\n";
    if ($error_message) {
        print "<UL>\n$error_message\n</UL>\n";
    }
}

sub print_form {
    print "<FORM>\n";
    print "<TABLE BORDER=0>\n";
    print "<TR><TD>Name:</TD>\n";
    print "<TD><INPUT TYPE=\"text\" NAME=\"name\" VALUE=\"$name\">\n";
    print "</TD></TR>\n";
    print "<TR><TD>Street address:</TD>\n";
    print "<TD><INPUT TYPE=\"text\" NAME=\"address\" ";
    print "VALUE=\"$address\" SIZE=40 MAXLENGTH=80></TD></TR>\n";
    print "<TR><TD>City:</TD>\n";
    print "<TD><INPUT TYPE=\"text\" NAME=\"city\" ";
    print "VALUE=\"$city\"></TD></TR>\n";
    print "<TR><TD>State:</TD>\n";
    print "<TD><INPUT TYPE=\"text\" NAME=\"state\" ";
    print "VALUE=\"$state\" SIZE=2 MAXLENGTH=2></TD></TR>\n";
    print "<TR><TD>Zip</TD>\n";
    print "<TD><INPUT TYPE=\"text\" NAME=\"zip\" ";
    print "VALUE=\"$zip\" SIZE=5 MAXLENGTH=5></TD></TR>\n";
    print "<TD>Credit card:</TD>\n<TD>\n<SELECT NAME=\"cc_type\">\n";
    foreach $key (sort {$a <=> $b} keys %cc_types) {
        print "<OPTION VALUE=\"$key\">", $cc_types{$key}, "\n";
    }
    print "</SELECT>\n</TD>\n";
    print "<TR><TD>Credit card number:</TD>\n";
```

continues

16

LISTING 16.4   continued

```
        print "<TD><INPUT TYPE=\"text\" NAME=\"cc_number\" ";
        print "VALUE=\"$cc_number\"></TD></TR>\n";
        print "<TR><TD>Expiration date:</TD>\n";
        print "<TD><INPUT TYPE=\"text\" NAME=\"exp_month\" ";
        print "VALUE=\"$exp_month\" SIZE=2 MAXLENGTH=2>\n";
        print "<INPUT TYPE=\"text\" NAME=\"exp_year\" ";
        print "VALUE=\"$exp_year\" SIZE=2 MAXLENGTH=4>\n";
        print "<TR><TD></TD>\n";
        print "<TD><INPUT TYPE=\"submit\" VALUE=\"Complete Checkout\">";
        print "</TD></TR>\n";
        print "</TABLE>\n";
        print "</FORM>\n";
    }

    sub print_page_start {
        print $query->header;
        print "<HTML>\n<HEAD>\n<TITLE>$page_title</TITLE>\n";
        print "</HEAD>\n<BODY>\n";
        print "<H1 ALIGN=\"center\">$page_title</H1>\n";
    }

    sub print_no_cart {
        print "<P>There are no items in your shopping cart.</P>\n";
    }

    sub print_success {
        print "<P>Your order is complete.</P>\n";
    }

    sub print_page_end {
        print "<P><CENTER><B>";
        print"<A HREF=\"catalog.pl\">return to catalog</A></B></CENTER></P>\n";
        print "</BODY>\n</HTML>\n";
    }
```

This program is a typical form handling program. It's somewhat similar to the other programs presented this hour in the preliminary variables that are set up, and in how it fetches information about the contents of the user's cart. Let's look at the areas where it differs from those other programs. It begins by fetching the contents of the user's cart. If the user does not have anything in their shopping cart, then the page prints an error message. Someone who has nothing in their cart can't check out.

If the user does have items in their shopping cart, I check for the presence of the cc_type form field in the user's request in order to determine whether the order form has been submitted. The reason why I chose this particular field is that it's a select list, so the user always has to select a value from the field. The other fields on the form are text boxes, so they're not suitable for testing in this way. The user could submit the form without entering anything in the text field I chose to test, and then I would assume that they didn't submit the form even though they really did.

Once I've determined whether the user did or didn't submit the form, I can have the script take the appropriate action. If they did submit the form, there's one more decision to be made. Did the user submit valid data? The valid_form subroutine is used to make this determination. This valid_form subroutine uses regular expressions to verify that the user entered valid information. Most of the tests just make sure that the user entered something in the field other than just spaces. The zip code is tested to make sure that the user entered only numbers in the field. The credit card expiration date is actually tested to verify that the user entered appropriate values for the month and year.

16

If the user's form submission is valid, then the program empties their shopping cart and inserts their order into the order entry system. The cart is emptied using the empty_cart subroutine, which begins on line 81. The subroutine just opens the cart file, copies all of the records into memory, empties the file, and then prints all of the records not associated with the user's session ID back to the file. The insert_order subroutine is just a placeholder in this script. There is no back office system to hook this script into, so the customer's order is thrown away. Obviously, if you were using this script on a real site, you'd want to store the user's order somewhere. (In Hour 20, I'll demonstrate how you can insert an order into a relational database.)

If the user's form input was not valid, then print an error message and require them to correct the errors and submit the form again in order to have their order processed. The same subroutine, print_form, is used to print the empty form or to print the form if an error occurs.

Summary

The purpose of this hour was to illustrate how session management works using a real world example. Shopping carts are a feature common to almost all electronic commerce sites, and are one of the classical cases of an application that must keep track of the user's session. In these examples, you learned how cookies are used to keep track of a user's identity as they use an online catalog, and how that identity is correlated with data stored on the server.

Q&A

Q How do I verify the user's credit card account to make sure that the number they entered is valid and that we can charge the order to their credit card?

A Generally, you contract with a third party to do the credit card validation for your site. When the user submits the order form, you connect with the payment processing company's computer and submit the credit card number and amount of the transaction in order to verify that the customer's credit card is valid and can accept the charge. There are a number of companies that provide this service. Two of the most popular are CyberCash (`http://www.cybercash.com`) and CyberSource (`http://www.cybersource.com`). Most companies that provide this service will give you sample code that you can integrate into your programs to communicate with their servers.

Q What role does SSL play in this?

A SSL (secure sockets layer) is a protocol that allows Web browsers and Web servers to communicate in a secure manner. All of the data sent between the browser and server is encrypted so that if someone intercepts the network traffic, they won't be able to determine what data was being transmitted. SSL should be used whenever a user is submitting personal information to the Web server. Examples include credit card numbers, or the user's social security number. When you set up an online store, you should place the checkout script on a secure server. For more information, check out Hour 22, "Securing CGI Scripts."

Q Is it OK to store all of the user's order information on the Web server?

A It's OK to store some order information on the Web server, but you should remove the user's payment information from the Web server as soon as possible after the order is submitted. Storing credit card numbers on a Web server is a very bad idea because Web servers are left exposed on the Internet and can be broken into by malicious individuals. You should forward payment information to a computer that is less exposed to the outside world in order to make sure that credit card numbers aren't stolen through your site.

Workshop

The quiz questions are designed to strengthen the knowledge you gain each hour. The exercises help you build on that knowledge by providing you with the opportunity to apply it to real problems. See Appendix A, "Answers" for the answers to the quiz questions.

Quiz

1. In the sample application, what happens to items that users have in their cart when the user leaves the site without completing their order?

Exercises

1. Enhance the shopping cart application so that the session ID is preserved in the query string in each link as well as being stored in the cookie.

2. Add a button to the cart page that allows users to remove all of the items from their cart at once.

16

Hour **17**

Content Publishing with CGI

CGI is generally associated with Web applications. The user interacts with the application using HTML forms, and the CGI application processes the data the user enters and produces the requested results. However, CGI is also widely used for content publishing. By building a content publishing system, you can separate your content and its presentation, and save yourself the trouble of maintaining thousands of HTML documents.

In this hour, you'll learn

- How content publishing systems are used
- Which types of content publishing systems you can create
- How to build a content publishing system

Why Content Publishing?

Back in the good old days, sites were pretty easy to manage. They generally consisted of a few HTML documents, and maybe some images. When you wanted to change the look and feel of a site, you loaded up Notepad and edited all the documents to reflect the changes you wanted to make. As sites grew larger, other techniques and tools were developed to make life easier for site maintainers. You can get tools to make sure that all the links on your site work, and multifile search and replace tools to make it easier to update your entire site at once.

These days, though, many Web sites consist of so many individual documents that it's just not practical to keep everything in separate HTML files. Making changes to the entire site is too difficult, and even keeping track of that many files and directories is an unenviable chore. Verifying that all the links on your site work is a total nightmare.

Separating Content and Presentation

The solution to this problem is to store the data that will appear on your pages in a format other than HTML, and then use a program to generate the HTML dynamically. The main advantage here is that content and presentation of that content separated. You can change the templates that dictate how your content is presented without making any changes to the content itself. This also allows you to change the look and feel of any number of pages with a change to a single template.

Clearly, when you're dealing with very large volumes of content, this is the way to go. There are a number of other advantages provided by building a content publishing system as well. It makes it easier to allow users to create and update pages through a Web-based application instead of editing HTML files by hand. It also makes it easier to create dynamic, personalized sites.

Building in an Editorial Process

Another advantage of a content management system is that you can create an editorial process using software. When users are directly editing HTML files, it's difficult to make sure that content has been reviewed and approved before it is published. When you use a content management system, you can add editorial steps to the publishing process to make sure that no unapproved content is published to your site.

Let's look at how this might work. A story begins its life when a writer visits your publishing application and submits his story using an HTML form. The next time that writer's editor logs into the system, she sees that a new story awaits her review. At that point, she can review the story, make any required changes, and then approve or reject the story. If she rejects it, the writer will be notified and can revise the story, or if she approves it, it will be published or moved along to the next step in the approval process.

Types of Content Publishing Systems

No two content publishing systems are exactly alike, but they can be categorized based on various criteria. One important criterion for categorization is the time when the

HTML is generated. Some systems generate the HTML whenever the page is requested, others generate the HTML periodically and store it on disk. Others generate the HTML the first time a page is requested, and then save it on disk until the template or content changes, at which time it's generated again the next time that page is requested.

There are advantages to each of these approaches. Let's talk about each of them individually. First let's look at systems that generate all of their pages on-the-fly. In a system like this, every time a user requests a page, the data required to build the page is retrieved and placed in the HTML template. Every user receives a page custom created for him.

This type of system makes it very easy to add personalization to your site. Because all the pages are already being created dynamically for each user, customizing the page for that user doesn't change the architecture of the system at all. The disadvantage of this system is that it's taxing from a performance standpoint. When a user requests a static page, the server just has to read the file and send it to the user. Generating every page with a CGI script can tax server performance.

For some sites, the best option is to generate the pages using a program, but then save the generated HTML on the Web server and then use those files statically. The advantage here is good performance. You can build your site whenever something changes, and then just serve it as a completely static site. Whenever you add new content or make a change, you can just "publish" those changes, and the new dynamically generated files will overwrite the old ones. The disadvantage is that you can't include truly dynamic content on these pages. The content is only as fresh as the last time it was published. The other disadvantage is that your content has to be published manually when you want to update it. Changes won't automatically be transferred into the content on the site.

The third option is to write a system that generates pages dynamically and then caches them until they change. When a change in the underlying content is detected, the page in the cache is deleted and a new page is generated to replace it. The great thing about these systems is that they offer the advantage of immediately making new content available to users while at the same time not generating any pages dynamically if it's not necessary. The main problem here is that the architecture is pretty complex to create. If you want to use this type of architecture, you should look into some of the third party content publishing solutions that support this type of functionality.

Data Storage for Content Publishing Systems

One of the big questions you face when you create a content publishing system is how to store the data associated with your site. Often, the site content itself is stored in a relational database. In Hours 18, "Working with Relational Databases," and 19, "How to Use the Structured Query Language," I explain how relational databases work, and how to use them for data storage with Web applications.

You can also use flat files for data storage on a Web site. In Hour 14, "Creating a CGI-Based Message Board," I explained how to create a message board for your Web site. All the message board content was stored in formatted text files and rendered using a CGI program.

Rather than developing your own file format, you can use XML to format the data for your publishing system. XML, the Extensible Markup Language, is a markup language similar to HTML. The difference is that rather than confining you to a particular set of tags, XML enables to write your own markup language by creating tags of your own. The only catch is that your language and the files created using that language must meet the rules specified by the XML standard. For lots more about XML, check out http://www.xml.com.

A Content Publishing Example

Let's look at an example of how a content publishing system might work. This example illustrates how an online publication like a magazine or newspaper might publish articles using a template system. In this case, the page will be generated every time the user visits the page. The system consists of three components: a story-input program (which allows writers to submit stories), the stories themselves, and a story-display program (which applies a template to a story and displays it in the browser).

First let's look at the template file and the data files. The template looks like a regular HTML file but it contains placeholders that take will be populated with content from the data files. The template file is included in Listing 17.1.

LISTING 17.1   The Story Template File

```
 1: <html>
 2: <head>
 3: <title>News: #STORY_TITLE#</title>
 4: </head>
 5: <body>
 6: <h1 align="center">#STORY_TITLE#</h1>
 7:
 8: <p><b>#DATE_FILED#</b></p>
 9:
10: <font size=2>#BYLINE#</font><br>
11:
12: #BODY_TEXT#
13:
14: <p>Copyright&copy; News 2000</p>
15:
16: </body>
17: </html>
```

Now let's look at the format of the data files . The story-display program writes files in this format. A sample data file is included in Listing 17.2.

LISTING 17.2   A Data File for the Content Publishing System

```
1:<DATE_FILED>Thu Mar 16 15:10:21 2000</DATE_FIELD>
2:<STORY_TITLE>A Sample Story</STORY_TITLE>
3:<BYLINE>Rafe Colburn</BYLINE>
4:<BODY>
5:Sample body text.<BR>
6:</BODY>
```

The tags in the data file correspond to the placeholders in the template. The story-display program can work with any template and data file, as long as the fields in the data file correspond to the placeholders in the template. The story-input program is specific to this particular data format, although you could write a more complex program that would work for any format.

The Story-Input Program

Let's start at the beginning of the editorial process. Before stories can be published or viewed by users, they have to be entered into the content management system. The story-input program accepts the user's form submission, performs some basic validation, and then creates the story file. In our system, there are no additional steps in the approval process. When the writer submits his story, it's published immediately. Let's look at the source code for this program, which is included in Listing 17.3.

LISTING 17.3   The Story-Input Program

```
 1: #!/usr/local/bin/perl
 2:
 3: use CGI;
 4: use CGI::Carp qw(fatalsToBrowser);
 5: $query = new CGI;
 6:
 7: $news_directory = "news";
 8:
 9: if ($query->param('action')) {
10:     &set_variables;
11:
12:     # The form to create a new topic has been submitted
13:     if ($action eq "new") {
14:         if (&valid_form) {
15:             &write_new_topic;
```

continues

LISTING 17.3   continued

```
16:                     $page_title = $title;
17:                     &print_page_start;
18:                     &print_success;
19:                     &print_page_end;
20:            }
21:            else {
22:                     $page_title = "New Topic";
23:                     &print_page_start;
24:                     &print_error;
25:                     &print_form;
26:                     &print_page_end;
27:            }
28:      }
29: }
30: else {
31:      $action = "new";
32:      $page_title = "Enter new topic";
33:      &print_page_start;
34:      &print_form;
35:      &print_page_end;
36: }
37:
38: sub set_variables {
39:      $action = $query->param('action');
40:      $title = $query->param('title');
41:      $byline = $query->param('byline');
42:      $body = $query->param('body');
43: }
44:
45: sub print_page_start {
46:      print $query->header;
47:      print "<HTML>\n<HEAD>\n<TITLE>$page_title</TITLE>\n</HEAD>\n";
48:      print "<BODY>\n<H1>$page_title</H1>\n";
49: }
50:
51: sub print_page_end {
52:      print "</BODY>\n</HTML>\n";
53: }
54:
55: sub print_form {
56:      print "<FORM METHOD=\"post\">\n";
57:      print "<INPUT TYPE=\"hidden\" NAME=\"action\" VALUE=\"$action\">\n";
58:      if ($action eq "new") {
59:          print "Headline: ";
60:          print "<INPUT TYPE=\"text\" NAME=\"title\" ";
61:          print "SIZE=40 MAXLENGTH=72 VALUE=\"$title\"><BR>\n";
62:      }
63:      print "Byline: ";
64:      print "<INPUT TYPE=\"text\" NAME=\"byline\" ";
```

```
65:      print "SIZE=40 MAXLENGHT=72 VALUE=\"$byline\"><BR>\n";
66:      print "Story: <BR>\n";
67:      print "<TEXTAREA ROWS=10 COLS=60 NAME=\"body\" WRAP=\"virtual\">";
68:      print "$body</TEXTAREA><BR>\n";
69:      print "<INPUT TYPE=\"submit\" VALUE=\"publish story\"><BR>\n";
70:      print "</FORM>\n";
71: }
72:
73: sub valid_form {
74:      $error_message = '';
75:      if ($title eq '' && $action eq 'new') {
76:          $error_message .= "You must enter a story title.<BR>\n";
77:      }
78:      if ($byline eq '') {
79:          $error_message .= "You must enter a byline.<BR>\n";
80:      }
81:      if ($body eq '') {
82:          $error_message .= "You must enter the body of your story.<BR>\n";
83:      }
84:      if ($error_message eq '') {
85:          return 1;
86:      }
87:      else {
88:          return undef;
89:      }
90: }
91:
92: sub write_new_topic {
93:      $news_file = time . $$ . '.txt';
94:      open (STORY, "> $news_directory/$news_file")
95:          or die "Can't open $news_directory/$news_file";
96:      print STORY "<DATE_FILED>" . scalar(localtime(time)) .
"</DATE_FIELD>\n";
97:      print STORY "<STORY_TITLE>$title</STORY_TITLE>\n";
98:      print STORY "<BYLINE>$byline</BYLINE>\n";
99:      print STORY "<BODY>\n";
100:      $body =~ s/\n/<BR>\n/g;
101:      print STORY $body;
102:      print STORY "</BODY>\n";
103:      close STORY;
104: }
105:
106: sub print_success {
107:      "<P>New story published.</P>\n";
108: }
109:
110: sub print_error {
111:      print "<FONT COLOR=#CC0000>\n";
112:      print "<P>Please correct the following errors:<BR>\n";
113:      print "$error_message\n</FONT></P>\n";
114: }
```

17

The program begins like nearly all of the scripts in this book, by pointing to the Perl interpreter and then importing the modules needed to run the program. As written, the program is set up to send fatal errors to the browser. If you use this script on your Web site, you'll want to turn that feature off before you make the script public. I also specify in which directory the program should place the new-story files.

This program is designed to serve two purposes. It can process a submission or print a new-story form. To determine which of these actions it should take, it looks at the action parameter. The new-story form contains a hidden field named action with a value of new. If the script finds that the action parameter is set to new, it attempts to process the form submission; otherwise, it prints the form.

Let's look at the decision structure for the program. On line 9, I check whether the action parameter exists. If it doesn't exist, I skip straight down to line 30 and print the new-story form. On line 31, I set the $action variable to new. This value will be included in the hidden form field on the form. I then set the page title, print out the beginning HTML for the page, print the form itself, and print the closing HTML for the page.

If the action parameter does exist, the set_variables subroutine is called. It just transfers the form data to regular variables so that it's less cumbersome to access. On line 13, an if statement checks whether the action parameter is set to new. This extra if statement is meaningless in this script because the only possible action is the submission of a new story. However, leaving it in there makes it easier to add other actions later, if I need to do so. (For example, it might make sense to allow users to edit existing stories using this script.)

On line 14, I determine whether the form submission was valid. This is accomplished by using a call to the valid_form subroutine as the expression in an if statement. The value returned by the subroutine is tested to determine whether the form input was valid. The subroutine itself, which begins on line 73, checks to make sure that the user entered a value in every field on the form. Whenever there's an empty form field, the script appends an error message to the variable $error_message. At the end of the subroutine, on line 84, the script checks the value of $error_message, and returns 1 if it's still empty, or undef if it isn't. A return code of undef indicates that an error occurred and that the script should print the error message.

If there was an error, the script prints the error using the print_error subroutine, and then displays the form again, prepopulated with all the values that the user entered. If the form submission was successful, the script saves the new-story file to disk, and prints a message indicating that the story was created successfully.

The `write_new_topic` subroutine begins on line 92. First, it creates a unique filename by combining the process ID of the CGI program and value returned by the `time` function. It then adds `.txt` to the filename, and attempts to open a file with that name in the directory specified at the beginning of the program. After the file is open, I print out all the data that the user submitted in a format that the story-display program can read.

The Story-Display Program

Now let's look at how the stories are displayed after they've been published. I've written a program that reads a template file and a data file, inserts the data into the template, and sends the results to the browser. The source code for the program appears in Listing 17.4.

LISTING 17.4   The Story-Display Program

```
 1: #!/usr/local/bin/perl
 2:
 3: use CGI;
 4: use CGI::Carp qw(fatalsToBrowser);
 5: $query = new CGI;
 6:
 7: $news_directory = "news";
 8:
 9: if ($query->param('story') && $query->param('template')) {
10:     $story = $query->param('story');
11:     $template = $query->param('template');
12:     &file_error unless (&open_story);
13:     &format_error unless (&parse_story);
14:     &file_error unless (&open_template);
15:     &format_error unless (&parse_template);
16:     &print_page_start;
17:     &print_story;
18:     print "<P>Return to the <A HREF=\"display.pl\">story list</A>.</P>\n";
19:     &print_page_end;
20: }
21: else {
22:     $page_title = "Story Index";
23:     &print_page_start;
24:     &print_story_index;
25:     &print_page_end;
26: }
27:
28: sub print_page_start {
29:     print $query->header;
30:     print "<HTML>\n<HEAD>\n<TITLE>$page_title</TITLE>\n</HEAD>\n";
31:     print "<BODY>\n<H1>$page_title</H1>\n";
32: }
33:
```

17

continues

Listing 17.4   continued

```
34: sub print_page_end {
35:     print "</BODY>\n</HTML>\n";
36: }
37:
38: sub print_story_index {
39:     eval {
40:         opendir (STORIES, "$news_directory")
41:             or die "Can't open $story_directory";
42:         @stories = grep (/^.+\.txt$/, readdir (STORIES));
43:         foreach $story (@stories) {
44:             $story =~ s/(.+)\.txt/$1/;
45:             &open_story;
46:             &parse_story;
47:
48:             # In this case, we assume that stories contain
49:             # a value called STORY_TITLE.
50:             if ($vals{'STORY_TITLE'}) {
51:                 print "<A HREF=\"story.pl?story=$story&template=story\">";
52:                 print $vals{'STORY_TITLE'}, "</A><BR>\n";
53:             }
54:         }
55:     };
56: }
57:
58: sub open_template {
59:     $template_file = $template . ".tmpl";
60:     eval {
61:         open (TEMPLATE, "< $template_file")
62:             or die "Can't open $template_file";
63:         @template_text = <TEMPLATE>;
64:     };
65:     if ($@) {
66:         $error = $@;
67:         return undef;
68:     }
69:     else {
70:         return 1;
71:     }
72: }
73:
74: sub open_story {
75:     $story_file = "$news_directory/" . $story . ".txt";
76:     eval {
77:         open (STORY, "< $story_file")
78:             or die "Can't open $story_file";
79:         @story_text = <STORY>;
80:     };
81:     if ($@) {
82:         $error = $@;
```

```
83:             return undef;
84:         }
85:     else {
86:             return 1;
87:         }
88: }
89:
90: sub parse_template {
91:     $template_text = join '', @template_text;
92:
93:     $template_text =~ s/\#(.+?)\#/$vals{$1}/sg;
94:
95:     # Return a value so that the parse was considered successful.
96:     1;
97: }
98:
99: sub parse_story {
100:     $story_text = join '', @story_text;
101:
102:     %vals = ();
103:     while ($story_text =~ /<(.+?)>(.+?)<\/.+?/sg) {
104:         $vals{$1} = $2;
105:     }
106:
107:     # Return a value so that the parse was considered successful.
108:     1;
109: }
110:
111: sub print_story {
112:     print $template_text;
113: }
114:
115: sub format_error {
116:     print $query->header;
117:     print "<HTML>\n<HEAD>\n<TITLE>Format Error</TITLE>\n</HEAD>\n";
118:     print "<BODY><H3>Format Error</H3>\n<P>$err</P>\n</BODY>\n</HTML>\n";
119:     exit;
120: }
121:
122: sub file_error {
123:     print $query->header;
124:     print "<HTML>\n<HEAD>\n<TITLE>File Error</TITLE>\n</HEAD>\n";
125:     print "<BODY><H3>File Error</H3>\n<P>$error</P>\n</BODY>\n</HTML>\n";
126:     exit;
127: }
```

This script does two things. It creates a list of all the stories in a directory, and it renders the stories by merging them with the appropriate templates. Let's look at the story-indexing functionality first. If the template and story parameters are not present in the query string, the script builds a list of available stories. The print_story_index subroutine, which begins on line 38, generates the list of stories.

First, print_story_index opens the directory specified on line 7 to get a list of the story files. Then, it retrieves a list of all the files with the extension .txt and copies them into the array @stories. After a list of stories has been obtained, the program iterates over each of the stories to retrieve the story title. The open_story and parse_story subroutines are used here, just as they will be when a single story is displayed. The script searches for a field in the stories called STORY_TITLE. If it's present, the program generates a link to that story including the story and template parameters. The story parameter is taken from the filename of the file currently being processed, and the template parameter is hard coded into the program.

The important thing about this part of the program is that it's not generic—it only works with content files that contain a STORY_TITLE field. The next section of the program, which generates the HTML for specific stories, is completely generic. It reads a template file and a data file and displays the formatted data. This code is only called if both the story ID and the template used to render the story are specified in the query parameters.

If they are, the program first calls open_story and parse_story to retrieve all the data associated with the current story. The open_story subroutine begins on line 74. First, it derives the name of the file in which the content is stored from the value of the story parameter. Then, the program attempts to open that file and retrieve all the data from it and store it in the @story_text array. If the program fails to open the file for some reason, the error is trapped and the program continues execution, thanks to the eval construct.

After the contents of the file have been retrieved, the parse_story subroutine is used to extract the data. parse_story, which begins on line 99, just iterates over all of the contents of the file extracting tag names and the data between the tags. It adds the content to a new hash I create called %vals. The tag name is used as the index for the hash, and the text between the tags serves as the value for that item in the hash. There's one problem with this scheme. If the actual content in the file includes opening and closing HTML tags, that data will also be copied into the %vals array, even if you don't need it. For that reason, when working with HTML documents it might make more sense to use some alternative layout scheme other than the HTML-like tagging scheme I used in this application.

After the data has been extracted from the content file, I parse the template file. There are two subroutines that I use, open_template and parse_template. In the open_ template subroutine, I get the name of the template file by appending .tmpl to the value in the template parameter, and then I attempt to open that file. I then read all the data in the template file into the array @template_text. At that point, I execute the parse_ template routine.

All the tokens in the template are enclosed within # symbols. To replace the tokens with the data, I search for strings within those symbols, and then replace the token with the value in %vals that matches the string. So, if the program finds #STORY_TITLE# in the template file, it is replaced with the value stored in $vals{'STORY_TEMPLATE'}. After all the tokens have been replaced with the corresponding values from the content file, the print_story subroutine prints the resulting page.

Third-Party Content Management Systems

As you might imagine, content management is a big problem for many Web sites. There are many products on the market that attempt to solve this problem so that you don't have to write your own software to manage your Web site's content. There are also some free applications that attempt to solve this problem as well. Rather than writing your own application to manage the content on your site, it may make sense to use one of the existing packages to save yourself some time.

This is by no means a complete list of these systems. There are probably hundreds of these types of products available today. I'm only going to discuss a few of the most popular ones. One important thing to remember is that once you choose a content management system, you're going to be married to it. Most of these systems have little in common. They support different programming languages, template formats, and ways of storing the actual content. After you've committed to one of them, moving your content to a different system can be a long and arduous process.

The three most important criteria you'll want to have in mind when you look at these systems are your budget, your schedule, and the capabilities you're looking for.

Content management systems range in price from free to hundreds of thousands of dollars. Price isn't directly correlated to capability, either. Some of the free systems are very powerful, whereas some very expensive systems are hard to use and inflexible. If you know your budget, you can probably eliminate some systems based on their price right off the bat.

The second issue is your schedule. Content management systems tend to follow the standard curve, familiar to most software users, of built-in functionality versus flexibility. Consider the difference between C and Perl. In C, you can write programs to do just about anything, but writing programs to perform even the simplest of tasks takes quite a bit of work, at least compared to Perl. On the other hand, Perl isn't as flexible as C. In C, people write operating systems and compilers. In Perl, people tend to write string processing scripts and CGI programs. Because Perl is built for those sorts of tasks, it has a lot of built-in functionality that makes writing those specific types of programs easy.

17

Getting back to my point, the issue you face when selecting a content management system is how much time you have to get it up and running. Given infinite time (and development resources) you could write a content management system yourself that would be perfect for your site. It would do exactly what you want to do. If you have a month to get the site up and running and only yourself to work on it, it probably makes more sense to use a system with tons of built-in functionality. You may have to compromise on how flexible it is and settle for doing without some features that you might have wanted, but the time you save in using an existing system will probably be worth it.

The third issue is the capabilities of the content management system you choose. This issue is probably the most important because ultimately the system you select must provide the capabilities you require or it won't do you any good. One important issue is the programming language that the content management system uses. Most systems can be programmed using at least one programming language; you should find out which languages are supported and make sure that you're comfortable with them. Other capabilities you'll want to look at are the ability to cache content that doesn't need to be generated dynamically every time a page is requested, and workflow capabilities that allow you to manage the publishing process.

Now let's look at a few specific content management systems that are available.

Vignette StoryServer

Vignette StoryServer is a commercial content management system that is very popular with large publishing sites. It costs anywhere from tens of thousands of dollars to hundreds of thousands of dollars, and the implementation time for a new site is significant. In return for the time and cash investment, Vignette provides a powerful system that allows you to build sites that can be used to serve millions of hits and allow many authors to participate in the publishing process.

Vignette StoryServer runs under Solaris and Windows NT, and requires a relational database for data storage. The supported databases are Oracle, Sybase, and Microsoft SQL Server. All StoryServer programming is done in TCL, and Vignette provides some macros that allow you to accomplish common tasks without programming. All the site content and all the templates are stored in the relational database. In order to develop templates, you must use Vignette's tools. For more information, you should check out http://www.vignette.com.

Mason

Mason is a free content management system written in Perl. It allows you to use templates to publish documents, and to create HTML documents with Perl embedded in them that is executed when the page is rendered. It also provides caching capabilities. You can find out more about Mason at `http://www.masonhq.com`.

Userland Frontier

Userland Frontier is a different sort of content management system. Although it has a built-in Web server, it is most commonly used in environments where pages are built in Frontier and then saved and served as static files. Frontier has a built-in scripting language—UserTalk, and Macintosh users can also program Frontier using AppleTalk. It also stores all the templates, scripts, and user data internally in a built-in object database. Frontier is a commercial product, but is significantly less expensive than StoryServer. The Frontier home page is at `http://www.userland.com`.

Zope

Zope is a content management system built around the Python programming language. Python is a developer-friendly language built on the principles of object orientated programming. Zope uses these principles to provide a powerful content management system. Like Frontier, Zope has a built-in Web server and object database. You can also run Zope in CGI mode to use it with other Web servers, and use other relational databases for data storage. Like Mason, Zope is completely free. The Zope home page is `http://www.zope.org`.

Summary

The goal of this hour was to introduce you to the world of content management. Static Web sites are increasingly going the way of the dinosaur, and these days, it's more common to see Web sites that enable you to separate your content from the manner in which it is presented, so that you can make changes to your site without editing hundreds of individual HTML documents. In this hour, I provided an example of a simple content management system written using a couple of CGI scripts. I also discussed some of the pre-built content management systems that are available, and how to evaluate them.

Q&A

Q How does XML fit into the content management picture?

A XML is a markup language that is designed to be more structured than HTML. Unlike HTML, XML documents must conform to a particular document type definition in order to be considered valid. These document type definitions, or DTDS, really allow you to write markup languages of your own, using the tags and structure that you specify. The advantage of XML is that it can be processed easily by computer programs. After an HTML document has been published, it's not easy to extract the data from the document. Using XML, it should be just as easy to get data out of a document as it is to put it into it. Because of its flexible functionality and rigid structure, XML is a good source format for documents that will be converted to HTML by a content management system.

Q What do I do with the content that's already part of my static site?

A There's no easy answer to this question. One of the biggest challenges in moving from a static system to a content management system is converting all your HTML documents into whatever format your content management system uses. If your pages all follow a very similar format, you might be able to write scripts that read your HTML documents and store them in the new format. If they don't, you might have to convert a lot of your content manually, which is a pretty huge job. However, when you compare the amount of time it will take to the time it takes to redesign a large static site, you may find it's worth it. Some sites just leave all their static content as it is, and generate all the new content using their content management system.

Workshop

The quiz questions are designed to strengthen the knowledge you gain each hour. The exercises help you build on that knowledge by providing you with the opportunity to apply it to real problems. See Appendix A, "Answers" for the answers to the quiz questions.

Quiz

1. Why was it a questionable decision to use HTML-style tags as delimiters for the content files in the example?

2. On what types of sites is caching HTML documents not a good idea?

Exercises

1. Create a new template and content file format and modify the sample programs to use them.

PART V

Integrating Databases and CGI

Hour

HOUR 18

Working with Relational Databases

These days, most complex Web sites use a relational database for data storage. They are widely used to store transaction data and user account information, and in many cases, they're used to store the actual content that will be published on the Web site as well. Over the course of the next two hours, I'll explain how relational databases work, and how you can build Web applications that use relational databases. In this hour you'll learn:

- What the relational model for databases is
- Structured Query Language (SQL)—the means to accessing data in a relational database
- How the database design process works
- What types of data are supported by relational databases

The Relational Database Model

Today, the dominant paradigm in the world of databases is the relational model. The fundamental attribute of the relational model is that data is stored within tables. Each *table* consists of rows and columns; each *row* represents a single record, and the *columns* contain the data that make up each record. The intersection of a row and column is referred to as a *field*. Each field contains a single value.

The relational theory, which was originally described by mathematician E. F. Codd in his paper, "A Relational Model of Data for Large Shared Data Banks," does not use the terms *table*, *row*, and *column*. When he spoke of these elements, he referred to tables as *relations,* rows as *tuples,* and columns as *attributes.*However, in this book, I will refer to them as tables, rows, and columns because the world of Structured Query Language (SQL) uses that terminology, and besides, those words are a lot more familiar to most people.

Table 18.1 contains an example of what a table about movies might look like. As you can see, each column contains a particular type of data, and each row makes up a single record.

TABLE 18.1   A Sample Table

ID	Title	Studio	Budget
1	Mineral House	Giant	20
2	Prince Kong	MPM	3.25
3	The Code Warrior	MPM	10.3
4	Bill Durham	Delighted Artists	10.1

So, in the sample table, each row is made up of four columns, ID, Title, Studio, and Budget. The value in each field is a single, atomic piece of data.

> You could place a list of several values, separated by commas, in a single field. However, the database would treat that list as a single value; you would need to extract the individual values after retrieving the list from the database.

A relational database is made up of groups of tables, which are linked together through relationships. For example, if there were another table in the database that contained information on each studio, you could look up information on the studio that produced each of the movies by cross referencing the Studio column in Table 1.1 with the column that contained the studio name in the second table.

By taking advantage of relationships between tables, you can avoid duplicating data in a database. Rather than including the city where each studio is located in Table 1.1 (where the data would be duplicated among each movie from the same studio), you could include it in the table specifically related to studios, and then cross-reference the two tables to obtain that information when you need it.

The practice of designing your databases so that information is not needlessly duplicated is referred to as *normalization*. Not only are normalized databases more space-efficient than non-normalized databases, but they don't suffer from the data inconsistency that can occur without normalization. Duplicated data means that every program that performs an update operation must remember to access the data in every location.

Structured Query Language

One requirement of the relational model is that while a database may support multiple languages, at least one of those languages must be capable of performing all of the tasks relating to the manipulation, definition, and administration of databases. For this reason, in nearly every case, all the configuration and administrative data for database management systems is actually stored within tables in the database itself.

For the vast majority of relational database systems, Structured Query Language (SQL) fulfills the language requirement of relational database systems. The full SQL standard is more than 600 pages long, and no commercial relational database system fully conforms to the standard. This hour and the next cover the details of the language that are most commonly implemented in popular relational databases.

SQL is made up of three types of statements: statements that are used to manipulate data, statements for data definition, and statements for database administration. I'll discuss some of the statements that are common to most relational databases.

Statements for Data Manipulation

Within the category of statements for data manipulation, there are two types of commands: commands that are used to retrieve data from a database, and commands that modify data within a database. Let's look at the statements within these categories.

There is a single statement that is used to retrieve data stored within a database, SELECT. Thanks to the rich capabilities of SQL, however, incredibly complex SELECT statements can be written to perform complex queries on data within a database. Listing 18.1 contains an example of a simple SELECT statement and its results from the database.

18

I display both the query and its results in these listings in order to make it easy for you to see what happens when you enter these queries, even if you don't have access to a relational database containing these tables yourself.

LISTING 18.1   A SELECT Statement

```
 1: SELECT *
 2: FROM Studios
 3:
 4: STUDIO_ID STUDIO_NAME            STUDIO_CITY          ST
 5: --------- --------------------   -------------------  --
 6:         1 Giant                  Los Angeles          CA
 7:         2 MPM                    Burbank              CA
 8:         3 Delighted Artists      Austin               TX
 9:         4 FKG                    Apex                 NC
10:         5 Metaversal Studios     Los Angeles          LA
```

Because the SELECT statement is used to retrieve data from a database, it's usually referred to as a *query*.

The statements available for manipulating data within a database are UPDATE, INSERT, and DELETE. As you probably can guess, the UPDATE statement is used to make changes to records, the INSERT statement is used to create new records in a table, and the DELETE statement is used to remove records from a table. There are examples of these three types of statements in Listing 18.2.

LISTING 18.2   Data Manipulation Statements

```
 1:
 2: UPDATE Studios
 3: SET studio_city = 'Houston'
 4: WHERE studio_state = 'TX'
 5:
 6: 1 row updated.
 7:
 8: DELETE FROM Studios
 9: WHERE studio_name = 'Giant'
10:
11: 1 row deleted.
12:
```

```
13: INSERT INTO Studios
14: (studio_id, studio_name, studio_city, studio_state)
15: VALUES
16: (5, 'Big Pictures', 'Culver City', 'CA')
17:
18: 1 row created.
```

Statements for Data Definition

Statements used for data definition create or alter the structure of the database, or allocate resources to a database. First among these statements is CREATE. The CREATE command can be used to create databases, views, and tables. Listing 18.3 contains an example of the CREATE statement, used to create a table.

LISTING 18.3   Creating a Table Using the CREATE Statement

```
1: CREATE TABLE example
2: (name            VARCHAR2(60),
3: rank             CHAR(10),
4: serial_number    NUMBER)
5:
6: Table created.
```

In some databases, after an element like a table has been created, it can be changed using an ALTER statement. For example, if you had wanted to make the serial_number a character field instead of a number field, the ALTER command could be used to change the data type of the column, as shown in Listing 18.4.

LISTING 18.4   An Example of the ALTER Command

```
1: ALTER TABLE example
2: MODIFY serial_number CHAR(10)
3:
4: Table altered.
```

Statements for Database Administration

The other category into which SQL commands fall is database administration commands. These commands are used to grant and remove privileges from users, and to perform other tasks related to general database operation rather than specific manipulation of elements within the database.

In most cases, the configuration of the database is stored within tables in the database itself that are accessible only to the database administrator's account. When this is the case, you can use the standard data manipulation commands to configure the database.

Database Design

As you can tell by now, the relational model is completely centered around tables. All data in a database is stored in tables, and all queries receive their results in tables. Therefore, when you're thinking about how to organize your data, it's important to think about how to group your data within tables. Here are some important rules that apply:

- All data must be returned by the database in a tabular format.
- Each field must contain a single value.
- For the purposes of data integrity, every row must contain a value (or group of values) that uniquely identifies that row.
- A relationship between two tables is represented by part or all of the data in a column. In other words, the column data that expresses a relationship must appear in corresponding columns of both tables.

Strangely enough, the default behavior of most databases is to make the third and fourth rules optional. Not all of the rows in your tables must be unique, and there need not be a formal link between related tables. However, both of these rules help to preserve the integrity of data in your database. The third rule, which states that every row must be unique, is important because it eliminates redundancy in your database. In the relational world, redundancy is always a bad thing. Whenever you have redundant data, whenever you need to update that data, you have to remember to update it in every place that it exists. Failing to update one instance of the same data when you update another causes your data to get out of sync, and eliminates the integrity of that data.

Adhering to the final rule assures that your database has referential integrity. *Referential integrity* is simply the principal that when you have data in one table that refers to data in another, the data it refers to really exists. In some cases, it may be prudent to intentionally break these rules. However, when you do so you should be sure you know why you're breaking the rules and what the pitfalls of doing so are.

The value (or group of values) that uniquely identifies each row is referred to as the *primary key*. When the primary key from one table corresponds to a column in another table, it expresses a relationship between the two tables, and the corresponding column (or columns) in the other table is referred to as a *foreign key*. I will return to the topic of these keys when I start discussing the nuts and bolts of database design in this hour.

Before delving further into the topic of design, let me introduce a new term: schema. The *schema* of a database is a list of all the tables in the database, along with the keys and columns in each of those tables. The *schema* of a table includes the table name, a list of the columns in the table, and an indication of the keys.

The notation used to portray the schema for a table contains the name of the table, followed by the names of the columns within parentheses. The primary key of the table should be underlined with two lines. Here's an example:

```
studios (name, city, state)
```

Characteristics of Good Databases

When you think about it, the characteristics of well-designed databases are self-evident. Good databases make it easy to retrieve the data you need, exhibit high integrity so that the data remains consistent after updates, and provide optimal performance in responding to queries.

Naturally, although a good database exhibits all three of these qualities, there are tradeoffs among them. For example, it might make it easy to retrieve data if you store it all in a single table; however, this can lead to poor performance, and can lead to needless duplication of data that hurts the integrity of your database. On the other hand, splitting up your data into many tables can ensure that you never run into problems with data integrity, but can make it tiresome to write queries that return the data you need, and can also be detrimental to performance. Designing a database that is solely focused on good performance over concerns of organization and integrity is probably likely to be unsatisfactory as well.

It's up to you to create the proper recipe for your database. You should be mindful of all three of the qualities listed here when you design your database, balancing each of them as appropriate for your application. In the end, the ultimate positive characteristic of any database is that it provides high levels of user satisfaction, and that it reliably meets its requirements.

Symptoms of Bad Databases

All too often, it's easier to point out the wrong way to do things than to explain how to do them correctly. Not surprisingly, the symptoms of a bad database are more or less the opposites of the good qualities described previously.

It's quite possible to design a confusing database with bad performance and poor integrity. Hopefully this hour will help you to avoid doing so. Symptoms of a poorly designed database include

- Tables or columns with confusing or unclear names.
- Database design that requires users or programmers to enter the same data more than once, or change the value of the same piece of data in multiple places when it is updated.

- Allowing data in the database to get out of sync, so that multiple queries seeking the same piece of information return different results.
- Poor performance.
- Difficulty in determining the relationship between pieces of data.
- Duplicate rows within a single table.

The Design Process

Regardless of what type of information will eventually be stored in your database, the design procedure generally follows a standard set of steps. Let's take a look at a list of the steps involved in database design:

1. Information gathering. Obviously, before you can design a database, you need to know exactly what will be stored in the database.

2. Taking inventory. After you've found all the information you'll store in the database, you need to create a laundry list of all the types of data you've found, and the attributes of those types.

3. Entity-relationship modeling. Arrange the data into individual entities and attributes of those entities. Determine how the entities are related.

4. Determine which level of normalization is required for your database. Apply the normalization rules to your data.

5. Write the SQL code necessary to create the database, and then create the database in your relational database system.

6. Determine which users should have access to your data, and then grant the appropriate levels of access to the users.

7. Populate your database with data.

These are general steps that can be taken in the process of designing a database. They are by no means set in stone, and if another method works better for you, that is the method you should follow. In the end, it is the result that matters, not necessarily the route by which you arrived at that result.

Creating a Database

In some databases, before you can create individual tables within a database, it's necessary to create a new database and allocate space for storing the records. In most databases, the CREATE DATABASE command is used to initialize a new database. Many database packages also provide graphical tools that can be used to create new databases. In fact, some low-end packages leave out the CREATE DATABASE command and require you to create databases through a graphical interface. In its most basic incarnation, the CREATE DATABASE statement looks like:

```
CREATE DATABASE Film_Industry
```

Oracle requires database names to be less than eight characters long, so if you're using Oracle, you can use a statement like:

```
CREATE DATABASE FI
```

There are lots of additional attributes that can be passed to the CREATE DATABASE statement that specify the physical location where the database style will be stored, log file information, and other information relating to the operation of the database. These options vary significantly between various database packages, so I'll cover them later on, when I talk about specific databases.

There are a number of other CREATE statements that can be used to specify various internal information for a database. For example, using the CREATE TABLESPACE command in Oracle, you can allocate more physical drive space for tables. The CREATE SCHEMA command can be used to create more than one table in a single statement. Generally, use of those commands is best left to database administrators. Most database programmers rarely create anything above the table level.

Choosing Which Database to Access

If you've created more than one database, your SQL statements need to specify the database in which to find tables. In most databases, you can prepend a table name with the database name and two periods to indicate that the table is in a database other than the one that is currently active. For example, in Microsoft SQL Server, if you're currently using a database called DB_ONE, but you want to retrieve data from a table within DB_TWO, you could use the following SELECT statement:

```
SELECT *
FROM DB_TWO..Some_Table
```

If you want to change the active database, most databases provide the USE or DATABASE command. For example, if you want to switch from DB_ONE to DB_TWO for a series of queries, you could just use:

```
USE DB_TWO
```

to make DB_TWO active. Similarly, the DATABASE command is used as follows:

```
DATABASE DB_TWO
```

18

Once you've made a database active, you can leave out the database specification in your queries, and just use the table name in the table list, like this:

```
SELECT *
FROM Some_Table
```

Creating a Table

In order to create a new table within a database, the CREATE statement is used. CREATE can be used to create more than tables, so you have to specify that you're creating a table when you use it. The basic structure of a CREATE statement is as follows:

```
CREATE TABLE Table_Name
(column_name    data type[(size)],
column_name     data type[(size)],
...)
```

The table specified by Table_Name will be created with the columns specified in the column listing. Each column name must be followed by a data type for that column. Most data types require that you specify a size for the field, but a few don't. I'll explain the details of the data types in the next section.

Let's take a look at a real table specification very quickly, before I get into the explanations of the individual data types. Listing 18.5 contains a CREATE statement that could be used to create a table to store information about movie studios.

LISTING **18.5**   A Statement to Create the Studios Table

```
1: CREATE TABLE Studios
2: (name        CHAR(20),
3: city         VARCHAR2(50),
4: state        CHAR(2),
5: revenue    NUMBER)
```

For now, don't worry about the data types listed in the table; I'll explain what they are in the next section. Look at the structure of the statement. This statement creates a table called Studios, with four columns: name, city, state, and revenue. There are a lot more options available when a table is created; I could have specified the primary key, or set up relationships with other tables, or placed constraints on the values that could be entered in the columns. For information on those options, you should refer to a book that deals specifically with databases.

Some good books covering relational databases are *The Practical SQL Handbook*, by Judith S. Bowman, Sandra L. Emerson, and Marcy Darnovsky, and *Special Edition Using SQL*, by me. You might also consider books that deal specifically with the database product that you're using.

Relational Data Types

Relational databases support different data types based on the type of information that you store within a column. These data types not only affect how data is stored on disk, but also, more importantly, how data is compared to each other. For example, if you are comparing two numbers, or two dates, you don't want to compare them alphabetically. Storage requirements are important as well. You don't want to reserve 255 bytes of space for the state field of a table, which you know will contain only the two letter abbreviation of a state's name. Similarly, you don't want to reserve only five bytes of space for a telephone number, which you know is 10 digits long.

Fortunately, relational databases provide you with a wide assortment of data types that you can assign to columns within your databases. There are data types for text strings, numbers, dates, and other objects, like binary data, and large text objects. Unfortunately, each relational database product has its own distinct set of data types, although there is some overlap between products.

In any case, the basic types of data which each database can store are basically the same—the main difference is in what those data types are named. Some databases offer a variety of subtypes for some of the types; for example, in addition to a basic numeric type, they offer specific types for integers, floating point numbers, and money. The following sections cover the three general types of data that are offered by nearly every database: string, numeric, and temporal. (There are several other common data types supported by relational databases, but they're used less often with Web applications.) To ascertain the necessary details, you should review the documentation specific to your database when you create tables.

18

String Data

Most databases offer two string data types, fixed length and variable length. The difference is that a fixed length field always occupies a given amount of space on disk, no matter how much data is placed in it, whereas a variable length string occupies only the amount of space consumed by its contents, no matter what its maximum size is.

The data type for fixed length strings is usually CHAR. When you create a fixed length string, you must specify the length of the string. For example, a column called state would be of the type CHAR(2). This column always uses two bytes of disk space, even if it is actually blank, or contains only one character. Similarly, a name field might be a fixed length field that can hold up to 20 characters. CHAR fields are automatically padded to fill out the bytes that are not consumed by data placed in them.

Strings can also be stored in variable length fields. These fields are generally specified using the identifier VARCHAR or, in the case of Oracle, VARCHAR2. Variable length fields must be specified with a maximum length. For example, the data type of a `city` field that can contain up to 50 characters would be VARCHAR(50). The difference between it and a field specified as CHAR(50) is that although the variable-length field can hold up to 50 characters, it will be resized to fit its actual contents. So, if a city name is 10 characters long, it will take up 10 bytes of space on disk, rather than the 50 that a CHAR(50) field would consume.

The maximum sizes for string fields vary widely among databases. Oracle allows CHAR fields up to 2000 bytes in length, and VARCHAR2 fields up to 4000 bytes in length. Some databases restrict you to 255 bytes in both types.

In some cases, you may need to store more data in a character field than either of the two data types I've already discussed will allow. Most databases provide a data type for large character objects. Oracle provides the CLOB (character large object) data type for text that won't fit within a VARCHAR2 field; CLOB will hold up to four gigabytes of data. Microsoft SQL Server provides the TEXT data type for large strings.

Numeric Data

The large majority of commercial databases differentiate between numeric and string data. Unlike string data, numeric data does not have to be enclosed in single quotation marks. You can also include numeric data in mathematical expressions.

Most databases provide at least two numeric data types, one for integers and another for floating point numbers. Some others provide more distinct numeric types, like MONEY, which always allots two numeric places after the decimal point. Table 18.2 contains a list of common numeric data types. The number of digits supported by these types varies. In many databases, you can specify how many digits a number contains, just as you can specify how many characters a CHAR field holds.

TABLE 18.2   Numeric Data Types in SQL

Type	Definition
DECIMAL	A floating point number.
FLOAT	A floating point number.
INTEGER(size)	An integer of specified length.
MONEY	A number which contains exactly two digits after the decimal point.
NUMBER	A standard number field, which can hold a floating point number.

Sometimes, you'll want to store numeric data as strings. For example, zip codes and phone numbers should be stored strings for two reasons. First, many numeric data types remove leading zeroes from the data, but a zip code might contain a leading zero. Second, a numeric data type cannot store non-numeric data, but you might want to allow phone numbers to contain alphabetic, dash, and parenthesis characters.

Temporal Data

Another distinct data type supported by most relational data types is temporal data—dates and times. The variation between databases is very wide when it comes to temporal data. The way dates are stored and displayed differs, and some databases support more temporal data types than others.

Basically, the three types of temporal data supported by relational databases are dates, times, and date-time combinations. Some databases support only a single date type, which combines both a date and time. Others support all three.

I'd like to take a moment to discuss the year 2000 problem and year 2000 compliance. The roots of the Y2K problem lie within a false assumption made by programmers, which was that their programs would be replaced before the turn of the century. Unfortunately, because of this, much of the code written until very recently only allocated two characters for the year portion of a date, and programs operated under the assumption that all years began with 19. So, at the turn of the century, these programs assume that the year is 1900 as opposed to 2000. The date data types in all modern databases allocate four digits for the year, but it is still possible to write applications that aren't Y2K-compliant. If you opt not to use a standard date field, and you use two digits to store the year, you can run into the Y2K problem, just as programmers going all the way back to the '60s have.

18

Summary

The purpose of this hour was to provide you with an overview of the relational database landscape. Many books have been written about relational databases themselves, so as you might imagine, not much detail was presented in this hour. Still, it should provide you with the foundation you need for writing Web applications that use relational databases for data storage. If you find yourself using relational databases a lot, you might want to look into purchasing a book that covers SQL or the relational database you're using.

Q&A

Q What is database normalization?

A Database normalization is the process of designing databases so they conform to certain rules, which prevent various data storage and retrieval problems. Generally, the rules prevent unnecessary duplication of data in a database.

Q How do I know if the database I'm using supports SQL?

A The key word to look for is "relational." Nearly all relational databases provide SQL support. The most popular databases—Oracle, Sybase, Informix, IBM DB/2, MySQL, Microsoft SQL Server, and even Microsoft Access—all support SQL to varying degrees.

Workshop

The quiz questions are designed to strengthen the knowledge you gain each hour. The exercises help you build on that knowledge by providing you with the opportunity to apply it to real problems. See Appendix A, "Answers" for the answers to the quiz questions.

Quiz

1. Which SQL statement is used to add a new table to a database?

2. What criteria must a column or combination of columns satisfy to be able to serve as a primary key?

3. How do CHAR and VARCHAR fields differ?

Exercises

1. Install a relational database for your own use. If you own Microsoft Office Professional, you can use Access. If you don't, check out MySQL (http://www.mysql.net).

HOUR 19

How to Use the Structured Query Language

The structured query language is the lingua franca of the relational database world. Nearly all relational databases use SQL for data retrieval, data modification, and database administration. While the SQL dialect used by various databases differs, once you know the basics of SQL, you should be able to use most any relational database. In this lesson, I'm going to discuss the statements associated with SQL and demonstrate how they are used in CGI programs.

This lesson includes the following:

- A brief overview of Structured Query Language (SQL)
- What the Open Database Connectivity (ODBC) standard is
- How to access relational databases from Perl programs using DBI and DBD

Structured Query Language

Structured Query Language (SQL) is a standard language for retrieving records from databases. The standard is maintained by the American National Standards Institute (ANSI), and is supported by most major database vendors, including IBM, Oracle, Informix, Sybase, and Microsoft.

You can embed SQL statements in your CGI programs that issue queries to databases and include the results in your Web pages. Because SQL is an open standard, your SQL statements will be portable so that they work no matter which database package you opt to use.

> Although most database vendors have created proprietary extensions to SQL that only work with their database package, your code will remain extremely portable if you stick with the standard SQL statements.

First, let me show you a sample table that I can refer to throughout this section. The table in Listing 19.1, which contains the records for four students, is named StudentData.

LISTING 19.1   The StudentData Table

```
1: SSN          FirstName    LastName    Class      Major        Tuition
2: 555123322    Joe          Smith       Freshman   Business     5000
3: 834781313    Michael      Albrecht    Freshman   Chemistry    3500
4: 777333111    Robert       Jones       Senior     English      10000
5: 316385989    Alicia       Brown       Junior     Business     5000
6: 123456789    Bill         Brown       Junior     History      7500
```

Now let's take a look at how SQL statements are built.

> The following sections describe just a few of the most useful SQL commands. I've written an entire book on using SQL that describes the language in full detail. The book, published by Que, is entitled *Special Edition Using SQL*. There are a number of other excellent books on SQL as well, including books that are written to cover specific database engines.

The SELECT Statement

The most common, and important, SQL statement is the SELECT statement, which is used to retrieve data from the database. The simplest SELECT statements are used to extract a list of columns from a specific table. Here's an example:

```
SELECT SSN, FirstName, LastName
FROM StudentData;
```

This statement retrieves the values in the three specified columns from every row in the StudentData table. By default, SELECT statements retrieve every row from the table in the FROM clause.

 To select all the columns in a table, instead of entering all the column names in the SELECT statement, you can use the * (asterisk) character.

To constrain the query so that only specific rows are returned, you can use the WHERE clause to set up conditions that filter the records based on the values in certain columns. Here's an example:

```
SELECT SSN
FROM StudentData
WHERE Tuition > 7000;
```

This query uses the greater-than conditional operator (>) to return the social security numbers of only those students who are paying more than $7000 tuition.

You can also select records based on textual values. For example, to retrieve the first and last names of all the members of the junior class, you would use the following statement:

```
SELECT FirstName, LastName
FROM StudentData
WHERE Class = 'Junior';
```

Table 19.1 contains a list of all the conditional operators that can be used in the WHERE clause of a SELECT statement.

19

TABLE 19.1   Operators For Use in Conditional SELECT Statements

Operator	Definition
=	Equal
<> or !=	Not equal
<	Less than
>	Greater than
<=	Less than or equal to
>=	Greater than or equal to

AND and OR

You can also create more complex expressions in your WHERE clauses using the AND and OR operators, which enable you to select records based on the values in more than one column. Let's take a look at a SELECT statement that retrieves the SSN of students who are freshmen and business majors:

```
SELECT SSN
FROM StudentData
WHERE Class = 'Freshman' AND Major = 'Business';
```

If you look back at the sample data in Listing 19.1, you can see that this query will return one row, the one for Joe Smith. Michael Albrecht and Alicia Brown each meet one of the two conditions, but neither satisfy both, so because of the AND operator, neither of those records is returned.

> You can use the UPPER or LOWER functions to create case-insensitive textual conditions. To make the previous query case insensitive, you could use either function on the column name and rewrite the value it is compared to appropriately, as follows:
>
> ```
> SELECT SNN
> FROM StudentData
> WHERE LOWER(Class) = 'freshman'
> AND LOWER(Major) = 'business'
> ```

Compound SELECT Statements

You can use multiple expressions with the AND and OR operators to create even more complex WHERE clauses. Take a look at this one, for example:

```
SELECT FirstName, LastName
FROM StudentData
WHERE Class = 'Senior' AND Major = 'English' OR Tuition < 5000;
```

The problem with this example is that it doesn't make the order in which these expressions are evaluated clear. The query could return different results depending on whether the AND expression is evaluated before the OR operator, or vice versa. In this case the AND operator is evaluated first. So, the query would be written in plain English as, "Either the student is a senior majoring in English, or the student's tuition is less than $5,000."

```
SELECT FirstName, LastName
FROM StudentData
WHERE (Class = 'Senior' AND Major = 'English') OR Tuition < 5000;
```

The parentheses make it clear that the two conditionals combined with the AND statement are one group. You can also use parentheses to group the operators in the statement so that it reads the last two expressions as a single group. Here's an example:

```
SELECT FirstName, LastName
FROM StudentData
WHERE Class = 'Senior' AND (Major = 'English' OR Tuition < 5000);
```

In this example, the results are different than they would be for the previous two queries. In plain English, it's written as "The student is a senior, and either their major is English or their tuition is less than $5,000." Whenever you create compound SELECT statements, you should use parentheses to group the expressions in order to make the code more readable and to ensure that the database engine knows exactly how you want the expressions evaluated.

IN, NOT, and BETWEEN

When you are writing compound SELECT statements, there are several other operators that you can use in WHERE clauses to build expressions. These include the IN, NOT, and BETWEEN operators. Let's take a look at the IN operator first. It compares a value to a list of values that you specify. If the value in the current row matches any of the values in the list, the IN expression evaluates as true. Conveniently, lists in SQL are identical to lists in Perl, so it's easy to remember the syntax. Here's an example:

```
SELECT SSN
FROM StudentData
WHERE Class IN ('Junior', 'Senior');
```

This SELECT statement will return any records in which the Class column contains a value of Junior or Senior. Take a look at a statement that uses the OR operator to do the same thing:

```
SELECT SSN
FROM StudentData
WHERE Class = 'Senior' OR Class = 'Junior';
```

As you can see, using the IN statement shortens the line of code. In this case, the advantage isn't too dramatic, but imagine if you wanted to use a list of 20 alternatives. The IN expression would radically decrease the amount of code you had to write, and make your code more readable.

Now let's look at the NOT operator, which reverses the meaning of any conditional expression. Take a look at the previous example, with the NOT operator inserted:

```
SELECT SSN
FROM StudentData
WHERE Class NOT IN ('Junior', 'Senior');
```

As you probably guessed, this example selects any records in which the value in the Class column is not equal to Junior or Senior.

19

> The NOT operator can be used with any operator, but it doesn't make much sense to use it with the mathematical operators—for each, there is already an inverse operator that does the opposite operation. For example, rather than using NOT < you can just use >=.

BETWEEN is used to check whether a column contains a value between the two values that are specified. Not surprisingly, NOT BETWEEN checks to see whether a value is not between the two specified values. BETWEEN provides a shorthand way of writing the following example:

```
SELECT SSN
FROM StudentData
WHERE (Tuition => 5000) AND (Tuition <= 10000);
```

The same statement written using the BETWEEN operator looks like this:

```
SELECT SSN
FROM StudentData
WHERE Tuition BETWEEN 5000 AND 10000;
```

The LIKE Comparison

LIKE is used to match the contents of a column to a pattern. The basic syntax of the LIKE command is very simple. LIKE uses the % sign for pattern matching. The % character matches any character or sequence of characters. Take a look at this example:

```
SELECT SSN
FROM StudentData
WHERE LastName LIKE 'S%';
```

This statement extracts any columns in which the LastName field starts with S. You can create all sorts of patterns using the LIKE command. For example, LIKE 'S%h' matches any last names that begin with *S* and end with *h*, like Smith.

> If you just want to match one character, most databases support the ? wildcard as well. The ? character will match any single character, so t?p will match top and tap, but not tarp.

Joins

When databases are designed, it is a good practice to only include a single type of information in each table. For example, you wouldn't include personal information about the students, information on classes, and all the student schedules within a single table. Instead, you would create three tables.

Using joins, you can retrieve data from each of the tables with one SELECT statement. A join is a query that retrieves data from more than one table, and correlates the data from the tables based on what's referred to as a joining condition.

> The previous paragraph was a gross oversimplification; there are two processes that are generally used in the design of relational databases, entity-relationship modeling, and normalization. *Entity-relationship modeling* is the process of looking at all the data that will be stored in your database and organizing it into tables that make sense from a relational database standpoint. *Normalization* is the process of further breaking your data down into tables in order to avoid data redundancy. For more information about these processes, you should consult resources on database design.

First, I'm going to create some sample data for the examples that I will use. I will be using the StudentData table shown earlier as well as two new tables, named Courses and StudentGradesStudentGrades.

Here's the Courses table:

```
SectionNumber     Dept       Professor
001               Math       Einstein
002               English    Whitman
003               Business   Trump
004               Biology    Salk
```

Here is an excerpt from the StudentGrades table consisting of a single student's grades

```
SSN           SectionNumber     Grade
555123322     001               A
555123322     002               C+
123456789     003               B
```

SectionNumber is the primary key of the Courses table. Each of the records in that table is uniquely identified by its SectionNumber, even if the course is in the same department and has the same professor. The SectionNumber is a foreign key inside the StudentGradesStudentGrades table, as is the SSN. Any value given as a SectionNumber in the StudentGrades must correspond to an existing record in the Courses table. Any value given inside the SSN column of the StudentGradesStudentGrades table must correspond to a record in the StudentData table. This is known as *referential integrity*.

Primary and foreign keys enable you to create relationships between tables so that you don't have to repeat data between them. Therein lies the power of relational databases. For example, I can find the names of a student's professors without having to include them in the StudentGradesStudentGrades table. The reason it's a bad idea to store the professor names in the StudentGrades table is that it would cause potential updating problems. If you wanted to change the professor for a course, you'd have to find every record in the table associated with the old professor and replace them with the new professor. Here's an example of how to look up the names of the professors for a particular student's courses:

```
SELECT Courses.Professor
FROM Courses, StudentGrades
WHERE (Courses.SectionNumber = StudentGrades.SectionNumber)
AND (StudentGrades.SSN = '555123322');
```

Unlike the SELECT statements I used previously, I select from two tables here, Courses and StudentGrades, because I need information from both of them to complete the query. In order to indicate which table I am taking each value from, I use *dot notation* to prefix the column name with the name of the table it comes from. This is only required when the column name isn't unique amongst all of the tables in the query, but I use it here to make my code easier to read.

This particular query returns Einstein and Whitman. The condition (Courses.SectionNumber = StudentGrades.SectionNumber) is referred to as the *joining condition* because it creates the relationship between the two tables. In this case, it is referred to as an *equijoin* because it joins the two tables based on a condition of equality.

Using DISTINCT

Let's say you want a list of the names of students who are enrolled in any course. When you're generating this list, you obviously only want each student to appear one time, no matter how many courses he or she is enrolled in. At the same time, you only want students who are actually enrolled in a course. If a student is enrolled in more than one course, then they appear multiple times in the StudentGrades table. The StudentData table contains records for all of the students, regardless of whether they're enrolled in any classes this semester. A joining query between StudentData and StudentGrades is required to retrieve a list of students who are enrolled in courses. To eliminate duplicates from this list, you use the DISTINCT operator. The duplication occurs for students who are enrolled in multiple courses. The most important thing to remember when you use the DISTINCT operator is to use it on the proper column. Look at this example:

```
SELECT DISTINCT StudentGrades.SSN, StudentData.FirstName,
➡StudentData.Lastname
FROM StudentGrades, StudentData
WHERE StudentGrades.SSN = StudentData.SSN;
```

First, notice that I use an equijoin that grabs all the first and last names where the SSN from the StudentData table is equal to an SSN from the StudentGrades table. Using the DISTINCT operator indicates that no matter how many times a particular SSN appears in the StudentGrades table, it will only be extracted once.

This SELECT statement returns a list of the SSN, first name, and last name for every student who appears in the StudentGrades table.

Sorting Output from SELECT Statements

You can use the ORDER BY operator to sort the output of a SELECT statement. Here's an example:

```
SELECT FirstName, LastName
FROM StudentData
ORDER BY LastName, FirstName;
```

This example takes the first and last name from every record in the StudentData table and alphabetizes them by the last name and first name. First, all of the records are sorted by last name, and then the records with the same last name are ordered by first name. You can also use ORDER BY on fields containing numbers, and they will be sorted into numerical order.

Adding, Deleting, and Modifying Records

In addition to using SQL to retrieve records, you can also use it to change the actual contents of databases. There are separate commands to add records to a table, delete records from a table, and modify records in a table. Compare these to the code that I used back in Hour 13 to add, delete, and modify entries in a flat-file database. The relational model and SQL make it much easier to perform these types of operations than writing code to accomplish the same tasks in a flat file.

Adding Records

Let's first look at how to add a record to a table. The INSERT statement is used to add a record (or records, if your database supports it) to a table. The record will be added to the "end" of the specified table. Technically speaking there is no first or last record in a relational database table. A record that appears first in the results of one query could turn up last in the next, unless you use the ORDER BY clause to specify the order in which they should appear. Most databases do store records sequentially in the order that they were inserted, but it's a bad idea to count on their being stored that way. Here's how I would add a student to the StudentData table:

```
INSERT INTO StudentData
VALUES (131333885, 'Todd', 'Wilson', 'Freshman', 'Biology', 15000);
```

If you only want to include some of the columns in the new record you are creating, or you want to specify them in an order other than the default, you need to include a list of the column names. (If you don't remember the order of the columns in a table, you can include a column list to make sure your INSERT statement will work.) For example, if I

19

wanted to create a new student record, except for the tuition, and list the columns in reverse order, I could use this INSERT statement:

```
INSERT INTO StudentData (Major, Class, LastName, FirstName, SSN)
VALUES ('Biology', 'Freshman', 'Wilson', 'Todd', 131333885)
```

By specifying the columns I want to populate as well as the values, I place the values in exactly the fields in which I want them to appear, even though I'm not populating every field. If you leave a column out of an insert statement, the default value for that column will be included. Generally, the default value for columns is null, unless you specify a different default when you create the table. Most databases allow to disallow null values for certain columns, and in those cases you must specify a value unless a default is set for that column.

Deleting Records

You can use the DELETE FROM command to delete records in a table. You can use any WHERE expression that works with the SELECT statement to choose records to delete. In fact, you will probably want to test the condition with SELECT before you use it with DELETE to make sure you're not deleting records that you really want to keep. Let's look at an example, in which I will try to delete the record I just inserted:

```
DELETE FROM StudentData
WHERE LastName = 'Wilson';
```

Of course, this will delete any students with the last name Wilson, so you probably wouldn't want to use it. Instead, you should probably either stick to deleting records based on the primary key, or use some other combination of values that you know will only match the records that you want to delete. You could be more specific about what you want to delete by using a compound statement like this:

```
DELETE FROM StudentData
WHERE LastName = 'Wilson'
AND FirstName = 'Todd'
AND CLASS = 'Freshman';
```

This still deletes all the freshmen named Todd Wilson, but you get the idea of how records can be deleted using compound conditional statements. Your best bet if you really wanted to delete just the record that I entered in the previous example would be to simply delete the record by matching the SSN:

```
DELETE FROM StudentData
WHERE SSN = 131333885;
```

Modifying Records

One way to modify a record is simply to delete it and then add a record with the same primary key and new values in the other fields. However, SQL provides a more convenient method than that. Using the UPDATE command, you can select records using WHERE and then change only the fields in the record that you specify.

Let's say a student has just completed a year of college and will be moving up a class. You can change their classification using the following command:

```
UPDATE StudentData
SET Class = 'Senior'
WHERE SSN = 123456789;
```

You can also change more than one record at a time by matching a field that is not a primary key. You can modify more than one field at a time by separating the name and value pairs using commas. Here's an example:

```
UPDATE StudentData
SET Class = 'Senior', Tuition = 10000
WHERE Class = 'Junior';
```

That command changes the class to senior and the tuition to 10,000 for every record with the class set to Junior in the database.

Database Interfaces

As you've already read, SQL is fairly standardized. Most of the SQL statements you write will work with any relational database. However, there's another layer of communication that I haven't yet discussed. SQL is what you use to issue commands to a database, but the next question you have to answer is how to connect to the database with your program so that you can issue those SQL statements and retrieve the results. All databases provide a native interface of some kind that you can use to communicate with the database. Unfortunately, those interfaces are proprietary. A program that is written specifically to communicate with an Oracle database will be totally unable to issue SQL statements to a MySQL database. Fortunately, there are ways around this problem. There are a number of database interfaces available that provide a uniform interface to your programs while at the same time using database-specific drivers to communicate with whatever database you're using. If you use one of these database interfaces to connect to the database, all you have to do is write your code to access the API provided by the database interface, which then connects to the appropriate database and issues your SQL statements.

The advantage of using these interfaces is that you can use the same code to connect to any database that has the appropriate driver available. The disadvantage is that it adds an extra layer of processing between the application and the database that can reduce performance. If you need the best performance possible, you should probably forego using a database interface and connect straight into the database using its native API. If you're more concerned with portability, writing your application to the database interface is probably the safer choice.

19

There are several of these types of interfaces available. Generally they are associated with various programming languages or operating system platforms. For example, ODBC is a database interface associated with the Windows platform. JDBC is a database interface used to provide connectivity to relational databases in Java programs. DBI is the database interface for Perl.

ODBC

ODBC is a generic database interface associated with the Windows platform. All of Microsoft's database products support ODBC (as do most other databases these days), and the ODBC drivers are built into Windows. If you're using any kind of database-related product under Windows, you can generally count on it supporting ODBC. UNIX users can purchase third-party ODBC drivers as well. Generally, ODBC drivers for UNIX come packed with applications that require ODBC support in order to work.

DBI and DBD

Using Perl to access a relational database requires two pieces: the DBI (Database Interface) module and a DBD driver. *DBI* is the interface from Perl to any relational database, and *DBD (Database Driver)* provides the code necessary to communicate with a particular database. There are DBD drivers available for all the popular relational databases.

Much like ODBC, DBI and DBD provide a level of abstraction between an application and a database. DBI provides a uniform means of accessing the data inside any database because the DBI interface is standard regardless of the database. Internally, DBI works with the DBD driver specific to the database you're using. DBD modules are available for most popular databases, including Oracle, Sybase, Informix, and MySQL. There is even a DBD driver for ODBC. When you use DBD and ODBC together, that means that there is an additional layer between the application and the database, as shown in Figure 19.1.

If you're using a database that supports ODBC, but does not have a DBD driver, you should use the DBD driver for ODBC. Obviously, there's no advantage to using ODBC at all if a DBD driver exists for your database.

You can download the DBI module and the appropriate DBD driver for your database from the Comprehensive Perl Archive Network (CPAN) at `http://www.perl.com/CPAN/`. DBI and DBD can be found in category 7 of the archive called Database Interfaces. After you've installed DBI on your system, you can view the DBI documentation by typing **perldoc DBI**.

FIGURE 19.1

Accessing a database via the DBD driver for ODBC.

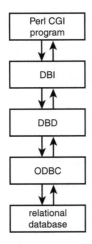

A Sample Program Using DBI and DBD

I'm going to write a simple CGI program that uses DBI and the MySQL DBD driver to connect to a database, send a SELECT statement, and print the output of the SELECT statement in an HTML table. The full source code for the program appears in Listing 19.2.

If your Web server doesn't already have a database engine installed and you want to experiment with a real SQL database, I suggest that you look at MySQL. It's available free of charge. If you like, you can pay for a support subscription. You can download MySQL and find the documentation at http://www.mysql.net.

19

LISTING 19.2   The dbiquery.pl Program

```
 1: #!/usr/local/bin/perl
 2:
 3: use DBI;
 4: use CGI;
 5: use CGI::Carp qw(fatalsToBrowser);
 6:
 7: $database = "database_name";
 8: $db_server = "database_hostname";
 9: $user = "user_name";
10: $password = "password";
11:
12: $query = new CGI;
13:
14: print $query->header;
```

continues

LISTING **19.2**   continued

```
15:
16: $dbh = DBI->connect("DBI:mysql:$database:$db_server", $user, $password);
17:
18: $statement = "SELECT * FROM StudentData ORDER BY SSN";
19:
20: $sth = $dbh->prepare($statement)
21:     or die "Couldn't prepare the query: $sth->errstr";
22:
23: $rv = $sth->execute
24:     or die "Couldn't execute query: $dbh->errstr";
25:
26: print "<HTML>\n<HEAD>\n<TITLE>Student Data</TITLE>\n</HEAD>\n<BODY>\n";
27:
28: print "<H1>Student Data</H1>\n";
29:
30: print "<TABLE BORDER=1>\n";
31: print "<TR>\n<TH>SSN</TH>\n<TH>Name</TH>\n<TH>Class</TH>\n";
32: print "<TH>Major</TH>\n<TH>Tuition</TH>\n</TR>\n";
33:
34: while (@row = $sth->fetchrow_array) {
35:     print "<TR>\n";
36:     print "<TD>$row[0]</TD>\n";
37:     print "<TD>$row[1] $row[2]</TD>\n";
38:     print "<TD>$row[3]</TD>\n";
39:     print "<TD>$row[4]</TD>\n";
40:     print "<TD>$row[5]</TD>\n";
41:     print "</TR>\n";
42: }
43:
44: print "</TABLE>\n";
45:
46: $rc = $sth->finish;
47: $rc = $dbh->disconnect;
48:
49: print "</BODY>\n</HTML>\n";
```

As always, the first step is to point to the Perl interpreter. Afterward, I import two modules. The CGI module is, of course, CGI.pm, which is used to import data from forms and generate HTML code automatically. The DBI module provides the methods necessary to access a database. On line 5, I import the CGI::Carp module so that any runtime errors encountered are automatically echoed to the browser.

After all the modules are imported, I create variables to hold all of the connection information for the database on lines 7–10. These variables are used in the connection string to establish a connection to the database. On line 12, I create a new query object for this program. On line 14, I print the HTML headers for the page.

On line 16, I open a database connection and assign it to the variable $dbh. To connect to the database, I use the connect method of the DBI module. There are three arguments that are passed to the connect method (they appear inside the parentheses). The first argument tells the connect method which database to connect to. In this case, the database type is mysql, and the database name is retrieved from the $database variable. The next two attributes are used to send the username and password for the database account being used.

The next step is to use the prepare method to get an SQL statement ready for execution. First, I create the statement on line 18. On line 20 and 21, I prepare the statement and assign the prepared statement to $sth. An or die construct (which appears on line 21) is used to trap any errors that occur when attempting to prepare the statement. The prepared statement can be executed later using the execute method. There are other methods for executing SQL statements as well. For example, you can prepare and execute statements at the same time by using the do method.

On lines 23 and 24, I actually execute the statement, assigning the resulting code to $rv. Calling the execute method on a prepared statement will execute that statement. Again, an or die construct is used to trap errors. The results of the query are then accessible through the $sth variable.

On lines 26 through 32, I print out the HTML that appears before the actual query results. Then, on line 34, a while loop that retrieves all the records returned by the query is initiated. The fetchrow_array method of the statement handle returns the next row of the query results in an array. In this case, that array is assigned to @row. In the body of the loop, the data retrieved is printed in an HTML table. After the loop's execution is complete, I close the table on line 44. On lines 46 and 47, I release the statement handler using the finish method, and close the database using the disconnect method of the database connection object.

19

Of course, there's a lot more you can do with DBI than just fetch rows from a database. DBI provides full SQL access to the databases that it supports. For more information, you might want to look at the book *Programming the Perl DBI*, by Alligator Descartes and Tim Bunce (published by O'Reilly and Associates).

Summary

This lesson gave you a broad introduction to designing and using relational databases. You should have come away with a good overview of the technologies involved in building a relational database and in accessing them using CGI.

Q&A

Q Isn't there a lot more to working with relational databases than this?

A Of course there is, but due to the enormity of the subject, the lesson was "A mile wide and an inch deep," as they say. If you're going to be working with databases a lot, you should really buy a book that discusses them in detail. You may want to look at the following books: *Special Edition Using SQL*, by Rafe Colburn; *Database-backed Web Sites*, by Philip Greenspun; *The Practical SQL Handbook*, by Judith S. Bowman, Sandra L. Emerson, and Marcy Darnovsky; or *Database Design for Mere Mortals: A Hands-On Guide to Relational Database Design*, by Michael J. Hernandez.

Q Are there easier ways to connect databases to the Web than those illustrated in this lesson?

A A booming field in the Internet software industry is the creation of *middleware* that makes it easy to connect databases to the Web. There is a mind-boggling list of products available to connect your Web server to your relational database. Hour 12, "Pros and Cons of Alternate Technologies," covered some of these products, although it seems new products in this category are released every day.

Workshop

The quiz questions are designed to strengthen the knowledge you gain each hour. The exercises help you build on that knowledge by providing you with the opportunity to apply it to real problems. See Appendix A, "Answers" for the answers to the quiz questions.

Quiz

1. What's the difference between a primary key and a candidate key?
2. What is the relationship between DBI and DBD?
3. What shortcut is used to select all the columns in a table?

Exercises

1. Obtain a copy of MySQL (or Microsoft Access or another relational database if you're using Windows NT server), create some tables, and try connecting them to the Web. If you already have access to a relational database, find out the schema and write some programs that grab information from the database.

Hour **20**

Creating an Online Store

In Hour 16, "Building a Simple Shopping Cart," I provided an example of an online store that demonstrated how one uses session management to create a shopping cart. In this hour, I'm going to extend that example to show how you can use a relational database to store all the data used by a Web site—specifically an online store. In this hour, you'll look at modified versions of the programs from Hour 16 that interface with a relational database.

In this hour you'll learn

- What the database schema for a basic online store looks like
- How to write a catalog script that works with a relational database
- How a database simplifies the shopping cart script
- How a real-life checkout script works

The Database Design

In Hour 16, I had to create some flat files to use for data storage. Those flat files will no longer be used; instead, I've created tables in a relational database that will house all the data associated with the online store. Before I can get into the changes I've made to the programs, I need to explain the database design, and provide you with the SQL queries I used to create those tables.

The two data files I used in Hour 16 were products.txt and cart.txt. The products.txt file contained a list of products sold by the online store. I've replaced it with a table named products. The cart.txt file, which was used to save session information for users with products in their shopping cart, has been replaced with a table named cart. I've also created two additional tables for use in the application, orders and order_products. These tables are used to store order information when orders are submitted.

All the sample programs in this hour communicate with a MySQL database. The queries are written in standard SQL, so they should work with any relational database that provides SQL support. However, you might have to alter the data types to get them to work with the relational database you use.

Let's look at the layout for each of these tables. Listing 20.1 contains the output of the MySQL desc commands that show the schema of the tables in the database.

LISTING 20.1 The Schema for the Tables Used by the Online Store

```
 1: mysql> desc products;
 2: +--------------+--------------+------+-----+---------+-------+
 3: | Field        | Type         | Null | Key | Default | Extra |
 4: +--------------+--------------+------+-----+---------+-------+
 5: | product_id   | int(11)      | YES  |     | NULL    |       |
 6: | product_name | varchar(25)  | YES  |     | NULL    |       |
 7: | product_desc | varchar(255) | YES  |     | NULL    |       |
 8: | product_price| float(10,2)  | YES  |     | NULL    |       |
 9: +--------------+--------------+------+-----+---------+-------+
10: 4 rows in set (0.01 sec)
11:
12: mysql> desc cart;
13: +------------+---------+------+-----+---------+-------+
14: | Field      | Type    | Null | Key | Default | Extra |
15: +------------+---------+------+-----+---------+-------+
16: | session    | int(11) | YES  |     | NULL    |       |
17: | product_id | int(11) | YES  |     | NULL    |       |
18: | quantity   | int(11) | YES  |     | NULL    |       |
19: +------------+---------+------+-----+---------+-------+
20: 3 rows in set (0.23 sec)
21:
```

```
22: mysql> desc orders;
23: +--------------+-------------+------+-----+---------+-------+
24: | Field        | Type        | Null | Key | Default | Extra |
25: +--------------+-------------+------+-----+---------+-------+
26: | order_id     | int(11)     | YES  |     | NULL    |       |
27: | name         | varchar(60) | YES  |     | NULL    |       |
28: | addr         | varchar(60) | YES  |     | NULL    |       |
29: | city         | varchar(40) | YES  |     | NULL    |       |
30: | state        | char(2)     | YES  |     | NULL    |       |
31: | zip          | varchar(5)  | YES  |     | NULL    |       |
32: | cc_number    | varchar(20) | YES  |     | NULL    |       |
33: | cc_type      | varchar(4)  | YES  |     | NULL    |       |
34: | cc_exp_month | char(2)     | YES  |     | NULL    |       |
35: | cc_exp_year  | varchar(4)  | YES  |     | NULL    |       |
36: +--------------+-------------+------+-----+---------+-------+
37: 10 rows in set (0.02 sec)
38:
39: mysql> desc order_products;
40: +------------+---------+------+-----+---------+-------+
41: | Field      | Type    | Null | Key | Default | Extra |
42: +------------+---------+------+-----+---------+-------+
43: | order_id   | int(11) | YES  |     | NULL    |       |
44: | product_id | int(11) | YES  |     | NULL    |       |
45: | quantity   | int(11) | YES  |     | NULL    |       |
46: +------------+---------+------+-----+---------+-------+
47: 3 rows in set (0.02 sec)
```

The first table is the products table. It's similar to the products.txt file that I used in Hour 16, except that I added the field product_name. The product_desc field is used to store a description of the product that will be displayed in the catalog, and the product_name field contains a short name that can be used in the shopping cart and on invoices.

The second table is the cart table, which is used to store session information about users who have items in their shopping carts. The cart table contains the same fields as the cart.txt file—session ID, product ID, and quantity.

There are two tables associated with orders, which will be used to store information when orders are completed. The first table, orders, is used to store general information about the order as a whole. The user's name, address, and credit card information are stored in the orders table. The second table is the order_products table. It's similar to the cart table—it stores the type and quantity of each product associated with an order.

The reason you need to store order information in two tables is that you want to store as little duplicate information in the database as possible, and at the same time, you want to avoid storing multiple data elements in a single field. Let's look at each of these problems individually.

20

The first problem involves storing duplicate data. You know that you need one record for each type of product in the order. However, if you also stored the general order information (name, address, and credit card) in each product record, you'd duplicate the general information if the order contained multiple product records.

The second problem involves storing multiple "atoms" of data in a single field. What would happen if you tried to squish all the product information for the order into a single order record? If the order included multiple products, one of the fields would contain multiple product IDs, and another would contain multiple quantities. This would violate a database design rule, called the First Normal Form, and introduce lots of problems into the process of retrieving data from the database. The most sensible option is to use both tables, and to associate the products in each order with the general order information using a common field, in this case, order_id.

Listing 20.2 shows the SQL queries used to create all the database tables.

LISTING 20.2   Create Statements for the Online-Store Database Tables

```
 1: create table cart
 2: (session_id varchar(25) not null,
 3: product_id integer not null,
 4: quantity integer not null);
 5:
 6: create table products
 7: (product_id integer primary key,
 8: product_name varchar(25) not null,
 9: product_desc varchar(25) not null,
10: product_price float(10,2) not null);
11:
12: create table order_products
13: (order_id varchar(25) not null,
14: product_id integer not null,
15: quantity integer not null);
16:
17: create table orders
18: (order_id varchar(25) primary key,
19: name varchar(60) not null,
20: addr varchar(60) not null,
21: city varchar(60) not null,
22: state char(2) not null,
23: zip char(5) not null,
24: cc_number varchar(20) not null,
25: cc_type varchar(4) not null,
26: cc_exp_month char(2) not null,
27: cc_exp_year char(4) not null);
```

The Catalog Script

Now that you've got a picture of what the relational database looks like, let's examine the modified catalog.pl program. This program offers the same functionality as the catalog program from Hour 16. It displays the catalogs for users, and process requests to add items to the user's shopping cart. It differs from the old script in that it opens a database connection instead of creating filehandles, and processes the results of SQL queries instead of parsing files. The source code for the new catalog.pl program appears in Listing 20.3.

LISTING 20.3 The Source Code for catalog.pl

```
 1: #!/usr/local/bin/perl
 2:
 3: use CGI;
 4: use CGI::Carp qw( fatalsToBrowser );
 5: use DBI;
 6:
 7: $query = new CGI;
 8:
 9: $database = "some_database";
10: $db_server = "db.example.com";
11: $user = "db_user";
12: $password = "db_password";
13:
14: if ($query->param('product_id')) {
15:     if ($query->cookie('session_id')) {
16:         $session_id = ($query->cookie('session_id'));
17:     }
18:     else {
19:         $session_id = time . $$;
20:     }
21:     &set_variables;
22:     &db_connect;
23:     &print_page_start;
24:     &add_to_cart;
25:     &get_products;
26:     &display_catalog;
27:     &db_cleanup;
28:     &print_page_end;
29: }
30: else {
31:     &print_page_start;
32:     &db_connect;
33:     &get_products;
34:     &display_catalog;
```

20

continues

LISTING 20.3   continued

```
35:       &db_cleanup;
36:       &print_page_end;
37: }
38:
39: sub add_to_cart {
40:     # First, make sure they don't already have the product
41:     # in their shopping cart.  If they don't have the cookie,
42:     # it's definitely not in their shopping cart.
43:
44:     if ($query->cookie('session_id')) {
45:     # Because they have a session, let's see if they
46:     # already have the product in their cart.
47:     $statement = qq[
48:            select quantity
49:            from cart
50:            where session_id = '$session_id'
51:            and product_id = $product_id];
52:     $sth = $dbh->prepare($statement)
53:         or die "Couldn't prepare the query:", $sth->errstr, "\n";
54:     $rv = $sth->execute
55:         or die "Couldn't execute select statement: ", $sth->errstr, "\n";
56:
57:     # If a record was found, you need to update it.  Otherwise
58:     # you can just insert a new record.
59:     if (($rec_quantity) = $sth->fetchrow_array) {
60:         $action = "update";
61:     }
62:     else {
63:         $action = "insert";
64:     }
65:     }
66:     else {
67:     $action = "insert";
68:     }
69:
70:     if ($action eq "insert") {
71:     $statement = qq[
72:            insert into cart
73:            values ($session_id, $product_id, $quantity)];
74:     $sth = $dbh->prepare($statement)
75:         or die "Couldn't prepare the query:", $sth->errstr, "\n";
76:     $rv = $sth->execute
77:         or die "Couldn't execute insert statement: ", $sth->errstr, "\n";
78:     }
79:     else {
80:     $new_quantity = $quantity + $rec_quantity;
81:     $statement = qq[
82:            update cart
83:            set quantity = $new_quantity
```

```
84:                where session_id = $session_id
85:                and product_id = $product_id];
86:      $sth = $dbh->prepare($statement)
87:         or die "Couldn't prepare the query:", $sth->errstr, "\n";
88:      $rv = $sth->execute
89:         or die "Couldn't execute update statement: ", $sth->errstr, "\n";
90:      }
91: }
92:
93: sub get_products {
94:      $statement = qq[
95:                select product_id, product_name,
96:                product_desc, product_price
97:                from products
98:                ];
99:      $sth = $dbh->prepare($statement)
100:     or die "Couldn't prepare the query:", $sth->errstr, "\n";
101:     $rv = $sth->execute
102:     or die "Couldn't execute select statement: ", $sth->errstr, "\n";
103: }
104:
105: sub set_variables {
106:     $product_id = $query->param('product_id');
107:     $quantity = $query->param('quantity');
108: }
109:
110: sub db_connect {
111:     $dbh = DBI->connect("DBI:mysql:$database:$db_server", $user,
         $password);
112: }
113:
114: sub db_cleanup {
115:     $rc = $sth->finish;
116:     $rc = $dbh->disconnect;
117: }
118:
119: sub display_catalog {
120:     print "<CENTER>\n<TABLE BORDER=1 CELLPADDING=4>\n";
121:     print "<TR>\n<TH>Description</TH>\n<TH>Price</TH>\n</TR>\n";
122:
123:     while (@row = $sth->fetchrow_array) {
124:         ($product_id, $product_name, $product_desc,
125:      $product_price) = @row;
126:         print "<TR>\n";
127:         print "<FORM>\n";
128:         print "<INPUT TYPE=\"hidden\" NAME=\"product_id\" ";
129:         print "VALUE=\"$product_id\">\n";
130:         print "<TD>$product_desc</TD>\n<TD>$product_price</TD>\n";
131:         print "<TD><INPUT TYPE=\"text\" NAME=\"quantity\" ";
132:         print "VALUE=\"1\" SIZE=2></TD>\n";
```

20

continues

LISTING 20.3   continued

```
133:            print "<TD><INPUT TYPE=\"submit\" VALUE=\"add\"></TD>\n";
134:            print "</FORM>\n";
135:            print "</TR>\n";
136:        }
137:        print "</TABLE>\n</CENTER>\n";
138: }
139:
140: sub print_page_start {
141:        if ($session_id) {
142:            $cookie = $query->cookie(-name=>'session_id',
143:                                     -value=>$session_id);
144:            print $query->header(-cookie=>$cookie);
145:        }
146:        else {
147:            print $query->header;
148:        }
149:        print "<HTML>\n<HEAD>\n<TITLE>PC Product Catalog</TITLE>\n";
150:        print "</HEAD>\n<BODY>\n";
151:        print "<H1 ALIGN=\"center\">PC Product Catalog</H1>\n";
152: }
153:
154: sub print_page_end {
155:        print "<P><CENTER><B>";
156:        print"<A HREF=\"cart.pl\">view cart</A></B></CENTER></P>\n";
157:        print "</BODY>\n</HTML>\n";
158: }
```

Let's take a look at the changes that were made to the catalog.pl script to get it to work with the relational database. First, I added some new variables to the beginning of the script on lines 9–12. These variables provide information about the database that will be used by the program. They specify the name of the database, the hostname of the database server, and the username and password used to connect to the database. The locations of the product and cart files have been removed because they're no longer used.

Opening and Closing Database Connections

I've added two additional subroutines to this script. These subroutines appear in all the scripts in this hour because they're used whenever I want to communicate with the database. The two subroutines are db_connect and db_cleanup. The db_connect subroutine is used to open a new connection to the database, and the db_cleanup script cleans up resources used by the connection and then closes the connection.

In db_connect, I assign the database connection to the variable $dbh. The connect method of the DBI object accepts the connection string for the server as an argument, along with the database username and password. The connection string contains the database driver name, database server hostname, and the name of the database itself.

Displaying the Product List

In the old script, the product file was parsed, and the contents of the file were displayed as a catalog. In this case, I use a SQL query to retrieve the contents of the `products` table, and then I iterate over the results of that query to display the catalog. These steps take place in different subroutines. The query is prepared and executed in the `get_products` subroutine. Let's take a look at the query itself:

```
select product_id, product_name, product_desc, product_price from products
```

The query simply selects the four columns from the `products` table, returning all the rows. There are two steps in the query process. First, I use the prepare method to prepare the statement for execution, and then I call the `execute` method to execute the statement. Errors that occur with both of these statements are trapped using an `or die` clause. If either the preparation of the statement or the execution fails, the program will exit with an error message.

After all the product records have been fetched, I print the catalog using the `display_catalog` subroutine. In the old version, I iterated over the lines in the catalog file; in this case, I process the rows returned by the query one at a time. The `while` loop that processes the query results begins on line 119. Let's look at the condition associated with the `while` loop:

```
while (@row = $sth->fetchrow_array)
```

The `while` loop continues until there are no longer any rows left to pull out of the result set using the `fetchrow_array` method. It processes the result set one row at a time, and assigns the values in the row to the `@row` array in the order that the columns were specified in the query. To make this clear, let's look at the next statement in the subroutine:

```
($product_id, $product_name, $product_desc,  $product_price) = @row;
```

As you can see, the list of variable extracted from `@row` conforms to the select list in the SQL statement used to fetch the product list. The values in these variables are used to populate the catalog.

Adding Items to the Shopping Cart

Now let's look at what happens when you an add an item to the shopping cart and you're using a relational database. There's one important decision to make in the `add_to_cart` subroutine: whether to use an `insert` statement to add a new record to the cart or an `update` statement to change the quantity in an existing record. First, the script checks for

20

a session ID. If there's no session ID, the script assumes that the user doesn't already have any records in the cart table, and thus an insert statement should be used.

If the user had a cookie, the next step is to determine whether there's already a record for that session ID and product. A select statement is executed that retrieves the quantity of items associated with the user's session ID and the product that was selected. The script then counts how many rows were returned by the query. If no rows were returned, the script assumes that it should insert a new record. If a row was returned, the script adds the quantity being added to the quantity of items already in the user's cart, and updates the cart table with that value. After the item is added to the cart, the script prints out the catalog.

The Shopping Cart Script

The cart.pl program has two purposes—to list the contents of the user's shopping cart and to remove items from the cart. When I kept everything in text files, this program was pretty complex because it had to correlate products listed in the cart.txt file with product information stored in the products.txt file. In this case, I use a single query to fetch the contents of the cart and the product information for each of the products in the cart at once. A delete statement is used to remove items from the user's shopping cart. All of the database connection code in this script is identical to that in catalog.pl. In other words, I included the db_connect and db_cleanup subroutines, imported the DBI module, and set the variables necessary to connect to the database. The full source code for the cart.pl program appears in Listing 20.4.

LISTING 20.4   The Source Code for cart.pl

```
 1: #!/usr/local/bin/perl
 2:
 3: use CGI;
 4: use CGI::Carp qw( fatalsToBrowser );
 5: use DBI;
 6:
 7: $query = new CGI;
 8:
 9: $database = "some_database";
10: $db_server = "db.example.com";
11: $user = "db_user";
12: $password = "db_password";
13:
14:
15: if ($query->cookie('session_id')) {
16:     $session_id = ($query->cookie('session_id'));
17: }
18:
```

```
19: if ($query->param('action')) {
20:     if ($query->param('action') eq 'remove') {
21:         $page_title = "Shopping Cart";
22:         &db_connect;
23:         &remove_item;
24:         &print_page_start;
25:         &get_cart_contents;
26:         if ($sth->rows) {
27:             &print_cart;
28:         }
29:         else {
30:             &print_no_cart;
31:         }
32:         &print_page_end;
33:         &db_cleanup;
34:     }
35: }
36: else {
37:     $page_title = "Shopping Cart";
38:     &print_page_start;
39:     &db_connect;
40:     &get_cart_contents;
41:     if ($sth->rows) {
42:         &print_cart;
43:     }
44:     else {
45:         &print_no_cart;
46:     }
47:     &print_page_end;
48:     &db_cleanup;
49: }
50:
51: sub db_connect {
52:     $dbh = DBI->connect("DBI:mysql:$database:$db_server", $user,
          $password);
53: }
54:
55: sub db_cleanup {
56:     $rc = $sth->finish;
57:     $rc = $dbh->disconnect;
58: }
59:
60: sub remove_item {
61:     $product_id = $query->param('product_id');
62:     $statement = qq[
63:                     delete from cart
64:                     where session_id = '$session_id'
65:                     and product_id = $product_id
66:                     ];
67:     $sth = $dbh->prepare($statement)
```

20

continues

LISTING 20.4   continued

```
 68:             or die "Couldn't prepare the query:", $sth->errstr, "\n";
 69:         $rv = $sth->execute
 70:             or die "Couldn't execute select statement: ", $sth->errstr, "\n";
 71: }
 72:
 73: sub get_cart_contents {
 74:     $statement = qq[
 75:                         select cart.product_id as product_id,
 76:                         quantity, product_name, product_price
 77:                         from cart, products
 78:                         where session_id = '$session_id'
 79:                         and cart.product_id = products.product_id
 80:                         ];
 81:     $sth = $dbh->prepare($statement)
 82:         or die "Couldn't prepare the query:", $sth->errstr, "\n";
 83:     $rv = $sth->execute
 84:         or die "Couldn't execute select statement: ", $sth->errstr, "\n";
 85: }
 86:
 87: sub print_cart {
 88:     print "<CENTER>\n<TABLE>\n<TR>\n";
 89:     print "<TH>Product ID</TH>\n<TH>Product Name</TH>\n";
 90:     print "<TH>Price</TH>\n<TH>Quantity</TH>\n</TR>\n";
 91:     while (@row = $sth->fetchrow_array) {
 92:         ($rec_product_id, $rec_quantity, $rec_product_name,
 93:          $rec_price) = @row;
 94:         print "<TD>$rec_product_id</TD>\n";
 95:         print "<TD>$rec_product_name</TD>\n";
 96:         print "<TD>$rec_price</TD>\n";
 97:         print "<TD>$rec_quantity</TD>\n";
 98:         print "<TD>\n<FORM>\n";
 99:         print "<INPUT TYPE=\"hidden\" NAME=\"action\" VALUE=\"remove\">\n";
100:         print "<INPUT TYPE=\"hidden\" NAME=\"product_id\" ";
101:         print "VALUE=\"$rec_product_id\">\n";
102:         print "<INPUT TYPE=\"submit\" VALUE=\"remove\">\n";
103:         print "</TD>\n";
104:         print "</TR>\n";
105:     }
106:     print "</TABLE>\n";
107: }
108:
109: sub print_page_start {
110:     print $query->header;
111:     print "<HTML>\n<HEAD>\n<TITLE>$page_title</TITLE>\n";
112:     print "</HEAD>\n<BODY>\n";
113:     print "<H1 ALIGN=\"center\">$page_title</H1>\n";
114: }
115:
```

```
116: sub print_no_cart {
117:     print "<P>There are no items in your shopping cart.</P>\n";
118: }
119:
120: sub print_page_end {
121:     print "<P><CENTER><B>";
122:     print"<A HREF=\"catalog.pl\">return to catalog</A></B></CENTER></P>\n";
123:     print "</BODY>\n</HTML>\n";
124: }
```

Displaying the Shopping Cart

First let's look at how the cart is displayed. The code here is similar to that used in catalog.pl, in that it's split between two subroutines. The get_cart_contents subroutine retrieves the user's cart from the database. The program then checks to see whether the user has anything in his cart. If he does, the print_cart subroutine is used to print it out.

The most interesting thing here is the query used to retrieve the contents of the user's cart from the database. In this case, I use a joining query that retrieves data from both the products and cart table using a single select statement. Let's take a look at the query:

```
select cart.product_id as product_id,
quantity, product_name, product_price
from cart, products
where session_id = '$session_id'
and cart.product_id = products.product_id
```

First, let's look at the select list. Because this query retrieves data from two tables, and both tables contain a column called product_id, I have to specify from which table I want to retrieve the product_id column using dot notation. Using cart.product_id indicates that I want the product_id column from the cart table. In this case, it doesn't matter which table I retrieve the column from because product_id is the joining condition for this query. The query retrieves rows where the product_id values match between the tables. I'll explain this in a bit. I use the as keyword to associate the name product_id with cart.product_id. This makes it easier to retrieve the value in that column later.

As you can see, the from clause of this query contains two column names. When you join two tables, they are actually merged to create one giant table that contains the Cartesian product of both tables. In other words, if you join two 10 row tables, you'll come out with one 100 row table to be used by the query, which contains every combination of rows between the two tables.

In the where clause, I use two conditions. The first is the joining condition. Its purpose is

20

to throw out all of the rows in the joined table that are irrelevant. In this case, I want to correlate all the items in the cart with the product information associated with those items. So, any rows where the `product_id` column from the `cart` table doesn't match the `product_id` column from the `products` table are discarded. The condition used to accomplish this is `cart.product_id = products.product_id`. The second condition in the `where` clause discards any rows that aren't associated with the current user's session. So, the query results include the contents of the user's cart along with the product information associated with them.

After the contents of the user's shopping cart have been fetched, the next step is to determine whether the user actually had anything in his shopping cart. Line 26 of the script contains a simple condition that tests for whether the `$sth->rows` expression evaluates as true. If no rows were returned by the query, the expression is false; otherwise, the user does have items in his cart and the expression is true.

Assuming the expression is true, the `print_cart` subroutine is executed. The `print_cart` subroutine, which begins on line 87, is very similar to the `display_catalog` subroutine in `catalog.pl`. It uses a `while` loop to process the records returned by the query one at a time, and extracts them from the result set using `fetchrow_array`. The individual data in the fields is extracted from the `@row` array and printed.

Removing Items from the Shopping Cart

When the cart is displayed, a form is created for each item that allows the user to remove that item by clicking on a button. If the `cart.pl` program is called by a form submission that includes the `action` parameter, and the parameter is set to `remove`, the `remove_item` subroutine is called. The `remove_item` subroutine executes a single query:

```
delete from cart
where session_id = '$session_id'
and product_id = $product_id
```

This query simply deletes any rows in the `cart` table that match the user's session ID and the product ID of the item that he wanted to remove.

The Checkout Script

In Hour 16, I didn't write code to do anything with the order information the user entered after the checkout form was processed. In this hour, I'm inserting the order data into the database, so you can see how the back-end processing often works for online stores. As you've probably guessed, I had to make the same changes to this script that I had to make to the other scripts in order to get them to talk to the database. Before I look at the script's new functionality, let's look at the source code, which appears in Listing 20.5.

LISTING 20.5   The Source Code to `checkout.pl`

```perl
1: #!/usr/local/bin/perl
2:
3: use CGI;
4: use CGI::Carp qw(fatalsToBrowser);
5: use DBI;
6:
7: $query = new CGI;
8:
9: $database = "rafeco_rc3";
10: $db_server = "db4.pair.com";
11: $user = "rafeco_w";
12: $password = "vmppa55r";
13:
14: %cc_types = ('AMEX' => 'American Express',
15:             'VISA' => 'Visa',
16:             'MC' => 'Mastercard',
17:             'DISC' => 'Discover');
18:
19: if ($query->cookie('session_id')) {
20:     $session_id = $query->cookie('session_id');
21: }
22: else {
23:     $page_title = "Checkout: Error";
24:     &print_page_start;
25:     &print_no_cart;
26:     &print_page_end;
27:     exit;
28: }
29:
30: &db_connect;
31:
32: &get_cart_contents;
33:
34: if ($cart_query->rows) {
35:     if ($query->param('cc_type')) {
36:     &set_variables;
37:     if (! &valid_form) {
38:         $page_title = "Checkout Complete";
39:         &print_page_start;
40:         &insert_order;
41:         &empty_cart;
42:         &print_success;
43:         &print_page_end;
44:     }
45:     else {
46:         $page_title = "Checkout: Please correct errors";
47:         &print_page_start;
48:         &print_error;
```

continues

LISTING 20.5   continued

```
49:            &print_form;
50:            &print_page_end;
51:       }
52:       }
53:       else {
54:       $page_title = "Checkout";
55:       &print_page_start;
56:       &print_form;
57:       &print_page_end;
58:       }
59: }
60: else {
61:       $page_title = "Error: Your cart is empty";
62:       &print_page_start;
63:       &print_no_cart;
64:       &print_page_end;
65: }
66:
67: &db_cleanup;
68:
69: sub db_connect {
70:       $dbh = DBI->connect("DBI:mysql:$database:$db_server", $user,
➥$password);
71: }
72:
73: sub db_cleanup {
74:       if ($sth) {
75:       $rc = $sth->finish;
76:       }
77:       if ($cart_query) {
78:       $rc = $cart_query->finish;
79:       }
80:       $rc = $dbh->disconnect;
81: }
82:
83: sub get_cart_contents {
84:       $statement = qq[
85:               select product_id, quantity
86:               from cart
87:               where session_id = '$session_id'
88:               ];
89:       $cart_query = $dbh->prepare($statement)
90:       or die "Couldn't prepare the query:", $cart_query->errstr, "\n";
91:       $rv = $cart_query->execute
92:       or die "Couldn't execute select statement: ",
93:       $cart_query->errstr, "\n";
94: }
95:
96: sub insert_order {
```

```
97:     # Create a unique Order ID
98:     $order_id = time . $$;
99:
100:    # Insert all of the items in the user's cart into the
101:    # order_products table
102:
103:    while (@row = $cart_query->fetchrow_array) {
104:    ($product_id, $quantity) = @row;
105:    $statement = qq[
106:            insert into order_products
107:            values ('$order_id', $product_id, $quantity)
108:            ];
109:    $sth = $dbh->prepare($statement)
110:        or die "Couldn't prepare the query:", $sth->errstr, "\n";
111:    $rv = $sth->execute
112:        or die "Couldn't execute insert statement: ",
113:        $sth->errstr, "\n";
114:    }
115:
116:    # Create a record for the order itself
117:    $statement = qq[
118:            insert into orders
119:            values ('$order_id', '$name', '$address',
120:                '$city', '$state', '$zip',
121:                '$cc_number', '$cc_type',
122:                '$exp_month', '$exp_year')
123:            ];
124:    $insert = $dbh->prepare($statement)
125:    or die "Couldn't prepare the query:", $insert->errstr, "\n";
126:    $rv = $insert->execute
127:    or die "Order insert failed: ",
128:    $insert->errstr, "\n";
129: }
130:
131: sub empty_cart {
132:    $statement = qq[
133:            delete from cart
134:            where session_id = $session_id
135:            ];
136:    $sth = $dbh->prepare($statement)
137:        or die "Couldn't prepare the query:", $sth->errstr, "\n";
138:    $rv = $sth->execute
139:        or die "Couldn't execute delete statement: ", $sth->errstr, "\n";
140: }
141:
142: sub print_empty_cart {
143:    print "<P>You cannot check out until you have placed items ";
144:    print "in your shopping cart.</P>\n";
145:    print "<P>Return to the <A HREF=\"catalog.pl\">catalog</A>.</P>\n";
146: }
```

20

continues

LISTING 20.5   continued

```
147:
148: sub set_variables {
149:     $name = $query->param('name');
150:     $address = $query->param('address');
151:     $city = $query->param('city');
152:     $state = $query->param('state');
153:     $zip = $query->param('zip');
154:     $cc_type = $query->param('cc_type');
155:     $cc_number = $query->param('cc_number');
156:     $exp_month = $query->param('exp_month');
157:     $exp_year = $query->param('exp_year');
158: }
159:
160: sub valid_form {
161:     $error_message = '';
162:     $error_message .= "<LI>You must enter your name\n"
163:         if ($name =~ /^\s*$/);
164:     $error_message .= "<LI>You must enter your address\n"
165:         if ($address =~ /^\s*$/);
166:     $error_message .= "<LI>You must enter your city\n"
167:         if ($city =~ /^\s*$/);
168:     $error_message .= "<LI>You must enter a valid zip code\n"
169:         if ($zip !~ /^\d+$/);
170:     $error_message .= "<LI>You must enter a valid month of expiration\n"
171:         if ($exp_month > 12 || $exp_month < 1);
172:     $error_message .= "<LI>You must enter a valid year of expiration\n"
173:         if ($exp_year < 2000 || $exp_year > 2010);
174:     $error_message .= "<LI>You must enter a valid credit card number\n"
175:         if ($cc_number !~ /^\d+$/);
176:     return $error_message;
177: }
178:
179: sub print_error {
180:     print "<P>Please correct the following errors:</P>\n";
181:     if ($error_message) {
182:     print "<UL>\n$error_message\n</UL>\n";
183:     }
184: }
185:
186: sub print_form {
187:     print "<FORM>\n";
188:     print "<TABLE BORDER=0>\n";
189:     print "<TR><TD>Name:</TD>\n";
190:     print "<TD><INPUT TYPE=\"text\" NAME=\"name\" VALUE=\"$name\">\n";
191:     print "</TD></TR>\n";
192:     print "<TR><TD>Street address:</TD>\n";
193:     print "<TD><INPUT TYPE=\"text\" NAME=\"address\" ";
194:     print "VALUE=\"$address\" SIZE=40 MAXLENGTH=80></TD></TR>\n";
```

```
195:        print "<TR><TD>City:</TD>\n";
196:        print "<TD><INPUT TYPE=\"text\" NAME=\"city\" ";
197:        print "VALUE=\"$city\"></TD></TR>\n";
198:        print "<TR><TD>State:</TD>\n";
199:        print "<TD><INPUT TYPE=\"text\" NAME=\"state\" ";
200:        print "VALUE=\"$state\" SIZE=2 MAXLENGTH=2></TD></TR>\n";
201:        print "<TR><TD>Zip</TD>\n";
202:        print "<TD><INPUT TYPE=\"text\" NAME=\"zip\" ";
203:        print "VALUE=\"$zip\" SIZE=5 MAXLENGTH=5></TD></TR>\n";
204:        print "<TD>Credit card:</TD>\n<TD>\n<SELECT NAME=\"cc_type\">\n";
205:        foreach $key (sort {$a <=> $b} keys %cc_types) {
206:        print "<OPTION VALUE=\"$key\">", $cc_types{$key}, "\n";
207:        }
208:        print "</SELECT>\n</TD>\n";
209:        print "<TR><TD>Credit card number:</TD>\n";
210:        print "<TD><INPUT TYPE=\"text\" NAME=\"cc_number\" ";
211:        print "VALUE=\"$cc_number\"></TD></TR>\n";
212:        print "<TR><TD>Expiration date:</TD>\n";
213:        print "<TD><INPUT TYPE=\"text\" NAME=\"exp_month\" ";
214:        print "VALUE=\"$exp_month\" SIZE=2 MAXLENGTH=2>\n";
215:        print "<INPUT TYPE=\"text\" NAME=\"exp_year\" ";
216:        print "VALUE=\"$exp_year\" SIZE=2 MAXLENGTH=4>\n";
217:        print "<TR><TD></TD>\n";
218:        print "<TD><INPUT TYPE=\"submit\" VALUE=\"Complete Checkout\">";
219:        print "</TD></TR>\n";
220:        print "</TABLE>\n";
221:        print "</FORM>\n";
222: }
223:
224: sub print_page_start {
225:        print $query->header;
226:        print "<HTML>\n<HEAD>\n<TITLE>$page_title</TITLE>\n";
227:        print "</HEAD>\n<BODY>\n";
228:        print "<H1 ALIGN=\"center\">$page_title</H1>\n";
229: }
230:
231: sub print_no_cart {
232:        print "<P>There are no items in your shopping cart.</P>\n";
233: }
234:
235: sub print_success {
236:        print "<P>Your order is complete.</P>\n";
237: }
238:
239: sub print_page_end {
240:        print "<P><CENTER><B>";
241:        print"<A HREF=\"catalog.pl\">return to catalog</A></B></CENTER></P>\n";
242:        print "</BODY>\n</HTML>\n";
243: }
```

20

Before I talk about the code that inserts orders into the database, which comprises the bulk of the changes to this script, I'll mention a couple of other smaller changes I made. In the old script, I had to read the cart file to figure out whether the user had any items in his shopping cart. In the new program, I retrieve the contents of the shopping cart using the get_cart_contents subroutine. It contains a query that retrieves a list of the items in the user's cart, and the quantity of each of those items.

I assign this query result set to $cart_query, so that it doesn't conflict with any of the other queries in the script, which are assigned to $sth. Before the checkout form can be displayed, I make sure that the user's cart contains at least one item by verifying that the result set for $cart_query contains some records.

Storing Orders in the Database

After the items in the user's cart have been retrieved, and the user's form input has been validated, you're ready to store the user's order in the database. Storing the order is a two step process. First, all the items in the user's cart are stored in the order_products table. Then, the information the user entered in the checkout form is stored in the orders table. Both the items in the order_products table and the order in the orders table are identified using an order ID, which is generated in the same way that the session IDs are created in the catalog.pl program.

Let's look at the two steps in more detail. To store the items in the user's cart as part of the order, I use a while loop that iterates over the results of the query that retrieved all the items from the user's cart. Inside the while loop, I insert the current item into a new row in the order_products table. Here's the query:

```
insert into order_products values ('$order_id', $product_id, $quantity)
```

The $order_id variable is set at the beginning of the insert_order subroutine. The product ID and quantity are taken from the query results.

After all the items in the order are stored in the database, I insert the order information that the user entered into the orders table. The insert statement used to create the record is:

```
insert into orders values ('$order_id', '$name', '$address', '$city',
 '$state', '$zip', '$cc_number','$cc_type', '$exp_month', '$exp_year')
```

When the order information has been stored, all that's left is to remove the items associated with the user's session from the cart table. A single delete statement takes care of that job by deleting all the rows associated with the user's session ID.

Summary

In Hour 16, I used an online store to demonstrate how session management works in Web applications. I've reworked those scripts in this hour to demonstrate how to use a relational database to store data associated with a Web application. I took each of the scripts from Hour 16 and replaced the calls to flat files with relational database queries. In the course of this hour, you saw how `insert`, `update`, `delete`, and `select` statements are used within the context of a Web application.

Q&A

Q Is it possible to use a mixture of relational database tables and flat files to store application data?

A Yes, it is. However, if you're using a relational database to store any data associated with your application, I'd recommend that you store all your data there. Relational databases provide a lot of advantages over flat files for data storage.

Q Are there any performance issues associated with accessing relational databases from CGI scripts?

A Yes. Well, there's one issue in particular that you should know about. As you know, every time a CGI program is requested, a new process is started to execute the CGI program. This means that you have to open a new database connection every time the script is called, and close the database connection when it exits. This can create performance problems, particularly with some databases.

Q What do I need to test out these sample programs?

A In addition to the Web server software and a Perl interpreter, you'll need a relational database. To download MySQL (it's free and available for both Windows and UNIX), go to `http://www.mysql.net`.

Workshop

The quiz questions are designed to strengthen the knowledge you gain each hour. The exercises help you build on that knowledge by providing you with the opportunity to apply it to real problems. See Appendix A, "Answers" for the answers to the quiz questions.

20

Quiz

1. Why did I use a joining query in the `cart.pl` script?

2. Why did I use two different variables as statement handlers in the `checkout.pl` script?

Exercises

1. Create a script that allows you to add new items to the product catalog through a Web interface.

PART VI

Additional CGI Tips and Tricks

Hour

Hour **21**

Working with HTTP

When you enter a URL in the location field of your Web browser, more often than not it begins with http. The http stands for Hypertext Transfer Protocol, the *modus operandi* that Web servers and Web browsers follow in order to talk with each other. This hour covers the inner workings of http to provide you with a good understanding of the basic building blocks of the Web.

This hour includes:

- A discussion of how the HTTP protocol works.
- A detailed description of an HTTP transaction.
- Information about response codes and response headers from an HTTP server.
- How content types work on the Web.
- A brief discussion of secure Web connections.

HTTP Basics

HTTP (Hypertext Transfer Protocol) is a protocol—a set of rules that computers use to communicate over a network. It is designed to enable HTTP clients (such as Web browsers) to request information or services from HTTP servers (better known as Web servers).

HTTP is a connectionless protocol. This means Web browsers and Web servers don't establish a connection to each other; instead, they send individual messages back and forth. A connection-oriented protocol works like the telephone system. When you call someone on the telephone, a connection is established. You can then talk to each other over that connection until one of you hangs up. On the other hand, connectionless protocols work like the postal service (except much more quickly). You and I can send each other letters as long as we know the correct address to write on the envelope. The important difference here is that like the postal service, every message sent between the client and server requires the full address to be delivered to the proper destination. On the other hand, connection-oriented protocols only require this information when the connection is initially established. Because HTTP is connectionless, no "state" information is maintained between messages. In other words, there is no built-in way to tell what information the client and server have exchanged in the past.

HTTP follows a request/response model. A Web browser (or any client) sends a request to a Web server. The server then processes the request and sends the appropriate response. All HTTP sessions are structured as a set of requests and responses.

HTTP uses content typing. This means that every entity sent to a Web browser by the Web server has some content type associated with it. These types are modeled on the MIME Internet mail protocol, and will be discussed fully later in the hour. Appendix B, "MIME Types," includes a list of common content types. By sending a content type along with every entity sent to the Web browser, the Web server tells the Web browser what sort of thing that entity is—an HTML document, a GIF image, a sound file, or a standalone application program. Most browsers have a configurable list of helper applications that tell the browser how to handle the various content types sent by Web servers.

What Takes Place During an HTTP Session

Now you'll learn exactly what happens when a Web browser requests a document from a Web server. Understanding the details of how Web browsers and servers communicate will come in handy later when I'm discussing how to build CGI scripts that take advantage of this architecture. An illustration of the steps in this process appears in Figure 21.1.

Step 1: Establish a TCP Connection

Before the HTTP protocol can go to work, the computer that is running the Web browser has to connect over the network to the computer running the Web server. This connection is established using the TCP protocol which, along with the Internet Protocol (IP), is used by most application protocols for communication. For this reason, the Internet is referred to as a TCP/IP network. HTTP is a higher-level protocol than TCP, which is, in turn, a higher-level protocol than IP. As a rule, higher-level protocols can't communicate until a connection is established at the lower level. HTTP is an application-level protocol, which means that it is at the highest level in the TCP/IP model.

FIGURE 21.1

The steps in an HTTP session.

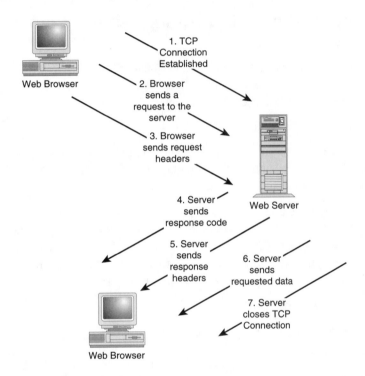

I'm not going to cover what goes into connecting at the IP and TCP levels in gruesome detail, but here's a short overview. If the URL entered in the Web browser was http://www. example.com, the first thing the client computer would do is perform a DNS (Domain Name Service) lookup on the name of machine in the URL (the contents of a URL were discussed in detail in Hour 1, "Overview of CGI Programming").

A DNS lookup is basically equivalent to looking up a phone number in a telephone book. Then the DNS server converts the hostname in the URL into an IP address. Every computer on the Internet has a unique IP address, consisting of four numbers between 0 and 255. An example of an IP address is 192.9.200.155. If the name is successfully looked up by the DNS server, the client will try to connect to the Web server using TCP; if the DNS lookup fails, the HTTP request will fail.

21

If you are connecting to a Web server over the Internet, chances are the request will travel through a number of routers in the process of connecting to the destination Web server. Routers are computers that connect independent networks to one another. If the TCP connection is made, the HTTP session itself can start, and the server will begin sending data to the client. If the Web server is unreachable, the HTTP request will fail.

Step 2: The Web Browser Sends a Command to the Server

After the TCP connection has been established, the Web browser sends a command to the Web server. The command includes a method, a resource identifier, and an HTTP version number. An example of a request line is

```
GET /cgi-bin/vote.cgi HTTP/1.0
```

The method describes the type of request that the browser is sending. There are three possible methods—GET, POST, and HEAD. In Hour 6, "Processing Input," I discussed the three request methods in detail.

The next element in the request is the URI, or Universal Resource Identifier. In almost every case, the URI is the absolute path to the requested file. The protocol and machine name are left out of the URI, and only the path to the resource remains. If the URL entered in the Web browser didn't include a path, the default path / is used. For example, entering the following URL in your Web browser:

```
http://www.example.com
```

would generate this request line:

```
GET / HTTP/1.0
```

The last part of the request line tells the version of the HTTP protocol for that request. Ordinarily, this is version 1.0, although the HTTP specification has been updated to version 1.1. Most Web servers still use version 1.0 for the sake of backward compatibility.

As you probably remember, if you are submitting form data using the GET method, it is added at the end of the requested URI. The form data is separated from the actual URI by a question mark.

Step 3: The Web Browser Sends Request Headers

After the browser sends its request line, it sends some other information to the Web server in the form of headers. This information usually includes identifying the browser that made the request, the content types that the browser accepts, and the URL that referred the user to the requested Web page. Appendix D, "Environmental Variables and Request Headers," contains an extensive list of client request headers, the environment variables that they stored in by the server, and to what the headers refer.

You can make use of the information provided in the request headers in your CGI scripts to serve specific pages based on which browser the user is running, or send special information based on where the user came from. All the response headers are optional, so the browser lets the server know that it has finished sending header information by sending a blank line.

After the browser has sent the header information, the request portion of the HTTP session has finished.

Step 4: The Web Server Responds

After the client has sent its request to the server, the server sends a response back to the client. The first line of the server's response looks like this:

```
HTTP/1.0 200 OK
```

The first part of the response is the protocol and version number. The version number indicates which version of the HTTP protocol that the response will be sent in because the syntax of the responses and headers differs between versions.

The last part of the response is the status code for the response. Most of the time, the response code is 200 OK, which means that the request was successful, and the response contains the data that the client requested. Another status code you may be familiar with is 404 Not Found, which means that the document referenced in the request does not exist.

Response codes are discussed in detail later in this hour in the section entitled, "Server Response Codes." Hour 23, "Creating Custom Error Documents," will discuss how to create CGI-based pages that are sent with error response codes.

Step 5: The Web Server Sends Response Headers

Just as the client sends information about itself along with the request, the server sends data to the user about itself and the requested document with the response. Appendix C, "Response Codes and Reason Phrases," is a list of items that can be included in HTTP headers. Response headers can be used to perform authentication, give the name and version of the server software, and set up "magic cookies."

The server's response headers also usually include the content type for the data being sent with the response, and the content length (in bytes) for the data. An example of a typical response header is:

```
Date: Tue, 26 Aug 1997 00:45:46 GMT
Server: Apache/1.2.4
Last-Modified: Thu, 14 Aug 1997 15:17:43 GMT
Content-Length: 7437
Content-Type: text/html
```

21

As you can see, this header includes the date and time that the response was sent, the name and version of the server software, the date that the requested URL was last modified, and the content length (in bytes) and content type for the resource being sent to the browser.

Step 6: The Web Server Sends the Data to the Browser

After the server has sent the header to the browser, it sends a blank line to indicate that it is finished. Then it sends the actual data that the user requested in the format described by the Content-type response header.

Step 7: The Web Server Closes the TCP Connection

Ordinarily, after the Web server has sent the requested data to the browser, it closes the TCP connection. However, if the browser or the server includes the line:

```
Connection: Keep-alive
```

in its header, the TCP connection will remain open after the data is sent. Then the browser can continue to send requests over the same connection. Keeping the connection alive saves the overhead of opening a new connection for each request, and conserves network bandwidth. Unlike HTTP 1.0, the default behavior of HTTP 1.1, the new version of the protocol, is to keep connections alive.

That's an overview of what transpires when a Web browser contacts a Web server and requests a document. Now that you have a good overview of what a Web transaction looks like, you can explore each part of the transaction and learn how to utilize them when you write CGI programs.

Server Response Codes

In the example I used previously, the server sent the response code 200 OK to the browser. There are a lot more server response codes that are commonly sent to the browser by Web servers. Table 21.1 contains the categories of server response codes. After I introduce the categories, I will discuss a few specific server response codes that are used frequently. A complete list of server response codes and what they indicate is included in Appendix C.

TABLE 21.1 Categories of Server Response Codes

Category	Description
Informational	The codes between 100 and 199 are informational response codes. They are only implemented under HTTP version 1.1. They indicate that the request from the browser has been received and is being processed.

Category	Description
Successful	Server response codes between 200 and 299 indicate that the client's request was successful. The request was received, understood, and processed.
Redirection	A response code in the range of 300 to 399 indicates that the client's request was not fulfilled, and further action must be taken on the part of the client to successfully complete the request. For example, if the requested page has moved, a redirection response code is sent to tell the client that it needs to request the page again from the new location.
Client Error	Response codes between 400 and 499 indicate that there is some error in the client's request. These errors can indicate that the page was not found, that the client's request used invalid syntax, or that access to the page was denied.
Server Error	A response code in the range of 500 to 599 indicates that there is a problem with the server that prevents it from fulfilling the request. Usually information is sent along with this response code that elaborates on the problem.

Table 21.2 contains a list of the codes that are used in the bulk of responses. The others are obscure, and you won't often see them used by Web servers.

TABLE 21.2 Common Server Response Codes

Response Code	Description
200 OK	Hopefully, this is the most common response from your Web site. It means that the client's request was successful, and that the requested document is being sent back to the user with the response.
401 Unauthorized	When a site is set up to use authentication, and the user fails to enter a correct user name and password, he is greeted with the 401 Unauthorized response.
403 Forbidden	The 403 Forbidden code is a generic response code that the server sends when the request can't be fulfilled but the server doesn't know why, or does know why but isn't allowed to tell. In practice, this code is often seen when the file permissions on the requested document are set up incorrectly. It means that the Web server process can't read the file, or in the case of CGI scripts, it doesn't have permission to execute the file.
404 Not Found	The 404 response code has attained fame on the World Wide Web because it indicates that the document you are requesting is no longer at the requested URL. Because almost no one ever sees the 200 OK status code when it is sent, this is probably the best known response code, and has, in fact, attained pop culture status.
500 Internal Server Error	Another common error response is 500 Internal Server Error. When a Web server is misconfigured, or there's a problem with a CGI script, this is the response code that is usually sent to the user.

21

Response Headers

In Hour 6, you looked at some environment variables that are derived from request headers commonly sent by Web browsers. There are also a number of headers that are usually sent to the browser by the server, and I will introduce some of the most important ones here. Appendix D includes an extensive list of headers that can be sent by both the browser and the server.

Cache-control

The Cache-control response header was added to HTTP 1.1 to provide more advanced methods of controlling the behavior of caching mechanisms like proxy servers. It is a more powerful replacement for the Pragma: no-cache response header, which is described a bit later. To prevent caching mechanisms from storing the entity sent with the response in their cache, you should use the Cache-control: no-cache response header.

Content-length

Content-length specifies the size of the entity that is sent to the browser with the response. The size is given in bytes.

Content-type

Content-type describes the media type and subtype of the entity sent with the response. Content types are covered in depth later in this hour.

Expires

The Expires header is used to specify when the information contained in the document will no longer be valid. Its value should be a valid time and date in the format specified by RFC 1123 (http://www.cis.ohio-state.edu/htbin/rfc/rfc1123.html). An example of this date format is:

```
Sat, 13 Sep 1997 10:42:00 GMT
```

This response header is designed to let browsers know that after a certain date, they should go back to the server to download a document instead of using a copy from the cache, if one exists.

Pragma

The Pragma header is used to send instructions to any proxy servers between the requesting browser and responding server. A proxy server is a computer that can be used to cache Web pages to conserve network usage. For example, a company may have a proxy server through which all of its Web traffic is routed. The proxy server can cache commonly requested pages so that these pages can be sent to servers from the proxy server's cache instead of being transferred over the Internet. In HTTP 1.0, the `Pragma: no-cache` header tells the proxy server to request the document from the remote server instead of loading it from its cache.

Server

The `Server` response header contains the name and version number of the server software that the responding Web server runs.

Set-Cookie

The `Set-Cookie` response header is used to send a magic cookie to the user's Web browser. Cookies are stored on the user's hard drive and are sent back to the Web server that sent them every time the user connects until they expire (an expiration date is required with every cookie). Cookies can be used to store a user's login name and password. When they visit your site in the future, they will be logged in automatically, or any other data that the server wants to store after the HTTP transaction. The use of cookies is discussed in depth in Hour 15, " Session (State) Management."

NPH Scripts

Most Web servers allow CGI programs the option of providing all the headers that are sent to the browser, completely bypassing the Web server itself (under ordinary circumstances, CGI scripts only provide the content type header). When the Web server calls a script in NPH (non-parsed header) mode, the script is responsible for generating all the headers that are sent to the browser.

Various Web servers identify NPH scripts in different ways. Most recognize any script with a name beginning with `nph-` as an NPH script. If they see a script with such a name, they treat it as an NPH script and send the output straight back to the browser. Your Web server might identify NPH scripts differently, you should check your Web server documentation for details.

After you know how to identify NPH scripts, the next question is what to do with them. Generally, NPH scripts are used to take advantage of features of HTTP that aren't supported by your Web server. At one time, NPH scripts were widely used to implement server push. Server push was a technique that allowed you to add animation to your Web pages by sending multiple GIFs from the server that overwrote each other onscreen. When Netscape added support for animated GIFs to its Web browser, the age of server push swiftly came to an end. Animated GIFs were easier to create (you didn't need to write a CGI script for the image) and required less bandwidth than server push.

21

The most important usage of NPH CGI scripts these days is to make `CGI.pm` scripts work with Microsoft IIS. `CGI.pm` only works under IIS if you generate the headers in NPH mode.

There are several methods that can be used to generate NPH headers with `CGI.pm`. The first method involves passing the `-nph` symbol to `CGI.pm` when you import it:

```
use CGI qw(-nph);
```

The second method is to set the `-nph` flag anywhere in the script before you print the headers by calling the `nph` method, like this:

```
CGI->nph(1);
```

The final method is to set the `-nph` flag when you actually print the headers, like this:

```
print $query->header(-nph=>1);
```

Content Types

All computer systems have a system that enables them to know what to do with files. On MS-DOS and Windows systems, the three letter extension tells the system the file type and often what to do with it. Files with the `.EXE` extension are executable files, the `.DOC` extension indicates that a file is a Word document, and `.HTM` tells the system that the file is an HTML document. Similarly, Macintosh systems store the file type and file creator in the resource fork.

It probably doesn't surprise you that every operating system has a method of specifying file types, and the method is different in each system. MS-DOS file extensions don't mean anything on the Macintosh, and Macintosh resource forks can't be transferred to computers running Windows. UNIX has a primitive file typing system that's not compatible with either platform.

In order to transfer files from one platform to another over the Internet, a common system of file types was designed. This system was originally designed for describing the contents of email messages that contain attachments, and is referred to as MIME—Multipurpose Internet Mail Extensions.

When the World Wide Web was created, the existing MIME standard was used as the foundation for sending file type information over the Web. Web browsers and Web servers on every platform have mechanisms for translating to and from their native file typing systems, so that when a Web server on a computer that runs Linux sends an Adobe PDF document to a user with a Macintosh computer, it can recognize the file type and know to open it with Adobe Acrobat Reader.

You've already seen some examples of how content types work. One of the first examples of content types that you've seen is the ENCTYPE attribute of the <FORM> tag. Remember that when you submit a form using the POST method, an entity with the form's contents is sent to the Web server with the request. The POST is accompanied by the `Content-type` and `Content-length` headers. The `Content-type` is the ENCTYPE that was specified in the form tag.

In some of the CGI scripts that were provided as examples in the previous hours, I also used content types. Every CGI script that returns a document also has to send the `Content-type` response header so that the browser knows what sort of document it is receiving. For example, when a CGI script dynamically generates an HTML document, it sends the `text/html` content type so that it will render the document as a Web page instead of just displaying the HTML source code.

How Servers Use Content Types

As you already know, when a browser requests a document or file from a Web server, the `Content-type` header is sent along with the entity in the response to tell the browser what type of entity it is. The question is, how does the server know the content type of the entity?

With CGI scripts, it's easy. The CGI script is supposed to generate the `Content-type` header for the server. If the CGI script generates an HTML file, it specifies `text/html`; if it creates a GIF, it sends `image/gif`. The server just passes the information along from the script to the browser.

What about other files? Web servers generally decide what content type to assign to files according to their extension, just like a computer running MS-DOS or Windows. Web browsers also have a table of content types that they refer to when they receive a response from the server. When they get the response, they take the appropriate action as defined in the table.

A common misconfiguration problem in Web servers is that they aren't configured to send the proper content type with `.EXE` files, so when a user tries to download an `.EXE` file (like an installer for an application), the contents of the file are displayed in the browser instead of being saved to the user's hard drive. Of course, because an executable file is a binary file, it just displays as pages and pages of garbage in the browser. If you run into this problem when you're surfing the Web, use the Save Link As command in your browser to download the link to your hard disk instead of displaying it.

If you're running the Apache server, you can view a list of content types and the extensions they're associated with in the <BLANK> file. You can add content types and file associates by editing this file and restarting your Web server. If a file type should be handled by the server and not sent to the Web browser directly, you can use the `AddHandler` directive. For example, if you want to place CGI programs in your document directories, this line in the `httpd.conf` file is used:

```
AddHandler cgi-script .cgi
```

21

Content-Type Categories

Each content type contains two parts—a type and a subtype. The type indicates the basic kind of file that is being sent, the subtype specifies the format of the file or which application created it. Take, for example, the content type text/html. The type is text, indicating that it is a normal text file, and the subtype is html, which indicates that it contains HTML source code. Most Web servers are configured to send the text/html content type for files with the extensions .htm and .html.

Table 21.3 contains a list of standard content types. The list of types is relatively short and isn't added to very often. On the other hand, the list of subtypes is always growing, and anyone can create a new subtype.

TABLE 21.3 Content Types

Type	Description
text	The text type contains messages that are in plain text. No special application is required to open plain text files as long as the computer supports the character set in which the file is written. Common subtypes of the text type are plain and html.
multipart	The multipart type is used to transmit a message consisting of multiple parts that can all be of a different data type. This type is usually used for email messages with attachments, which contain separate parts for the textual part of the message and the attachment. However, the ENCTYPE attribute of the FORM accepts multipart/form-data type as an acceptable option.
message	The message type is used for email messages. The most common subtype is rfc822, which indicates that the entity is an RFC 822–compliant email message. (RFC 822 is the IETF standard for the format of Internet email messages.)
image	The image type is used to indicate that the entity is an image file. Some of the popular image formats that you have probably used include image/jpeg and image/gif. There are all sorts of other subtypes of the image type that specify proprietary image formats.
audio	The audio type contains all sorts of audio file formats, including normal formats like Sun .AU files, .WAV files, and .AIFF files, as well as streaming audio files like RealAudio.
video	The video type is the type for all types of video files, including QuickTime, MPEG, and AVI files, along with streaming video formats like RealVideo, VExtreme, and VDOLive.
application	The application type is a catchall type for all types of file formats that don't fit into any of the other types. The basic application subtype is octet-stream, which indicates that the file is a standard binary file that shouldn't be interpreted by the browser when it is received. The typical action for application/octet-stream is to save it to disk. Despite the fact that the type is named application, all sorts of subtypes are document formats, including Adobe PDF files, Microsoft Office documents, and many, many more.

Nonstandard Types

When someone writes a new application for use on the Web, or creates a new file format, there is a provision for creating a new, nonstandard content type. Unlike standard types, which are present in standards documents and should be implemented in any piece of software that wants to stick to the standard, nonstandard types face a tougher road.

They are differentiated from standard types by prepending the prefix x- to the type or subtype section of the content type. For example, if you wanted to create a new image format called the All Blue Image format and it used the extension .ABI, you would also want to create a content type so that Web browsers would know how to handle .ABI files. As long as you use the x- prefix that's required for nonstandard types and subtypes, anything is fair game, although it's wise to do some research and make sure you're not using a type or subtype that's already being used by another format. You could choose image/x-allblue as your content type.

Ironically, some nonstandard types are probably more commonly used than many of the stan-dard types. One example is the content type for VRML worlds, which is x-world/x-vrml.

Secure Connections

One of the most common uses of Web applications is in electronic commerce. You can use CGI programs to enable people to manage their bank account, shop in an online mall, or donate to their favorite charity. One sticking point that users run into is that, by default, information sent via the Internet is not secure—if someone happens to intercept a message that you send to a friend, he can simply open it and read it. Imagine if that message contained your credit card numbers or other private information that you wouldn't want others to see.

Fortunately, many Web servers and Web browsers have the capability to create secure connections so that they can communicate privately. This enables your users to send sensitive data to your Web site and not have to worry about anyone sharing it while it's in transit.

The most common standard for providing secure connections over the Internet is the *Secure Sockets Layer*, or *SSL*, protocol. SSL is an application-level protocol (like HTTP) that is used to exchange data over the Web in a secure fashion. SSL uses a public key encryption system. Basically, what this means is that each party in the transaction has a public and a private key. When one party encrypts a message using the other's public key, only the person with the matching private key can decrypt it. Put simply, public key encryption provides a very secure method for exchanging data between two parties. When an SSL connection is established, both the client and the server exchange public keys, and verify them before the transaction is conducted. After each of the parties' keys has been verified, the data is exchanged securely.

21

Web servers also use documents that are referred to as "certificates" to verify their authenticity. For example, when you purchase a Netscape Web server, you also receive a digital certificate that verifies that you are who you claim to be. The certificate indicates that an independent third party, referred to as a certificate authority, verifies that the server holding the certificate is using its true identity. For example, if you connect to Amazon. com's online bookstore and try to place an order, when the SSL connection is made, a certificate is sent to your browser that confirms that the server you are connecting to really belongs to Amazon.com.

 There are two sources that provide the vast majority of certificates to people running secure servers on the Internet, VeriSign (http://www.verisign.com) and Thawte (http://www.thawte.com). VeriSign acquired Thawte in 1999.

The great thing about SSL is that as long as things are working correctly, all this business about encryption and digital certificates is completely transparent to the user. The only change you should notice is that your browser will indicate you are using a secure connection rather than a non-secure one. SSL servers also generally run on TCP port 443 instead of the default for HTTP, port 80.

The reason that this brief discussion of secure connections is included in this hour is that even though SSL isn't a part of the HTTP protocol, many CGI applications involve sending sensitive data over the Internet. So, if you plan on using CGI to build electronic commerce applications, you should be sure to implement them using a secure server so that your users feel comfortable conducting financial transactions, like purchasing things, using your site.

Summary

This hour provided you with knowledge of how the plumbing of the Web works. Understanding what actually takes place when you conduct a transaction over the Web enables you to create more powerful applications that can take advantage of this underlying structure.

Q&A

Q Is it really safe to conduct commercial transactions over the Web?

A In short, yes. Thanks to SSL, your data is extremely safe as it travels over the Internet. The odds of someone successfully intercepting the packets containing your data, and subsequently cracking the encryption, are quite slim. The dangers of fraud in Internet transactions are the same as those that plague traditional transactions, in that your credit card number is most at risk when it is handled by humans, or stored in an unsafe place.

Q Why was HTTP created as a connectionless protocol?

A HTTP is a connectionless protocol because connectionless protocols tend to be more scalable and efficient than connection-oriented protocols. With connectionless protocols, you don't have to worry about the overhead of keeping a connection open when it is not being used. Because most packets traveling over the Internet pass through a number of routers, it's easier and more efficient for each router to simply accept a packet and pass it on to the next router in the chain than to set up and maintain a connection that ties up a port on each of the routers between the server and client.

Workshop

The quiz questions are designed to strengthen the knowledge you gain each hour. The exercises help you build on that knowledge by providing you with the opportunity to apply it to real problems.

Quiz

1. What port does the HTTP protocol ordinarily run on?
2. What is the purpose of a DNS server?
3. What does a standard HTTP request line contain?
4. How can you tell a standard content type from a non-standard one?

Exercises

1. Learn more about how TCP/IP works. You can certainly write powerful CGI scripts without learning the internals of TCP/IP, but knowing about TCP/IP will help you understand how the Internet works. It will also help you figure out why you can't reach your favorite Web sites some of the time.
2. Find the RFCs on the Internet Web site at `http://www.internic.net`. Find the RFCs that define the HTTP protocol and read them to see how cryptic most standards documents are.

21

HOUR 22

Securing CGI Scripts

Over the course of this book, I've shown you many techniques for writing CGI programs to build Web applications. Here and there, I've mentioned security considerations that should be taken into account when you're writing CGI scripts. In this hour, I am going to focus solely on security because, no matter how cool or powerful your application is, if it opens easy-to-exploit holes that allow malicious folks to access your Web server, it's not worth installing. This hour discusses some methods for protecting your server and some common security holes found in CGI scripts. The following topics are covered in this hour:

- Why you should care about Web security
- Assessing risks and placing a value on your data
- Securing your Web server
- Common CGI security holes
- Writing security-friendly programs

Why Security?

The Internet is a large public network with millions of hosts distributed throughout the world. Under optimum conditions, any of those hosts is capable of reaching any of the others at any given time. The advantages of connecting your computers to this network are obvious. Not only can you retrieve all kinds of interesting and valuable information quickly and easily, but you can also publish information on the Web and make it easy for people around the world to access it.

Therein lies the rub. Whenever a user views a Web page on your site, downloads a file from your FTP server, or connects to your mail server, they are gaining access to a computer on your network. Under ideal circumstances, they are gaining access to only a very limited part of the system and are severely restricted in what they are allowed to do. Unfortunately, there are many ways to exploit software misconfigurations or applications with bugs and gain more access to the computer than you originally intended to allow.

The security problem is compounded by CGI scripts and other custom programs running on the Web server. Unlike publicly distributed software, which is generally well tested before it is released, the programs that you write to use on your Web site generally haven't been as well tested. Because of this, most Web sites that are successfully breached by intruders are exploited through poorly written or configured CGI programs.

The Crack-a-Mac Contest

In early 1997, a Swedish Macintosh consulting firm announced a contest on the World Wide Web offering a cash prize to anyone who could break into its Web server, which ran on a Macintosh, and modify the site's home page. The contest ran for an entire month, and nobody was able to hack into the Web server, so the firm ran the contest again.

The second time the company put on the contest, someone broke into the Web server and modified the site's home page, thanks to an improperly written CGI script. I'm including this story to illustrate how a minor inconsistency can lead your site to be compromised, and to put you in the proper mindset to think about information security.

The Web server software that was running on the Macintosh in the contest includes a security feature that prevents it from serving any files that have a specific creator code (creator codes on the Macintosh are basically analogous to extensions on Windows and UNIX files). A commercial CGI script was installed on the Web server that enabled the site's administrators to log in remotely and upload pages for the site. Naturally, the password file for the CGI program used the restricted creator code so that users from outside couldn't obtain the file.

22

Another CGI program was installed on the server; it was used to gather data from a Filemaker Pro database and publish it on the Web. Unfortunately, this CGI program didn't share the same restrictions as the Web server when it came to publishing particular types of files. The cracker exploited the database connectivity program to grab the password file for the site update application, and then logged into the site update application and uploaded a new version of the home page, thus winning the contest.

What's the point of this story? It's designed to put you in the mindset of people who are paid to think about information security. The Web server, the database connectivity application, and the site update application all had decent enough security by themselves, but when they were placed on the same computer, holes were created. There are a few lessons that can be taken from this story:

- The more complex a system, the greater the chance for security loopholes in the system. You should always use as few CGI programs as possible, and make those programs as simple as possible.

- When designing a system, don't take things for granted. The authors of the site update tool assumed that because they used a creator code that restricted the Web server from sending their password file, they didn't need to encrypt the password file. If they had used strong encryption on the password file, chances are the cracker couldn't have used the entries in the password file even after he obtained it.

- Don't open unnecessary doors to your system. The sponsors of the Crack-a-Mac contest assumed that because the Mac OS is very secure by default, they could install CGI programs like the site update tool. Although updating your site remotely can be convenient, when you provide this capability you provide yet another door through which unauthorized users can attack your system. You should think long and hard before you write or install any programs that provide additional access to your Web server.

Risk Assessment

Despite all the movies and books about the glamorous lives of hackers and the people who catch them, computer security really centers on something extremely boring: risk assessment. Basically, risk assessment involves deciding how much your data is worth and how much you are willing to spend to protect it.

For example, pictures of your wedding that you scanned in and posted on your Web site probably have a very low value. The originals are stored somewhere else, you can replace them online rather quickly, and chances are that making them available 24 hours a day and 7 days a week is not very important. So you probably won't be spending thousands of dollars to make sure your wedding pictures are secure and available.

On the other hand, suppose you're in charge of the Web site for a bank. Obviously, you have a lot of information in databases that you don't want disseminated to the general public. In fact, you probably want to make sure that nobody breaks into your Web site at all because making people feel they can trust the bank with their money is important.

In such a situation, you would probably take all the steps necessary to make your site as secure as possible. You would encrypt all the transactions handled by the Web site, and you would be extra careful to make sure that your Web server and network are extremely secure, probably disallowing access to the machine from the outside world except via HTTP (and HTTPS).

Most Web sites fall somewhere in between these two examples. When you're designing your Web site, you should do your best to place an accurate value on the data on the Web site. You should also take into account any business losses that could stem from having your home page redesigned by some clever hacker, like the U.S. Department of Justice or Central Intelligence Agency did.

Remember that if someone broke into your Web site and replaced the hard work you did on your company's home page with offensive material, aside from the monetary value of the actual data on the Web server, the value of your company's reputation should be taken into account. This is especially important in the age of electronic commerce. Security breaches on your Web site can be a crippling blow to your company's image.

Securing Your Web Server

Before you can begin to think about securing your CGI programs, be sure that your Web server is reasonably secure at the operating system level. There are all kinds of guidelines for securing the operating system on which your Web server runs that I won't go into here. Entire books on UNIX and Windows NT security exist, and if you're in charge of the computer on which the Web server runs, you should do some research and make sure that the computer is protected against attack. Macintosh users have it easy here because the Mac OS doesn't run any network services by default, so it's nearly immune to attacks over the Internet. (If a computer isn't listening for network connections, it isn't vulnerable to network attack.)

There are some guidelines to follow to secure your actual Web server software, however. First and foremost is that you should never, under any circumstances, allow the Web server on a computer running UNIX to run with root privileges. Correspondingly, you should never allow a Web server running under Windows NT to run with Administrator privileges. When you install Windows NT Web servers, they are generally configured to run under an unprivileged account.

root is the name of the account on UNIX systems that has full access to the entire system. The root user is authorized to run, modify, or delete any file on the system. If an attacker gains root access on your system, he has complete control of the computer. The root account is also referred to as the superuser account. The equivalent account on Windows NT is Administrator.

When the Web server runs with root privileges, mistakes made in writing CGI scripts or configuring the server are magnified greatly because a user can exploit those mistakes to directly compromise your system. Usually, Web servers run as nobody, a special account that is used to run servers with no privileges. If you want to run your Web server on port 80, which is the default port for HTTP connections, you must launch the Web server with root privileges. When the Web server is launched as root and is listening on port 80, it forks individual processes that handle HTTP requests. These processes should not run with root privileges.

Keep Your Software Up-to-Date

You should always keep your server software and operating system up-to-date. This doesn't necessarily mean running the newest version of the software, but it does mean keeping track of any security holes that are discovered and installing the appropriate updates or patches to close them. For example, many people run older versions of Linux or FreeBSD even though new versions are released all the time. The Computer Emergency Response Team (http://www.cert.org) releases security advisories whenever a new security problem is found within a common operating system. By subscribing to CERT's mailing list, you can receive all its advisories as soon as they are issued. You can also find lots of security information at http://www.securityfocus.com.

Store Your CGI Scripts Together

Most Web servers provide two options for storing your CGI scripts: you can either keep them all together under the cgi-bin/ directory, or you can store them under your document directory with your HTML files and images. Although storing them along with your documents might make sense from an organizational standpoint, from a security standpoint, you should always store them under cgi-bin/.

There are several reasons why you should keep your CGI scripts under cgi-bin/. The first is that you can prevent them from being downloaded by users. Your server knows to try to execute files in the CGI directory instead of sending them directly to the user, no matter which extension they have. That means there's no chance that a user will try to execute one of your CGI programs and see the source code to your Perl script instead.

On the other hand, if you store your CGI programs in your document directory along with your regular HTML files and images, the only way the server knows whether to run the program as a CGI script or send it to the user as a text file is by the extension. If your server isn't configured properly, or if you accidentally save your CGI program with the wrong extension, users will be able to download the files instead of executing them.

Another concern is being able to locate your CGI scripts when you must edit or disable them. If CGI scripts are scattered throughout your file system, keeping track of how many you have and what they do is difficult. If you keep all your CGI programs in one location they'll be easier to find when the time comes to audit your server and look at all the CGI scripts.

File Permissions

There are some rules of thumb you can use to set the file permissions properly for files on your Web server. Your best bet, in terms of security, is to make file permissions as restrictive as possible. The fewer the people who can read, write, and execute the files on your Web server, the better off you are.

Earlier I said that you should run the Web server as nobody, which is a special unprivileged account. Another option is to create a special account like www or web that has extremely restricted privileges. You should change the ownership of all the files under your Web root directory to the www account, and set up the server's log files and configuration files so that only the www account can write to them. Then, you can run the Web server under the www account instead of nobody.

If you're really ambitious, you can also create a group for users who are allowed to create content for your Web site. Then, you can change the file permissions for all the files in the document root so that only a member of the Web group can write to them. Hour 1, "Overview of CGI Programming," contains a discussion of UNIX file permissions.

 Hour 3, "Downloading, Installing, and Debugging CGI Scripts," contains a discussion of UNIX file permissions.

If you're running your Web server under Windows NT, you can also set up your file permissions to restrict access to Web files to the user that the Web server runs as.

Server Options That Are Bad for Security

Several features available for most Web servers are not conducive to good security. You should turn off any features that you don't plan to use, but you should also take a hard look at the following options before you decide to leave them turned on.

22

You should probably always turn off the automatic directory listings feature that ships with most Web servers. As a user, I find it helpful at times to get listings of directories that don't contain the default document. As a server administrator, however, I probably don't want users randomly surfing through the document directories on my server, especially because backups of access control documents or CGI scripts can be viewed if they don't have the correct extension. You should always remove any unused files from your document directories, but turning off directory listings can provide an added measure of security.

Most Web servers can also be set up to follow symbolic links to directories outside the document root. For example, you could set a symbolic link in the document root to a directory under your home directory and store Web documents there. While this may make things convenient for you, it's a really bad idea. If your server is set up to follow symbolic links, it can be easy to make mistakes and set links to system directories where Web users can get access to files that will make it easier for them to break into your system. Most Web servers offer the capability to extend the document root by setting up pointers to directories outside the server root in the configuration files. You should always use this method.

The SSI directive `exec` can also pose a major security risk because it can execute any system command and echo the output to the Web browser. If you are running your Web server as an unprivileged user, users can't do much with the `exec` command that could compromise your server, but you should still turn it off for all of the directories in which it is not required.

Common CGI Security Holes

You can make several common mistakes when you code CGI scripts that can make it easy for intruders to break into your Web server. If you avoid these pitfalls, you'll be way ahead of the game when it comes to protecting your server from attack.

A Note on How CGI Works

One thing you might not realize is that users can always access your CGI scripts without using the interface you've provided when they know where the CGI script is. For example, you might be using `MAXSIZE` attributes on all your text entry fields, and you might validate all the form input using JavaScript before it's sent to the CGI script, but users can bypass all that if they choose to, especially if your form uses the `GET` method.

Remember that the `GET` method sends all the form data to the server encoded as part of the URL. When a user sees how the form data is encoded and sent to the server, she can go to the location field of her browser and enter any input that she wants as part of the URL, bypassing your form altogether.

Things are only a bit tougher if you use the POST method. A determined user can simply write an HTML page that calls your CGI script and saves it on his hard drive. He then can place any data in the form that he wants and send it to your CGI script.

Because of the ease of bypassing the HTML front-ends to CGI scripts, you can never make assumptions about what kind of input you'll be getting from users. You should always take this into account when you're writing CGI programs.

The Buffer Overflow Problem

One trap that's easy to fall into is allocating a fixed amount of memory to gather input from a user. An attacker can send a lot more data than you planned for and crash the program, sometimes opening security holes that can be exploited to gain access to your system. This problem most often crops up in C or C++ programs. Here's an example of some improperly written code:

```
#include <stdlib.h>

#include <stdio.h>

static char query_string[1024];

char* read_POST() {


    int query_size;
    query_size=atoi(getenv("CONTENT_LENGTH"));
    fread(query_string,query_size,1,stdin);
    return query_string;

}
```

In the example, the programmer allocates 1024 bytes of memory for the user's input. If the form from which the programmer is gathering input contains TEXT input fields with no MAXSIZE attribute, or TEXTAREA fields, the user can send any amount of data he wants, so it would be easy for him to exceed the hard limit of 1024 bytes that the developer used. Even if the form contains only static fields like radio buttons or even hidden fields, the user can create a submission of her own to call the script and include any data she wants.

The programmer should have allocated the space for the information that the user posted dynamically in order to avoid the buffer overflow bug. Here's the correct method of writing the previous code:

```
char* read_POST() {


        int query_size=atoi(getenv("CONTENT_LENGTH"));
        char* query_string = (char*) malloc(query_size);
        if (query_string != NULL)
```

```
        fread(query_string,query_size,1,stdin);
      return query_string;
  }
```

When you're writing any C program, you should also avoid using the strcpy() and strcat() functions in general because they're susceptible to the buffer overflow problem. strncpy() and strncat() are safer choices because they enable you to specify the maximum length of the string that you're manipulating.

Don't Send Raw Input to Shell Commands

In order to make it easy to use shell commands in your programs, most UNIX programming languages provide functions that will escape to a shell and execute commands. These are very handy, but you should be very careful when you use them in your programs. Look at some Perl code that illustrates what a problem this can be.

Suppose you're going to provide a Web-based interface to the finger command from your Web site. You would provide a field in which the user could enter a username to finger, and then launch the finger command from within your CGI script. The CGI script would print the output of the finger command in the browser window.

```
$user_to_finger = $data_from_form  # Taken from the form input
print "Content-type: text/plain\n\n";
open (FINGER, "finger $user_to_finger |");
while (<FINGER>) {
    print;
}
```

If the person enters a username in the form as he is supposed to, the script simply tries to finger that person and print the output to the Web page.

However, what happens if the user enters rafe; cat /etc/passwd? The script will run both commands and pipe the output back to the browser, so the user will have the contents of your server's password file. Now, imagine that the server administrator has committed another cardinal sin and is running the Web server under the root user ID. If the user enters rafe; rm -rf / in the text field of the form, your server will suddenly develop big problems (for the non-UNIX savvy, this will attempt to delete all the files on the server).

As you can see, improper use of shell escapes can lead to big problems in a hurry. If you do use any shell escapes in your programs, you should be absolutely certain that there's no way the user can send input to them. C functions that run shell processes include system() and popen(). In Perl, the system() and exec() functions launch shell processes, and the eval() function runs the code in the function argument through the Perl interpreter. As shown in the previous example, using pipes with the open function can also expose you to risk. The exec and eval commands are used in shell scripts to spawn another process to run shell commands. Characters enclosed in backtick (`) characters are evaluated as shell commands in Perl scripts and shell scripts as well.

Obviously, shell escapes are far too useful to completely avoid when you're writing CGI scripts. For example, if you've used the gd library to write a program that creates graphs and you want to call it from within a CGI script, you must execute the program using a shell escape. The main problem with shell escapes is not using them in your programs, but passing them input sent by users. You should always filter user input to ensure that users haven't tried to insert commands into the input before you pass it along to external programs.

Using File Paths Is Risky

Any time you use direct file paths in your Web pages or you let users enter paths in a form, you expose yourself to risk. Suppose you write a script that loads text files from somewhere on your file system and formats them using a CGI script. The argument passed to the script is the path to a file on the server. If you enable users to enter the path information (either through a field on the form or by doctoring the URL in the location field on the browser), they can enter paths to any file on the system that the server is capable of reading. For example, suppose your program is set to automatically look for files in the /home/documents directory.

If the user entered the path ../../etc/passwd in the URL, a poorly written script would send the password file to the user. Whenever you write a CGI program that uses path information, you should always check to make sure that .. expressions haven't been slipped into the path.

Don't Place the Perl Interpreter in `cgi-bin`

At one time, it was recommended that the perl.exe program for Windows NT be placed in the cgi-bin directory in order to execute CGI scripts written in Perl. For example, to run a CGI script named search.pl, you would use the URL /cgi-bin/perl.exe?&search.pl. Unfortunately, placing the Perl executable in the cgi-bin directory enables any user to run arbitrary snippets of Perl code on the server, thanks to the -e command-line flag. For example, the user could enter the following URL to delete all the files in the server's directory:

```
/cgi-bin/perl.exe?&-e+unlink+%3C*%3E
```

As you can see, placing perl.exe in your CGI directory is a recipe for disaster. The same holds true for any other command interpreter.

This practice is very antiquated. The Perl installer for Windows has improved, as has support for Perl scripts by most Windows Web servers.

Security Hole with DOS Batch Files

When DOS batch files are used as CGI programs with Windows NT, users can append an extra command to the URL and they will be executed after the batch file has executed. Suppose you've written a simple batch file called `output.bat` that prints a message on the screen. A user can simply type the URL:

```
/cgi-bin/output.bat?&dir
```

Both the batch file and the `dir` command will run. This security hole is closely related to the problem with passing user input to shell commands on UNIX servers. The best way around this problem is just to avoid using DOS batch files as CGI programs.

Keep Your Server Information Private

As cool as it sounds to add gateways to all types of UNIX utilities like `who`, `finger`, `ifconfig`, `netstat`, or any other programs that print system information, it generally isn't a good idea. The more information about your server that you give out, the easier it is for crackers to break into your system. Even providing a list of usernames is a good start if someone is actively trying to break into your server.

Safe Programming

Now that you've looked at some of the common holes that can make it easy for crackers to break into your server, look at some good programming practices that can help ensure that your scripts are secure.

Running Shell Commands Without Using the Shell

I warned you of the dangers of using shell commands within your CGI scripts, and especially of the dangers of using user input in shell commands. Now I'm going to show you a method by which you can still run shell commands without running the risk of having the shell's command-line parser examine the command you want to execute.

The risks associated with using shell commands involve the shell's command-line parser. When the shell receives a command line, it interprets some characters as instructions to the shell itself. These are referred to as *meta-characters*. Take the following command line for example:

```
ls -al | grep "passwd"; cat `find . -name "thisfile"`
```

The pipe (|), semicolon, and backtick (`) characters are all meta-characters. They are meant to indicate something to the shell itself, unlike the other characters on the line, which are used to invoke commands or pass information to the command being invoked. The security risk involved with running commands through the shell is that users will send meta-characters that thwart the intended purpose of the shell escape. By the way, the preceding command line contains two commands separated by the semicolon. The first gets a full directory listing of the current directory, and prints only lines that contain the string `passwd`. The second uses the `find` command to search the directory tree, beginning with the current directory, for any files with names that contain `thisfile`. It then prints the contents of those files.

One of the easiest ways to get around problem meta-characters is to simply discard them before you send the command to the shell. Here's a list of meta-characters that the shell uses:

```
& ; ` ' \ " | * ? ~ < > ^ () [] {} $ \n \r
```

By using a regular expression to scan for the meta-characters and remove them, you can prevent users from doctoring commands. You should note that the list of meta-characters includes \n and \r, which are newline characters.

This is a fairly rudimentary method of avoiding the risks involved with the shell escape characters. A better method is to use regular expressions to whittle down the user input to exactly the data you need. For example, if you requested an email address or the path to a file, you can use regular expressions and the binding operator (=~) to make sure that the user's input is valid before you send it along to the command line.

In Perl, you can also call external programs without going through the shell (which enables you to avoid any nasty effects embedded meta-characters can have). To do so, instead of sending the command to the shell as one long string, you can send the command name and each argument sent to the command as separate strings in a list. For example, instead of using this command:

```
system "grep rafec /etc/passwd";
```

You would use the following construct:

```
system "grep", "rafec", "/etc/passwd";
```

Summary

Remember that when you write CGI programs for use on the Web, they can potentially be accessed by millions of people. At least a few thousand of those people probably don't have the best intentions, so you should always have security in mind. By keeping the guidelines presented in this lesson in mind, and by testing your CGI scripts rigorously, you can avoid intrusion by most crackers.

Q&A

22

Q **What are denial of service attacks?**

A Denial of service attacks are designed to deny access to a computer rather than to break into it. They usually involve sending a lot of data over a network to a computer so that it's overwhelmed and can't respond to legitimate requests. There have also been some bugs that enable malicious people to send certain commands to a computer that cause it to crash. Most of these attacks work on the network level and are usually corrected by patches released by operating system vendors. This is one reason why you should always stay up-to-date on the latest security issues.

Q **How can I stay up-to-date on security issues?**

A There are a number of excellent Web sites that provide security information. Security Focus (`http://www.securityfocus.com/`) provides all sorts of security news and information, and is home to the well known Bugtraq mailing list. Windows NT users might find the NTBugtraq (`http://www.ntbugtraq.com`) site and mailing list more useful.

Q **What should I do if someone breaks into my Web server?**

A Don't panic. If you suspect that someone has broken into your system, you should consult the CERT Intruder Detection Checklist available at

`http://www.cert.org/tech_tips/intruder_detection_checklist.html`

Following the steps on this checklist should reveal whether your system has been compromised, but it may not, depending on how skillful the attacker is. It may be necessary to bring in a professional security consultant to get a handle on things.

If you find that your system has been compromised, you should take the system offline and follow the instructions in CERT document, "Recovering from a UNIX Root Compromise," assuming your server runs a UNIX derivative. The document is available at

`http://www.cert.org/tech_tips/root_compromise.html`

Workshop

The quiz questions are designed to strengthen the knowledge you gain each hour. The exercises help you build on that knowledge by providing you with the opportunity to apply it to real problems. See Appendix A, "Answers" for the answers to the quiz questions.

Quiz

1. Why is it important to scan form input for meta-characters?
2. Why is it a bad idea to store CGI scripts under the document root directory?
3. What causes a buffer overflow?

Exercises

1. Search the Internet for security information on the operating system that runs on your server. Each operating system has distinctive security issues, and you should always be sure that you've corrected any known problems with the operating system that you use on your server.
2. Check out the CERT intruder detection checklist and be sure your system hasn't already been compromised. Familiarize yourself with the logging mechanisms and other security facilities provided with your server's operating system to make sure you know what to do if your system is compromised.

HOUR 23

Creating Custom Error Documents

What can make your Web site more user friendly when something goes wrong? The answer is displaying a custom error document. When an error occurs, the Web server usually displays a default error document. Most Web servers allow you to specify that custom documents be substituted for the default ones. In this hour, I'll discuss how to configure your Web server to use custom error documents as well as how to write CGI scripts that display them.

In this hour, you'll learn:

- What exactly error documents are
- How to set up your Web site to use custom error documents
- What custom error documents should contain

What Is an Error Document?

Whenever you request a URL that no longer exists, or you enter the wrong username and password trying to view a page that is protected using basic authentication, you're met with an error document. Most Web servers have default error documents for each type of error, and also allow the server administrator to configure things so that another document or CGI program can be called to override the default documents. The document in Figure 23.1 is the default document for a 404 Not Found error from the Apache server.

FIGURE 23.1

A typical document generated for a 404 Not Found error.

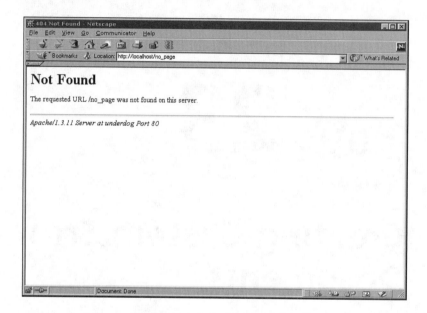

Documents like the one in Figure 23.1 get the point across that there is a problem with the request. However, they don't do much to help the user find their way to the content that they were looking for, or resolve the problem in a way that would make them eager to return to your Web site.

This problem is exaggerated by the fact that many Internet users find pages using a search engine. If you've ever reorganized your content and changed the URLs for some of your pages, there's a good chance that users will find the old URLs to those pages through a search engine and come up empty when they try to visit your site. Chances are, if a user tries to visit your site and sees an error document instead, they won't come back anytime soon. Obviously, when you're designing a site, it's a good idea to try to structure it so that as few URLs as possible change over time. Sometimes older content is moved aside as a site is revised, however, and it helps to make it as easy as possible for users to find current content when the page they're looking for isn't available.

To minimize the shock when a user encounters an error on your site, you can create custom error documents. These documents can simply include a link to your home page and an email address for reporting the problem, or they can automatically look up the new location of the page and redirect users to that location. In any case, by creating customized error documents, you can give users the opportunity to locate useful information on your site, even if their first attempt to enter the site fails. Figure 23.2 is an example of a customized document that is generated when a user tries to access a non-existent page on the Gamespot Web site.

FIGURE 23.2

A customized 404 Not Found error document from the Gamespot Web site.

As you can see, the error document still uses the site's overall look-and-feel, and provides links to areas of the site that might be of interest to the user. Even though the user requested a page that does not exist, the document they are presented with is still somewhat inviting. That's a big improvement over the default error document in Figure 23.1, which practically screams "Go away!"

> Users of recent versions of Microsoft Internet Explorer will see the error documents provided by Microsoft instead of the error documents you create, unless they've explicitly turned off that setting in browser options.

Configuring Your Web Server for Custom Error Documents

Before you can use custom error documents, you have to set up your Web server to send your custom documents instead of sending the default ones. Custom error documents can be plain HTML documents or they can be generated dynamically using CGI scripts. This section includes instructions on setting up pointers to custom error documents on several popular Web servers.

The Apache Web Server

The Apache Web server has very robust support for custom error documents. You can specify custom error documents in a wide variety of contexts. For example, you can modify the global configuration files to specify specific error documents for the entire server, for virtual hosts served by the server, or for specific directories on the server. You can also modify the .htaccess files to specify custom error documents for Web pages that are governed by that file.

> In order to specify custom error documents from within an .htaccess file, you must have the FileInfo override turned on for the Web server.

The ErrorDocument directive is used to specify the location of custom error documents, as well as the errors to which they are sent in response. The ErrorDocument directive is a member of the core group of configuration directives, so any Apache Web server installation should support the directive. If you want to specify a new ErrorDocument for the entire server, you should probably place this directive in the httpd.conf file. In the past, this directive would have been placed in the srm.conf file, but these days all the server-wide configuration directives live in httpd.conf; srm.conf has fallen into disuse.

The syntax for the ErrorDocument directive is

```
ErrorDocument error-code document-location
```

Error responses can be configured in four different ways:

- Print the message hard coded into the server. This is the default response.
- Print a different message, specified using the ErrorDocument directive.
- Redirect the user to a local URL.
- Redirect the user to a URL on another Web server.

The default configuration simply prints a basic error message and sends it to the user, which is not very exciting or informative. The second option, a custom message, is configured by placing the text of the message on the same line in the configuration file as the ErrorDocument directive. To change the error message for a 404 error, for example, all you have to do is add the following line to a configuration file that affects the URL the user is looking for:

```
ErrorDocument 404 "Sorry, I couldn't find that document..."
```

The third option sends the visitor to another URL on the Web site. To specify the Web site, all you have to do is add the relative location of the error document to a configuration file using the ErrorDocument directive:

```
ErrorDocument 404 /cgi-bin/404_response.cgi
```

The final option is to send the user to an external Web site. Any ErrorDocument line in which the document location begins with http: is considered to be an external link, even if the URL points to a document on the local Web server:

```
ErrorDocument 404 http://home.netscape.com
```

Links to external error documents will not work for 401 Unauthorized errors because of the way basic authentication works.

Netscape Web Servers

You can specify custom error documents for Netscape Web servers using the Netscape Server Manager's graphical interface. Here are the steps in specifying new default error documents for the server:

1. Select Server Preferences, Error Responses.

2. From the Resource Picker, choose the server resource you want to configure.

3. Select the error response you want to customize.

4. Type the absolute path name of the file that you want to run (the path should start at the document root). If the file you are going to run is a CGI program, select the CGI box.

5. Make changes to any other error responses that you want to customize.

6. Click OK.

7. Click Save and Apply to write the changes to the server configuration file.

23

You can also set up specific error messages for individual directories and files using `.nsconfig` files. These files are used to set configuration options for a directory and all of its child directories. In addition to specifying custom error messages for particular documents, these files can also be used to set the MIME type for files, restrict access to the directory, or require a password to access a directory. I am going to show you how to specify custom error documents in a `.nsconfig` file. Here's an example of a very simple `.nsconfig` file:

```
<Files *>
ErrorFile reason="Unauthorized" code="401" path="/cgi-bin/forbidden.cgi"
ErrorFile reason="Not Found" code="404" path="/cgi-bin/notfound.cgi"
</Files>
```

The sample file consists of two `ErrorFile` directives enclosed in the `<Files>` tag. The `<Files>` tag contains a pattern, and all the directives enclosed in the tag affect only files that match the pattern. In the example, I use a pattern of `*`, which matches all files. I could have used a tag like `<Files *.html>` instead, which would match only files with the `.html` extension. So, if I were to use the `*.html` pattern, the custom `ErrorFile` directives listed previously would only come into play when a user requested an HTML file.

Netscape supports custom configurations of four different types of errors: Unauthorized (401), Forbidden (403), Not Found (404), and Server Error (500).

The syntax of the `ErrorFile` directive is

```
ErrorFile reason="reason_string" code="error_code" path="absolute_path_to_file"
```

Using HTML to Create a Basic Error Document

At a minimum, an error document should tell the user what went wrong, provide a link to your site's home page, and send an email to the site administrator. Errors are logged by the server, but it's still polite to give users the opportunity to tell you what went wrong when they tried to view your page.

For example, Listing 23.1 shows what a basic error document for 404 Not Found errors could be.

LISTING 23.1   A Sample Error Document for a 403 Error

```
1: <HTML>
2: <HEAD>
3: <TITLE>Document Not Found</TITLE>
4: </HEAD>
5: <BODY>
```

```
 6: <H1>Document Not Found</H1>
 7: <P>The document you requested is no longer available at the location that
 8: you specified.  You can return to our <A HREF="/index.html">home page</A>
 9: or send email to the <A HREF="mailto:siteadmin@example.com
10: </A>site administrator</A>.</P>
11: </BODY>
12: </HTML>
```

You could create similar documents for the other error messages. An error that practically demands a custom document is the 401 Unauthorized response. If you are using basic authentication, you should create a custom document for users who aren't authorized, so they can either figure out why they're not allowed in, or go to a page where they can apply to be allowed in.

> Your custom error documents should reflect the look-and-feel of your Web site. If people have been to your site before and they get an error document that looks like your site, they'll get the "Hey, I'm in the right place" feeling even though their request turned up an error. Hopefully the user can follow a link on your error document and be on their way to the information they're seeking.

Using CGI to Create an Advanced Error Document

CGI offers you a lot of flexibility in creating custom error documents that you just don't get from building a plain HTML error document. The problem with straight HTML is that no matter which page the user requested, or how he got to the page, he still gets the same error message. Through the use of CGI scripts, you can create dynamic error documents that provide customized content depending on what the user is looking for.

Environment Variables for Error Documents

When a CGI program is called as the result of an error, Apache (and other NCSA-compliant Web servers) set three environment variables that aren't part of the normal CGI environment. These variables contain information about the user's request that are helpful in constructing an error document. These environment variables are described in Table 23.1.

TABLE 23.1   Environment Variables for Error Documents

Variable	Contains
REDIRECT_REQUEST	The full request that caused the error, including the request method, path to the file, and protocol.
REDIRECT_URL	The URL that actually caused the error.
REDIRECT_STATUS	The status code that would have been sent to the user had the request been successful.

Linking Back from the Error Document to the Referring Page

One common feature of error documents, particularly those received with 404 errors, is a link back to the referring page. This enables the user to at least go back to the page that they came from, and perhaps inform the person who runs that site (assuming it's not a search engine) that their link is no longer working.

The page with the link that led to the current page is stored in an environment variable by the Web server, so that you can use it in your CGI scripts. Thanks to the presence of the HTTP_REFERER variable, creating a document that links back to the referrer is really quite simple. Listing 23.2 contains sample code that demonstrates how to create the referrer link. The document generated by the script is shown in Figure 23.3.

LISTING 23.2   An Error Document that Sends the User Back to the Referring Page

```
 1: #!/usr/bin/perl
 2:
 3: print "Content-type: text/html\n\n";
 4: print "<HTML>\n<HEAD>\n<TITLE>Document Not Found</TITLE>\n</HEAD>\n";
 5: print "<BODY BGCOLOR=#FFFFFF>\n";
 6: print "<H1>Document Not Found</H1>\n";
 7: print "<P>The document you requested is no longer available at the \n";
 8: print "location that you specified.  You can return to our \n";
 9: print "<A HREF=\"/index.html\">home page</A> or send email to the \n";
10: print "<A HREF=\"mailto:siteadmin\@example.com\">Site Administrator</A>.
\n";
11: print "</P>\n";
12: if ($ENV{'HTTP_REFERER'}) {
13:     $referrer = $ENV{'HTTP_REFERER'};
14:     print "<P>You can also go back to the referring page:<BR>\n";
15:     print "<A HREF=\"$referrer\">$referrer</A></P>\n";
16: }
17: print "</BODY>\n</HTML>\n";
```

The @ character has to be escaped using the \ character within strings in Perl. If you leave an @ inside a quoted string without escaping it first, your program will fail to compile with a syntax error.

FIGURE 23.3

An error document containing a link back to the referring page.

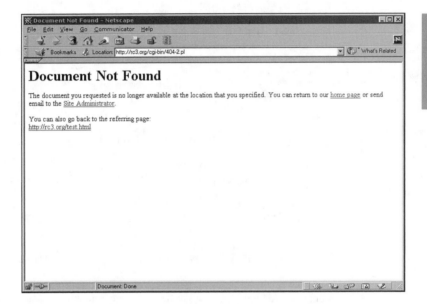

23

Creating Custom Links from the Error Document

Let's say you have a relatively small site with only a few directories of HTML documents. For each of these directories, a known file provides links to all the documents under that directory. In addition to, or instead of, providing links back to the referring page, you can create a program that selects the appropriate page within the site to send the user to, and create a link to that page.

Basically, this program takes a look at the requested path and compares it to the paths of the existing sections of the site. If the requested path matches, the program supplies a link to a page that hopefully contains current information that the user will find useful. On the other hand, if the user has entered a path that doesn't fit into any of the known sections of the site, the program provides them with a link back to the referring page. Listing 23.3 contains the source code for the program.

LISTING 23.3 A 404 Handling Program that Redirects Users to the Proper Section
of a Site

```perl
 1: #!/usr/local/bin/perl
 2:
 3: print "Content-type: text/html\n\n";
 4: print "<HTML>\n<HEAD>\n";
 5: print "<TITLE>404 Not Found</TITLE>\n";
 6: print "</HEAD>\n<BODY BGCOLOR=#FFFFFF>\n";
 7: print "<H1>404 Not Found</H1>\n";
 8: print "<P>The document that you requested was not found on the server.
</P>\n";
 9: print "<P>You can try looking at the index for that\n";
10: print "section of the website: </P>\n";
11:
12: print "<P>\n";
13: (undef, $main_path) = split /\//, $ENV{'REDIRECT_URL'};
14:
15: if ($main_path eq "football") {
16:     print "<A HREF=\"/football/index.html\">Football Index</A>\n";
17: }
18: elsif ($main_path eq "baseball") {
19:     print "<A HREF=\"/baseball/index.html\">Baseball Index</A>\n";
20: }
21: elsif ($main_path eq "basketball") {
22:     print "<A HREF=\"/basketball/index.html\">Basketball Index</A>\n";
23: }
24: else {
25:     print "<A HREF=\"/index.html\">Go to the home page.</A>\n";
26: }
27: print "</P>\n";
28:
29: print "<P>or return to the ";
30: print "<A HREF=\"", $ENV{'HTTP_REFERER'}, "\">referring page</A>.</P>\n";
31: print "</BODY>\n";
32: print "</HTML>\n";
```

First, the program prints out the first part of the Web page. It then examines the
requested URL to see under which directory the file being searched for is located (the
program assumes that the site is logically organized with a separate subdirectory for each
topic). The program prints a link to the appropriate index page for each subdirectory. If
the link isn't under one of the known subdirectories, the program prints out a link to the
home page for the site. The document generated by the script is shown in Figure 23.4.

FIGURE 23.4

An error document that points the user to an appropriate page.

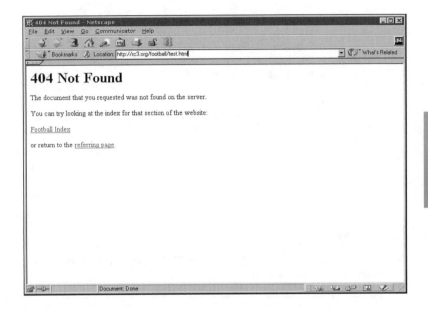

Of course, I could write a more complex program that examines the path even more closely and tries to make a really educated guess about what the user was looking for. If the user tried a URL that ended with an .htm extension, for example, the custom error message could check to see whether there is a file in the same location with an .html extension instead, and point the user toward that file. Listing 23.4 contains the source code to the program.

LISTING 23.4   A Program that Attempts to Determine the Proper Extension for a Missing File

```
1: #!/usr/bin/perl
2:
3: print "Content-type: text/html\n\n";
4: print "<HTML>\n<HEAD>\n";
5: print "<TITLE>404 Not Found</TITLE>\n";
6: print "</HEAD>\n<BODY BGCOLOR=#FFFFFF>\n";
7: print "<H1>404 Not Found</H1>\n";
8: print "<P>The document that you requested was not found on the server.
</P>\n";
9: print "<P>You can try looking at the index for that\n";
10: print "section of the website: </P>\n";
11: print "<P>\n";
12: $extension = substr($ENV{'REDIRECT_URL'},3);
13: if ($extension eq "htm" or $extension eq "HTM") {
14:     if ($extension eq "htm") {
```

continues

LISTING 23.4   continued

```
15:            $path_to_file = $ENV{'DOCUMENT_ROOT'} . $ENV{'REDIRECT_URL'} . "l";
16:        }
17:        elsif ($extension eq "HTM") {
18:            $path_to_file = $ENV{'DOCUMENT_ROOT'} . $ENV{'REDIRECT_URL'} . "L";
19:        }
20:        if (-e $path_to_file) {
21:            print "Perhaps the file you're looking for is located at \n";
22:            print "the following URL:\n";
23:            print "<A HREF=\"", $path_to_file, "\">", $path_to_file, "</A>\n";
24:        }
25:        else {
26:            print "You can go to our <A HREF=\"/index.html\">home page</A>.\n";
27:        }
28: }
29: print "</P>\n";
30: print "<P>or return to the";
31: print "<A HREF=\"", $ENV{'HTTP_REFERER'}, "\">referring page</A>.</P>\n";
32: print "</BODY>\n";
33: print "</HTML>\n";
```

Like the other two programs, this one first prints the standard HTML section of the error document. It then takes a look at the URL that was requested. If the extension of the requested file is .htm (or .HTM), the program tries to check and see whether the file exists with the .html extension instead. It does this by putting the DOCUMENT_ROOT and REDIRECT_URL environment variables together in order to get the absolute path to the file, and putting the l on the end to create the filename to test. The program then uses if (-e $path_to_file), which tests to see whether the file location stored in the $path_to_file variable exists (-e is an operator that checks for the existence of a file).

If the file the user is looking for exists (with the new extension), the script points the user in the direction of the file. If the file doesn't exist, a link back to the home page is printed instead. A link back to the referring page is offered as well.

> Some of the environment variables used in these three examples may not be available with certain Web servers. You should research the environment variables that are set by the server for the CGI environment and find the appropriate ones to get the information you need. To find out which environment variables are available for your CGI scripts, create a small CGI program that includes the statement print %ENV;, which prints the names of all the environment variables and their contents.

Handling a "Not Found" Error

Most Web sites are redesigned periodically to add new information to the site, reorganize existing information, and update the look-and-feel. Most of the time when a site is redesigned, some stuff gets moved around. A popular page that was buried deep within the site might get moved closer to the top, and various sections of the site are generally moved around as part of the process.

Unfortunately, this has a big impact on visitors who've bookmarked pages within your site, and also on potential visitors who are pointed to your site by search engines. The indexes in search engines generally aren't up to date. There are hundreds of millions of pages on the Web, and it's nearly impossible to keep track of all of them. Not only is it difficult for sites to keep track of all the new pages on the Web, but it's also challenging for them to know when to discard old ones. In any cases, pages that were moved or removed months ago might still be in the indexes of popular search engines, waiting for users to find them.

One solution to this problem that's often advocated is simply never killing links on your site. You never know who's linking to you, so it's best to just keep everything around indefinitely for fear of driving visitors away. Rarely is this a workable solution 100 percent of the time. Let's say you move from a static HTML site to a template-driven system. Rather than applying new designs to every old static HTML page on your site, it's easier just to remove them.

This example contains a script that can ease the pain of moving resources from one place to another on your site. It has a list of old URLs and the new URLs that they map to. When a user tries to pull up a page using the old URL, it looks it up in the list and automatically refers them to the new URL, with a reminder that they should change their bookmark to reflect the new location.

First, let's look at the data file used by the program. Each line represents a record in the file. The old URL and new URL make up each record, and are separated by tabs. Here is the data file:

```
/some_page.html  /some_other_page.html
/toc.html        /sitemap.html
```

Note that the file could just as easily contain hundreds of lines of data. In this case, there are only two URLs that have been moved. Now let's review the source code for the script, which appears in Listing 23.5.

23

LISTING 23.5   A 404 Script that Redirects Users from Old File Locations to New Ones

```perl
 1: #!/usr/local/bin/perl
 2:
 3: use CGI;
 4: use CGI::Carp;
 5:
 6: $query = new CGI;
 7: $new_urls_file = "new_urls.txt";
 8:
 9: # REDIRECT_URL is a special environment variable set when an
10: # error occurs
11: $requested_url = $ENV{'REDIRECT_URL'};
12:
13: open (URLS, "< $new_urls_file")
14:     or die "Can't open $new_urls_file";
15:
16: while (<URLS>) {
17:     ($old_url, $new_url) = split /\t/;
18:     if ($old_url eq $requested_url) {
19:         $new_location = $new_url;
20:         last;
21:     }
22: }
23:
24: close URLS;
25:
26: print $query->header();
27: print "<HTML>\n<HEAD>\n<TITLE>";
28:
29: if ($new_location) {
30:     print "Page Moved";
31: }
32: else {
33:     print "Requested URL Not Found";
34: }
35:
36: print "</TITLE>\n</HEAD>\n<BODY>\n";
37:
38: if ($new_location) {
39:     print "<H1>Page Moved</H1>\n";
40:     print "<P>The page you're looking for has moved.\n";
41:     print "It is now located at:</P>\n";
42:     print "<CENTER><P><FONT SIZE=+1>";
43:     print "<A HREF=\"$new_location\">$new_location</A>";
44:     print "</FONT></P></CENTER>\n";
45: }
```

```
46: else {
47:     print "<H1>Requested URL Not Found</H1>\n";
48:     print "<P>The URL you requested does not exist or has been moved.\n";
49:     print "If you'd like, you can return to the \n";
50:     print "<a href=\"/\">home page</a>.</P>\n";
51: }
52:
53: print "<P>If you have questions or would like to report a problem \n";
54: print "send email to <a href=\"mailto:webmaster\@rc3.org\">";
55: print "webmaster\@rc3.org</a>.</P>\n";
56: print "</BODY>\n</HTML>\n";
```

23

The basic structure of the script should be pretty familiar to you, but I'd like to go over some features specifically. First, the location of the data file is specified on line 7. The location of the file is stored in the variable $new_urls_file. On line 11, I retrieve the URL that the user originally requested from the REDIRECT_URL environment variable, and store it in $requested_url.

On line 13, I open the data file. The while loop that begins on line 16 iterates through all the records in the data file and compares the old URLs to the URL that the user requested. If it matches, the $new_location variable is set to the URL of the new location of that page. The last command indicates that the loop should exit at that point. This means that if the same old URL appears twice in the file, the first new URL assigned to it will be used.

At this point, it's time to start printing out the HTML for the page. First the header and initial HTML is printed. When the script reaches line 29, it determines whether a new URL was found that corresponds to the requested URL. If so, then the "Page Moved" title is printed. If not, the title indicates that the file was not found.

The same logic appears on line 38. If there is a new URL corresponding to the URL requested, that URL is printed along with a link to the new location for the page. If not, a generic Page Not Found message is printed. After that, a brief message containing the site administrator's email address and the ending HTML are printed. An error document for a page that has moved appears in Figure 23.5, and an error document for a missing file appears in Figure 23.6.

FIGURE 23.5
The 404 document for a URL that moved to a new location.

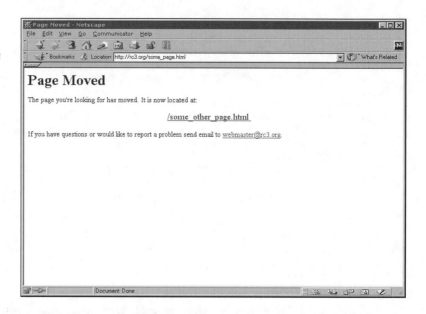

FIGURE 23.6
The 404 document for a missing URL.

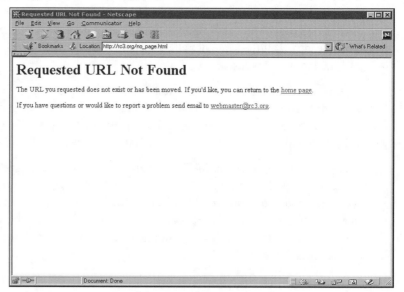

Handling an "Unauthorized" Error

As you learned earlier in the book, the 401 Unauthorized error is sent to the user when she fails to enter the correct username or password for a site that requires the user to log in. Unfortunately, the default error documents for the 401 error aren't very descriptive, as you can see from Figure 23.7.

FIGURE 23.7

A standard error document from the 404 Unauthorized error.

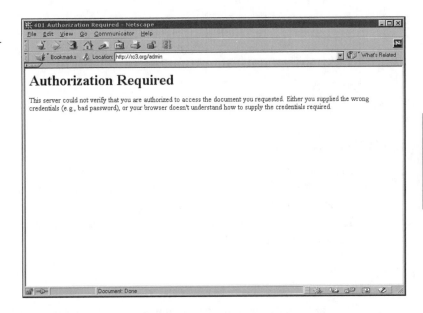

If your site uses authentication, you should provide users with an error document that explains why access to the page wasn't granted if they fail to log in correctly. Furthermore, if you run a public site, you should explain how users can gain access on the error document.

Custom error documents for 404 errors are often dynamically created by CGI scripts, depending on which page the user was looking for, and usually include a link back to the referring page. On the other hand, error documents for 401 errors can usually be regular HTML files that explain to users why they can't access the page, or what they need to do to register.

Listing 23.6 shows an example of an HTML document that you could use as the document that appears for 401 errors.

LISTING 23.6   An Error Document for a 401 Error

```
 1: <HTML>
 2: <HEAD>
 3:     <TITLE>Unauthorized</TITLE>
 4: </HEAD>
 5: <BODY>
 6: <H1>Unauthorized</H1>
 7: <P>
 8: Sorry, the username or password you entered was incorrect.  You can go
```

continues

LISTING 23.6   continued

```
 9: back to the <A HREF="/restricted_site/">restricted site</A>, or go to
10: the <A HREF="/register.html">registration page</A>.
11: </P>
12: </BODY>
13: </HTML>
```

Summary

In this hour, you learned how to configure Web servers to use custom error documents, and I gave you some ideas for creating custom error documents to use on your Web site. Informative error documents can really reduce the support load on your Web site because users have a better chance of figuring out what's going on when they try to load a page but get an error instead.

Q&A

Q Can I create custom error documents for errors other than 401 and 404?

A Yes, but it's not as important to do so as it is for the two most common errors. One is 403 Access Denied, which is returned when the browser doesn't have permission to access the requested file and is usually caused by a file permission problem. The other is 500 Server Error, which is almost always the result of a bug in a CGI script that prevents it from sending the appropriate header information.

Workshop

The quiz questions are designed to strengthen the knowledge you gain each hour. The exercises help you build on that knowledge by providing you with the opportunity to apply it to real problems. See Appendix A, "Answers" for the answers to the quiz questions.

Quiz

1. What causes 401 errors?

2. Why are custom error documents usually created by CGI scripts rather than static HTML documents?

Exercises

1. Try creating some custom error documents for your own server, if you administer one. Your users will appreciate it.

HOUR 24

Server Side Includes

Server Side Includes (SSI) are a kind of shortcut around CGI. As you know, a CGI program is external to your HTML page and can generate complex content, which is provided to the Web browser. A Server Side Include, on the other hand, is a simple command you place within an HTML page that adds functionality—such as reading an external file, inserting the current date or last file-modification date, or executing a program and inserting that program's output into your page. It's true that SSI doesn't provide nearly the same level of interaction for your users as CGI does. However, the number one advantage of SSI is that it saves you lots of work when you need the same HTML code snippet in many pages. Like CGI programs, Server Side Includes are processed on the server before a response sent to the browser.

The following topics are covered in this hour:

- How SSI works in general
- How to get SSI to work with some popular Web servers
- An overview of SSI directives
- Taking advantage of SSI in the design of a site
- Using Apache's extended server-side includes

How Server Side Includes Work

As you already know, when a user sends a request for a CGI script to the Web server, the server sends the request to the CGI script and then sends the data that the script returns back to the user that requested it. Server side includes work a bit differently. An SSI page is any page that the server parses for SSI directives. SSI directives are commands embedded in HTML comments that the Web server parses and replaces with whatever the directive calls for.

Unlike CGI programs, which are generally set apart in their own directory, cgi-bin, SSI pages are located in your Web directories with your regular HTML pages. Your Web server has to be configured to tell which files are regular HTML documents and which ones are SSI files. Generally, you configure your Web server to parse files with certain extensions for SSI directives. Most often, the extension .shtml is associated with SSI. If you want to use SSI with every page on your site, it might just be easier to configure your Web server to files with the .html extension for SSI directives.

When an SSI page is requested by a user, the Web server reads the file and interprets the directives in the file. It then substitutes the results of the directive in the file for the directive itself. For example, if you embed a directive in your file that looks up the current time and date, the Web server places the current time and date on the page in place of the directive.

The directives themselves look similar to HTML comments. They are embedded in the file wherever the information that the directive returns is to be displayed on the rendered page. Each directive is interpreted separately, so if you include lots of them in your pages, the performance of your Web server can suffer.

> Each SSI directive is interpreted individually, so if you include lots of them in your pages, the performance of your Web server can suffer.

Setting Up Your Web Server for SSI

Before you can start creating SSI pages for your Web site, you need to configure your Web server so that it can recognize which files to scan for SSI directives. The method for specifying which file extensions belong to SSI documents varies, depending on which Web server you're using and the platform on which it runs.

Configuring your Web server to scan all files with the .html extension for SSI directives can place an additional processing load on your Web server, but only administrators running extremely high-volume sites need to worry about it. Most Web servers are powerful enough that the increase in server load this directive causes won't affect the performance of the Web site. The rule of thumb is to go ahead and use SSI in designing your Web site if you want, but it should be the first thing you remove if your Web server's performance starts to degrade to a point where it's refusing connections.

There is also a security problem. Let's say that you have a guest book CGI program on your Web site that provides a form where visitors can enter a short message that will be displayed on a page. If your server is set up to parse all HTML documents for SSI directives, and the user enters a directive that deletes an important file (like your server's log file) or prints the server's password file as part of the page, that directive will be executed when the page is rendered. Anytime you set up your server to look for SSI directives in all of your HTML documents, you have to be doubly careful with input from forms.

Apache and NCSA

To configure the NCSA and Apache (which is a derivative of the NCSA server) Web servers to interpret SSI pages, you need to make changes to two configuration files.

First, you have to specify the extensions that you want to associate with SSI files in the appropriate configuration file. (Recent versions of Apache consolidate all configuration directives in `httpd.conf`; older versions and NCSA keep this type of stuff in `srm.conf`). To set up files with the `.shtml` extension as SSI documents, you should add the following line to the file:

```
AddType text/x-server-parsed-html .shtml
```

To specify other extensions as SSI documents, you can add additional lines to the configuration file, replacing the `.shtml` extension in the preceding example with the extension of other SSI documents.

If you want the Web server to parse all the HTML documents on your Web site for SSI directives before it sends them, you can add the following line to your configuration file:

```
AddType text/x-server-parsed-html .html
```

One problem with doing this is that it can place an additional processing load on your Web server. Most Web servers are powerful enough that the increase in server load won't affect the performance of the Web site.

There is also a security problem. Let's say that you have a guest book CGI program on your Web site that provides a form where visitors can enter a short message that will be displayed on a page. If your server is set up to parse all HTML documents for SSI directives, and the user enters a directive that deletes an important file (like your server's log file) or prints the server's password file as part of the page, that directive will be executed when the page is rendered. Anytime you set up your server to look for SSI directives in all your HTML documents, you have to be doubly careful with input from forms.

24

To use SSI on the Apache and NCSA Web servers, you also need to indicate which kinds of directives you will allow in the access configuration file. To allow directives that display environment variables and file statistics, enable the Includes feature. To allow directives that execute external programs, including system commands and CGI applications, enable the ExecCGI feature. The reason these two are split into different permissions is that enabling ExecCGI is a security risk, the Includes feature isn't. You should only enable ExecCGI if you have a very specific need to use it. Enabling Includes is safer, so you don't have to worry as much when you enable it. For example, to enable both of these options, you would embed the following line in either the httpd.conf, access.conf, or .htaccess file:

```
Options Includes ExecCGI
```

Netscape Web Servers

Netscape Web servers (both for UNIX and Windows NT) implement SSI exactly like the NCSA server and Apache. To enable SSI on your server, you should turn on parsing using the Administration Server.

Microsoft Internet Information Server

Microsoft IIS only supports the #include directive, which inserts the contents of a file into the Web page where the directive appears. You don't need to make any configuration changes to enable this feature.

O'Reilly's WebSite

O'Reilly's WebSite Web server software for Windows 95/98 and Windows NT provides support for SSI. To specify which extensions should be parsed for SSI directives, you should use the Mappings tab in the Server Admin program and add the content type wwwserver/html-ssi for those extensions.

WebStar

WebStar, the most popular Web server for the Macintosh platform, supports SSI via a plug-in, WebStar SSI. This plug-in is distributed with the WebStar application itself, so all you need to do is install it to use SSI.

Using SSI Directives

Let's look at a simple example of embedding SSI directives in a page. The syntax for SSI directives is very similar to HTML comments. There's a good reason for this. If for some reason you used SSI directives in a document that the Web server thought was a normal

HTML file, the Web browser would interpret the directives as comments instead of displaying them as part of the page. The basic format for SSI directives is:

```
<!—#command parameter="argument"—>
```

With SSI directives, punctuation counts. Be sure to use all the punctuation exactly as it appears in the preceding example. Specifically, it is important not to put a space between the <!— and the # sign, or between the closing quotation marks and the end of the directive, —>. SSI directives are also case-sensitive, so both the directive and the parameter should be lowercase.

flastmod

Listing 24.1 shows an example of a page that uses an SSI directive to indicate when the page was last modified.

LISTING 24.1   A Page That Includes the Flastmod Directive

```
 1: <HTML>
 2: <HEAD>
 3: <TITLE>Current Weather</TITLE>
 4: </HEAD>
 5: <BODY>
 6: The current weather is a balmy 108 degrees with 90% humidity. You can
 7: expect gale force winds for most of the day, accompanied by torrential
 8: rainstorms and tornado activity.
 9: Last modified: <!—#flastmod file="weather.shtml"—>
10: </BODY>
11: </HTML>
```

Figure 24.1 shows what this page looks like in a browser.

This page has a brief blurb about the current weather. At the bottom is the `flastmod` directive, which inserts the date and time when the file specified in the `file` parameter was last modified. In this case, the file being viewed, `weather.shtml`, is the one specified in the `file` parameter of the directory. This SSI directive is useful because it tells viewers of the page exactly how current that weather information is.

The `flastmod` directive can be used to insert the last modified date of any file, not just the one that's currently being viewed. For example, let's say you used the `include` directive to insert the file `weather.txt` into your document. The last modified date that is relevant to the user is probably the one for the `weather.txt` file, not for the HTML document that it is embedded in. To print that date, you would use this directive:

```
<!—#flastmod file="weather.txt"—>
```

24

FIGURE 24.1
An HTML page that uses an SSI directive to print the date the file was last modified.

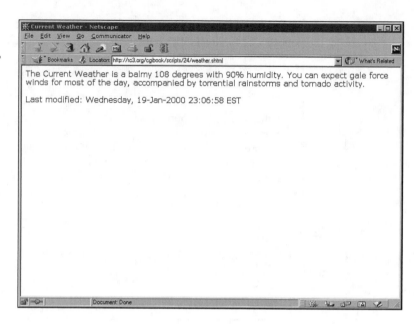

SSI Directives

The other SSI directives are similar to the `flastmod` directive in their basic syntax, but they provide lots of flexibility in designing dynamic Web pages.

#echo

The `echo` command inserts the value of an environment variable in the page. The syntax of the #echo directive is:

```
echo var="variable_name"
```

The variable can be any environment variable that's defined on the Web server, including any of the CGI environment variables set by the Web server. There are also several environment variables associated specifically with SSI. Table 24.1 lists SSI-specific environment variables.

TABLE 24.1 SSI Environment Variables

Variable	Contains
DOCUMENT_NAME	The filename of the current document.
DOCUMENT_URL	The URL of the current document.
QUERY_STRING_UNESCAPED	The query string sent with the request, decoded with all shell characters escaped using the backslash character.

Variable	Contains
DATE_LOCAL	The current date according to the server's clock.
DATE_GMT	The server's current date setting in Greenwich Mean Time.
LAST_MODIFIED	The date and time when the current file was last modified. The echo directive is an alternative to the flastmod directive. However, unlike flashmod, LAST MODIFIED applies to the current file only.

#include

You can use the #include directive to insert the contents of a text file directly into a document. For example, if you want to insert the current weather forecast on many pages on your site, but you don't want to make changes to every one of those places whenever the weather changes, you can use the #include directive to automatically read the contents of a file with the weather report into your pages whenever a user requests them.

There are two parameters for the include directive: file and virtual. The file directive specifies the location of the file you're including, relative to the location of the file in which the directive appears. So, to include a file named weather.txt in an HTML document that appears in the same directory, use this directive:

```
<!—#include file="weather.txt"—>
```

On the other hand, the virtual parameter specifies the location relative to the Web server's document root directory. If the weather report is located in the /reports/weather.txt subdirectory of the Web server, you can use this directive in any files that should include it:

```
<!—#include virtual="/reports/weather.txt"—>
```

#fsize

The #fsize directive inserts the size, in bytes, of the file specified in the file parameter. For example, to insert the size of a file called visitor.log into your page, you would use the directive:

```
<!—#fsize file="visitor.log"—>
```

#exec

The #exec directive inserts the output of an external program into the page. You can insert the output from a regular application or from a CGI script, depending on whether you use the cmd parameter or the cgi parameter. As you might imagine, the cmd parameter launches a normal application or command, and the cgi parameter launches a CGI script.

24

For example, let's say that you want to create a page that automatically provides a list of users logged into the Web server. The easiest way to do this is to run the who command (if you're on a UNIX system). To insert the output from the who command into your Web page, include the following directive in your page:

```
<!--#exec cmd="/usr/bin/who"-->
```

On the other hand, sometimes you may want to use SSI to include the output from a CGI script on your page. To capture the output of a CGI script using an SSI directive, you use the cgi parameter instead of the cmd parameter. For example, the directive to insert the output of a CGI script called guestbook.cgi is:

```
<!--#exec cgi="/cgi-bin/guestbook.cgi"-->
```

You might use this if you want to write a very simple CGI script, perhaps one that returns the current price of a particular stock. Rather than writing a script to generate all of the HTML for a page and insert the stock price, you can simply insert this SSI directive into the page and execute a script that prints only the number that you need. Another case where you might use this is one where you want to include CGI-generated information from a document that lives outside cgi-bin. If you run your own server, you can set things up so that you can put CGI scripts in the document directories, but if you don't, you might have to use the exec cgi directive as a workaround.

#config

The #config directive doesn't insert content into your Web page, but rather specifies the format that other directives use for their output. There are three parameters for the #config directive. The errmsg parameter specifies the error message when SSI directives fail, the sizefmt parameter specifies the format for the #fsize directive, and the timefmt parameter formats the output from directives that display a time and date, like #flastmod.

Listing 24.2 shows an HTML file that demonstrates how to use the #config directive to format the output of other SSI directives:

LISTING 24.2   A SSI Document That Uses the Config Directive

```
1: <HTML>
2: <HEAD>
3: <TITLE>Using the config directive</TITLE>
4: </HEAD>
5: <BODY>
6: <P>This is an example of an unconfigured date:
7: <!--#flastmod file="config.shtml"--></P>
8: <P><!--#config timefmt="%r on %A, %B %e"-->
```

```
 9: This is an example of a date with a configuration I specified:
10: <!—#flastmod file="config.shtml"—></P>
11: <P>There are a couple of options for the <B>sizefmt</B> option:<BR>
12: <!—#config sizefmt="bytes"—>
13: bytes: <!—fsize file="/vmlinuz"—><BR>
14: <!—#config sizefmt="abbrev"—>
15: abbrev: <!—fsize file="/vmlinuz"—><BR></P>
16: <P>You can also create custom error messages.</P>
17: <P>If you try to act on a file that doesn't exist, the default
18: message is: <BR>
19: <!—#fsize file="a_file_that_doesnt_exist"—></P>
20: <P>On the other hand, we can create a custom error message:<BR>
21: <!—#config errmsg="Whoops, the file doesn't exist!"—>
22: <!—#fsize file="this_file_doesnt_exist"—></P>
23: </BODY>
24: </HTML>
```

24

Figure 24.2 shows this page rendered in a browser.

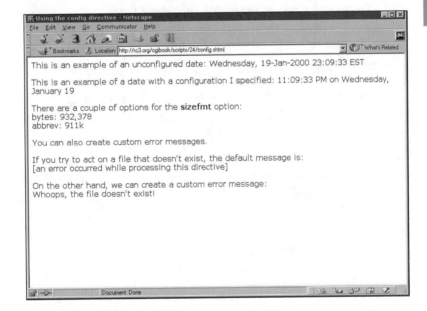

Let's take a look at each of the parameters for the #config directive.

errmsg

The errmsg parameter enables you to set an alternative error message for SSI directives that fail to execute properly. Let's say you try to perform an #fsize on a file that doesn't exist. By default, the Apache server prints [An error occurred while processing this directive] instead of printing the file size. This error message doesn't really tell the user much. You can change the error message to something that's a bit more informative to the user:

```
<!—config errmsg="Whoops, the file doesn't exist."—>
```

sizefmt

When you use the #fsize directive to display the size of a file on a Web page, by default the size is displayed in bytes. You can use the #config directive to display the size rounded to the nearest kilobyte instead. To change the display to kilobytes, use this command:

```
<!—#config sizefmt="abbrev"—>
```

To change it back to bytes, you can use this command:

```
<!—#config sizefmt="bytes"—>
```

timefmt

The most flexible configuration attribute is timefmt, which enables you to change the way the date and time are displayed by SSI directives. Let's look again at the example I used earlier:

```
<!—#config timefmt="%r on %A, %B %e"—>
```

This directive changes to time format so that it appears in the browser as follows:

```
07:41:45 PM on Saturday, September 20
```

There are a number of codes that the timefmt parameter replaces with actual time and date information when the page is rendered. In order to create a new display format, you can choose the codes that you want to use and arrange them, along with any text you want to include in the new format. Table 24.2 contains a list of the variables that are available.

TABLE 24.2   SSI Time Codes

Code	Example	Definition
%a	Mon	Abbreviated day of the week
%A	Monday	Day of the week
%b, %h	Aug	Abbreviated month name
%B	August	Month name
%d	01	Day
%D	08/01/97	Numerical date
%e	1	Day without the leading zero

Code	Example	Definition
%H	18	Hour (in 24-hour format)
%I	07	Hour (in 12-hour format)
%j	365	Day of the year
%m	08	Month number
%M	55	Minutes
%p	AM	AM or PM
%r	08:17:59 AM	12-hour time string
%S	31	Seconds
%T	18:25:31	24-hour time
%U, %W	26	Week of the year
%w	7	Numerical day of the week (starts on Sunday)
%y	97	Two digit year
%Y	1997	Four digit year
%Z	CDT	Time zone

To create a custom date format, just select the items you want and place them in the order you want. For example, if you want a date that says `Monday, May 4, 1997 at 06:30 PM`, use this directive:

```
<!—#config timefmt="%A, %B %e, %Y at %I:%M %p"—>
```

Designing Pages Using SSI

Now that you understand the mechanics of SSI, let's take a look at how to use them to create dynamic sites and to make your sites easier to maintain.

Using the `#include` Directive

The most commonly used SSI directive is `#include` because it can save tons of labor for Web designers, especially when the time comes to update a site long after it was designed.

Let's say you've created a site that has 200 HTML pages. Some of them are index pages that provide links into the site, and others are pages with articles or other content for the user to read. However, one thing that they all have in common is a navigation bar and copyright statement at the bottom of the page. When you create the site, it's easy enough to use a common template that contains the copyright statement and navigation bar, so that all your pages are consistent. However, the first time the CEO of your company says that there needs to be a link to his home page from the navigation bar, or that the wording of the copyright statement exposes you to potential lawsuits from everyone in the dog food industry, you probably have a lot of work ahead of you.

This is where the #include directive comes in. Instead of including identical blocks of HTML code in every page on the site (or even in most of them), it's a lot easier to use the same #include directive in every page to link to one block of code. So, when the CEO asks you to make a change to the navigation bar, you just go to the included file on the disk and make the change there. It's then reflected in all the pages that load the file when they are parsed.

Let's look at an example that shows how you'd use the #include directive in an HTML document. Bear in mind that you're only going to see a single HTML document here, but you could use the #include directive in any number of documents on your site to link to the included file.

First, look at the HTML file shown in Listing 24.3.

LISTING 24.3   An HTML Document That Uses SSI to Include a Footer

```
 1: <HTML>
 2: <HEAD>
 3: <TITLE>An example page</TITLE>
 4: </HEAD>
 5: <BODY>
 6: <H1 ALIGN=CENTER>An Example of Server Side Includes</H1>
 7: The actual content of the page appears here. <P>
 8: You can enter all the information that's unique to the page
 9: in the body of the document, and then you can place all the
10: standard information in a separate file that you link into
11: the page using the #include directive.<P>
12: <!-#include file="included.html"-->
13: </BODY>
14: </HTML>
```

Figure 24.3 shows what the Web page with the included data looks like when rendered in a browser.

For the most part, this page appears to be a normal HTML file. However, at the bottom of the page where there normally might be some standard footer information, like a link to the home page or to the page maintainer's email address, there's the #include directive instead. When the page is requested by a browser, the #include directive loads the following code into the page:

```
<HR WIDTH=70%>
<B><A HREF="home.html">home</A>  |
```

```
<A HREF="toc.html">table of contents</A> |
<A HREF="search.html">search</A></B>
<P>
All contents of this site are copyright&copy; 1999.
```

FIGURE 24.3

An HTML page that loads its footer using SSI.

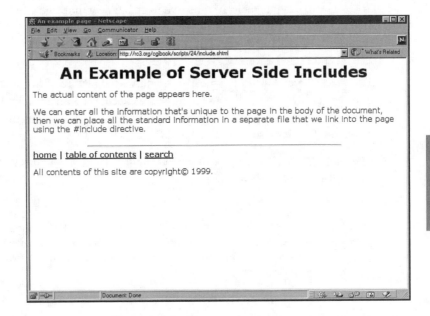

As you can see from the preceding example, using SSI can make it easy to automatically load any boilerplate information that your site requires into pages. More importantly, it's easy to change that information later.

> It's best to use absolute links and image paths in files that will be included in other files, because the included file and the including file may not be in the same place. Relative links are resolved from the location of the including file, and if an included file is used in files in more than one location, relative links are liable to break.

Last Modified Dates

One of the keys to building useful Web sites is timeliness. If the information on your Web site is outdated, visitors probably won't be too interested in giving it a second look. Another key is to tell users how current the information on your page is. Many popular Web pages now include the current date somewhere on their home page, indicating that the page changes every day and that the user can find current information inside.

You can use the #echo directive to display the LAST_MODIFIED variable, which displays the date that the current page was last changed. You can also use the #flastmod directive to insert the date specified in the file parameter into the page.

You can also use the #config directive to create new time and date formats that are more readable or look better on your page.

Using the #exec Directive

The #exec directive isn't the most commonly used feature of SSI, but it is probably the most powerful. Because the #exec directive executes commands on the Web server, it can be a significant security risk, especially if the person who creates the Web pages isn't careful about which sorts of commands he uses.

By using the cmd parameter with the #exec directive, you can insert the output from UNIX shell commands into your Web pages.

> Output from SSI is interpreted as part of the HTML page. Because the output from UNIX commands isn't formatted in HTML, unless you use the <PRE> tag around the exec directive, the resulting HTML page can look pretty strange.

Figure 24.4 shows how Listing 24.4 looks when rendered by a browser.

LISTING 24.4   Using the <PRE> Tag

```
 1: <HTML>
 2: <HEAD>
 3: <TITLE>A #exec Directive</TITLE>
 4: </HEAD>
 5: <BODY>
 6: <P>Here's what the <TT>ls -al</TT> command looks like without
    ➥formatting:</P>
 7: <P><!—#exec cmd="ls -al"—></P>
 8: <P>On the other hand, here's what it looks like formatted with the PRE
 9: tag:</P>
10: <P><PRE>
11: <!—#exec cmd="ls -al"—>
12: </PRE></P>
13: </BODY>
14: </HTML>
```

FIGURE 24.4

This page illustrates the importance of using the <PRE> tag to format the output of UNIX commands.

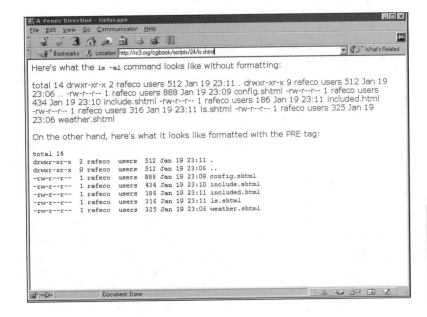

XSSI

XSSI, or Extended SSI, is a group of advanced SSI directives that are built into the `mod_include` module included with versions 1.2 and later of the Apache Web server. These directives enable you to create more powerful server-parsed HTML documents than you can by using standard SSI directives.

First, the following sections provide a brief overview of the directives that are available with XSSI.

printenv

The `printenv` directive takes all the environment variables that are currently available in the Web server's environment and dumps them to the screen. This is mainly useful for debugging purposes. If you're trying to use environment variables with other XSSI directives, or with a CGI script, you can use the `printenv` directive to make sure that the values in the environment variables are what you expect them to be. The usage of `printenv` is as follows:

```
<!—#printenv —>
```

set

The set directive assigns a value to a variable. You can use the variables with if statements later in the document. Here's an example of the set directive:

```
<!—#set var="color" value="blue" —>
```

if Directives

You can use XSSI to embed if directives within your documents. This enables you to create pages that can change the data that is displayed based on a criteria evaluated using the if directive.

There are actually four separate directives associated with if directives: if, elif, else, and endif. The if directive tests to see whether a condition is true, and if it is, the HTML enclosed by the XSSI directive is displayed. The elif directive is only executed if the previous if directive was false. If so, the elif directive is executed as though it were a normal if directive. The HTML enclosed within an else directive is displayed if the previous if (or elif) directive was false. The endif directive indicates the end of an if directive (or a group of if, elif, and else directives).

Here's an example of how if directives can be used:

```
<!—#if expr="$color = \"blue\"" —>
<P>The color is blue.</P>
<!—#elif expr="$color = \"red\"" —>
<P>The color is red.</P>
<!—#else—>
<P>I don't know what the color is.</P>
<!—#endif—>
```

The backslashes are used in the first two directives to escape the internal quotation marks so that they're not interpreted as ending the expression.

There are several test conditions that can be evaluated using the if statement, other than just =. Table 24.3 contains a list of conditionals that can be used with the if directive.

TABLE 24.3   XSSI Conditional Expressions

Expression	Tests
(string)	Returns true if string exists.
string1 = string2	Returns true if the two strings are identical.
string1 != string2	Returns true if the two strings are not identical.
string1 < string2	Returns true if the first string is smaller than the second one.
string1 <= string2	Returns true if string1 is smaller than or identical to string2.

Expression	Tests
string1 > string2	Returns true if string1 is larger than string2.
string1 >= string2	Returns true if string1 is identical to, or larger than string2.
!string	! is the not operator. It reverses the truth of the condition. So (!string) returns true if string doesn't exist. Or, !(string1 = string2) returns the same result as string1 != string2.
(string1) && (string2)	&& is the and operator. Both of the conditions being tested must be true for the entire expression to be true. In this example, both string1 and string2 would have to exist for the expression to be true.
(string1) || (string2)	|| is the or operator. If one or both of the expressions evaluate as true, the entire expression is true. In the example, if either string1 or string2 exists, it returns true.

24

Here's a quick example of how you could use the if directive to send different content depending on the name of the file:

```
<!—#if expr="\"$DOCUMENT_NAME\" = \"index.html\"—>
This is the root directory of the Web server.
<!—#else—>
This is not the root directory of the Web server.
<!—#endif—>
```

The code looks at the $DOCUMENT_NAME environment variable, which contains the filename of the current document. If the name is index.html, it displays the first sentence, and if it isn't, it displays the second sentence.

Summary

SSI is a kind of shortcut around CGI. It provides you with some of the same dynamic page-building features as CGI, but it doesn't allow nearly the level of interaction for your users. The number one advantage of SSI is that it can save you lots of work when you need to use the same snippet of HTML source code in many pages. You can create that snippet as a separate file and use SSI directives to load them into each page.

Q&A

Q What's the difference between using the exec directive to include the input from a command and using it for a CGI script?

A When you execute a command using the exec directive, the command is executed using /bin/sh and is not passed the data that is ordinarily provided to a CGI script by the server. On the other hand, when you exec a CGI script using SSI, the script is run in the normal CGI environment. All the environment variables, the query string, and the extra path information are passed to the script.

Q Are there server-parsed HTML technologies other than SSI?

A There are lots of other server-parsed HTML products, including Active Server Pages, Meta-HTML, and ColdFusion. Many of these products are discussed in Hour 12, "Pros and Cons of Alternate Technologies."

Workshop

The quiz questions are designed to strengthen the knowledge you gain each hour. The exercises help you build on that knowledge by providing you with the opportunity to apply it to real problems. See Appendix A, "Answers" for the answers to the quiz questions.

Quiz

1. What is the difference between #include and #exec?

2. Why is it sometimes a bad idea to parse all your HTML documents for SSI directives?

3. How do you set a variable using SSI?

Exercises

1. Create an SSI document that sends different data depending on the time of day. Hint: use the DATE_LOCAL environment variable.

2. Create a page that includes data from a command, a CGI script, and a file.

PART VII
Appendixes

Appendix

APPENDIX A

Answers

Hour 1

Quiz

1. Which was the first Web server to support CGI?
2. What is the primary advantage of compiled languages over interpreted languages?
3. What is the name of the technique used to translate special characters in query strings to characters that are acceptable to the Web server?

Quiz Answers

1. NCSA HTTPD.
2. They provide better performance.
3. URL encoding.

Hour 2

Quiz

1. What are the two dominant Web server operating systems?
2. Which two URLs can be used to address the Web server on the local machine, regardless of its domain name and IP number?
3. What is the name of the directory where CGI scripts are usually installed?

Quiz Answers

1. UNIX and Windows NT.
2. `http://localhost/` and `http://127.0.0.1`.
3. `cgi-bin`.

Hour 3

Quiz

1. What does the letter d at the beginning of a UNIX file permission string indicate?
2. When you run Perl at the command line, what do the c and w flags do?
3. True or false: You can simulate both the GET and POST methods when you run CGI programs from the command line.

Quiz Answers

1. A d at the beginning of a set of UNIX file permissions indicates that the file in question is a directory, not a normal file.
2. The c flag for the Perl interpreter compiles the script without executing it, and the w flag turns on compiler warnings, which report problems that won't keep your script from compiling, but could cause problems later on.
3. True.

Hour 4

Quiz

1. How do the > and >> redirection operators differ?
2. What are the two arguments passed to a foreach loop?
3. Under what circumstance would you use the eq comparison operator?

Quiz Answers

1. The > operator redirects the output to a new file, or overwrites the file if it exists; the >> operator appends the output to the file if it exists.

2. foreach loops accept the variable name under which the items from the evaluated list will be stored, and the list of values that will be evaluated by the loop as arguments.

3. The eq operator is used to test the equality of strings.

Hour 5

Quiz

1. Why is the password field type insecure?

2. What is the purpose of the MULTIPLE attribute when used in a SELECT field?

3. How do you include default text in a TEXTAREA field?

4. True or false: A form must include a Submit button in order for the form to be submitted?

Quiz Answers

1. Because the user's input is masked on the screen, the password is stored and sent to the server as plain text.

2. The MULTIPLE attribute enables users to select more than one item in a multiline select list.

3. Default text is included in text areas by entering it between the opening and closing <TEXTAREA> tags.

4. False.

Hour 6

Quiz

1. What is the pack function used for when manually decoding form input in Perl?

2. True or false, you can capture user input using extra path information.

3. Which character is used to separate multiple arguments when you pass information to the server using command-line arguments?

A

Quiz Answers

1. The `pack` function is used to translate the ASCII codes for characters to the characters that they represent.

2. False, extra path information must be written into a link on a page when the page is sent to the user.

3. There is no specific character for separating arguments. You can choose pretty much any character you want to separate the arguments, but you have to split them up yourself when you read them into your program.

Hour 7

Quiz

1. What are the two primary advantages of using JavaScript for form validation?

2. Why is it important to validate user-submitted data in your CGI programs even if your forms are validated with JavaScript?

3. What is the difference between the + character and the * character in regular expressions?

Quiz Answers

1. JavaScript validation allows you to catch errors before they are submitted to the server, reducing the processor load on the server. It also provides instant feedback to users, saving them the trouble of submitting forms to discover errors in their input.

2. You should include form validation code in your CGI scripts even if you use JavaScript to validate input because some users have JavaScript turned off or use browsers that don't support it.

3. The + character matches one or more of the wildcard specified before it; the * character matches 0 or more of the wildcard specified before it.

Hour 8

Quiz

1. Which RFC document define the standard for Internet email messages?

2. What does the `-t` flag for `sendmail` indicate?

3. Which two roles does `sendmail` play on a typical server?

4. Why must temporary files be used with Blat?

Quiz Answers

1. RFC 822 defines the standard for the format of email messages.

2. It tells `sendmail` to read the list of email recipients from the message itself, not from the command line.

3. It is used to send email messages from the command line, and runs as a daemon to accept remote SMTP connections.

4. Blat does not accept email messages passed to it through standard input.

Hour 9

Quiz

1. Why must you not pass unprotected user input to a shell command?

2. How does Un-CGI know which script to execute when it is called from a Web browser?

3. What special handling does Un-CGI perform on form fields with names that begin with an underscore?

Quiz Answers

1. Users can send shell commands to your scripts through form fields. If you pass those commands to the shell, they can cause security problems.

2. Un-CGI determines which script to execute using extra path information.

3. Un-CGI automatically strips any leading or trailing whitespace from values submitted through fields with names beginning with an underscore.

Hour 10

Quiz

1. Which method in `CGI.pm` is used to generate the `<FORM>` tag that begins forms?

2. Which subroutine in `cgi-lib.pl` is used to import form variables into a CGI program?

3. True or false: `cgi-lib.pl` supports cookies.

A

Quiz Answers

1. The start_form method is used to produce a <FORM> tag with CGI.pm.
2. The ReadParse subroutine places all the form variables submitted to a script in a hash.
3. False, there is no cookie support in cgi-lib.pl.

Hour 11

Quiz

1. What is the difference between the cgiFormSelectSingle() and cgiFormRadio() functions in cgic?
2. Why is it important to make sure that you allocate enough space for strings in CGI programs written in C?

Quiz Answers

1. There is no difference between the two functions.
2. If you try to store a string in a variable that is not large enough to hold it, a buffer overflow occurs.

Hour 12

Quiz

1. What is the difference between technologies like ISAPI and CGI?
2. What are the three parts of ASP pages?
3. True or false: PHP is only available as an Apache module.
4. True or false: Java servlets are a closed standard supported only by a Sun product.

Quiz Answers

1. Technologies like ISAPI are direct interfaces to the Web server; libraries written to use it are actually executed within the context of the Web server executable itself. CGI is an interface for executing programs external to the Web server and capturing the output to send to users.
2. Components, scripts, and HTML pages.
3. False.
4. False.

Hour 13

Quiz

1. How do you open a file for output in Perl?
2. What is a delimiter?

Quiz Answers

1. Using the output redirection operator, like this:

```
open (FILEHANDLE, "> $file_name);
```

2. A delimiter is a character or series of characters used to separate records, or fields within a record, in a database.

Hour 14

Quiz

1. Why are both the time and process ID included in filenames generated by `post.pl`?

Quiz Answer

1. Both the time and process ID are included in the filename to ensure that the filename is unique. If only the process ID is used, a filename could be reused when the process table begins at 0 again (after a reboot or when all the numbers are used). If only the output of `time` is used, duplicate filenames will result if the CGI program is called more than once per second.

Hour 15

Quiz

1. What is the purpose of the `domain` attribute of a cookie?
2. How are the names and passwords for basic authentication encoded?
3. How can users spoof hidden form fields and send values other than those that you've specified?
4. How do you remove an existing cookie?

A

Quiz Answers

1. The `domain` attribute of a cookie is used to specify which servers the cookie is sent to when requests are sent.

2. When you use basic authentication, usernames and passwords are encoded using Base64.

3. Users can get around the fixed values in hidden form fields by modifying the form so that they can change the values in those fields, or by simply writing their own request that mimics the form and sending it to the server.

4. Cookies are removed by sending a cookie with a same name and an expiration date in the past.

Hour 16

Quiz

1. In the sample application, what happens to items that users have in their cart when the user leaves the site without completing their order?

Quiz Answer

1. Nothing happens to them in this application. If this were a real application, you would need to write some code that automatically expired old sessions and removed those items from the user's cart.

Hour 17

Quiz

1. Why was it a questionable decision to use HTML-style tags as delimiters for the content files in the example?

2. On what types of sites is caching HTML documents not a good idea?

Quiz Answers

1. Using HTML-style tags in the content format was probably not a good idea because if the user includes HTML tags in his input, they will be interpreted by the program that displays the content as content fields themselves.

2. It's not a good idea to cache HTML documents on personalized sites where every page is customized for the users.

Hour 18

Quiz

1. Which SQL statement is used to add a new table to a database?
2. What criteria must a column or combination of columns satisfy to be able to serve as a primary key?
3. How do CHAR and VARCHAR fields differ?

Quiz Answers

1. CREATE TABLE is used to add a table to a database.
2. A column (or group of columns) must be unique for every row in a table in order to serve as the primary key for that table.
3. CHAR fields consume all of the memory allocated to the field regardless of how much data is actually stored in the field. Data in VARCHAR fields only consumes the memory used by the data stored in the field.

Hour 19

Quiz

1. What's the difference between a primary key and a candidate key?
2. What is the relationship between DBI and DBD?
3. What shortcut is used to select all the columns in a table?

Quiz Answers

1. The primary key is the candidate key specified as the unique identifier for each row. Candidate keys are all the potential unique identifiers for each row.
2. DBI provides a consistent interface to all databases for which there is a specific DBD driver.
3. Using * as the select list for a query will return all of the columns in a table.

Hour 20

Quiz

1. Why did I use a joining query in the cart.pl script?
2. Why did I use two different variables as statement handlers in the checkout.pl script?

A

Quiz Answers

1. I used a joining query to retrieve the list of products in the user's cart and the information about the products at the same time.

2. I used two different statement handlers because I needed to execute some insert statements while I was still dealing with the result set from a select statement, I and didn't want to overwrite those results.

Hour 21

Quiz

1. What port does the HTTP protocol ordinarily run on?

2. What is the purpose of a DNS server?

3. What does a standard HTTP request line contain?

4. How can you tell a standard content type from a non-standard one?

Quiz Answers

1. The HTTP protocol normally runs on port 80.

2. DNS servers are used to look up the domain names associated with IP addresses, and the IP addresses associated with domain names. They're also used to determine which mail server is associated with a particular domain name.

3. Request lines contain the request method, URL requested, and the HTTP version used by the browser.

4. Non-standard content types are prefixed with x-.

Hour 22

Quiz

1. Why is it important to scan form input for meta-characters?

2. Why is it a bad idea to store CGI scripts under the document root directory?

3. What causes a buffer overflow?

Quiz Answers

1. You must scan form input for meta-characters so that they aren't passed on to the shell and interpreted, causing trouble.

2. Storing CGI programs in a document directory can be dangerous because it's possible that the source code could be downloaded by users.

3. A buffer overflow is caused when more data is placed in a variable than it was designed to hold.

Hour 23

Quiz

1. What causes 401 errors?

2. Why are custom error documents usually created by CGI scripts rather than static HTML documents?

Quiz Answers

1. 401 errors occur when a user fails to submit the correct username and password when he tries to access a page protected using Basic Authentication.

2. Custom error documents are often built using CGI scripts so that they can make use of the URL of the page the user tried to view, or the referring URL.

A

Hour 24

Quiz

1. What is the difference between #include and #exec?

2. Why is it sometimes a bad idea to parse all your HTML documents for SSI directives?

3. How do you set a variable using SSI?

Quiz Answers

1. The #include directive reads the contents of a file into a page; the #exec directive executes a program and includes its output in a page.

2. Parsing all your HTML files for SSI directives can hinder the performance of your Web server. For most servers, it doesn't add enough overhead to become an issue.

3. The #set directive is used to set a variable using XSSI.

APPENDIX B

MIME Types

Table A.1 lists some the file extensions and MIME Content-types supported by many popular Web servers. If your server does not list an extension for a particular content type, or if the type you want to use is not listed at all, you will have to add support for that type to your server configuration.

TABLE B.1 MIME Types and HTTPD Support

MIME Type	What It Is (If Noted)	File Extensions
application/acad	AutoCAD Drawing files	dwg, DWG
application/arj		arj
application/clariscad	ClarisCAD files	CCAD
application/drafting	MATRA Prelude drafting	DRW
application/dxf	DXF (AutoCAD)	dxf, DXF
application/excel	Microsoft Excel	xl
application/i-deas	SDRC I-DEAS files	unv, UNV
application/iges	IGES graphics format	igs, iges, IGS, IGES
application/mac-binhex40	Macintosh BinHex format	hqx

continues

TABLE B.1   continued

MIME Type	What It Is (If Noted)	File Extensions
application/msword	Microsoft Word	word, w6w, doc
application/mswrite	Microsoft Write	wri
application/octet-stream	Uninterpreted binary	bin
application/oda		oda
application/pdf	PDF (Adobe Acrobat)	pdf
application/postscript	PostScript	ai, PS, ps, eps
application/pro_eng	PTC Pro/ENGINEER	prt, PRT, part
application/rtf	Rich Text Format	rtf
application/set	SET (French CAD standard)	set, SET[sr]
application/sla	Stereolithography	stl, STL
application/solids	MATRA Prelude Solids	SOL
application/STEP	ISO-10303 STEP data files	stp, STP, step, STEP
application/vda	VDA-FS Surface data	vda, VDA
application/x-csh	C-shell script	csh
application/x-director	Macromedia Director	dir, dcr, dxr
application/x-dvi	TeX DVI	dvi
application/x-gzip	GNU Zip	gz, gzip
application/x-mif	FrameMaker MIF Format	mif
application/x-hdf	NCSA HDF Data File	hdf
application/x-latex	LaTeX source	latex
application/x-netcdf	Unidata netCDF	nc,cdf
application/x-sh	Bourne shell script	sh
application/x-stuffit	Stuffit Archive	sit
application/x-tcl	TCL script	tcl
application/x-tex	TeX source	tex
application/x-texinfo	Texinfo (Emacs)	texinfo,texi
application/x-troff	Troff	t, tr, roff
application/x-troff-man	Troff with MAN macros	man
application/x-troff-me	Troff with ME macros	me
application/x-troff-ms	Troff with MS macros	ms
application/x-wais-source	WAIS source	src
application/x-bcpio	Old binary CPIO	bcpio
application/x-cpio	POSIX CPIO	cpio

MIME Type	What It Is (If Noted)	File Extensions
application/x-gtar	GNU tar	gtar
application/x-shar	Shell archive	shar
application/x-sv4cpio	SVR4 CPIO	sv4cpio
application/x-sv4crc	SVR4 CPIO with CRC	sv4crc
application/x-tar	4.3BSD tar format	tar
application/x-ustar	POSIX tar format	ustar
application/x-winhelp	Windows Help	hlp
application/zip	ZIP archive	zip
audio/basic	Basic audio (usually μ-law)	au, snd
audio/x-aiff	AIFF audio	aif, aiff, aifc
audio/x-pn-realaudio	RealAudio	ra, ram
audio/x-pn-realaudio-plugin	RealAudio (plug-in)	rpm
audio/x-wav	Windows WAVE audio	wav
image/gif	GIF image	gif
image/ief	Image Exchange Format	ief
image/jpeg	JPEG image	jpg, JPG, JPE, jpe, JPEG, jpeg
image/pict	Macintosh PICT	pict
image/tiff	TIFF image	tiff, tif
image/x-cmu-raster	CMU raster	ras
image/x-portable-anymap	PBM Anymap format	pnm
image/x-portable-bitmap	PBM Bitmap format	pbm
image/x-portable-graymap	PBM Graymap format	pgm
image/x-portable-pixmap	PBM Pixmap format	ppm
image/x-rgb	RGB Image	rgb
image/x-xbitmap	X Bitmap	xbm
image/x-xpixmap	X Pixmap	xpm
image/x-xwindowdump	X Windows dump (xwd) format	xwd
multipart/x-zip	PKZIP Archive	zip
multipart/x-gzip	GNU ZIP Archive	gzip

continues

B

TABLE B.1   continued

MIME Type	What It Is (If Noted)	File Extensions
text/html	HTML	html, htm
text/plain	Plain text	txt, g, h, C, cc, hh, m, f90
text/richtext	MIME Richtext	rtx
text/tab-separated-values	Text with tab-separated values	tsv
text/x-setext	Struct enhanced text	etx
video/mpeg MPEG, mpeg	MPEG video	mpeg, mpg, MPG, MPE, mpe,
video/quicktime	QuickTime Video	qt, mov
video/msvideo	Microsoft Windows Video	avi
video/x-sgi-movie	SGI Movieplayer format	movie
x-world/x-vrml	VRML Worlds	wrl

Appendix C

Response Codes and Reason Phrases

Status codes and their corresponding explanations (reason phrases) are yet another part of the HTTP specification. Normally, a Web user will only notice status codes when something has gone wrong (for instance, the ubiquitous 404 File Not Found error). However, Web programmers should have at least a passing familiarity with them.

To start off the discussion, here's an actual HTTP transaction. Only the names and IP's have been changed to protect the innocent:

```
rdice$ telnet www.mywebsite.com 80
Trying 255.255.255.255...
Connected to www.mywebsite.com.
Escape character is '^]'.
GET /~rdice/
HTTP/1.0 200 Document follows
Date: Tue, 09 Dec 1997 18:11:55 GMT
Server: NCSA/1.5
Content-type: text/html
```

```
<HTML><HEAD><TITLE>My Home Page</TITLE><HEAD>
<BODY><H1>Thanks for visiting Richard's Home Page</H1>
<P>The Universe has apportioned you instant karma for this.</BODY></HTML>
Connection closed by foreign host.
```

Notice that this isn't the way users normally see a Web page. When they fire up a Web browser program (also known as a "Web client"), they only see the *results* of what's out there, protected from all the raw data the Web might have to offer.

We programmers know better.

That session can be divided up into three parts. In the first part, the italicized text is created as a normal part of a telnet session, as launched from a UNIX command prompt. At the command prompt I specified the name of the Web server and the port to access. The default port for HTTP Web services is 80.

The second part, the boldface line, is what I typed. I "pretended" to be a very, very simple Web client and told the server to "GET" the index file in the ~rdice directory. This whole command is virtually equivalent to typing either of the following within a Web client:

```
http://www.mywebsite.com/~rdice/
http://www.mywebsite.com:80/~rdice/
```

In the final part, the Web server (in this case I see that it's NCSA/1.5) returns to me the document I requested. But first the server generates a header section. A Web client such as Netscape or MSIE won't show this to the user, but it's certainly there. The first line of the header is the status code of the HTTP session. In this case, we see that the status code is 200, and that the successfully retrieved document follows the header.

Here is an example of an unsuccessful HTTP transaction:

```
rdice$ telnet www.mywebsite.com 80
Trying 255.255.255.255...
Connected to www.mywebsite.com.
Escape character is '^]'.
GET /~rdice/thisfiledoesntexist.html
HTTP/1.0 404 Not Found
Date: Tue, 09 Dec 1997 20:30:03 GMT
Server: NCSA/1.5
Content-type: text/html

<HEAD><TITLE>404 Not Found</TITLE></HEAD>
<BODY><H1>404 Not Found</H1>
The requested URL /~rdice/thisfiledoesntexist.html was not found on this server.
</BODY>
Connection closed by foreign host.
```

Here is the 404 error at work. Note that all the HTML shown here was automatically generated by the server in response to a 404 condition. Many Web servers can be configured to provide custom pages, rather than the canned HTML shown here, if a given error status code is encountered.

Status codes are provided in four blocks. Codes from 200 to 299 are *success* codes. Codes from 300 to 399 are *redirection* codes. Codes from 400 to 599 are *error* codes, but they come in two blocks. The block from 400 to 499 are error codes where, most likely, the Web client has performed the error. The block from 500 to 599 are error codes where the server has determined that it itself has failed in some way. Note that the vast majority of these codes are reserved for future use. In fact, a few defined errors aren't all that defined regarding what situations they are to be used in.

The following is a table of status codes and the description phrases. This information is adapted from the Web site of the World Wide Web Consortium, the source of HTML, HTTP, and all things Web. My thanks to the authors and the W3C for all their good work. Please visit

`http://www.w3.org/Protocols/HTTP/HTRESP.html`

for more information regarding status codes.

Status Code	Brief Description	Status Block	Description
200	OK	Success	Request was fulfilled.
201	Created	Success	Following POST command, indicates success.
202	Accepted	Success	Request has been accepted for processing, but processing has not been completed.
203	Partial Information	Success	Information regarding request is derived from secondary source.
204	No Response	Success	Server has received and processed request, but there's no information to send back.
301	Moved	Redirection	Requested data has been permanently moved to new URL.
302	Found	Redirection	Suggests referring to different URL for document, but it's not there.
303	Method	Redirection	Same as 302, but provides additional information on method for accessing redirected document.

continues

Status Code	Brief Description	Status Block	Description
304	Not Modified	Redirection	Document has not been modified as expected. Meant to support efficient caching.
400	Bad request	Client error	Request had bad syntax or was inherently impossible to satisfy.
401	Unauthorized	Client error	Parameter to this message gives specification of acceptable authorization schemes. Client should retry request with suitable Authorization header.
402	Payment Required	Client error	Parameter to this message gives specification of acceptable charging schemes.
403	Forbidden	Client error	Request is forbidden, likely due to file or directory permissions.
404	Not found	Client error	Server has not found anything matching URL supplied by client.
500	Internal Error	Server error	Server encountered unexpected condition that prevented it from fulfilling request.
501	Not implemented	Server error	Server does not support required facility.
502	Service temporarily overloaded	Server error	Server cannot process request due to high load traffic. Likely temporary.
503	Gateway timeout	Server error	Server has decided to stop waiting for service it must depend upon to fulfill request. Equivalent to Internal Error 500 but possesses more diagnostic value.

Many of these status codes won't appear in everyday Web interaction. You really have to try to make these conditions occur.

One practical consideration of HTTP status code handling is authentication handling. On NCSA-based Web servers, this is usually done with an .htaccess scheme. Microsoft IIS relies on native integration with the Windows NT user database. The programmer can directly control authentication handling by using status codes and no-parse header scripts. Consider the following Perl program, called nph-authenticate.cgi:

```
#!/usr/bin/perl5

print <<END;
```

```
HTTP/1.0 401 Unauthorized
Server: NCSA/1.5
Content-type: text/html
WWW-Authenticate: Basic realm="ByPassword"

<HEAD><TITLE>Authorization Required</TITLE></HEAD>
<BODY><H1>Authorization Required</H1>
Browser not authentication-capable or
authentication failed.
</BODY>
END

exit 0;
```

A telnet scheme reveals pretty much exactly what you would expect, given the preceding source code:

```
rdice$ telnet www.mywebsite.com 80
Trying 255.255.255.255...
Connected to www.mywebsite.com.
Escape character is '^]'.
GET /nph-authenticate.cgi
HTTP/1.0 401 Unauthorized
Server: NCSA/1.5
Content-type: text/html
WWW-Authenticate: Basic realm="ByPassword"

<HEAD><TITLE>Authorization Required</TITLE></HEAD>
<BODY><H1>Authorization Required</H1>
Browser not authentication-capable or
authentication failed.
</BODY>
Connection closed by foreign host.
```

This telnet session shows that the Web server returned exactly what the nph- CGI program printed. This doesn't usually happen with CGI programs. Usually, the programmer is responsible for writing a program that creates a valid Content-type header line, but not the whole header. The "nph-" prefix in the name of the CGI program is what triggered the server not to parse and add to the header. The special significance of the "nph-" prefix is common across all popular Web servers.

Because the programmer controls the status code and the WWW-Authenticate lines, a custom-built password protection scheme can be created. These bits of information instruct your browser to "pop up" a username/password box where the user enters her username and password. When the "OK" button is clicked, the nph- CGI program is re-activated, this time with authentication information. It is then up to the nph- CGI program to perform whatever authentication lookup is desired. (This activity isn't shown in nph-authenticate.cgi.)

C

APPENDIX D

Environment Variables and Request Headers

CGI Environment Variables

CGI programs receive information in a variety of forms. One of the most useful of these forms is the set of CGI environment variables. Based on the contents of these variables, a CGI program can make meaningful decisions regarding how best to interact with the Web client that invoked the CGI program.

CGI environment variables are provided to the CGI program by the parent Web server process. The server creates these variables using information derived from three different sources:

- The incoming HTTP request packet. This provides REMOTE_ADDR information.
- The Web server program itself. For instance, the SERVER_SOFTWARE variable is provided by the Web server.
- The HTTP request header provided to the Web server by the Web client. For instance, REQUEST_METHOD, CONTENT_TYPE, QUERY_STRING, and more

information is taken from the HTTP request header by the Web server and placed into environment variables.

Some environment variables will be populated from combinations of the above sources. REMOTE_HOST requires REMOTE_ADDR, plus the ability of the server to resolve a name for the given IP address. PATH_TRANSLATED comes in part from the Web client-requested URL, and in part from the directory structure of the server as determined by the Web server software.

Some HTTP request header-derived environment variables aren't strictly required by the CGI specification. However, the CGI specification does outline a method for the Web client to extend the standard set of environment variables provided to the CGI program by the Web server. A very popular CGI environment variable that is derived from this extension is HTTP_USER_AGENT. This environment variable contains the name of the Web client software that is being used to invoke the CGI program, and is essential in the creation of CGI programs that generate browser-specific Web pages. Extension-derived variables are denoted by an HTTP_ prefix.

The following is a table of the standard CGI specification environment variables, along with a few highly popular extension-derived variables. This information comes from the NCSA CGI Specification home page at http://hoohoo.ncsa.uiuc.edu/cgi/.

CGI Environment Variable	Description
AUTH_TYPE	The protocol-specific authentication method used to validate the user, if applicable.
CONTENT_LENGTH	The byte count of the attached comment provided by the Web client. See the CONTENT_TYPE environment variable.
CONTENT_TYPE	The type of data content attached to the Web client-created HTTP header, if any. Examples are POST and PUT.
HTTP_ACCEPT	The MIME types that the client will accept, as given by HTTP response headers. This is an extension variable, not part of the basic CGI environment variable specification but in extremely common use.
HTTP_USER_AGENT	The browser the client is using to send the request. This is an extension variable, not part of the basic CGI environment variable specification but in extremely common use.
GATEWAY_INTERFACE	The revision of the CGI specification to which this server complies.
PATH_INFO	Extra path information, as given by the Web client.
PATH_TRANSLATED	A Web server-created translated version of PATH_INFO, which takes the path and does any needed virtual-to-physical mappings.

CGI Environment Variable	Description
QUERY_STRING	The information that follows the ? in the URL that referenced the CGI program in question.
REMOTE_ADDR	The IP address of the remote host making the request.
REMOTE_HOST	The DNS name of the remote host making the request. If the server cannot obtain this information, you may observe two different actions: either the server will leave this variable unset, or it will give it the same value as REMOTE_ADDR.
REMOTE_IDENT	This variable will be set to the remote user name retrieved from the server if the HTTP server and client both support RFC 931 identification.
REMOTE_USER	If the server supports user authentication and the script is protected, this is the username they have authenticated as.
REQUEST_METHOD	The method used to make the HTTP request, most likely GET or POST.
SCRIPT_NAME	A virtual path to the script being executed, used for self-referencing URLs.
SERVER_NAME	The server's hostname, DNS alias, or IP address as it would appear in self-referencing URLs.
SERVER_PORT	The port number to which the HTTP request was sent.
SERVER_PROTOCOL	The name and revision of the protocol the request came in with. This will virtually always be HTTP.
SERVER_SOFTWARE	The name and version of the Web server software answering the request.

Here's a quick, easy, and useful Perl program that I call show_env_var.cgi, which will dump all applicable environment variables:

```
#!/usr/bin/perl5

print "Content-type: text/plain\n\n";

while ( ($key,$value) = each %ENV ) {
        print "[$key]\t[$value]\n";
}

exit 0;
```

Note that %ENV is the hash array that Perl uses to store environment variable information.

Here is the output I received (through my Web browser!) after running the preceding code on an installation I use. Names and IP addresses have been changed:

D

```
[SERVER_SOFTWARE]        [NCSA/1.5]
[GATEWAY_INTERFACE]      [CGI/1.1]
[DOCUMENT_ROOT] [/var/spool/www]
[REMOTE_ADDR]   [255.255.255.255]
[SERVER_PROTOCOL]        [HTTP/1.0]
[REQUEST_METHOD]         [GET]
[REMOTE_HOST]   [www.mywebsite.com]
[QUERY_STRING]  []
[HTTP_USER_AGENT]        [Mozilla/4.04   (WinNT; U) via Harvest Cache version
2.1-beta-internal-41]
[PATH]  [/bin:/usr/bin:/usr/ucb:/usr/bsd:/usr/local/bin:.]
[HTTP_CONNECTION]        [Keep-Alive]
[HTTP_ACCEPT]   [image/gif, image/x-xbitmap, image/jpeg, image/pjpeg, image/png,
*/*]
[HTTP_ACCEPT_LANGUAGE]
[SCRIPT_NAME]   [/show_env_var.cgi]
[SERVER_NAME]   [www.mywebsite.com]
[HTTP_ACCEPT_CHARSET]   [iso-8859-1,*,utf-8]
[SERVER_PORT]   [80]
[HTTP_HOST]     [www.mywebsite.com]
[HTTP_VHOSTING_AGENT]   [255.255.255.255 via www.mywebsite.com:80 to
www2.mywebsite.com:80]
[SERVER_ADMIN]  [admin@mywebsite.com]
```

There are two points about the environment variables listed above that I would like to
make. First, some environment variables prefaced with HTTP_ are extension variables, but
they are added by the Web server and not due to the contents of the HTTP request
header. Second, the PATH environment variable is indeed an environment variable, but it's
not a CGI environment variable. This is an artifact of the environment of the Perl script.

HTTP Request Headers

When a user types a URL into their Web client and "sends it on its way" to fetch a Web
page, the Web client uses that URL to create an HTTP request header. This request
header is sent to the Web server, which then decodes the header and sends back an
appropriate HTTP reply.

I provided many examples of simple request headers in Appendix B. They consisted of a
single GET line. Request headers can be far more complex and extensive than that. Here
is the header that my Netscape Web client produced when I asked it to fetch the root
index at a fictitious Web site:

```
GET / HTTP/1.0
Connection: Keep-Alive
User-Agent: Mozilla/4.04   (WinNT; U)
Host: www.mywebsite.com
Accept: image/gif, image/x-xbitmap, image/jpeg, image/pjpeg, image/png, */*
Accept-Language: en
Accept-Charset: iso-8859-1,*,utf-8
```

The first line of this request header should look familiar enough. It's the single GET header command I used in the previous appendix, with a little bit extra to specify the version of HTTP acceptable to the client. Notice that these bits of the header find their way into the REQUEST_METHOD and SERVER_PROTOCOL CGI environment variables. The User-Agent header line states that the Web client being used is Mozilla, which is an alias for Netscape. The three Accept header lines are turned into the HTTP_ environment variables shown in the preceding listing. Note that if I were to specify a URL of

```
http://www.mywebsite.com/mycgiprogram.cgi?this=that
```

and access it via a link from another page, the HTTP request header would be changed slightly:

```
GET /mycgiprogram.cgi?this=that HTTP/1.0
Referer: http://www.mywebsite.com/refererlink.html
Connection: Keep-Alive
User-Agent: Mozilla/4.04    (WinNT; U)
Host: www.mywebsite.com
Accept: image/gif, image/x-xbitmap, image/jpeg, image/pjpeg, image/png, */*
Accept-Language: en
Accept-Charset: iso-8859-1,*,utf-8
```

Note that the query string isn't explicit at this point. It's still hidden within the GET line. The Web server is responsible for decoding this information and placing it within the QUERY_STRING environment variable. The Referer header line will have its contents placed in the HTTP_REFERER environment variable.

A quite different HTTP request header is generated when a form is posted to a CGI program as an ACTION. First, here is the HTML source code:

```
<html><head><title>a test form</title></head>
<body>
<form method=post action=http://www.mywebsite.com/test.cgi>
<input type=text name=texttest value="first bit 'o' stuff"><br>
<textarea name=textareatest rows=4 cols=30> 2nd bit o stuff,
this time in a textarea.</textarea>
<input type=submit name=submit value=submit>
</form></body></html>
```

Here's the HTTP request header generated from this form:

```
POST /test.cgi HTTP/1.0
Referer: http://www.mywebsite.com/formtest.html
Connection: Keep-Alive
User-Agent: Mozilla/4.04    (WinNT; U)
Host: www.mywebsite.com
Accept: image/gif, image/x-xbitmap, image/jpeg, image/pjpeg, image/png, */*
Accept-Language: en
Accept-Charset: iso-8859-1,*,utf-8
Content-type: application/x-www-form-urlencoded
Content-length: 105
```

D

```
mytest=first+bit+%27o%27+stuff&bubba=2nd+bit+o+stuff%2C%0D%0Athis+time+in+a+text
area.%0D%0A&submit=submit
```

The first thing you'll notice is that POST is the method used, rather than GET. Also, a few new headers have been added. Content-type informs the Web server that there is content attached to the header of the MIME type application/x-www-form-urlencoded. This is the formal name of the standard encoding scheme encountered all the time in CGI programming. Next, the header divulges the length in bytes of the attached content. Finally, we see the content of the submitted form, with spaces translated into +'s and special characters translated into a %-escaped hex code. This content is provided to CGI programs through the STDIN file stream.

Here is a condensed reference list of the list of HTTP Request Headers, as taken from the W3C Web site:

```
http://www.w3.org/Protocols/HTTP/HTRQ_Headers.html
```

Please refer here for the exact header specification and more detailed descriptions.

Header	Description
From:	The name of the requesting user in Internet email format.
Accept:	A semicolon-separated list of representation schemes (Content-Type metainformation values) that will be accepted in the response to this request.
Accept-Encoding:	Similar to Accept, but lists the Content-Encoding types that are acceptable in the response.
Accept-Language:	Similar to Accept, but lists the Language values that are preferable in the response.
User-Agent:	Gives the name of the original Web client software used, untainted by proxies. Although optional, this header should be included.
Referer:	An optional header field, meant to tell the server the URL of the document from which the requested URL was obtained.
Authorization:	Contains authorization information, which might be needed to access certain protected Web documents.
ChargeTo:	Contains account information for the charging of currency. Introduced for the sake of electronic commerce support.
If-Modified-Since:	This request header is used with the GET method to make it conditional. If the requested document has not changed since the time specified in this field, the Web server will send a Not Modified 304 reply instead of the requested document.
Pragma:	Pragma directives for the sake of intermediary and proxy servers.

APPENDIX E

Summary of Regular Expressions

A regular expression is a way of specifying a pattern that filters text and only matches particular strings. Once a string has been matched, it can be extracted from the larger body of text or replaced with another string. In Perl, another common technique is to use regular expressions as conditions in `if` statements so that the statement evaluates as True if a particular text string contains text that matches the expression.

Regular expressions are a powerful but arcane tool for processing text. It's easy to get started using them, and once you've got a handle on the syntax they have almost limitless capabilities for pattern matching. Many UNIX utilities use a form of regular expression as a pattern-matching mechanism (for example, `egrep`), and a large part of Perl programming is mastering regular expressions.

Like arithmetic expressions, regular expressions are made up of a sequence of legal symbols linked with legal operators. Table E.1 lists all of these operators and symbols. If you're interested in investigating regular expressions more deeply, read Jeffrey E. F. Friedl's *Mastering Regular Expressions*, published by O'Reilly and Associates.

TABLE E.1 Regular Expression Meta-characters, Meta-brackets, and Meta-sequences

Meta-Character	Description
^	Matches the beginning of a string or, if the /m option is used, the beginning of a line. It is one of two pattern anchors, the other being $.
.	Matches any single character except for the newline (unless the /s option is specified, in which case the newline will also be matched).
$	Matches the end of a string or, if the /m option is used, the end of a line. It is one of two pattern anchors, the other being ^.
|	Lets you specify two values that can cause the match to succeed. For instance, m/a|b/ means that the $_ variable must contain the a or b character for the match to succeed.
*	Indicates that the item immediately to its left should be matched 0 or more times in order to be evaluated as True. Thus, .* matches any number of characters.
+	Indicates that the item immediately to its left should be matched 1 or more times in order to be evaluated as True.
?	Indicates that the item immediately to its left should be matched 0 or 1 times in order to be evaluated as True. When used in conjunction with the +, ?, or {n, m} meta-characters and brackets, it means that the regular expression should be non-greedy and match the smallest possible string.

Meta-Brackets	Description
()	The parentheses let you affect the order of pattern evaluation and acts as a form of pattern memory.
(?...)	If a question mark immediately follows the left parentheses, it indicates that an extended mode component is being specified (new to Perl 5).
(?#comment)	Extension: comment is any text.
(?:regx)	Extension: regx is any regular expression, but parentheses are not saved as a back reference.
(?=regx)	Extension: Allows matching of zero-width positive look-ahead characters (that is, the regular expression is matched but not returned as being matched).
(?!regx)	Extension: Allows matching of zero-width negative look-ahead characters (that is, negated form of (=regx)).
(?options)	Extension: Applies the specified options to the pattern, bypassing the need for the option to be specified in the normal way. Valid options are: i (case-insensitive), m (treat as multiple lines), s (treat as single line), and x (allow white space and comments).

{n, m}	The braces let you specify how many times the item immediately to the left should be matched. {n} means that it should be matched exactly n times. {n,} means it must be matched at least n times. {n, m} means that it must be matched at least n times but not more than m times.
[]	The square brackets let you create a character class. For instance, m/[abc]/ will evaluate to true if any of a, b, or c is contained in $_. The square brackets are a more readable alternative to the | meta-character.

Meta-Sequences	Description
\	Escapes the character that follows so that any special meaning normally attached to that character is ignored. For instance, if you need to include a dollar sign in a pattern, you must use \$ to avoid Perl's variable interpolation. Use \\ to specify the backslash character in your pattern.
\nnn	Any octal byte, where nnn represents the octal number. This allows any character to be specified by its octal number.
\a	Alarm character that, when printed, produces a warning bell sound.
\A	Represents the beginning of the string. Its meaning is not affected by the /m option.
\b	Represents the backspace character inside a character class. Otherwise, it represents a word boundary, or the spot between word (\w) and non-word (\W) characters. Perl thinks that the W meta-sequence matches the imaginary characters of the end of the string.
\B	Matches a non-word boundary.
\cn	Any control character (where n is the character; for example, \cY for Ctrl+Y).
\d	Matches a single digit character.
\D	Matches a single non-digit character.
\e	The escape character.
\E	Terminates the \L or \U sequence.
\f	The form feed character.
\G	Matches only where the previous m//g left off.
\l	Changes the next character to lowercase.
\L	Changes the following characters to lowercase until a \E sequence is encountered.
\n	The newline character.
\Q	Quotes regular expression meta-characters literally until the \E sequence is encountered.

E

\r	The carriage return character.
\s	Matches a single white space character.
\S	Matches a single non-white space character.
\t	The tab character.
\u	Changes the next character to uppercase.
\U	Changes the following characters to uppercase until a \E sequence is encountered.
\v	The vertical tab character.
\w	Matches a single word character. (Word characters are the alphanumeric and underscore characters.)
\W	Matches a single non-word character.
\xnn	Any hexadecimal byte.
\Z	Represents the end of the string. Its meaning is not affected by the /m option.
\$	The dollar character.
\@	The ampersand character.
\%	The percent character.

APPENDIX F

ASCII Table

Dec X_{10}	Hex X_{16}	Binary X_2	ASCII	Dec X_{10}	Hex X_{16}	Binary X_2	ASCII
000	00	0000 0000	null	026	1A	0001 1010	→
001	01	0000 0001	☺	027	1B	0001 1011	←
002	02	0000 0010	☻	028	1C	0001 1100	∟
003	03	0000 0011	♥	029	1D	0001 1101	↔
004	04	0000 0100	♦	030	1E	0001 1110	▲
005	05	0000 0101	♣	031	1F	0001 1111	▼
006	06	0000 0110	♠	032	20	0010 0000	space
007	07	0000 0111	•	033	21	0010 0001	!
008	08	0000 1000	◘	034	22	0010 0010	"
009	09	0000 1001	○	035	23	0010 0011	#
010	0A	0000 1010	◙	036	24	0010 0100	$
011	0B	0000 1011	♂	037	25	0010 0101	%
012	0C	0000 1100	♀	038	26	0010 0110	&
013	0D	0000 1101	♪	039	27	0010 0111	'
014	0E	0000 1110	♫	040	28	0010 1000	(
015	0F	0000 1111	☼	041	29	0010 1001	)
016	10	0001 0000	►	042	2A	0010 1010	*
017	11	0001 0001	◄	043	2B	0010 1011	+
018	12	0001 0010	↕	044	2C	0010 1100	,
019	13	0001 0011	‼	045	2D	0010 1101	-
020	14	0001 0100	¶	046	2E	0010 1110	.
021	15	0001 0101	§	047	2F	0010 1111	/
022	16	0001 0110	▬	048	30	0011 0000	0
023	17	0001 0111	↨	049	31	0011 0001	1
024	18	0001 1000	↑	050	32	0011 0010	2
025	19	0001 1001	↓	051	33	0011 0011	3

Dec X_{10}	Hex X_{16}	Binary X_2	ASCII	Dec X_{10}	Hex X_{16}	Binary X_2	ASCII
052	34	0011 0100	4	078	4E	0100 1110	N
053	35	0011 0101	5	079	4F	0100 1111	O
054	36	0011 0110	6	080	50	0101 0000	P
055	37	0011 0111	7	081	51	0101 0001	Q
056	38	0011 1000	8	082	52	0101 0010	R
057	39	0011 1001	9	083	53	0101 0011	S
058	3A	0011 1010	:	084	54	0101 0100	T
059	3B	0011 1011	;	085	55	0101 0101	U
060	3C	0011 1100	<	086	56	0101 0110	V
061	3D	0011 1101	=	087	57	0101 0111	W
062	3E	0011 1110	>	088	58	0101 1000	X
063	3F	0011 1111	?	089	59	0101 1001	Y
064	40	0100 0000	@	090	5A	0101 1010	Z
065	41	0100 0001	A	091	5B	0101 1011	[
066	42	0100 0010	B	092	5C	0101 1100	\
067	43	0100 0011	C	093	5D	0101 1101	]
068	44	0100 0100	D	094	5E	0101 1110	^
069	45	0100 0101	E	095	5F	0101 1111	–
070	46	0100 0110	F	096	60	0110 0000	`
071	47	0100 0111	G	097	61	0110 0001	a
072	48	0100 1000	H	098	62	0110 0010	b
073	49	0100 1001	I	099	63	0110 0011	c
074	4A	0100 1010	J	100	64	0110 0100	d
075	4B	0100 1011	K	101	65	0110 0101	e
076	4C	0100 1100	L	102	66	0110 0110	f
077	4D	0100 1101	M	103	67	0110 0111	g

F

Dec X_{10}	Hex X_{16}	Binary X_2	ASCII	Dec X_{10}	Hex X_{16}	Binary X_2	ASCII
104	68	0110 1000	h	130	82	1000 0010	é
105	69	0110 1001	i	131	83	1000 0011	â
106	6A	0110 1010	j	132	84	1000 0100	ä
107	6B	0110 1011	k	133	85	1000 0101	à
108	6C	0110 1100	l	134	86	1000 0110	å
109	6D	0110 1101	m	135	87	1000 0111	ç
110	6E	0110 1110	n	136	88	1000 1000	ê
111	6F	0110 1111	o	137	89	1000 1001	ë
112	70	0111 0000	p	138	8A	1000 1010	è
113	71	0111 0001	q	139	8B	1000 1011	ï
114	72	0111 0010	r	140	8C	1000 1100	î
115	73	0111 0011	s	141	8D	1000 1101	ì
116	74	0111 0100	t	142	8E	1000 1110	Ä
117	75	0111 0101	u	143	8F	1000 1111	Å
118	76	0111 0110	v	144	90	1001 0000	É
119	77	0111 0111	w	145	91	1001 0001	æ
120	78	0111 1000	x	146	92	1001 0010	Æ
121	79	0111 1001	y	147	93	1001 0011	ô
122	7A	0111 1010	z	148	94	1001 0100	ö
123	7B	0111 1011	{	149	95	1001 0101	ò
124	7C	0111 1100	¦	150	96	1001 0110	û
125	7D	0111 1101	}	151	97	1001 0111	ù
126	7E	0111 1110	~	152	98	1001 1000	ÿ
127	7F	0111 1111	Δ	153	99	1001 1001	Ö
128	80	1000 0000	Ç	154	9A	1001 1010	Ü
129	81	1000 0001	ü	155	9B	1001 1011	¢

Dec X_{10}	Hex X_{16}	Binary X_2	ASCII	Dec X_{10}	Hex X_{16}	Binary X_2	ASCII
156	9C	1001 1100	£	182	B6	1011 0110	╢
157	9D	1001 1101	¥	183	B7	1011 0111	╖
158	9E	1001 1110	₧	184	B8	1011 1000	╕
159	9F	1001 1111	ƒ	185	B9	1011 1001	╣
160	A0	1010 0000	á	186	BA	1011 1010	║
161	A1	1010 0001	í	187	BB	1011 1011	╗
162	A2	1010 0010	ó	188	BC	1011 1100	╝
163	A3	1010 0011	ú	189	BD	1011 1101	╜
164	A4	1010 0100	ñ	190	BE	1011 1110	╛
165	A5	1010 0101	Ñ	191	BF	1011 1111	┐
166	A6	1010 0110	ª	192	C0	1100 0000	└
167	A7	1010 0111	º	193	C1	1100 0001	┴
168	A8	1010 1000	¿	194	C2	1100 0010	┬
169	A9	1010 1001	⌐	195	C3	1100 0011	├
170	AA	1010 1010	¬	196	C4	1100 0100	─
171	AB	1010 1011	½	197	C5	1100 0101	+
172	AC	1010 1100	¼	198	C6	1100 0110	╞
173	AD	1010 1101	¡	199	C7	1100 0111	╟
174	AE	1010 1110	«	200	C8	1100 1000	╚
175	AF	1010 1111	»	201	C9	1100 1001	╔
176	B0	1011 0000	■	202	CA	1100 1010	╩
177	B1	1011 0001	■	203	CB	1100 1011	╦
178	B2	1011 0010	■	204	CC	1100 1100	╠
179	B3	1011 0011	│	205	CD	1100 1101	=
180	B4	1011 0100	┤	206	CE	1100 1110	╬
181	B5	1011 0101	╡	207	CF	1100 1111	╧

F

Dec X_{10}	Hex X_{16}	Binary X_2	ASCII	Dec X_{10}	Hex X_{16}	Binary X_2	ASCII
208	D0	1101 0000	⊥⊥	234	EA	1110 1010	Ω
209	D1	1101 0001	⊤	235	EB	1110 1011	δ
210	D2	1101 0010	⊤⊤	236	EC	1110 1100	∞
211	D3	1101 0011	⊩	237	ED	1110 1101	ø
212	D4	1101 0100	⊦	238	EE	1110 1110	∈
213	D5	1101 0101	⊩	239	EF	1110 1111	∩
214	D6	1101 0110	⊪	240	F0	1110 0000	≡
215	D7	1101 0111	╫	241	F1	1111 0001	±
216	D8	1101 1000	╪	242	F2	1111 0010	≥
217	D9	1101 1001	⌐	243	F3	1111 0011	≤
218	DA	1101 1010	⌐	244	F4	1111 0100	⌠
219	DB	1101 1011	■	245	F5	1111 0101	⌡
220	DC	1101 1100	▄	246	F6	1111 0110	÷
221	DD	1101 1101	▌	247	F7	1111 0111	≈
222	DE	1101 1110	▐	248	F8	1111 1000	°
223	DF	1101 1111	▀	249	F9	1111 1001	•
224	E0	1110 0000	α	250	FA	1111 1010	·
225	E1	1110 0001	β	251	FB	1111 1011	√
226	E2	1110 0010	Γ	252	FC	1111 1100	^{n}
227	E3	1110 0011	π	253	FD	1111 1101	^{2}
228	E4	1110 0100	Σ	254	FE	1111 1110	■
229	E5	1110 0101	σ	255	FF	1111 1111	
230	E6	1110 0110	μ				
231	E7	1110 0111	γ				
232	E8	1110 1000	Φ				
233	E9	1110 1001	θ				

INDEX

X-Z